VOWEL PATTERNS IN LANGUAGE

Linguists researching the sounds of languages do not just study lists of sounds but seek to discover generalizations about sound patterns by grouping them into categories. They study the common properties of each category and identify what distinguishes one category from another. Vowel patterns, for instance, are analyzed and compared across languages to identify phonological similarities and differences. This original account of vowel patterns in language brings a wealth of cross-linguistic material to the study of vowel systems and offers new theoretical insights. Informed by research in speech perception and production, it addresses the fundamental question of how the relative prominence of word position influences vowel processes and distributions. The book combines a cross-linguistic focus with detailed case studies. Descriptions and analyses are provided for vowel patterns in over twenty-five languages from around the world, with particular emphasis on minor Romance languages and on the diachronic development of the German umlaut.

RACHEL WALKER is an associate professor in the Department of Linguistics at the University of Southern California. She is the author of *Nasalization, Neutral Segments and Opacity Effects* (2000), and has contributed numerous articles to journals and books.

In this series

85. JOHN COLEMAN: *Phonological representations: their names, forms and powers*
86. CHRISTINA Y. BETHIN: *Slavic prosody: language change and phonological theory*
87. BARBARA DANCYGIER: *Conditionals and prediction*
88. CLAIRE LEFEBVRE: *Creole genesis and the acquisition of grammar: the case of Haitian creole*
89. HEINZ GIEGERICH: *Lexical strata in English*
90. KEREN RICE: *Morpheme order and semantic scope*
91. APRIL MCMAHON: *Lexical phonology and the history of English*
92. MATTHEW Y. CHEN: *Tone Sandhi: patterns across Chinese dialects*
93. GREGORY T. STUMP: *Inflectional morphology: a theory of paradigm structure*
94. JOAN BYBEE: *Phonology and language use*
95. LAURIE BAUER: *Morphological productivity*
96. THOMAS ERNST: *The syntax of adjuncts*
97. ELIZABETH CLOSS TRAUGOTT AND RICHARD B. DASHER: *Regularity in semantic change*
98. MAYA HICKMANN: *Children's discourse: person, space and time across languages*
99. DIANE BLAKEMORE: *Relevance and linguistic meaning: the semantics and pragmatics of discourse markers*
100. IAN ROBERTS AND ANNA ROUSSOU: *Syntactic change: a minimalist approach to grammaticalization*
101. DONKA MINKOVA: *Alliteration and sound change in early English*
102. MARK C. BAKER: *Lexical categories: verbs, nouns and adjectives*
103. CARLOTA S. SMITH: *Modes of discourse: the local structure of texts*
104. ROCHELLE LIEBER: *Morphology and lexical semantics*
105. HOLGER DIESSEL: *The acquisition of complex sentences*
106. SHARON INKELAS AND CHERYL ZOLL: *Reduplication: doubling in morphology*
107. SUSAN EDWARDS: *Fluent aphasia*
108. BARBARA DANCYGIER AND EVE SWEETSER: *Mental spaces in grammar: conditional constructions*
109. HEW BAERMAN, DUNSTAN BROWN AND GREVILLE G. CORBETT: *The syntax–morphology interface: a study of syncretism*
110. MARCUS TOMALIN: *Linguistics and the formal sciences: the origins of generative grammar*
111. SAMUEL D. EPSTEIN AND T. DANIEL SEELY: *Derivations in minimalism*
112. PAUL DE LACY: *Markedness: reduction and preservation in phonology*
113. YEHUDA N. FALK: *Subjects and their properties*
114. P. H. MATTHEWS: *Syntactic relations: a critical survey*
115. MARK C. BAKER: *The syntax of agreement and concord*
116. GILLIAN CATRIONA RAMCHAND: *Verb meaning and the lexicon: a first phase syntax*
117. PIETER MUYSKEN: *Functional categories*
118. JUAN URIAGEREKA: *Syntactic anchors: on semantic structuring*
119. D. ROBERT LADD: *Intonational phonology, second edition*

120. LEONARD H. BABBY: *The syntax of argument structure*
121. B. ELAN DRESHER: *The contrastive hierarchy in phonology*
122. DAVID ADGER, DANIEL HARBOUR AND LAUREL J. WATKINS: *Mirrors and microparameters: phrase structure beyond free word order*
123. NIINA NING ZHANG: *Coordination in syntax*
124. NEIL SMITH: *Acquiring phonology*
125. NINA TOPINTZI: *Onsets: suprasegmental and prosodic behaviour*
126. CEDRIC BOECKX, NORBERT HORNSTEIN AND JAIRO NUNES: *Control as movement*
127. MICHAEL ISRAEL: *The grammar of polarity: pragmatics, sensitivity, and the logic of scales*
128. M. RITA MANZINI AND LEONARDO M. SAVOIA: *Grammatical categories: variation in Romance languages*
129. BARBARA CITKO: *Symmetry in syntax: merge, move and labels*
130. RACHEL WALKER: *Vowel patterns in language*

Earlier issues not listed are also available

CAMBRIDGE STUDIES IN LINGUISTICS

General Editors: P. AUSTIN, J. BRESNAN, B. COMRIE,
S. CRAIN, W. DRESSLER, C. J. EWEN, R. LASS,
D. LIGHTFOOT, K. RICE, I. ROBERTS, S. ROMAINE,
N. V. SMITH

Vowel Patterns in Language

VOWEL PATTERNS IN LANGUAGE

RACHEL WALKER
University of Southern California

CAMBRIDGE UNIVERSITY PRESS
Cambridge, New York, Melbourne, Madrid, Cape Town,
Singapore, São Paulo, Delhi, Tokyo, Mexico City

Cambridge University Press
The Edinburgh Building, Cambridge CB2 8RU, UK

Published in the United States of America by Cambridge University Press, New York

www.cambridge.org
Information on this title: www.cambridge.org/9780521513975

© Rachel Walker 2011

This publication is in copyright. Subject to statutory exception
and to the provisions of relevant collective licensing agreements,
no reproduction of any part may take place without the written
permission of Cambridge University Press.

First published 2011

Printed in the United Kingdom at the University Press, Cambridge

A catalogue record for this publication is available from the British Library

ISBN 978-0-521-51397-5 Hardback

Cambridge University Press has no responsibility for the persistence or
accuracy of URLs for external or third-party internet websites referred to in
this publication, and does not guarantee that any content on such websites is,
or will remain, accurate or appropriate.

Contents

	Acknowledgments	*page* ix
1	**Introduction**	**1**
2	**Preliminaries: functional grounding**	**12**
2.1	Introduction	12
2.2	Stressed and unstressed syllables	14
2.3	Initial syllables	18
2.4	Final syllables	22
2.5	Morphological roots and stems	24
2.6	Specific vowel qualities	26
2.7	Summary and predictions	32
3	**Generalized licensing**	**36**
3.1	Introduction	36
3.2	The concept of licensing	36
3.3	Prominence-based licensing configurations	40
3.4	Formalism	44
3.5	Achieving the licensing configurations	53
3.6	Morpheme-specific licensing	59
3.7	Summary	63
4	**Typological predictions**	**64**
4.1	Introduction	64
4.2	Disyllables	66
4.3	Trisyllables	70
4.4	Non-local effects	75
4.5	Interactions with other faithfulness constraints	77
4.6	Summary	80
4.7	Appendix	80
5	**Indirect licensing**	**89**
5.1	Introduction	89

5.2	Control by the licensing position	91
5.3	Assimilation within the licensing position	110
5.4	Sources of trigger control	135
5.5	Alternatives	140
5.6	Conclusion	143

6	**Identity licensing**	**145**
6.1	Introduction	145
6.2	Preservation of vowel properties in the licensing position	147
6.3	Preservation of vowel properties in the licensing position and non-licensing position	158
6.4	Assimilation at a distance in the licensing position	166
6.5	Non-local effects in review	182
6.6	Alternatives	185
6.7	Conclusion	191

7	**Direct licensing**	**193**
7.1	Introduction	193
7.2	Effacement or deficiency of vowel properties in a non-licensing position	194
7.3	Preservation of vowel properties originating in licensing and non-licensing positions	212
7.4	Alternating vowel properties in the licensing position	216
7.5	Direct licensing phenomena in review	230
7.6	Alternatives	234
7.7	Conclusion	235

8	**Maximal licensing**	**238**
8.1	Introduction	238
8.2	Maximal licensing harmony from a strong position	240
8.3	Case study: Servigliano	256
8.4	Conclusion	293

9	**Conclusion and final issues**	**297**
9.1	Licensing and vowel patterns	297
9.2	Vowel patterns and prominence in the future	300
9.3	Final remarks	313

	Notes	314
	References	329
	Language Index	351
	Subject Index	353

Acknowledgments

The material in this book has taken shape over the course of several years, and many colleagues and students have provided valuable input and assistance during that time.

First, I am grateful to Keren Rice for the many useful comments she provided in a review of this work.

I wish to acknowledge the students who made contributions to this research. I am grateful to Erika Varis for her extensive research assistance and comments on the manuscript, Ben Parrell for his research assistance with Servigliano, and Michal Temkin Martinez for her assistance with OTSoft. I would also like to thank those students for feedback during presentations at USC while this work was being developed, as well as Rebeka Campos-Astorkiza, Alvaro Cerrón-Palomino López, Fang-Ying Hsieh, Cristian Iscrulescu, Henry Nandelenga, Magdalena Pire-Schmidt, Daylen Riggs, Sergio Robles-Puente, Meghan Sensenbach, Laura Tejada, and Sasa Tomomasa. Several colleagues at USC have influenced my thinking about aspects of this research: Dani Byrd, Louis Goldstein, Abigail Kaun, and Ania Łubowicz; Mario Saltarelli offered valuable help with Romance data and patterns, and Elena Guerzoni provided generous assistance with translations and suggestions about the formalism.

I would like to thank a number of other people for their help with data and questions about languages studied in this work: Michele Brunelli (central Veneto), Daniel Büring (Modern German, and for suggestions about formalism), Stefano Canalis (dialects of Italy), Rodolfo Cerrón-Palomino (Jaqaru), Brad Koenig (Esimbi), and Joe Salmons (Germanic umlaut, and for suggestions about its relation to the theoretical approach). I had the opportunity to present some of this work at PhonologyFest at Indiana University. I would like to thank the host, Stuart Davis, and the course and workshop participants for useful comments. Other venues at which parts of this research were presented include the UC Santa Cruz Linguistics Ph.D. Alumni Conference, the Southern California Workshop on Phonetics/Phonology at Pomona College, the 45th meeting of the Chicago Linguistic Society, and the annual meeting of the Linguistic Society of America in Baltimore. I am grateful to the organizers of those events and to audience members for valuable questions and feedback. I have also benefitted from discussions on topics related to this research with Jill Beckman, Bruce Hayes, Jaye Padgett, Joe Pater, Cathie Ringen, and Sharon Rose. Of course, any errors in this work are my own.

I am grateful to my editor at Cambridge University Press, Andrew Winnard, for his guidance and his support for this project.

The seeds of my interest in this area were planted when I was a student at the University of Toronto. I owe special thanks to Keren Rice for many stimulating discussions over the years and for her mentorship. Elan Dresher, Carrie Dyck, and Tom Wilson provided important early sources of inspiration for me on the topic of vowel patterns.

For financial support of this research I wish to express thanks to the USC College of Letters, Arts and Sciences, and to the USC Provost's Office for an award from the Advancing Scholarship in the Humanities and Social Sciences Initiative.

Finally, thanks to my family, especially my husband Geoff Duke, for their unflagging support. It is to my family that I dedicate this book.

1 *Introduction*

This book investigates phonological vowel patterns, that is, restrictions on which vowel sounds can occur where in a language. Such patterns intersect with two main themes of this work, characterized in (1).

(1)   a. How word position affects the way in which vowels function in a pattern.
            b. How aspects of the perception and production of speech affect vowel patterns.

Vowel patterns that interact with word position are pervasive in language. For example, many languages show some form of systematic reduction in the range of distinctive vowel qualities in unstressed syllables. This type of pattern occurs in languages such as Russian, Italian, and English. Instances of vowel reduction processes are witnessed when stress shifts under affixation. In Standard American English, primary stress (signified by an accent) is assigned to the first syllable in *phótograph*, where the vowel is pronounced as [oʊ]. In the related word, *photógraphy*, where stress is assigned to the second syllable, the pronunciation of the vowel in the first syllable is reduced to [ə], designating a mid-central quality that often occurs in unstressed syllables in all forms of English (Ladefoged 1993: 84f.). Other vowel qualities can reduce to [ə] in an unstressed syllable, as in *expláin* [eɪ] versus *explanátion* [ə] or *emphátic* [æ] versus *émphasis* [ə], causing a number of vowel distinctions to be merged in some unstressed contexts.

Instances of vowel quality reduction in unstressed syllables are illustrative of a relation between vowels and positional prominence. Positions in the word that display a prominence maximum or minimum (e.g. stress peak/stress trough) are often focal in patterns that affect vowel properties. Reduction of vowel quality is not the only type of systematic process that is sensitive to positional prominence. As will be illustrated below, several other kinds of vowel patterns are attested in the world's languages that are conditioned by the relative prominence of the position in which the vowel occurs. Investigating the breadth of these systems is essential to test and advance phonological theory.

2   Introduction

This gives rise to the primary investigatory questions that guide this research, given in (2).

(2) a. Why are only certain kinds of interactions between vowels and positional prominence attested in spoken language?
     b. What is the range of systematic vowel patterns in spoken language that are sensitive to positional prominence?
     c. What do these patterns reveal about the theoretical mental constructs that form the basis for the phonological system that governs speech sounds in a language?

Bearing on the question in (2a), prior preliminary investigation has identified a set of patterns that share a common result, namely, they avert distinctive vowel qualities that are only expressed in non-prominent syllables (Walker 2004, 2005). These fall here under the rubric of *prominence-based licensing* phenomena, and investigating their extent in language and their properties is a focus of this book. Growing out from the preliminary investigation is a hypothesis that the vowel patterns under study are in large part perceptually driven: prominence-based licensing patterns serve to reduce perceptual difficulty in language. Vowels that occur in a non-prominent syllable supply fewer cues or less salient cues for listeners to perceive the properties that distinguish them from other vowels; for instance, unstressed syllables tend to be shorter in duration and lower in amplitude than stressed syllables. Foundation for this hypothesis also stems from other studies of vowel patterns with different typological focus (Suomi 1983; Kaun 1995, 2004; Majors 1998; Crosswhite 2001, 2004) and from wide-scope studies on position-sensitive neutralization of speech sounds (e.g. Steriade 1995a, 1999a,b).

The hypothesis that vowel patterns can be influenced by perception predicts that a prominence-based licensing pattern could efface vowel qualities in a non-prominent position, with the result that the communication of particular distinctive properties in a non-prominent syllable would be sacrificed. It also predicts the possibility that a pattern could augment the perceptibility of a distinctive vowel quality by causing it to be produced in a prominent syllable, possibly as well as in a non-prominent syllable. A pattern that singles out vowels in prominent syllables for effacement – in the absence of augmenting a non-prominent vowel quality – is not predicted to occur. Also not predicted is a pattern that singles out only the most perceptible vowel qualities for augmentation or loss. For example, because of its open jaw position, the low vowel [a] tends to be longer and greater in amplitude than non-low vowels, so it is not expected to be singled out in this way. An exception could be expected in word-final position, where contextual laryngeal and aerodynamic weakening effects can interfere with the perception of low vowels (Barnes 2006). In conformity with these predictions, prominence-based licensing patterns that selectively augment or efface [a] are not found, except when it occurs in word-final position. In contrast, because the high vowels [i] and [u] tend to be shorter than non-high vowels and have a lower amplitude, the perception-driven hypothesis predicts that certain prominence-based licensing patterns could be specific to them, as is indeed attested. However, as will be taken up in chapter 2, it is not always an easy task to determine the relative perceptual difficulty of vowel qualities. Sometimes the vowel qualities involved in a given contrast each have some different advantages and disadvantages, which could lead to variability across languages in which quality is singled out in prominence-based licensing phenomena.

Improved perceptual cues are not the only enhancements that a prominent position affords. Articulations may be stronger and longer, for instance, in stressed syllables and in initial and final positions. However, the nature of these effects varies across languages and sometimes even across speakers of the same language. This could suggest either that certain prominent positions facilitate production or that the occurrence of stronger and longer articulations causes a position to function as prominent. Articulatory enhancements are likely to lead to certain improved perceptual cues, so these effects can be interactive. Moreover, particular prominent positions are suggested to be psycholinguistically prominent, that is, they play an important role in processing of speech for purposes of recognition or production. For example, word-initial positions show increased salience or facilitation in word recognition and retrieval, and they display evidence of a special status in the phonological encoding of sounds for speech production. Again, these effects may be interactive such that certain types of heightened psycholinguistic salience could facilitate or be facilitated by enhanced perceptual cues and articulation.

All of these factors, perception, articulation, and processing, can contribute to the relative markedness of a vowel, and possibly other factors can contribute as well. A guiding idea pursued in this work is that the positions that function as prominent in vowel patterns are ones that tend to facilitate the perception, production, and processing of speech (Steriade 1995a, 1999a,b; Beckman 1997, 1999; Crosswhite 2001, 2004; Smith 2005). The emphasis here will be chiefly on perception, although, as just described, this interacts with articulation and processing. Given the hypothesis that the patterns under study largely serve to reduce perceptual difficulty, it is expected that distinctive qualities in marked vowels will be likely to occur in prominent positions or come to occur in them, and they will otherwise be prone to effacement. Prominent positions that recur in vowel patterns across languages include stressed syllables, initial syllables, morphological roots and stems, and, with some mixed effects, final syllables. Although positional prominence is postulated to be grounded in concrete properties, the positions in question typically function as prominent in phonology in an abstract and categorical manner. For example, a stressed syllable is generally singled out in a prominence-sensitive phonological pattern without regard to fluctuations in its physical or psycholinguistic prominence due to variation in speaker or occasion. Furthermore, while all of the syllables in question may be potentially eligible to function as prominent in some respect, which particular position is selected to serve as prominent can vary from language to language, and sometimes even varies from pattern to pattern within a language. In characterizing prominence-based licensing phenomena, the *prominent or licensing syllable* is the one that serves as prominent for that pattern and *non-prominent or non-licensing syllables* are syllables that form the complement to the prominent syllable, even if they include syllables that may function as prominent in other respects or in other languages. Thus, for instance, the stressed syllable may serve as prominent for a given prominence-based licensing pattern, in which case all unstressed syllables will function as non-prominent for licensing in that pattern, including, if unstressed, initial, final, and root/stem syllables.

In order to shed light on the question in (2b), this work undertakes a typological investigation of prominence-based licensing vowel patterns across languages. Over 25 distinct patterns are studied, providing a broad empirical basis for developing and testing the theory. The aim is to investigate a range of patterns in the form of case studies, with varying degrees of depth.

It is significant that distinctive vowel qualities that are expressed solely in non-prominent syllables are prevented through diverse processes. A sampling of different types of vowel patterns that are sensitive to prominence is provided in (3). They include deletion (where a vowel is dropped), reduction (where a distinction in vowel quality is lost), metathesis (where a vowel and consonant change order), and assimilation (where a vowel becomes more like another in the word; also known as a harmony pattern). In transcriptions in this book I generally follow IPA conventions, although I indicate stress with accent marks rather than the diacritic [ˈ]. Tones are indicated by numbers following the syllable: '1' low, '5' high, '51' falling, and '15' rising.

(3)   a. Vowel deletion:
        In northern dialects of Modern Greek, [i] and [u] are deleted when they are unstressed in certain contexts. For example, the high vowel in the first syllable of [pín-a-mi] 'we were drinking' is deleted when unstressed in [é-pn-a] 'I was drinking' (Joseph 1990).

b. Vowel reduction:
   In Belarusian, a Slavic language, the vowels /e/ and /o/ lower to [a] in an unstressed syllable, as evidenced in the following word pairs [r̯éki] /[rakā] 'rivers/river,' [nóɣi]/[naɣá] 'legs/leg' (Krivitskii and Podluzhnyi 1994; Crosswhite 2001).
c. Vowel–consonant metathesis:
   In certain Romance dialects of northern Italy, [i] in a final unstressed syllable shows an apparent metathesis with a preceding consonant to create a diphthong in the stressed syllable. Examples from old Piedmontese are given alongside their forms in Standard Italian (SI): [káin] (SI [káni]) 'dog (m pl),' [dráip] (SI [dráppi]) 'cloth (m pl)' (Rohlfs 1966). Since the vowel that undergoes metathesis here is a suffix, this could be considered a process of infixation.
d. Assimilation of a vowel in a non-prominent position to one in a prominent position:
   In Macuxi, a Carib language, the central vowel [ɨ] undergoes assimilation for backness and rounding with a stem vowel in casual speech. The prefix /pɨ-/ 'noun class A marker' is produced with the vowel [ɨ] in [pɨ-riwɔ́] 'arrow (of someone),' but it displays assimilation in [pu-moiɔ́] 'egg (of someone)' and [pi-siɔ́] 'leg (of someone)' (Carson 1982). (Numbers indicate lexical pitch accents here.)
e. Assimilation of a vowel in a prominent position to one in a non-prominent position:
   i. In the Romance dialect of central Veneto, a high vowel in an unstressed syllable causes mid vowels [e] and [o] to raise to [i] and [u], respectively, when they occur in a preceding stressed syllable. This is evidenced by the word pairs [kantése]/[kantísimo] 'sing (1sg/1pl impf. subj.),' [kantór]/[kantúri] 'choir singer (m sg/pl)' (Belloni 1991; Brunelli 2000a; Walker 2005).
   ii. Lango, a Nilotic language, presents a case involving the morphological root. A vowel in the final syllable of the root assimilates in its tongue root advancement to a suffix vowel with an advanced tongue root, as seen in the pair [cɔ̀ŋɔ̀1]/[cɔ̀ŋo̱1-niɔ́] 'beer/your (sg) beer' (Woock and Noonan 1979; Kaplan 2008a).

Observe that the patterns in (3a), (3b) and (3d) cause effacement of a vowel quality in a non-prominent position, and patterns (3c) and (3e) cause augmentation of a vowel quality that originated in a non-prominent position.

In addition to phonological processes that can produce vowel alternations in related forms, prominence-based licensing patterns involving vowels can exist as static distributions over the lexicon. These include position-sensitive patterns that show a static lack of contrast, where certain vowel qualities are absent in non-prominent positions, and static sequential dependencies, where certain qualities can occur in a vowel in a non-prominent position only when those qualities are also present in a vowel in a proximate prominent position. Some examples of static patterns are given in (4). Both of these examples involve the word-initial syllable as the prominent position and they are drawn from Altaic languages, which are suffixing. The word-initial syllable thus remains constant across words with the same stem.

(4)   a. Static lack of contrast
In Ola Lamut, non-high round vowels [o], [oː], [ɔ], and [ɔː] occur only in word-initial syllables. Words like the following are attested: [olək] 'lie, deception,' [ɔran] 'reindeer,' [oːlə-] 'to become weak,' [ɔːta] 'sea wave,' whereas words with non-high round vowels in a non-initial syllables are absent (Li 1996).
    b. Static sequential dependencies
In Classical Mongolian, non-high round vowels [ø] and [o] occur in non-initial syllables of the root only when all preceding syllables contain non-high round vowels, as in [kømøske] 'eyebrow(s),' [nomoɣodqa] 'to tame.' In addition, non-high unround vowels can follow round ones, as in the final syllable of the preceding examples and in [køke] 'blue', [qola] 'far, distant' (Svantesson 1985; Walker 2001b).

I will refer later to sequential dependencies, like the one exemplified in (4b), as 'passive licensing.' Not all sequential dependencies are static. The one in Classical Mongolian happens to be static, because the initial syllable does not change under the attachment of affixes (which are suffixes in this language), and non-high round vowels never occur in suffixes. However, there are languages that show passive licensing patterns with alternations. In C'Lela, a Benue-Congo language, high vowels occur in certain suffixes when word final only if they follow a root with a high vowel, and this restriction causes alternations in the suffix vowel. What distinguishes these patterns from ones with active assimilation is that when the conditions for the sequential dependency are not met, the vowel in the non-prominent position is neutralized to another quality rather than undergoing assimilation with the vowel in the prominent position.

Relevant to question (2c), which asks what these patterns reveal about the theoretical mental constructs, a goal of this work is to develop a formal account that captures the commonalities among prominence-based licensing systems. The proposal is that the patterns share an imperative modeled in the form of a family of prominence-based licensing constraints, a construct that elaborates on prior concepts of segmental and subsegmental licensing constraints, conditions, or properties in language (e.g. Itô 1988, 1989; Goldsmith 1989, 1990; Lombardi 1994, 1995). The constraints are united under a generalized prominence-based licensing constraint schema. They bar certain types of phonological structure – such as certain vowel properties – that occur solely in a weak position, a type of positional markedness requirement (Zoll 1998a). In line with the foregoing discussion, the phonological structure in question is prone to be marked in some way.

With respect to subsegmental features – which characterize different vowel qualities – an important component of this proposal is the claim that features are licensed provided that some member of the chain to which the feature belongs is affiliated with a given licensing position. A chain for a feature consists of the feature and any duplicated coindexed occurrences of it in a structure. This allows the possibility of *identity* licensing, where licensing for a feature in a non-prominent position is achieved by a duplicated feature in a prominent position, as represented schematically for a feature specification [αF] in (5a). ('α' is a variable over values {+, -} for [F].) Identity licensing has the potential to operate at a distance over unaffected intervening material. Other possible licensing configurations are *indirect* licensing, in (5b), where a feature has associations with a prominent position and a non-prominent position, and *direct* licensing, in (5c), where a feature is contained wholly within a prominent position. (The labels 'direct' and 'indirect' follow Steriade 1995b).

(5)

a. Identity licensing   b. Indirect licensing   c. Direct licensing

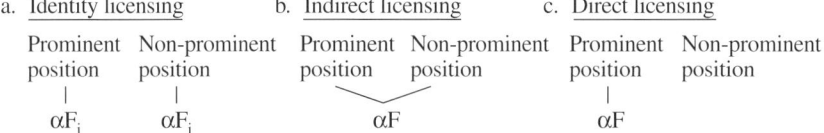

The licensing constraints are situated within the set of assumptions that constitute Optimality Theory (OT; Prince and Smolensky 2004). A basic principle of this outcome-centered framework is that systematic properties of a language are represented in terms of constraints that are imposed over the phonological output. Licensing constraints can block phonological structures that violate them or they can drive patterns where changes occur that prevent a violation. They thus are well suited to address both prominence-based licensing phenomena that involve active processes, as well as ones that exist as static distributions in a language. Further, because constraints in OT are ranked and violable, prominence-based licensing constraints may be violated within a language in order to satisfy competing constraints with which they conflict.

The OT model differs from process-centered frameworks in which grammars are organized around the individual processes that manipulate phonological forms, such as vowel deletion or vowel reduction, rather than being organized around the well-formedness of outputs of the grammar. A core result of this study is that the reduction of perceptual difficulty in prominence-based licensing patterns is accomplished by various processes across languages. This is consistent with the emphasis of OT on *common outcomes achieved by diverse means* (McCarthy 2002; Prince and Smolensky 2004). Alternative formal perspectives on these phenomena that concentrate on the means (process) and not the end (outcome) miss the insight that they are linked by a common factor with a shared form of linguistic knowledge.

Whereas the function of prominence-based licensing constraints constitutes the formal pivot that unites the vowel patterns under focus in this work, positional prominence also figures in the analysis in the context of positional faithfulness constraints (e.g. Casali 1997, 1998; Beckman 1997, 1999; Lombardi 1999, 2001). Positional faithfulness constraints bar changes in the properties of segments or other phonological constituents when they occur in a specific privileged position, such as a stressed syllable. These constraints play a role in the treatment of position-sensitive trigger control for assimilation and in position-sensitive resistance to neutralization. To be clear about the terminology used here, a *trigger* refers to a segment to which another assimilates, and a *target* refers to a segment that undergoes an assimilation. In many (but not all) assimilations driven by prominence-based licensing, a vowel in a privileged position is the trigger and a vowel in a non-prominent position is a target. This intersects with the theme concerning how word position affects the way vowels function in a pattern.

Pushing beyond vowel patterns that are driven by prominence-based licensing, the scope of the investigation is extended to vowel patterns that involve what is characterized in this work as *maximal licensing*. In maximal licensing patterns, certain vowel properties are driven to be expressed in every vowel in a word, not just in a prominent position. Maximal licensing constraints are proposed that can drive vowel harmony that is potentially unbounded in its extent of operation within a word. Like prominence-based licensing phenomena, maximal licensing tends to restrict marked structure, such as vowel qualities that show comparative perceptual difficulty or that occur in a weak context. The themes that underscore prominence-based licensing are thus more widely applicable.

This book is organized as follows. Chapter 2 explores possible functional grounding for asymmetries in positional prominence and vowel markedness with basis in the way that speech is perceived, produced, and processed. The discussion pulls together an overview of prior research on these topics. The positions under focus that can serve as prominent for some phonological purpose are stressed syllables, initial syllables, final syllables, and morphological roots and stems. In counterpoint, contexts that can serve as weak are unstressed syllables, final syllables, and affixes. Final syllables thus show a dual behavior across languages, and even within them. The relative markedness of specific vowel qualities, especially in weak position, draws discussion, with particular focus on contrasts for vowel height. Predictions for prominence-based licensing phenomena are delineated.

Chapter 3 introduces the formal framework for the analysis of prominence-based licensing patterns involving vowels. The chapter opens with background on the concept of licensing of segmental properties in phonological theory. A schema for generalized prominence-based licensing constraints is introduced that has the capacity to promote each of the three proposed licensing configurations: direct, indirect, and identity. Formal and substantive restrictions on the arguments within a licensing constraint are considered. A limited set of additional constraints that interact with prominence-based licensing constraints is presented, and demonstrations are provided to show how different constraint interactions, corresponding to different constraint rankings, can play out to obtain the three licensing configurations. The chapter closes with discussion of a means to obtain morpheme-specific effects in prominence-based licensing.

Chapter 4 examines typological predictions that are made by prominence-based licensing constraints in conjunction with a set of other constraints that are relevant to a typology that includes licensing-driven assimilation. In OT, the predicted typology of patterns is derived from all possible rankings of the constraint set, known as a 'factorial typology.' Typological properties are explored using factorial typologies that were algorithmically generated using OTSoft, Version 2.1 (Hayes *et al.* 2003). The generalizations that are discovered as properties of the formal system are identified. Primary interactions of a prominence-based licensing constraint with some additional constraints, besides those applicable to assimilation patterns, are also considered. Sample licensing patterns in languages discussed in later chapters are listed to illustrate particular predictions.

Chapters 5, 6, and 7 focus on the description and analysis of vowel patterns that involve prominence-based licensing. Chapter 5 addresses vowel patterns that are characterized by indirect licensing, chapter 6 deals with patterns that include identity licensing configurations, and chapter 7 deals with vowel patterns that show only direct licensing. Each of these chapters introduces a core constraint ranking structure for the patterns under focus. Following that, a series of case studies is presented, comprised language data to illustrate the patterns, discussion of relations to the overarching themes, and formal analyses.

A number of related topics cross-cut these chapters, including sources of strength, weakness, and control, local and non-local interactions, markedness-driven blocking, interactions with the lexical status of material, and morpheme-specific triggering and blocking, among others.

Romance dialects spoken in Italy and Spain form an area of concentration in chapters 5, 6, and 7, although they are by no means the only languages under study. The Romance 'dialects' in question are in fact minor Romance languages; they are descended from Latin and not varieties of Standard Italian or Spanish. Romance dialects were selected for study because they cast light on how satisfaction of prominence-based licensing constraints can play out in different ways within related languages. An important type of vowel pattern that a number of Romance dialects display is known as *metaphony*, where a post-tonic high vowel causes raising of a preceding stressed vowel.[1] (A post-tonic vowel is one that occurs following a stressed vowel.) An example is the raising harmony in the central Veneto dialect, introduced in (3e). Metaphony is significant for the typology of prominence-based licensing patterns, because it involves a vowel in a prominent position undergoing assimilation to a vowel in a non-prominent position, sometimes at a distance. Metaphonic patterns can therefore serve to discriminate the different roles of positional markedness and positional faithfulness constraints and facilitate investigation of locality.

Another topic that spans these chapters is the evolution of umlaut in German. Like Romance metaphony, umlaut in Old High German began as an assimilation that was triggered by a post-tonic vowel and affected a stressed vowel; in umlaut the assimilation chiefly involves fronting. In the progress from Old High German to Modern Standard German, umlaut traversed through each of the three proposed licensing configurations, starting with indirect licensing, followed by identity licensing, and ending with direct licensing in the language spoken today. This provides a lens on a scenario of diachronic evolution in a prominence-based licensing pattern.

Chapter 8 turns to maximal licensing patterns where a weak vowel trigger causes harmony that propagates in an unbounded fashion rather than targeting a vowel in a prominent position. Maximal licensing harmony can be triggered by a vowel in a weak position and/or by a vowel that displays some weak property or combination of properties. First, two patterns are examined where the trigger resides in a strong position, which is the locus of contrast for a particular weak property. A comprehensive case study is then developed for the Servigliano dialect, which includes two maximal licensing patterns with triggers that are weak by virtue of their properties and/or their position. In all,

Servigliano displays four distinct vowel patterns that each show some sensitivity to relative weakness and/or positional prominence. As such, it provides an excellent testing ground for constraints that drive prominence-based licensing and maximal licensing.

Chapter 9 assesses results of this work and highlights some topics that merit attention in future research.

2 *Preliminaries: functional grounding*

2.1 Introduction

This chapter provides background on possible phonetic and psycholinguistic bases for positional licensing effects and vowel markedness. As introduced in chapter 1, this discussion ties into a hypothesis that positions or contexts that show the capacity to asymmetrically license distinctive phonological properties are liable to be ones that facilitate perception or production. Thus, restrictions on marked or perceptually difficult properties in vowels and other phonological elements are predicted to be more likely in positions where they suffer some functionally based disadvantage, and positions that show a capacity for licensing are predicted to present some advantage.[1]

Quite generally, this discourse builds upon research in which certain phonological constraints are proposed to have a basis in what Kingston and Diehl (1994) call 'phonetic knowledge,' that is, "the speakers' partial understanding of the physical conditions under which speech is produced and perceived" (Hayes and Steriade 2004: 1). Interpreting the basis for phonological constraints' functional underpinnings more broadly with respect to the human speech processing system renders also relevant levels such as speech planning and lexical access in production and perception. Related research that explores versions of phonology that are phonetically and/or psycholinguistically based includes work by Archangeli and Pulleyblank (1994), Steriade (1995a, 1999a,b, 2001, 2009), Boersma (1998), Hayes (1999), and Smith (2005), among many others.[2]

There is theoretical debate about the way in which phonetics can influence phonology. For example, Evolutionary Phonology offers a different perspective from the teleological approach of phonetically based phonology just described (Blevins and Garrett 1998, 2004; Blevins 2004). Evolutionary Phonology postulates that phonetic optimization need not play a role in a phonological grammar or in phonological typology – the influence of phonetics on phonology in diachronic evolution is given priority as a source of explanation. See Hansson (2008) for a recent overview of the issues.[3]

Discriminating empirically between a theory that permits phonetic knowledge to have an active role in shaping constraints and one that postulates that the role of phonetics in phonology is wholly diachronic requires careful and focused study. Some empirical evidence that poses problems for the latter perspective is discussed by Hayes and Steriade (2004) and Zuraw (2007). This involves such diverse phenomena as characteristics of child phonology, misperceptions of place in preconsonantal nasals, characteristics of certain patterns of metathesis, and infixation patterns in loanwords. Given this kind of evidence, I adopt the position that constraints are possible that are induced making use of a speaker's phonetic knowledge. This does not exclude the possibility that phonetics could play a role in language change; indeed, I assume that phonological patterns with phonetic origin could evolve diachronically. Many of the phonological patterns under consideration in this work are compatible with either theoretical standpoint. Although testing the distinct predictions of these particular theories is not the emphasis of this study, further investigation of these issues would be valuable.

A theory that assumes the existence of phonetically driven phonological constraints must reckon with the means by which phonetics and phonology are related. Models or scenarios by which to implement synchronic functional grounding in the set of constraints whose ranking forms the phonological grammar have been discussed by Boersma (1998), Hayes (1999), Steriade (1999b, 2001), Smith (2005), and Flack (2007a, c). In agreement with Hayes, I take constraints justified on the grounds of phonetic functionalism to be ones that reflect principles of good design in that they optimize speech so that it is easier to articulate or easier to perceive contrasts. Likewise, constraints with a psycholinguistic grounding would be ones that render speech easier to process in some respect. An important question is whether the influence of phonetics on phonology is direct or indirect. Following Hayes, I assume that the relationship is not direct; rather, grammar design is mediated by structural constraints that can produce effects of formal symmetry in the phonological system (see also Gordon 2004, 2006). Thus, while many phonological contextual restrictions show functional underpinnings, for instance, in that they facilitate ease of articulation and distinctness of contrastive elements, there is a gap between what Hayes characterizes as 'raw phonetics' and phonological constraints.[4] This is tied to observations that phonological phenomena show more categorical effects and are characteristically less variable than phonetic phenomena.

To be clear, I do not hypothesize that every phonological constraint or synchronic phonological pattern is functionally grounded. See Hayes (1999) for discussion of ungrounded constraints, which may arise under various circumstances, such as through a sequence of historical changes, or under historical circumstances of language contact. A hypothesis that I pursue in this book is that prominence-based licensing phenomena show functional grounding at the stage when they originate as phonological patterns. In some cases, later historical changes could have obscured the grounding in the present-day pattern, so that it might no longer be induced on the basis of functional principles. The patterns on which I focus in this work are chiefly ones for which the synchronic functional grounding is evident. Nevertheless, certain morpheme-specific phonological patterns are considered for which the pattern can be considered to have functional grounding, but it is restricted to a subset of the morphemes of the language (§3.6).

In what follows I consider specifics that may be connected to the increased prominence of four positions: stressed syllables, initial syllables, final syllables, and morphological roots or stems. I also consider particulars that bear on the comparative weakness of unstressed syllables and final syllables. Interestingly, final syllables show mixed effects of strength. I then turn to the relative markedness of specific vowel properties, especially in a weak position. Particular attention is paid to the topic of vowel height in a weak position. For certain contrasts, phonological patterns and their possible phonetic bases point to some variation for which quality serves as marked. I close with predictions concerning prominence-based licensing systems.

2.2 Stressed and unstressed syllables

In addition to their function in metrical systems, stressed and unstressed syllables often show asymmetries in other types of phonological phenomena. Because the strength of stressed syllables and the weakness of unstressed syllables will both be relevant in patterns studied in this work, I consider matters relating to each here.

Phonological processes or distributions often show some sort of privilege for the stressed syllable, often displayed in the form of retention of structure or resistance to phonological change. Likewise, the content of stressed syllables is often preserved in child language and in the formation of prosodic morphemes, such as truncations or reduplicants. Stressed syllables can also exhibit privilege such that the stressed position is the target of change, for instance it can be the target of augmentative processes that operate within the stressed syllable or of processes that augment weak material by causing it to shift to the stressed syllable or overlap with it. Further, stressed syllables can serve as the point of prominence for infixation phenomena. A sampling of the phenomena in question are listed in (1).

(1) Examples of phonological patterns that display privilege for the stressed syllable
   a. *Deletion*: Vowels in stressed syllables resist synchronic deletion (e.g. Miglio 2005) and they resist deletion in language change (e.g. Grandgent 2002).
   b. *Contrast*: Certain segmental contrasts are displayed or preserved in stressed syllables (e.g. Trubetzkoy 1969; Beckman 1999; Crosswhite 2001, 2004; Barnes 2006).
   c. *Fortition/lenition*: Segments resist lenition or show fortition in a stressed syllable (Kirchner 2001; Lavoie 2001; González 2003).
   d. *Augmentation*: Stressed syllables are heavy or become heavy; stressed syllables display a high tone; stressed syllables display a preference for high sonority nuclei; stressed syllables that lack an onset or have a high sonority onset are avoided (Smith 2005).
   e. *Harmony*: Segments in a stressed syllable control vowel harmony or nasal harmony (e.g. Majors 1998; Beckman 1999); segments in a stressed syllable are the target of vowel harmony (e.g. Calabrese 1988; Walker 2005).
   f. *Metathesis*: Unstressed vowels at a word boundary undergo consonant–vowel metathesis to become aligned with the stressed syllable (Blevins and Garrett 1998, 2004); metathesis of certain consonants occurs following a stressed vowel (Hume and Seo 2004).
   g. *Infixation*: Stressed syllables are the destination for infixation (Yu 2007).
   h. *Prosodically based morphemes*: Stressed syllables are singled out in reduplication or truncation (Nelson 2003).
   i. *Truncations in child language*: Stressed syllables are preserved in truncations produced in children's developing language (Kehoe and Stoel-Gammon 1997; Curtin 2002).

In addition to phenomena that privilege the stressed syllable, the comparative weakness of the unstressed syllable can give rise to phenomena that restrict or efface content in unstressed contexts, such as vowel reduction processes. In some cases, vowels in an unstressed syllable can serve as the trigger for assimilation with the result that particular distinctive properties become extended over multiple syllables in a word, sometimes specifically overlapping with the stressed syllable.

The asymmetry between the strength of stressed syllables in comparison to unstressed syllables in phonology correlates with phonetic differences in the strength of these positions. Fougeron (1999) surveys research on variations in articulations in relation to the presence of stress in some languages, including French and English. She finds that consonants in a stressed position may display a longer closure, higher jaw position,[5] higher tongue position, and higher velum position. Further, a laryngeal gesture may be longer in a stressed syllable than in an unstressed syllable, as Goldstein (1992) finds for /h/ in English. Stressed vowels show a lower jaw position, and effects on the tongue position are such that they tend to make vowels more peripheral. Also, muscular activity in the lips is increased. Fougeron notes, however, that these effects can show some speaker-specific variation.

In terms of their acoustic properties, unstressed syllables tend to be shorter in duration and lower in amplitude than stressed syllables, and they tend to lack a salient pitch contour, although with some language-dependent differences (e.g. Lehiste 1970). Stressed syllables thereby supply richer cues for the perception of segments and suprasegmental characteristics (e.g. Steriade 1999a; Crosswhite 2001, 2004; Walker 2005). This is in line with patterns in which a greater range of contrasts is found in stressed syllables than in unstressed ones.

In contrast to stressed syllables, in durationally impoverished unstressed syllables, articulatory targets might not be reached, causing a compression of the articulatory and acoustic space. For example, the shorter durations that tend to occur in unstressed syllables may cause undershoot of a height target for non-high vowels (Flemming 2004, 2005; Barnes 2006). The result could be a lowering of F1 in an unstressed non-high vowel, or a raising of the floor of the vowel space, reducing dispersion of vowel height contrasts. This is supported by experimental studies of Swedish (Lindblom 1963), Catalan (Herrick 2003), and Russian (Padgett and Tabain 2005). For Russian, it was found that not only did the floor of the vowel space raise in unstressed syllables, but the ceiling also lowered in non-palatalized vowels, causing further compression. The reduced space for realization of contrasts may be connected to the occurrence of fewer contrasts in unstressed syllables. Nevertheless, whether undershoot drives phonological reduction patterns in vowels is the subject of debate.[6]

Coarticulation is another area of asymmetry between stressed and unstressed syllables. Studies on English and Dutch have shown that unstressed vowels are more vulnerable to vowel-to-vowel coarticulation than stressed ones (e.g. Fowler 1981; van Bergem 1994; Majors 1998); however, the effects show some variation across speakers and they vary with the vowel quality involved. The tendency for primacy of stressed vowels in coarticulation is consistent with vowel harmony patterns in which an unstressed vowel assimilates to a stressed one (Majors 1998).[7] From the angle of perception, in harmony patterns that involve assimilation between a stressed syllable and an unstressed syllable, the harmonizing property will have greater duration than if it were in either syllable alone, providing more opportunity for its accurate perception (see Cole 1998 for related discussion). Harmony of a distinctive property from an unstressed syllable stands to gain more by extending its duration. On the other hand, all else being equal, harmony from a stressed vowel to an unstressed one could be expected if coarticulation were the motivating source. Both types of harmony patterns are actually attested, suggesting that perception and production could both be important.

In addition to the copious evidence that supports the phonetic prominence of stressed syllables in comparison to unstressed ones, there is some evidence from psycholinguistic studies to support the salience of stressed syllables, although there are perhaps some bounds on its role in processing. One study concerns tip-of-the-tongue (TOT) states. Browman (1978) found that segments near the beginning of the stressed syllable show better recall than content later in the syllable and than syllable-initial clusters in unstressed syllables. In the area of lexical access, a variety of studies suggest that stressed syllables play a role in locating word boundaries or in triggering lexical access attempts; see Smith (2005: 220f.) for an overview. Goldstein's (1977) study of experimentally generated misperceptions in words and short phrases found a higher incidence of misperceptions in unstressed syllables than in stressed ones. Further, in a study where participants were tasked with detecting mispronunciations, these were detected more often in stressed syllables than in unstressed syllables (Cole and Jakimik 1980). Cole and Jakimik attribute this result to the increased salience of segmental distinctions in stressed syllables (p. 968). Goldstein reaches a similar conclusion and suggests that the effect is at least partly due to the greater phonetic ambiguity in unstressed syllables (p. 53). On the whole, the role of stressed syllables in word recognition appears to be somewhat limited. In particular, Smith argues that stressed syllables do not play a fundamental role in early-stage word recognition, unlike the initial syllable and root material, discussed below.

Other studies have investigated the role of stress in phonological encoding. Research by Shattuck-Hufnagel (1986, 1992) has investigated the role of stress in segmental speech errors in English. She found that vowels that occur in a position of primary lexical stress are more likely to interact in errors than vowels that do not share stress, and likewise consonants occurring before a stressed vowel show more interaction than consonants occurring in different positions. Shattuck-Hufnagel observes that the effect of stressed position seemed to be stronger for vowels than for consonants. This difference was demonstrated for German by Berg (1990). The interaction between stress and incidence of speech errors seems to vary across languages. Whereas there are more speech errors involving stressed syllables in English and German, errors occur equally often in stressed and unstressed syllables in Spanish (Berg 1991, 1998). Further, the data discussed by Shattuck-Hufnagel are equivocal about whether errors support prominence for stressed syllables in processing or just information about whether they are stressed. Patterns of errors in English involving syllabic sonorants and non-main-stress vowels suggest that it is stress similarity that affects the likelihood of participation in an error (i.e. likelihood increases if both segments are in a stressed syllable or both are unstressed), rather than main stress alone conditioning a greater incidence of errors. However, more study of the issue is needed. At a minimum, this supports the need for sensitivity to stress in the processing representations used for phonological planning in some languages.

Of course, there is not necessarily just a two-way distinction of prominence for the dimension of stress. Beyond metrical systems, primary stressed syllables could show more prominence than ones with secondary stress in phonological or phonetic patterns. Magen (1997) found evidence in English that primary stress can cause more coarticulation in a non-adjacent syllable with secondary stress than the reverse. In addition, unstressed syllables might show differences in strength according to their position in the word. Unstressed syllables at word boundaries could show strength associated with those positions. Also, some languages show phonological asymmetries in strength in pretonic syllables versus post-tonic syllables, sometimes specifically associated with immediate pretonic or immediate post-tonic position. A number of Slavic and Romance languages show greater strength in pretonic syllables (e.g. Maiden 1995; Crosswhite 2001; Bethin 2006); however, this is not a universal property of language (Kaplan 2008a). Phonological patterns connected with these asymmetries in Romance are taken up in chapter 8. Whether they correlate with asymmetries in phonetic strength or psycholinguistic salience remains to be explored for many languages, although some experimental work in this direction has been undertaken (see chapter 8).

2.3   Initial syllables

Numerous phonological patterns support the special status of the initial syllable or initial segments. A sampling of such phenomena is outlined in (2).

(2)   Examples of phonological patterns that display privilege for initial material
   a. *Deletion*: Vowels in the first syllable of words or morphemes resist deletion in vowel hiatus environments (Casali 1997, 1998); in language change, unstressed vowels in an initial syllable resist deletion in contrast with unstressed vowels in certain other positions in the word (e.g. Grandgent 2002).

b. *Contrast*: Certain segmental contrasts are displayed or preserved in initial position or in an initial syllable (Trubetzkoy 1969; Steriade 1995a, 1999a; Beckman 1999; Fougeron 1999).
c. *Fortition/lenition*: Segments resist lenition or show fortition in initial position (Fougeron 1999; Kirchner 2001; Lavoie 2001).
d. *Augmentation*: Onsetless syllables are avoided in initial position; high sonority onsets are avoided in initial syllables (Smith 2005).
e. *Local consonant assimilation*: Assimilation among adjacent consonants is controlled by a segment in the initial syllable (Beckman 1999).
f. *Consonant cooccurrence restrictions*: Restrictions on the cooccurrence of homorganic consonants are enforced more strongly for consonant pairs that include a root-initial consonant (Frisch 1996, 2000).
g. *Harmony*: Vowels in a word-initial syllable or root-initial syllable control harmony (e.g. Suomi 1983; Kaun 1995; Beckman 1997, 1999; Walker 2001b; Krämer 2003; Barnes 2006).
h. *Metathesis*: Word-initial segments resist metathesis (Hume 1998); metathesis shifts particular consonants to the initial position of a vowel-initial root (Alber 2001).
i. *Infixation*: First consonant or first vowel is the destination for infixation (Yu 2007).
j. *Prosodically based morphemes*: Initial material is singled out in reduplication or truncation (Nelson 2003).

The privileged status of initial syllables, or in some cases specifically word-initial consonants or vowels, has been variously argued to have a basis in the psycholinguistic salience and phonetic strength of this context.

The claim that word-initial phonological units are privileged or prominent in phonology with at least partial basis in the psycholinguistic prominence of this position is discussed by Beckman (1997, 1999), Casali (1997), Fougeron (1999), Alber (2001), Nelson (2003), and Smith (2005).[8] Psycholinguistic evidence for the increased salience of initial material is discussed by Nooteboom (1981), Hall (1988), and Hawkins and Cutler (1988). Numerous studies have shown that word beginnings are important for word recognition and lexical retrieval. For example, using fragments of one or two syllables in length, Nooteboom found that initial fragments make better cues for word recognition than final fragments. In research on TOT states, Brown and McNeill (1966) demonstrated that word-initial letters were most likely to be matched in words of similar sound that were provided by experiment participants. In another TOT study, Browman (1978) reported better recall of units at the beginning and end of the item than internal material. Cole and Jakimik (1980) found that listeners detect a mispronunciation in the second syllable more rapidly than in an initial syllable. They interpret this as supporting a hypothesis that words are accessed from the sounds that begin a word. Under this view, reaction times are faster for errors in second syllables, because the set of word candidates has already been narrowed based on information in the first syllable. On the other hand, an error in the first syllable provides misleading information so that the error cannot be detected until information from a subsequent syllable is obtained. In research involving speech shadowing tasks, Marslen-Wilson (1975) and Marslen-Wilson and Welsh (1978) found that mispronunciations are less likely to be replaced in initial portions of words, which suggests that mispronunciations are better perceived at word beginnings.

Initial syllables can also play a special role in language production. In research on certain kinds of speech errors, Fay and Cutler (1977: 514–16, n. 15) found that vowels in the first syllables of target and error words were more likely to be identical than vowels in the stressed syllables of target and error words in forms where the first syllable and stressed syllable do not coincide. A series of experiments by Shattuck-Hufnagel (1992) using tongue-twisters with speakers of English to elicit speech errors demonstrated that consonants that share the status of being in word onset position are more likely to participate in a speech error than consonants in two different word positions. Also, Berg (1998) notes that word onsets are most often affected in slips of the tongue in the Germanic languages. Shattuck-Hufnagel argues that this tendency supports making available reference to the word onset in the model for phonological planning. Research by Frisch (1996, 2000) on consonant errors in English found that word onsets are more prone to errors when the consonants are similar, but not when they are dissimilar. He also found a trend for more errors to occur between similar stressed word onsets than between similar stressed onsets in the second syllable, suggesting that the effect of similarity is stronger in word onset context, at least for speech errors. He interprets this as an effect of sequential encoding (Sevald and Dell 1994), where word onsets have a special status because they have no preceding context in the word to produce interference. Another study by Meijer (1996) with speakers of English found results suggesting that word onset consonants are the most prone to participating in errors in general. Based on those results, Meijer postulates that word onsets receive a higher level of activation in phonological encoding. As with stressed positions, however, these effects seem to vary across languages: Berg (1991) found that in Spanish, word onset consonants are less prone to participate in slips of the tongue than word-medial onsets.

Smith (2005) attributes the phonological strength of the initial syllable specifically to its importance for early-stage word recognition, that is, "the stage of speech processing in which a set of lexical entries that are similar to the incoming acoustic signal is initially activated" (p. 86, n. 38). She argues that positions of this kind tend to resist neutralization of contrasts in augmentation phenomena, except for neutralizations that serve to facilitate word segmentation by marking word beginnings in the speech stream. In this respect, Smith distinguishes psycholinguistically strong positions from ones that show phonetic strength. In the latter positions, phonetic strengthening effects can cause resistance to neutralization, such as reduction, but they can also be the source of neutralization, for example, by lengthening. In a departure from this viewpoint, Barnes (2006) argues that initial syllables show effects of phonetic prominence enhancement. He further takes the position that the strength-based asymmetries shown by initial syllables are due to their phonetic characteristics.

In his discussion of phonetic evidence for the prominence of segments belonging to the initial syllable, Barnes points out that many cases of initial syllable strength can be attributed to fixed initial stress. Apart from stress, phonetic strengthening of segments at the beginning of prosodic constituents has been documented, but the particulars of the phenomenon are language specific and effects tend to be stronger at higher prosodic levels. Strengthening in domain-initial consonants has been observed for languages such as English, French, Korean, and Taiwanese. Depending on the language, these effects include an increase in the magnitude of the supralaryngeal gestures and glottal opening gestures, lengthening, greater amplitude, and effects involving VOT and airflow, among other enhancements (e.g. Goldstein 1992; Pierrehumbert and Talkin 1992; Fougeron and Keating 1996; Fougeron 1999; Keating *et al.* 1999; Cho and Jun 2000). In addition, in research reviewed by Fougeron (1999), vowels in absolute word-initial position show some strengthening in comparison to word-internal vowels in Finnish and English. Finnish vowels were found to be longer and more peripheral. Some languages, such as English, German, Finnish, and Czech, enhance initial vowels with glottal articulation.

In many languages, domain-initial strengthening effects appear to be limited to the first segment of the word in domain-initial position (Cho and Jun 2000), and in this respect, they are weaker than domain-final strengthening effects, which often shows effects further into the word. For example, in English, vowels in word-initial syllables with onsets did not show significant lengthening or strengthening effects (Fougeron and Keating 1996; Byrd 2000; Barnes 2006). In conformity with this finding, Barnes points out that a number of phonological patterns tied to the strength of the initial position single out just initial consonants or absolute word-initial vowels. On the other hand, a study of Turkish by Barnes found evidence of domain-initial strengthening of vowels in initial syllables with onsets. Specifically, vowels in initial syllables show greater duration than ones in the second syllable. Perhaps somewhat surprisingly, Barnes found the greatest effect in word-initial context, in contrast to higher order prosodic constituents. Barnes also notes that in Turkmen, a related language, vowels in word-initial syllables are realized with a longer duration than in comparable word-internal syllables, regardless of the location of stress. On the basis of his study and others in this area, Barnes concludes that domain-initial phonetic strengthening effects vary in their extent across languages.

Apart from the debate about the psycholinguistic or phonetic origins of the special status of initial material, perspectives differ on the particular units in phonological theory to which the privileged initial material is relativized. Beckman (1997, 1999) proposes that root-initial syllables show privilege in phonology with respect to faithfulness effects.[9] On the basis of phonological patterns of positional augmentation, Smith (2005) argues that the initial syllable of the morphological word serves as a strong position. Research by Casali (1997, 1998) on vowel elision in hiatus contexts leads him to postulate a special status for word-initial and morpheme-initial segments. For the purposes of the vowel patterns studied in this book, initial prominence effects will generally concern material in the first syllable of words. Morphological categories will be noted where they are relevant to the pattern.

2.4 Final syllables

Final syllables are another position that can display evidence of prominence. Some examples of relevant phonological patterns are listed in (3).

(3) Examples of phonological patterns that display privilege for final material
 a. *Deletion*: Vowels in final syllables resist deletion in language change (Grandgent 1927).
 b. *Contrast*: Certain segmental contrasts are displayed or preserved in the final syllable or in final position (Steriade 1999a; Barnes 2006).
 c. *Tones*: Contour tones preferentially occur in final syllables (Zoll 1998a; Zhang 2002, 2004; Gordon 2006).
 d. *Local consonant assimilation*: Word-final consonants control laryngeal assimilation in a final cluster (Petrova *et al.* 2006).
 e. *Harmony*: Vowels in a final syllable control harmony (Hyman 1998; Cerrón-Palomino López 2003; Krämer 2003; Sasa 2009).
 f. *Infixation*: Final syllables or final vowels are the destination for infixation (Yu 2007).
 g. *Truncations in child language*: Final syllables are preserved in truncations produced in children's developing language (Kehoe and Stoel-Gammon 1997; Curtin 2002).

Phenomena such as these have led some researchers to postulate the existence of phonological positional privilege for a word-final segment (Petrova *et al.* 2006) or a word-final syllable (e.g. Curtin 2002).

As with word beginnings, there is evidence from psycholinguistic studies to support the salience of word endings. Evidence from studies on word recognition is discussed by Petrova *et al.* They point out that word beginnings and word endings were found to be equally good for cuing recognition of a word when the rest of the word is masked by noise (Nooteboom and van der Vlugt 1988), and rhyming items were demonstrated to facilitate identification of spoken words (Milberg *et al.* 1988). The importance of word-final material has also been demonstrated in TOT studies. As mentioned in §2.3, Browman (1978) reported that units at the boundaries of items were better recalled in TOT states than internal material. Similar findings with respect to letters at the beginnings and ends of words were reported by Brown and McNeill (1966) and Koriat and Lieblich (1974).

Final syllables also show prominence in first language acquisition. In truncated productions of polysyllabic words by children, a preference was observed for retention of final syllables over non-final unstressed syllables for English, Dutch, and Polish (Kehoe and Stoel-Gammon 1997; Curtin 2002). In addition to suggesting that this pattern could have an origin in phonetic strengthening in final syllables, some of which is greater in infant-directed speech than in adult-directed speech, Curtin hypothesizes that final syllable prominence could have a basis in a recency effect for syllables in phrase-final or sentence-final position. She suggests this could increase the likelihood that final syllables would be extracted and stored in first language acquisition compared to syllables in non-final positions. Barnes (2006: 78) speculates that the special psycholinguistic status of final syllables evidenced in children's early speech could lead to analogous prominence effects in the phonological systems of adults.

In some languages, final syllables show increased phonetic prominence. As Barnes discusses, a phonetic basis for final syllable strength lies in domain-final lengthening and strengthening (see also Zhang 2002). Experimental studies have established the occurrence of final lengthening in many languages. Barnes speculates that it might be a universal characteristic displayed by languages, and it might be a general property of motor performance (Johnson and Martin 2001). However, lengthening effects tend to be more robust at the boundaries of higher level phrases, and implementation differs across languages. For example, Barnes points to a study by Delattre (1966), which shows that English, French, German, and Spanish differ in the magnitude of final lengthening in comparable constituents.

In contrast to their above-mentioned strength, final syllables also show weakness. For a review of phonological phenomena that are associated with final weakness, see Barnes (2006). Barnes reconciles this by pointing out that alongside their potential for certain properties of phonetic strength, final positions tend to show certain phonetic properties that reduce perceptual robustness. These include drops in pitch and intensity, and total or partial loss of voicing or the occurrence of breathy or creaky voice. These characteristics have the potential to obscure perception of vowel quality, which can cause final syllables to pattern as weak. Barnes observes that final weakening effects could be specific to vowels in final open syllables, since vowels in a final closed syllable could be protected to some extent by their increased distance from the phrase boundary. The mixed strength and weakness of final positions correlates with their variable display of strength across and within languages, and it can produce conflicting or variable markedness effects.

2.5 Morphological roots and stems

An abundance of research supports the primacy of root or stem material in phonological patterns. An assortment of the types of patterns that show such effects is listed in (4).

(4) Examples of phonological processes that display privilege for root or stem material
   a. *Deletion*: Lexical stem vowels resist deletion in vowel hiatus environments (Casali 1997, 1998).
   b. *Contrast*: Roots display or preserve more phonological contrasts or marked structure than non-root morphemes (e.g. McCarthy and Prince 1994a, 1995; Dyck 1995; Steriade 1995b; Beckman 1999, Walker 2001a; Urbanczyk 2001, 2006; Ussishkin and Wedel 2002; Smith 2005; Barnes 2006; Campos-Astorkiza 2009).
   c. *Accent*: Lexical stresses or accents affiliated with the root are preserved (Revithiadou 1999; Alderete 2001a, b).
   d. *Fusion*: Preservation of root material is prioritized in segmental fusion (Kawahara 2003).
   e. *Local consonant assimilation*: Root consonants control nasal place assimilation (Hyman 2001, 2008).
   f. *Harmony*: Material affiliated with the root or stem controls vowel harmony or consonant harmony in non-root segments (Clements 1980; Ringen and Vago 1998; Baković 2000; Hansson 2001; Walker 2001a; Krämer 2003; Rose and Walker 2004); a segment in the root is the target of harmony (Kaplan 2008a, b).
   g. *Prosodically based morphemes*: Root material is singled out in reduplication (McCarthy and Prince 1993a; Spaelti 1997; Urbanczyk 2001, 2007).

A body of research on cyclic effects and lexical phonology also lends support to stem prioritization in various capacities. See Cole (1995) for an overview.

Psycholinguistic evidence supports the prominence of roots. Smith (2005) provides a comprehensive review of the psycholinguistic literature on this topic in the context of its relation to phonological patterns (see also Beckman 1999 and Kaplan 2008a). A main finding that emerges is support for the claim that the root forms the primary base for lexical storage and access. For example, various experimental studies have shown that for frequency-sensitive aspects of language processing, the frequency of a given item is affected by other forms containing the same root. A word recall study for English *-ly* adverbs formed from high frequency and low frequency adjectives showed that ease of recall of low frequency adverbs is influenced by the frequency of the adjective root (Rosenberg *et al.* 1966). In their interpretation of results of a priming experiment for English, Kempley and Morton (1982) likewise find that frequency of root morphemes influences recognition of inflected words. Smith discusses other studies on related topics for Dutch and Italian (2005: 212).

Other types of study also suggest that lexical storage is organized around the root. For instance, experimental research on Dutch by Jarvella and Meijers (1983) measured the response time for judgments of whether certain verb forms were the same or different in either the stem or the inflectional form (e.g. past tense or past participle) of a cuing verb. Judgments were faster for stem decisions than for form decisions. Their results suggest that verb roots are accessed more easily than inflectional affixes, and they are compatible with a lexical processing system that is root centered. Other studies have shown that inflected words that contain a given root can prime the bare root as effectively as the bare root can prime itself in English (e.g. Stanners *et al.* 1979; Fowler *et al.* 1985). Feldman and Moskovljević (1987) find related results for Serbo-Croatian.

Smith's (2005) review of research relating to words with derivational affixes yields a somewhat more complex picture for their relation to roots. While Smith notes that the available experimental evidence is not entirely conclusive, she nevertheless finds that evidence points towards a privileged role for the root in processing of words with derivational morphology. Specifically, lexical access seems to involve identifying roots within affixed forms. At the same time, Smith also discusses experimental results suggesting that forms with derivational morphology could have their own lexical entry independent of the lexical entry for the root. The possibly different status of derivational affixes from inflectional affixes in language processing could perhaps be connected to the potential for stems with derivational morphology to function as a 'base' for certain phonological processes or formations, but more research on this topic is needed before firm conclusions can be reached.

Alongside reported effects of root strength and the comparative weakness of affixes, cases exist where affixes show evidence of phonological strength, apparently separate from phonetically based word-edge strength effects. Such patterns have not generally been interpreted as signaling affix prominence; rather they have engendered proposals that certain patterns could arise from a need to avoid neutralization of a morphological contrast involving the affix or a need to improve its perceptibility. For discussion of possible cases of this kind involving vowel patterns, see Majors (1998), Crosswhite (2001), Kurisu (2001), Dillon (2004), Miglio (2005), and Barnes (2006).

2.6 Specific vowel qualities

I turn now to markedness of specific vowel properties, especially in weak position, and their possible phonetic basis. This issue is relevant because although some licensing-based vowel patterns take scope over all distinctive vowel properties in the language, the majority either efface or augment specific vowel properties in a weak position. I consider marked vowel properties to be directly related to typological patterns obtained through the action of markedness constraints that penalize certain vowel properties, either in particular contexts or without contextual restrictions. Such patterns typically reflect vowel properties that are relatively less frequent within and across languages. Marked vowel properties could be eliminated in the course of a derivation, for example through being the target of deletion or neutralization. On the other hand, a contextually marked vowel property could trigger assimilation if that caused it to shed the contextual characteristics that render it marked. Vowel properties that are relatively less marked tend to be associated with epenthesis. For general discussion of aspects of segmental markedness and its diagnostics, see Rice (1999, 2007) and de Lacy (2002, 2006). A few examples of some marked vowel properties, couched in terms of feature specifications, are given in (5). These are cases of contextual markedness in that they either involve a vowel property in a particular position or one in combination with another vowel property.

(5)   Examples of contextually marked vowel feature specifications
      a. [*round*]:
         [+round] is more marked in a non-high vowel than in a high vowel (Kirchner 1993; Kaun 1995, 2004).

b. [*ATR*]:
[−ATR] is more marked in a high vowel than in a non-high vowel; [+ATR] is more marked in a low vowel than in a non-low vowel (e.g. Calabrese 1988; Archangeli and Pulleyblank 1994; Baković 2000).
c. [*high*]:
[+high] can be more marked than [−high] in an unstressed syllable (Walker 2005); [−high] can be more marked than [+high] in an unstressed syllable (Crosswhite 2001, 2004).

Some cases of markedness involving a vowel property in combination with another are straightforward, such as those in (5a–b), whose markedness patterning is generally consistent across different phonological phenomena and across languages. Prior research has considered the phonetic basis for these examples. As concerns (5a), Kaun has argued on the basis of experimental research that lip rounding is more perceptually subtle in vowels with a lower jaw height than in higher vowels. Thus, rounding in a non-high vowel could be considered marked. A physical basis for the markedness asymmetries in (5b) has been discussed by Archangeli and Pulleyblank. They observe that because the tongue is incompressible, a gesture in one dimension often results in a compensatory gesture in another dimension. This plays out in interactions between height and tongue root advancement such that in advancing the tongue root, the tongue body tends to raise, and in retracting the tongue root, the tongue body tends to lower.

Unlike the ubiquitous cases in (5a–b), not every pairing of vowel properties shows a clear markedness asymmetry. For example, different studies come to different conclusions about whether [+ATR] or [−ATR] mid vowels are more marked (Archangeli and Pulleyblank 1994; Miglio 2005). Some context-sensitive cases seem to show variable markedness. As listed in (5c), there appears to be variation as to whether [+high] or [−high] is more marked in the context of an unstressed syllable. Further, the relative markedness of features considered independent of context can be a vexed matter. Rice's (1999) wide-ranging review of diagnostics for featural markedness finds that they do not regularly produce the same results across languages, even when the languages share the same inventory. Her survey points to the existence of some variation for which features may be unmarked within a class. For instance, for a contrast between front and back vowels, languages can differ in whether front vowels or back ones serve as unmarked with respect to asymmetric assimilation.[10] Independent of context, the relative markedness of vowels that have an advanced versus retracted tongue root also seems to be variable. Nevertheless, Rice finds that cross-linguistic generalizations exist in that not all feature specifications can serve as unmarked. For example, she observes that [labial] does not serve as the least marked place of articulation for consonants in an inventory that shows a labial/coronal/velar opposition.

In what follows, I focus on the issue of the markedness of different vowel heights in an unstressed syllable or other weak position, which will be especially relevant to many of the licensing patterns considered in this work. I will consider markedness predictions both on the basis of phonetic grounding and phonological patterning.

With respect to perception, there is reason to suppose that either unstressed high vowels or mid vowels could present difficulty. All else being equal, high vowels are expected to be lower in amplitude and shorter in duration than non-high vowels, because of their narrower aperture and lesser jaw lowering. Lehiste (1970) reports that the intrinsic intensity of high vowels in English is less than that of non-high monophthongs with the same backness (after Lehiste and Peterson 1959). The same is true of Hungarian for vowels compared with others of the same length (Fónagy 1966; Lehiste 1970). In addition, Lehiste points out that a correlation has been confirmed in numerous languages between intrinsic duration and tongue height such that high vowels are shorter (in English, German, Spanish, Swedish, and Thai, among others). These effects could cause high vowels to be less perceptible or salient than non-high vowels (Majors 1998; Smith 2005; Walker 2005). On the other hand, high vowels could be more perceptible because they tend to improve dispersion (e.g. Lindblom 1986, 1990) and because of their focalization of acoustic energy, which could enhance their salience[11] (Schwartz et al. 1997; see also Stevens 1989 on quantal effects).[12] Nevertheless, the extent to which focalization produces an effect in weak positions, such as unstressed syllables, deserves more study. As for low vowels, in cross-linguistically common inventories with three, five, or seven vowels that include a single low vowel /a/, the diagnostics of intrinsic amplitude and duration, dispersion, and focalization converge on a categorization of /a/ as not perceptually difficult in comparison to vowels of other heights. However, in word-final position this situation can change, as I discuss later in this section.

Other phenomena point to the possibility that either high or mid vowels could serve as marked in a weak position. One criterion for a marked vowel quality is that it is unlikely to be epenthetic. Rice observes that high vowels are often epenthetic (e.g. Navajo) but in some languages epenthetic vowels are mid (e.g. Spanish). Epenthetic vowels do not have a contrastive function, and they often occur in phonologically weak positions. These patterns suggest that when perception of a height contrast is not at stake, high vowels may be unmarked in a weak position, but this is not a universal generalization.

Patterns of vowel deletion provide another diagnostic. It can be supposed that deletion that asymmetrically affects vowels with particular qualities eliminates marked vowels (de Lacy 2002, 2006).[13] In patterns that delete unstressed vowels, often high vowels or all non-low vowels are prone to deletion. In the history of Latin, unstressed high and mid vowels were frequently deleted, but [a] was generally retained (Grandgent 2002; note also Hermann 1997), e.g. *frigdária* for *frìgidária*, *cornáre* for *coronáre*, but *mìrabília*. Further examples where elision occurred include *cóm(i)tem*, *dèl(i)cátus*, *fráx(i)nus*, *pérs(i)ca*, *fíb(u)la*, *póp(u)lus*, *séd(e)cim*, *còll(o)cáre*. In many present-day dialects of northern Italy, unstressed vowels except [a] are extensively deleted where syllable structure allows (Maiden 1997), e.g. Bolognese [dmáŋga] 'Sunday' < *[doménika], [zbdɛl] 'hospital' < *[ospitále]. These patterns point to non-low vowels, especially high ones, being disfavored in unstressed syllables of Latin and certain of its descendents. In late Latin the vowels [i]/[e] and [u]/[o] were often used indiscriminately in post-tonic syllables (Grandgent 2002). This suggests that the contrast between high and mid vowels in post-tonic syllables was perceptually difficult, and these same vowels were susceptible to deletion. The cause for the perceptual difficulty could be tied to compression of the height dimension in the absence of stress (see §2.2). The low vowel /a/ could be less vulnerable to deletion or confusion with other vowels because it has the lowest height, and hence tends to have the greatest intrinsic amplitude and duration. Also, as the only low vowel and the only central vowel in Latin, it lacks a minimally contrastive vowel paired for backness/rounding or height.

While Latin unstressed vowel patterns point to a weak contrast between high and mid vowels in this context, which could be construed as a basis for classifying them as marked, diagnostics do not uniformly designate one of these heights as more marked. The fact that many Romance dialects show partial or full raising of mid vowels in unstressed vowel neutralization (e.g. Maiden 1997; Crosswhite 2001) could indicate that unstressed high vowels are less marked, either with respect to prominence (Crosswhite 2001, 2004) or articulatory effort (Flemming 2004). This is in keeping with a viewpoint that peripheral vowels (e.g. /i a u/) are less marked than non-peripheral vowels, (e.g. /e o/) (Steriade 1995b; Crosswhite 2001, 2004). However, in many Romance dialects, high vowels trigger height assimilation in the stressed syllable, and sometimes the triggers are restricted to high vowels that are in contrast with mid vowels (Dyck 1995; Rice 1999; Campos-Astorkiza 2009). Rice and de Lacy identify triggering of assimilation as a characteristic of marked elements. These triggering effects are therefore suggestive of an opposite conclusion, namely, that the high unstressed vowels are more marked. As interpreted here, these patterns can be construed as avoidance of a high vowel whose contrastive height property is expressed solely in an unstressed position.

It is worth considering whether asymmetries in triggers of vowel assimilation could have a basis in coarticulatory patterns that are sensitive to vowel quality. For example, [i] has been found to have the strongest coarticulatory influence in German and Italian (Butcher and Weiher 1976; Farnetani et al. 1985). Also, cross-linguistically [i] tends to show the weakest coarticulatory effects from other vowels (Beddor et al. 2001, 2002). Iverson and Salmons (2003) suggest that umlaut in Old High German, which is triggered by high front [i j], has a source in the coarticulatory properties of these vocoids (see §5.3). In Walker 2005, I speculate that the coarticulatory characteristics of [i] could contribute to this vowel's function as a trigger of metaphony in Romance dialects of Italy and Spain, although most likely as an ancillary factor. In metaphony patterns, a high vowel causes height assimilation in a preceding stressed vowel. However, the occurrence of harmony from unstressed [i] but not stressed [i] seems to require explanation apart from coarticulation.[14] Indeed the opposite could be expected if coarticulation were the only motivating force (see §2.2). Experimental research by Majors (1998) found that unstressed /i/ was more prone to coarticulatory influence from an adjacent stressed vowel than vice versa for some speakers of English. Also, the strong coarticulatory influence of [i] cannot be the only basis for high vowel triggers given that [u] can trigger metaphony; indeed, in some languages [u] serves as the only trigger (e.g. in the dialect of Lena). These characteristics support the conclusion that high unstressed vowels serve as marked in metaphonic-type patterns, and that prominence-based licensing plays a driving role in such systems.

As mentioned above, low vowels do not typically present greater perceptual difficulty than higher vowels. As we might expect, this generalization is principally tied to inventories in which /a/ is the only low vowel. When it comes to contrasts involving backness and rounding, both of which affect F2, high vowels tend to exhibit greater perceptual distance than lower ones (Sands 2004). Not surprisingly, then, in Esimbi, a language that displays three low vowels, as well as front and back mid vowels and three high vowels, a prominence-based licensing pattern that realizes vowel height contrasts in the initial syllable singles out non-high vowels as a class. Here, the crowding of the low vowels presents a greater challenge for the perception of contrasts among non-high vowels than in a language whose only low vowel is /a/. That the markedness of /a/ is sensitive to the presence or absence of other contrastive low vowels is consistent with the claim of Flemming (2002, 2004) that markedness as it pertains to perception is a property of contrasts and cannot be determined by assessment of individual sounds independent of the contrastive inventory.

Furthermore, the feature [+low] could serve as perceptually marked in the context of a final unstressed open syllable. Barnes (2006: 144f.) discusses a number of languages in which word-final /a/ undergoes reduction. In several cases, he lists /a/ as the only vowel to undergo reduction in this position. For example in Kullo (Omotic), word-final /a/ raises to [ʌ], in Muinane (Witotoan) and Goajiro (Arawakan) word-final /a/ undergoes variable raising to [ə]. Jiménez (1998) discusses Valencian varieties where word-final unstressed /a/ undergoes neutralization to [ɛ], [ɔ], or [ə]. Barnes notes an asymmetry between word-final open and closed syllables in Standard Malay. Neutralization in the final syllable results in the vowels [i ə u] in an open syllable but [e a o] in a closed syllable. He suggests that the vowels in a final open syllable may be more susceptible to certain types of phonetic attrition than vowels in a closed syllable by virtue of their closer proximity to the boundary (see §2.4).

We may wonder why lower vowels in particular could be disadvantaged in a word-final open syllable. Barnes identifies two possible reasons for vowel raising in word-final context. One is that breathy phonation – which can occur as an effect in final position – has been linked to raising in some languages (Gordon and Ladefoged 2001). Another has to do with the phasing of laryngeal and aerodynamic weakening in a final vowel and the target of its supralaryngeal gesture. Barnes examines Russian /a/ and /o/ in an unstressed syllable, which are realized anywhere between [ɐ] and [ə] in phrase-final position. He finds that amplitude in the final vowel decreases over the course of its production, becoming extremely weak towards the end. At the same time, Barnes observes that the peak F1 for the vowel seems to be delayed, coming later relative to the onset of the vowel. Assuming that gestures undergo slowing approaching the boundary, Barnes suggests that the combination of gestural slowing and amplitude decay cause the F1 peak to be attained during a portion of the vowel where perceptibility is significantly decreased. Thus, despite final lengthening, perception of the peak F1 is more difficult. During the earlier portion of the vowel, where perceptibility is stronger, the vowel has not yet reached its F1 target. Barnes speculates that this could cause listeners to misperceive the vowel as higher, leading to raising. This effect is specific to final position. Barnes found that pretonic /a/ showed a robust amplitude throughout, including at its F1 peak.

To summarize, with respect to vowel height, it seems that in weak positions, especially ones with reduced duration, high and mid vowels can be confusable and each have intrinsic aspects that could reduce their perceptibility. Properties of the word-final position can also interfere with the perception of low vowels. In this book I will interpret this as opening the possibility that there may be variation across languages in which quality is the focus of a pattern that reduces markedness. As we will see, this is consistent with the variable avoidance of these vowel qualities expressed solely in weak position across prominence-based licensing patterns. Nevertheless, much remains to be explored in issues surrounding markedness of specific vowel qualities in weak contexts, and its relation to the phonological aspect under focus, such as perception of a contrastive property, ease of articulation, metrical prominence, and so on. These remain matters on which more research is needed.

2.7 Summary and predictions

As introduced in chapter 1, factors of perception, production, and processing could all contribute to determining positions that function as prominent and segmental markedness. While the emphasis in this work is chiefly on the perceptual basis for position-sensitive vowel patterns, there is interaction with effects of production and processing. In view of that, this chapter has reviewed phonetic and psycholinguistic evidence that is hypothesized to be related to or give rise to certain types of prominence and markedness asymmetries in phonology. Four types of prominent positions were considered: stressed syllables, initial syllables, final syllables, and morphological roots or stems. Overall, stressed syllables show especially robust phonetic strength, whereas for initial positions and roots there is an abundance of evidence for psycholinguistic strength. However, some of the psycholinguistic evidence concerning initial content is for word onsets rather than initial syllables. Initial material also shows some phonetic strengthening effects, although this is variable across languages. There is some psycholinguistic evidence for the prominence of stressed syllables, but it is less substantial than for initial material and roots, possibly signaling a fundamentally different status for stressed syllables in processing. Final syllables show effects of phonetic strengthening in the form of final lengthening, although the implementation of such effects differs from language to language. There is also some evidence that final material is psycholinguistically prominent, although on the whole the effects are not as robust as for word beginnings. The strength of final syllables may be counteracted by phonetic final weakening effects, with the result that final syllables could be expected to show mixed effects with respect to strength and weakness.

The relative markedness of specific vowel qualities was also considered, especially in a weak position. For some characteristics, the assessment of relative markedness is consistent across languages and phenomena, and it falls in line with expectations that arise from what we know about the articulation or perception of the sounds involved. However, for other comparisons the predictions based on phonetic properties or from diagnostics based on phonological patterns do not point in a uniform direction. Here, it seems that languages can show some variation.

Asymmetries in positional prominence and vowel quality markedness lead to predictions about types of prominence-based licensing patterns that are expected and those that are not, outlined in what follows. These predictions bear on fundamental guiding questions of this work concerning the nature of phonological interactions between vowels and positional prominence and their functional grounding.

Given the evidence for the increased prominence of stressed syllables, initial positions, and roots/stems, we could expect each of them to show the potential to serve as licensors in prominence-based licensing phenomena. As we will see in later chapters, this is borne out. The prediction for final syllables is less clear-cut. Given their mixed strength, they might be expected to serve as a licensor or as prominent in other positional prominence constraints, but the expectation here is weaker. Indeed, Barnes observes that final syllables rarely if ever serve as the only prominent syllable within the word domain, as, for instance, stressed syllables sometimes do. For the vowel patterns studied in this book, a system was not found in which final syllables serve as a prominent position for purposes of prominence-based licensing, although patterns in which final syllables serve as prominent for positional faithfulness are identified. Whether the lack of prominence-based licensing patterns in which the final syllable serves as the licensing position is a systematic generalization about language or just results from the rarity of final syllables as a uniquely prominent position, remains to be seen, but the typological trend is consistent with Barnes' observations.

Positions that are relatively weak are also expected to figure in certain ways in prominence-based licensing phenomena. Phonological content in contexts that show comparative weakness could be expected to be singled out as the subject of licensing-based restrictions. Such contexts include unstressed syllables (possibly particular ones), final syllables (again, possibly with mixed effects), and affixes, especially those that are inflectional. Given the potential for action-at-a-distance in an identity-licensing configuration, we could expect licensing patterns where a particular weak position, such as a final syllable, interacts with a prominent position, such as a stressed syllable, across intervening material. We will see that these predictions too are borne out.

Certain types of systems are also unexpected with respect to positional asymmetries. Positions that are non-prominent are not expected to be singled out as licensors in positional licensing phenomena. This holds of contexts defined as the complement to a prominent position or that are especially weak, such as non-initial syllables, unstressed syllables, affixes, and inflectional morphemes. Likewise, material contained within a prominent position, such as a stressed syllable, initial syllable, or root/stem, are not expected to be singled out as the subject of a prominence-based licensing restriction, as is consistent with the patterns studied here.

The markedness of specific vowel properties results in quality-sensitive predictions for prominence-based licensing phenomena. It is expected that vowel properties that are marked (in some context) could be the subject of a prominence-based licensing restriction, especially if they are perceptually difficult. For example, lip rounding is considered to be more perceptually subtle in a non-high vowel than a high one. Consistent with this asymmetry, certain prominence-based patterns studied in this work prevent forms in which rounding in a non-high vowel is expressed solely in a weak position. No patterns were found where round high vowels alone were prevented by a licensing restriction, nor are they expected.

Another type of quality-sensitive prediction is that there could be exceptions to a prominence-based licensing process (i.e. blocking or a different solution) specifically when the result would otherwise have been a marked vowel. For example, there is wide consensus that [−ATR] is more marked in a high vowel than in a non-high one, and we could expect licensing-driven raising phenomena to be prevented or altered when they would generate a [−ATR] high vowel. Such patterns are indeed attested. Exceptions are not predicted when the result would otherwise have been a comparatively unmarked vowel.

Where the relative markedness for the qualities involved in a given vowel contrast is variable, we could expect variation across languages or perhaps even within them as to which vowel quality serves as marked (i.e. restricted) in licensing-based patterns. One such example is high versus mid vowels in a weak position, each of which has been suggested to present some perceptual difficulty. In the prominence-based licensing patterns studied in this book that involve height contrasts, high vowels in weak position are often the ones involved. We might perhaps expect high vowels to show more frequent activity than mid vowels in these phenomena based on the overall frequency with which this class of segments is active in phonology. Mielke's (2008) survey of phonologically active classes, which includes segments that undergo or trigger a phonological process or that display a static distributional restriction, ranks high vowels as the third most common natural class, whereas mid vowels rank nineteenth.

Low vowels in a weak position do not show asymmetric perceptual weakness, except in word-final open unstressed syllables. This is consistent with an apparent cross-linguistic generalization that prominence-based licensing patterns do not single out height in low vowels apart from in final position. The patterns investigated in this book find that low vowels are usually included only when all vowels in the system in weak position are involved. Barnes' research suggests that a low vowel could be perceptually disfavored in a word-final context. Consistent with his observations, prominence-based licensing patterns are observed that work to prevent distinctive properties of a low vowel from being expressed in this context alone. In addition to raising that occurs in word-final low vowels, vowel harmony is attested that targets these vowels in particular. What we do not expect to find is patterns that restrict low vowels in positions other than word-final to the exclusion of vowels at other heights, particularly when back/round contrasts are absent among low vowels.

Summing up on comparatively marked content, a general prediction is that material that is unambiguously more marked (e.g. more perceptually difficult) could be singled out for restriction in prominence-based licensing phenomena. If content that is less marked (e.g. more perceptually robust) is subject to a licensing restriction, its more marked counterpart is expected to also be restricted. For properties where markedness is variable across languages, the possibility is open for variation in the value restricted in prominence-based licensing patterns.

3 *Generalized licensing*

3.1   Introduction

This chapter centers on the formal framework for prominence-based licensing patterns. It contains the chief theoretical claims of this book. Three representations for prominence-based licensing of vowel properties are advocated: direct licensing, indirect licensing, and identity licensing. The generalized licensing constraint schema that is advanced has the capacity to drive each of these configurations. The analysis of licensing effects within and across languages is developed within Optimality Theory. Which particular licensing representation occurs in a language is determined by the interaction of licensing constraints with other constraints in the grammar. Generalized licensing constraints thereby capture a common factor that is active across prominence-based licensing patterns, despite differences in the specifics that the patterns display.

This chapter is organized as follows. §3.2 provides background on the concept of licensing in phonology. The three licensing configurations advanced in this work are introduced in §3.3. In §3.4 the licensing constraint schema is presented. §3.5 demonstrates primary interactions of licensing constraints with other constraints, with emphasis on assimilation scenarios. Morpheme-specific licensing effects are addressed in §3.6. A summary is provided in §3.7.

3.2   The concept of licensing

Prominence-based licensing of segmental properties, as pursued in this work, involves formal restrictions in which the well-formed occurrence of some segmental property is contingent upon its expression – in part or in full – in some particular prominent position. This approach builds on a long-standing basis of research where segments or segmental properties that are subject to licensing effects are required to be structurally affiliated or bound in some way with a licensing unit, such as a prominent position, a particular prosodic constituent or configuration, etc. (Itô 1988, 1989; Goldsmith 1989, 1990; Lombardi 1994,

1995, 2001; Steriade 1995b; Zoll 1997, 1998a, among others).[1] Licensing constraints or conditions have variously been formulated as negative statements that serve to bar unlicensed structure, or as positive statements that call for the presence of a relation between a licensor and licensee. The means by which the licensee is affiliated with the licensor are often established by some path of association that connects elements of structure. For example, the affiliation could be considered accomplished if the licensor dominates the licensee, or vice versa (Zoll 1998a).

A classic pattern to which this model of licensing has been applied involves neutralization asymmetries in syllable margins. Many languages display more consonantal contrasts in onsets than in codas. Taking the case of coda neutralization of consonant place features, Itô and Mester (1993) employ a negatively formulated condition along the lines in (1).

(1)   <u>Coda place condition</u>
            *μ
            |
        [Place$_{cons}$]

This condition is interpreted as prohibiting consonant place features that exhaustively trace to a mora node in the prosodic structure, but it does not bar these features in a mora-dominated segment if they are also affiliated with a segment that lacks a mora (i.e. an onset). Expressed in terms of licensing, onsets license consonant place features but codas do not. Itô and Mester apply this to the case of Japanese. Apart from a placeless moraic nasal coda, the only consonants that can close a syllable in Japanese are geminates or nasals that are place-assimilated with a following onset consonant. The permissible structures where a consonant place feature occurs in a coda are illustrated in (2a–b); (2c) shows a structure that will be prevented by the coda place condition.

(2)

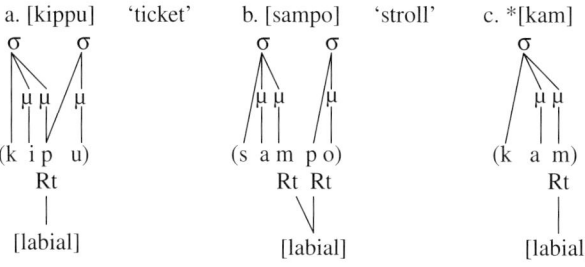

The figures in (2) depict syllable and mora nodes, plus the root and consonant place feature structure relevant for the coda consonants. The phonetic value of the segments is provided in parentheses, but this does not represent an actual layer of structure. In (2a), the place feature for the geminate is contained within a root that reports to the final μ node in the first syllable as well as to the σ node of the second syllable. Because the segment that contains the place feature is not contained wholly within a mora, the place feature escapes violating the coda place condition. In licensing terms, the affiliation of the geminate consonant with a non-moraic position in the second syllable causes its consonant place feature to be licensed. In (2b), a place feature is shared across a coda nasal and an onset stop. Here, again, the place feature is licensed, because one of the segments to which it belongs traces up to a syllable node without an intervening mora. The figure in (2c) shows an ill-formed structure in Japanese with a word-final labial nasal coda. This structure does not obey the coda place condition, because the place feature exhaustively traces up to a mora. Although not depicted, it should be clear that consonant place features occurring entirely within an onset consonant will be licensed.

The present work focuses largely on position-sensitive licensing of vowel properties. As discussed in chapter 2, the positions or contexts in which distinctive segmental properties are licensed tend to facilitate their perception or production. Most often, the primary cues for perception of vowel contrasts are internal, that is, they occur during the vowel, not in the transitions to neighboring segments. Likewise, contexts that facilitate vowel production tend to refer to positions in which the vowel occurs, not a neighboring context. The licensors thus tend to be prominent positions with which the vowel coincides, namely the salient positions discussed in chapter 2, such as stressed syllables, among others.

An important aspect of the interpretation of licensing demonstrated in (2), which is adopted in this work, is that licensing is accomplished if the licensee is wholly contained in the licensing position, or if it only partially overlaps with the licensing position. Thus, licensing of a vowel property by a stressed syllable will be satisfied when that property occurs solely within the stressed syllable and also when it is shared across a stressed syllable and one or more unstressed syllables. In an extension elaborated in the following sections, licensing for a property can further be satisfied if a coindexed occurrence of it is affiliated with the licensor. A second important aspect of licensing as instantiated in this work is that it is characterized as a positional markedness constraint (e.g. Zoll 1997, 1998a). A licensing constraint thus simply assesses whether there are elements in a form that are not licensed by a specific position. It does not make reference to whether the content of that licensing position was altered from its representation in the input, that is, it is blind to whether that position is faithful or not.

Another approach to certain types of positional licensing effects uses positional faithfulness constraints, which require that elements in a given strong position are faithful (e.g. Casali 1997, 1998; Beckman 1997, 1999; Lombardi 1999, 2001). For example, a faithfulness constraint for a feature [F] in a stressed syllable requires a segment in a stressed syllable to have identical values for [F] in the input and output. Unlike positional markedness, this approach predicts that positional licensing effects will always favor preservation of feature specifications that originate with a segment in a given strong position. Some predictions made by a positional markedness licensing constraint for [±F] in a stressed syllable versus those made by a corresponding positional faithfulness constraint are outlined in (3).

(3)

	Input	Output	Positional markedness for [±F] in σ́	Positional faithfulness for [±F] in σ́
i.	V V | | +F -F	V́ V \\ / +F	✓	✓
ii.	V V | | -F +F	V́ V \\ / +F	✓	✗
iii.	V V | | +F -F	V́ V \\ / -F	✓	✗
iv.	V V | | +F -F	V́ V | | +F -F	✗	✓
v.	V V | | +F +F	V́ V | | -F +F	✗	✗

The positional licensing effect under consideration is for [F] in a stressed syllable. In the outputs in (3i–iii) a [+F] or [−F] specification is associated with both a stressed and unstressed vowel. These scenarios all satisfy licensing as positional markedness. However, only (3i) satisfies licensing as positional faithfulness, because it is the only case where the vowel that is assigned stress has identical values for [F] in the input and output. In (3iv–v) the unstressed vowel has a specification for [F] that is not affiliated with a stressed syllable. This does not satisfy licensing as positional markedness. The scenario in (3iv) satisfies licensing as positional faithfulness, because the specification for [F] in the stressed syllable is faithful, but in (3v) positional faithfulness is not satisfied.

Positional markedness and positional faithfulness thus make rather different licensing predictions. Most notably, licensing as positional markedness predicts the possibility of licensing effects where the specification for [F] in the licensing position is altered to license a specification that originated in a position that does not license [F], as in (3ii–iii), but licensing as positional faithfulness does not predict these. We will see that patterns of licensing for vowel properties *are* attested where the licensing position is unfaithful for that property. Positional markedness therefore offers the appropriate characterization for the licensing effects under study.

On the other hand, positional faithfulness predicts that preservation of feature specifications that originate in strong positions can be enforced. Positional markedness is silent on this matter. Preservation of vowel properties that originate in a strong position will play a role in a number of patterns studied here. The strong position that shows asymmetric faithfulness does not always coincide with the position that serves as the positional markedness-based licensor for those properties. Positional faithfulness constraints will thus be required in order to obtain position-sensitive trigger control in assimilations and certain kinds of position-sensitive resistance to neutralization, but they will not be the driving force that underlies the prominence-based licensing phenomena under consideration. Discussion of surrounding issues is taken up in chapter 4 and in §5.5.

In chapter 8, the concept of licensing will be elaborated beyond positional effects alone. Maximal licensing effects are considered where all of the vowels in a word together serve as a licensor, and a penalty is levied for every vowel that does not contribute to the licensing of a given vowel property. Maximal licensing constraints will be applicable to unbounded assimilation patterns with a weak trigger. This differs from assimilation phenomena that are driven by prominence-based licensing, which show bounded effects.

3.3 Prominence-based licensing configurations

This section introduces the position-sensitive licensing configurations that form the core of the phonological representations advocated in this book. Under focus are prominence-based licensing patterns in which a property P of vowel quality is penalized if it fails to be expressed in a strong position. In the next section of this chapter, vowel properties are formalized as autosegmental features, consistent with the majority of work on licensing of segmental properties, but the discussion in this section is neutral on this point, as the licensing conceptualization could be applicable to formalizing articulatory properties as either features or gestures.

Prominence-based licensing bans representations containing *P* where it is not expressed in strong or prominent position, as schematized in (4a). Three configurations serve to express *P* in a prominent position, as schematized in (4b–d).

(4)   Prominence-based licensing configurations

a. Unlicensed *P*

Prominent Position	(…)	Non-prominent Position
Vowel property ¬P		Vowel property P

b. Direct Licensing

Prominent Position	(…)	Non-prominent Position
Vowel property P		Vowel property ¬P

c. Indirect Licensing

Prominent Position	(…)	Non-prominent Position
Vowel property P		

d. Identity Licensing

Prominent Position	(…)	Non-prominent Position
Vowel property P_i	(¬P)	Vowel property P_i

The top row of each figure contains cells representing prominent and non-prominent positions, for example, a stressed syllable versus unstressed, or a morphological root versus affix. For illustration, the non-prominent position is sequenced after the prominent position but their order does not matter. The second row contains cells that represent the presence or absence of a given property *P*. If a cell for *P* appears immediately below a position's cell, it signifies that *P* occurs in that position. In the configuration in (4a), *P* is not licensed, because it fails to be expressed in the prominent position. It is this type of configuration that licensing-driven patterns prevent. In the remaining three configurations, *P* is present in the prominent position. The configurations differ in what occurs in the non-prominent position. In the direct licensing configuration (4b), *P* appears only in the prominent position. Therefore the non-prominent position contains only properties that are ¬*P*. In indirect licensing (4c), *P* extends over both the prominent and non-prominent positions. The single cell for *P* spanning both positions signifies that *P* is continuously present, without interruption. In identity licensing (4d), coindexed instances of *P* are present in the prominent and non-prominent position. Coindexing signifies that the occurrences of *P* are separate but in a correspondence relation (McCarthy and Prince 1995). Correspondent occurrences of *P* may be separated by intervening material that is ¬*P*.

Among the three licensing configurations, direct licensing is the most restrictive. In patterns that exhibit only direct licensing, *P* occurs solely in the prominent position in licensing configurations. Patterns that exhibit indirect licensing typically also exhibit direct licensing where *P* occurs in the prominent position alone. Identity licensing is relevant for phenomena that involve action-at-a-distance, where *P* is present in a non-prominent position but is licensed by virtue of a corresponding element in a non-adjacent prominent position. Generally speaking, patterns that exhibit identity licensing at a distance also include indirect and direct licensing configurations for *P*.

As for the nature of *P*, chapter 2 laid the groundwork. The functional underpinnings for licensing patterns give shape to the kinds of properties that are expected to be subject to licensing-based restrictions. If a particular value for a property is more marked (e.g. presents more perceptual difficulty), or the property is more marked in some particular context (e.g. lip rounding is more perceptually difficult in a non-high vowel), we could expect restrictions that operate over those marked structures alone. It is also possible for all values of a property in a non-prominent position to be restricted, but a property that is unambiguously less marked is not expected to be restricted alone. Where the value that serves as marked in phonological patterns is variable for an opposition (e.g. high versus mid in unstressed vowels), we could expect either value for the property to be subject to restriction in a prominence-based licensing pattern in some language.

Let us turn now to patterns that exemplify the three licensing configurations. As introduced in chapter 1, Ola Lamut presents an example of direct licensing where non-high round vowels are restricted to word-initial syllables (Li 1996). Some examples of well-formed words are repeated in (5). Words with [o oː ɔ ɔː] in a non-initial syllable do not occur.

(5) olək   'lie, deception'
     ɔːta   'sea wave'

Classical Mongolian presents an example of indirect licensing (Svantesson 1985; Walker 2001b). Non-high round vowels occur in non-initial syllables only when all preceding syllables contain non-high round vowels. Examples introduced in chapter 1 are repeated in (6). Here, the property [+round] in combination with [−high] (in featural terms) is prevented when it does not overlap, in continuous fashion, with the initial syllable. Classical Mongolian presents both direct and indirect licensing configurations for [+round].

(6) kømøske   'eyebrow(s)'
     nomoɣodqa 'to tame'

køke 'blue'
qola 'far, distant'

The Romance dialect of Ascrea exemplifies identity licensing. In Ascrea, high suffix vowels [i u] cause raising of preceding stressed mid vowels (Fanti 1938–1940). In addition to producing height assimilation in an adjacent syllable (7a), assimilation affects a non-adjacent stressed syllable, across a vowel that does not undergo raising (7b). High vowels also occur in the stressed syllable when they originate in that position (7c–d). The assimilation in (7a) could involve indirect licensing by the stressed syllable for height in a high suffix vowel, whereas the one in (7b) must involve an identity licensing configuration. (Later in this chapter, I address a preference for indirect licensing when elements are adjacent, as in [7a].)

(7) a. metésse metíʃʃi 'reap (1sg/2sg impf. subj.)'
    b. tóreu̯a túreu̯u *túriu̯u 'cloudy (f sg/m sg)'
    c. mírʒa 'spleen (f sg)'
    d. fúme 'smoke (m sg)'

Identity licensing is motivated for (7b), because a licensed property ([+high]) is absent during the vowel that intervenes between licensor and licensee. Here, the representation involves separate but coindexed occurrences of [+high] in the stressed vowel and the suffix. This claim is connected to work by scholars who have argued that extension or spreading of features or gestures occurs only between segments that are articulatorily adjacent (e.g. Gafos 1999; Walker 2000a; Ní Chiosáin and Padgett 2001; see also related work by Flemming 1995). That assumption implies that discontinuous presences of a feature or gesture are not the product of spreading. Ní Chiosáin and Padgett obtain the effect of articulatory adjacency in feature extension with a locality statement, adapted in (8), which constrains possible phonological representations. Under this statement, a feature occurrence F ('featural event') that is associated to ('overlaps') more than one segment cannot skip an intervening segment.

(8) Let F be a featural event. For all segments, α, β, γ, if α precedes β, β precedes γ, α overlaps F and γ overlaps F, then β overlaps F.

Vowels in adjacent syllables are plausibly articulatorily adjacent in the usual case (Gafos 1999, Ní Chiosáin and Padgett 2001), but vowel articulations in non-adjacent syllables separated by a distinct feature value or gesture for the dimension in question are not. Indirect licensing involves a single featural event, whereas identity licensing involves two.

A central aim of this work is to bring together the three licensing configurations in (4b–d) as possible outcomes of a single prominence-based licensing constraint that prohibits unlicensed P. Integral to achieving this result is a construct that unites the relations for P to the licensing position in these representations. This construct is formalized as a chain, in which an element (e.g. feature, gesture, tone, segment) and all its correspondents in a representation form an entity (Walker 2004).[2]

(9)   *Chain*: Let X be an element belonging to a given representation R. Then X's chain, C(X), is composed of X and all its correspondent elements within R.

That correspondence operates directly among the vowel properties subject to licensing (e.g. features or gestures) rather than among the vowels to which they are associated is motivated by identity licensing phenomena, because only the properties subject to positional licensing show assimilation. If the sponsoring vowels were to correspond, a pressure would exist for all vowel properties to assimilate. This makes problematic predictions, as discussed in §6.6.

The prominence-based licensing configurations can now be characterized as having the following relation in common: some member of a vowel property's chain is expressed in the prominent position. Licensing for P is accomplished by the presence of some or all of each occurrence of P in the prominent position (as in direct and indirect licensing) or by the presence of a correspondent of P in the prominent position (as in identity licensing). This latter configuration connects to other analyses of assimilation at a distance using correspondence or copy among the assimilating elements (Gafos 1998, 1999; Walker 2000b, 2000c; Hansson 2001, 2007a; Rose 2004, Rose and Walker 2004, among others).[3]

3.4   Formalism

This section introduces the formal statement of the generalized constraint schema for prominence-based licensing. Also addressed are substantive and formal limitations on licensors and licensees. The analysis is couched within OT where grammars are composed of a ranking of violable constraints assessed over candidate output forms. When constraints stand in conflict, the higher-ranked of the constraints takes precedence over others. The ensuing discussion assumes familiarity with the basics of OT and the relational formalisms of Correspondence Theory (McCarthy and Prince 1995). For background on these theoretical constructs, see Kager (1999) and McCarthy (2002).

3.4.1 The prominence-based licensing constraint schema

The proposed generalized constraint schema for prominence-based licensing in (10) penalizes specific constituents that are not licensed. The formalization draws upon precursors by Zoll (1998a), Crosswhite (2001), and Walker (2004, 2005). Departing from that prior work, the constraint is formulated negatively so as to prohibit outputs that contain unlicensed constituents. (On advantages of negatively formulated constraints, see Morén 1999; de Lacy 2002; McCarthy 2003.) The schema is formulated to be potentially applicable to phonological elements of any type (e.g. features, gestures, tones, syllable structure, metrical structure, etc.). I use λ as a variable for the element type over which the licensing restriction holds. Following the markedness constraint schema proposed by McCarthy (2003), λ calls out the unlicensed constituent that forms the *locus of violation* of the constraint. I use π as a variable over prominent positions. In the schema, $P(\lambda_j)$ serves as a placeholder for certain restrictions on λ, such as restrictions on its context or value. This will be elaborated below. For patterns that do not display such a restriction, $P(\lambda_j)$ will be defined so that it is vacuous in effect. In the absence of any visible force of $P(\lambda_j)$, the constraint assigns a violation to every instance of λ, a given type of element, where that instance of λ belongs to a chain C(λ) for which no member coincides with a given type of prominent position π. The Coincide relation is characterized by Zoll (1998a: 108). Coincide(x, y) is true if x = y, if y dominates x, or if x dominates y. Constraints formulated according to this schema thus penalize members of weak chains, i.e. chains contained wholly in positions that form the complement of the prominent position.[4]

(10)   *Generalized Prominence-based Licensing constraint schema*: LICENSE(λ, π)
       *λ/¬LICENSE(λ, π) ≡ $_{def}$
       Let any occurrence of λ, a given type of constituent, in a chain $C_j(\lambda)$ be λ_j and p be an occurrence of π, a given type of prominent position.
       Then assign a violation to each λ_j if the following holds
       $\exists \lambda_j [P(\lambda_j)] \land \forall \lambda_j [\neg Coincide(\lambda_j, p)]$

An important aspect of the formalization is that it does not stipulate the particular means by which prevention of unlicensed constituents is accomplished. Therefore, the schema is neutral as to whether the constraint is satisfied by elimination of an unlicensed element or by one of the three licensing configurations. In practice, the simplified label that I will assign to a prominence-based licensing constraint is LICENSE(λ, π). For instance, a constraint LICENSE([back], ó) would penalize each token of the feature [back] belonging to a chain where no members of that chain coincide with a stressed syllable. The application of the schema to some specific examples of licensing constraints is provided later in this section, and their evaluation in the context of a tableau is illustrated in §3.5.

Relevant for this book are prominence-based licensing phenomena involving vowel properties, formalized in terms of features. For simplicity, I assume binary features, but the representations and constraints could be adapted to privative features. On licensing phenomena applicable to prosodic structure and tones, see Zoll (1998a) and Kager (2001, 2007). We will primarily be concerned with configurations in which the prominent position dominates a feature specification.[5] In cases where phonological features are licensed by a morphological constituent, such as a root or stem, I will assume that the domination relation is satisfied if the feature is realized within a segment that belongs to the licensing morphological constituent.

Under focus here are vowel patterns that circumvent perceptually difficult featural information. Such constituents could be features with a particular value or they could be ones in particular contexts. To capture effects of this kind, $P(\lambda_j)$ in the licensing constraint schema can be spelled out in one or more of the ways listed in (11). Specifically, $P(\lambda_j)$ can be spelled out as ID in (11a), or as ID in conjunction with one or more of the others. ID will always be satisfied, so it is vacuous in its effect on the evaluation of the constraint. Nevertheless it is included to allow a uniform constraint schema that contains $P(\lambda_j)$. The means of notating these restrictions in the constraint label are given for each.

(11) *Possible spell-outs for $P(\lambda_j)$ in prominence-based licensing for feature [F]:*
  a. ID, true if $[F]_j = [F]_j$
     Notation in constraint: None
  b. $[F]_j = [\alpha F]$, where α is a given value of [F], {+, –}
     Notation in constraint: LICENSE([αF], π)
  c. $[F]_j/[\beta G]$, where [F] and [G] are given features, β is a given value of [G], {+, –}, and [F]/[βG] means that [F] occurs in a segment that is [βG]
     Notation in constraint: LICENSE([F]/[βG], π)
  d. $[F]_j$/Weak, where Weak is a given weak position, and [F]/Weak means that [F] occurs in Weak
     Notation in constraint: LICENSE([F]/Weak, π)

A licensing constraint can be applicable to a feature F only when it has value α, or it can be applicable to all specifications of a vowel feature, i.e. the existence of a contrast for F, which may be avoided in a non-prominent position or context. Given the functional basis for licensing (see chapter 2), if a licensing constraint is restricted to [αF], [αF] is expected to have the capacity to serve as marked, and the opposite value [–αF] is not expected to be unambiguously more marked than [αF]. Likewise, a licensing constraint can restrict [F] (or [αF]) when it belongs to a chain in which it is associated with a segment that is specified [βG], where that combination or context serves as marked. The spell-out in (11d) characterizes a restriction on [F] (or [αF]) when it belongs to a chain where it is associated with a given weak position. In this case, the licensing constraint would assign violation(s) if the chain did not also coincide with the prominent licensing position named in the constraint.[6] The resulting typological prediction for prominence-based licensing is that if a less marked (e.g. perceptually stronger) vowel quality or context is subject to a licensing restriction, then its more marked (e.g. perceptually weaker) counterpart is too.[7] This is explored further in chapter 4.

To accommodate the larger set of variables that may be involved in a licensing effect for a feature, the expanded schema in (12) is given (with exemplification below).

(12)　*Prominence-based Licensing constraint schema with variables for feature values and contexts:*
　　*[F]/¬L<small>ICENSE</small>([F], π) ≡ _{def}
　　Let
　　　　[F] and [G] be given features,
　　　　α and β be given feature values,
　　　　any occurrence of [F] in a chain C_j([F]) be [F]$_j$,
　　　　p be an occurrence of π, a given type of prominent position,
　　　　weak be an occurrence of Weak, a given weak position,
　　　　[αF] mean that [F] has value α,
　　　　[F]/Weak mean that [F] occurs in Weak,
　　　　and [F]/[βG] mean that [F] occurs in a segment that is [βG].
　　Then assign a violation to each [F]$_j$ if the following holds
　　　　$\exists$ [F]$_j$ [P([F]$_j$)] $\wedge$ $\forall$ [F]$_j$ [¬Coincide([F]$_j$, p)]

A couple of instantiations of licensing constraints with restrictions on the value and context for F are illustrated in what follows. Later in this chapter, some cases are discussed that operate over a class of features rather than a single feature.

A licensing constraint with restrictions of types (11b, c) is active in Ola Lamut and Classical Mongolian. Both of these languages prevent unlicensed occurrences of [+round] in a non-high vowel. The prominent position for these patterns is the initial syllable. The constraint is defined in (13). It will penalize every specification of [+round] that occurs in a segment that is [−high] and that belongs to a chain that does not coincide with the initial syllable. Notice that the restriction of type (11a) ([round]$_j$ = [round]$_j$) is present because of the assumption that ID is always included. As it does not affect the force of the constraint, it will henceforth be omitted from constraint definitions. Since the labels for features and feature values are familiar, as is how they combine, I have not defined them in this constraint.

(13) LICENSE([+round]/[−high], $\sigma_{Initial}$)
Let
any occurrence of [round] in a chain C_j([round]) be [round]$_j$,
$s_{Initial}$ be an occurrence of $\sigma_{Initial}$, an initial syllable,
and [round]/[−high] mean that [round] occurs in a segment that is [−high].
Then assign a violation to each [round]$_j$ if the following holds
$\exists$ [round]$_j$ [[[round]$_j$ = [round]$_j$] ∧ [[round]$_j$ = [+round]] ∧ [[round]$_j$/[−high]]] ∧ $\forall$ [round]$_j$ [¬Coincide([round]$_j$, $s_{Initial}$)]

The licensing pattern in central Veneto, where a post-tonic high vowel causes raising of stressed /e o/ to [i u], involves the restrictions in (11b, d). Examples are provided in (14) (repeated from chapter 1).

(14) kantése   kantísimo   'sing (1sg/1pl impf. subj.)'
      kantór   kantúri   'choir singer (m sg/pl)'

The phenomenon involves licensing by a stressed syllable of the specification [+high] when it occurs in a post-tonic syllable. The constraint is given in (15). It assigns a penalty to each instance of [+high] in a post-tonic syllable whose chain does not coincide with a stressed syllable. Walker (2005) speculates that post-tonic syllables could be phonetically weaker than pretonic syllables in central Veneto. While this remains to be verified instrumentally, patterns in related dialects suggest that post-tonic syllables compose a weak segment of the word in this language group (Maiden 1991b, 1995, and see §8.3).

(15) LICENSE([+high]/$\sigma_{post-tonic}$, σ́)
Let
any occurrence of [high] in a chain C_j([high]) be [high]$_j$,
s_{tonic} be an occurrence of σ́, a stressed syllable,
$s_{post-tonic}$ be an occurrence of $\sigma_{post-tonic}$, a post-tonic syllable,
and [high]/$\sigma_{post-tonic}$ mean that [high] occurs in $\sigma_{post-tonic}$.
Then assign a violation to each [high]$_j$ if the following holds
$\exists$ [high]$_j$ [[[high]$_j$ = [+high]] ∧ [[high]$_j$/$s_{post-tonic}$]] ∧ $\forall$ [high]$_j$ [¬Coincide([high]$_j$, s_{tonic})]

It should now be clear how the constraint definitions unpack. Henceforth, constraint labels alone will be used, such as LICENSE([+round]/[−high], $\sigma_{Initial}$) and LICENSE([+high]/$\sigma_{post-tonic}$, σ́) for the constraints in (13) and (15), respectively.

3.4.2 Substantive limitations

Topics involving substantive phonological restrictions on licensing effects have been addressed in other research. While modeling these particular aspects is not the focus of this book, I draw upon the advances that have been made in these areas where relevant, as outlined in what follows.

First is the issue of which combinations of features and positions occur in prominence-based licensing effects. Specific universal restrictions on combinations are not imposed by the generalized licensing schema. Yet some pairings of features and positions are more ubiquitous than others. The availability of the restrictions in (11), grounded in speakers' phonetic knowledge of perceptual difficulty, makes headway in addressing which features may be subject to licensing. See chapter 2 for discussion on progress by Hayes (1999) and others on modeling the means by which formal phonological constraints are induced or selectively admitted using knowledge of phonetic and psycholinguistic principles. Progress on our understanding of which positions are best suited to favor particular perceptually weak or marked elements has been made by Steriade (1995a, 1999a, b, 2001) and Barnes (2006).

Steriade suggests that the expression of contrasts is favored in contexts that supply more perceptual cues or more informative perceptual cues. Which contexts are favored varies according to the contrast in question, and, for a given contrast, possible contexts can be arrayed in a hierarchy according to the strength of the cues that they offer.

Barnes' cross-linguistic study of positional neutralization finds that languages evolve in such a way as to yield phonological patterns with phonetic origins. He postulates that phonological representations can undergo change through reinterpretation of phonetic regularities in the system. The likelihood of reinterpretation that neutralizes a phonological distinction is increased in a context where two distinct phonological elements show overlap in a significant portion of their realizations. For example, a mid vowel could show phonetic raising in an unstressed syllable in some language, due, at least in part, to a shorter duration. This raising could cause the mid vowel to overlap in more instances with a high vowel, creating a circumstance with the potential for reinterpretation of the mid vowel as undergoing phonological neutralization with a high vowel in this context. Because a stressed syllable has greater duration, reinterpretation of this kind would be less likely to occur in that context. Barnes' view is that once a pattern is 'phonologized,' it is no longer sensitive to its phonetic basis (and see discussion of related work in §2.1). Whether one espouses this perspective or not, the idea that diachrony plays a role in giving shape to positional licensing effects can certainly contribute to addressing why certain pairings of features and positions are more likely to be attested.

A second issue involves the role of contrast in prominence-based licensing phenomena. As mentioned in §2.6, prominence-based licensing sometimes holds specifically of contrastive information. Dyck (1995) made this observation about metaphonic vowel height harmonies in Romance dialects, which are analyzed here as a kind of prominence-based licensing phenomenon. A relevant case occurs in the Asturian dialect of Lena, which shows a harmony wherein certain high suffix vowels cause raising of stressed /e o a/ to [i u e], respectively, as in (16) (Neira 1983; Campos-Astorkiza 2009).

(16) féa   fíu   'ugly (f sg /m sg)'
      tónto túntu   'dumb (mass/m sg)'
      sánta séntu   'holy (f sg/m sg)'

Like the metaphonies of central Veneto and Ascrea, this phenomenon can be analyzed as involving indirect licensing of vowel height features by the stressed syllable, at least when the trigger and target are in adjacent syllables. (On the analysis of stepwise raising, see §8.3.) In Lena, height features are only subject to licensing if they occur in an unstressed inflectional morpheme (Hualde 1989). In addition, Lena's metaphony pattern is sensitive to phonological contrast. Suffix vowels in Lena present a contrast between high and mid back vowels but not high and mid front vowels: /e a o u/. This differs from stems, which contrast five vowels /i e a o u/. In suffixes, the realization of /e/ ranges from [i] to [e], but its realization is not free (Granda Gutiérrez 1960; Dyck 1995; Campos-Astorkiza 2009). In some cases it is lexically fixed. It also shows sensitivity to contextual and analogical factors. Nevertheless, [i] and [e] do not present a contrastive distribution in inflectional suffixes, whereas [u] and [o] do, e.g. [frí-o]/[frí-u] 'cold (mass/m sg).' Concomitantly, [u] triggers productive raising (as shown in [16]), but [i] does not, as in [bénti] 'twenty' (cf. bentidós 'twenty-two,' which confirms the first syllable contains [e] outside of a harmony context). In the context of the licensing analysis, only features that are contrastive are subject to licensing, because these are the features that carry distinctive information.

A formal treatment of the sensitivity of licensing to phonological contrast is addressed by the contrast-coindexing proposal of Campos-Astorkiza (2009). The basics of this approach are reviewed here. Contrast coindexing causes segments to explicitly encode information about the dimensions for which they are contrastive in the system, represented by 'contrast coindices.' In Campos-Astorkiza's approach, encoding of contrast is sensitive to phonological and morphological contexts, which incorporates Dyck's insight that Lena's front vowels are non-contrastive for height in inflectional morphemes in particular. Campos-Astorkiza posits that licensing constraints can reference segments' contrast coindices, therefore restricting their application to segments that are contrastive for a particular dimension.

In the contrast-coindexing model, segments that are minimally contrastive for a particular dimension (e.g. height, voicing, etc.) are assigned indices for that dimension. Segments are minimally contrastive when they differ in a single dimension of contrast (Jakobson *et al.* 1952). Framed within OT, the contrast-coindexing analysis is couched within a systemic approach to contrast, where the candidates under assessment are composed not of single word forms but rather of sets of word forms that constitute candidate languages (e.g. Padgett 1997, 2003; Ní Chiosáin and Padgett 2001, 2009; Flemming 2002, 2004; Łubowicz 2003, 2010; Sanders 2003). Campos-Astorkiza augments the architecture for candidate generation and evaluation as in (17).

(17) GEN → CONTRAST → EVAL
           COINDEXING

  Candidate generation   Marking for minimal   Constraint ranking selects
                          contrast   optimal candidate

For each dimension of contrast, the contrast-coindexing function operates on the words in the candidate languages produced by GEN to index segments that minimally contrast for that dimension. The resulting set of candidates, with contrasts encoded in the segments' representation, is submitted to EVAL, where the optimal candidate output is selected. Note that as contrast coindices are assigned prior to EVAL, the indexing does not depend on the language's rankable constraints. Rather, the constraint hierarchy of EVAL selects the candidate language with the optimal system of contrast.

To illustrate, a candidate output relevant for Lena produced by GEN is shown in (18). This candidate is submitted to the contrast-coindexing function, where contrast coindices for the dimension of height, indicated by a subscript 'h', are assigned to inflectional vowels. To focus on the issue at hand, the candidate 'language' here is narrowed to hypothetical words composed from one of two roots and an inflectional suffix. Each word is taken to have a different meaning. The roots chosen here are ones that provide a context in which /–e/ is prone to be realized as [–i] in Lena, following a prepalatal consonant and following stressed [i] (Granda Gutiérrez 1960; Campos-Astorkiza 2009). Suffixes [u] and [o] are assigned contrast coindices for height as they minimally contrast for this property. Suffix [i] lacks a height contrast coindex, because it does not contrast with [e]. Suffix [a] is not assigned a constraint coindex for height, because it does not meet the criterion for a minimal contrast with non-low vowels for this dimension; it differs in both backness and height. In this regard, Campos-Astorkiza argues that dimensions of contrast are not the same as features. In practice, GEN will also generate candidates with a much larger set of words, and it will generate multiple candidate languages, each of which will have contrast coindices assigned to represent the contrasts within that candidate language. Henceforth, for ease of exposition, presentation of candidates as sets of word forms will be demonstrated only when relevant for a specific point.

(18) GEN → CONTRAST COINDEXING → EVAL
  pútʃ-i   pútʃ-i
  pútʃ-u   pútʃ-u$_h$
  pútʃ-o   pútʃ-o$_h$
  pútʃ-a   pútʃ-a
  kít-i   kít-i
  kít-u   kít-u$_h$
  kít-o   kít-o$_h$
  kít-a   kít-a

Since the lack of contrast between [i] and [e] is specific to suffixes, Campos-Astorkiza proposes that the contrast-coindexing function applies over stems and suffixes separately within words.

As a result of contrast coindexing, the contrastive status of segments will be marked in the representation. This permits the constraint in (19) to be formalized. The restriction to particular morphemes in Lena is addressed in §6.4 and generally for licensing constraints in §3.6.

(19) LICENSE([HEIGHT]/V$_h$[+high], ó)

Licensing here operates over all height features of a high vowel, because Lena's metaphony shows evidence for licensing of [−low] in raising of /a/ to [e] and of [+high] in raising of /e o/ to [i u]. '[HEIGHT]' is used to generalize over the class of vowel height features. (See Padgett 2002 on feature classes and treatment of partial class behavior.) Following Odden (1991) I assume that the class of height features includes [ATR]. This is not crucial for Lena, because [ATR] is not active in its system of height contrasts, but it will be relevant for Romance languages with seven-vowel inventories.[8] The constraint in (19) is interpreted as incurring a violation for each feature occurrence that is a member of the class HEIGHT that does not obey it. In addition, features that are subject to licensing must not only occur in a vowel that is [+high] but also one that bears a contrast coindex for height, as represented by 'V$_h$' in the constraint (after Campos-Astorkiza). This means that the vowel in question is minimally contrastive along the dimension of height. In Lena inflectional morphemes, [u] will bear the relevant contrast coindex but [i] will not, predicting that only [u] will trigger metaphony in this language.[9]

3.5 Achieving the licensing configurations

Licensing constraints interact with certain other constraints. This section considers some primary interactions that produce the three prominence-based licensing configurations: direct, indirect, and identity. Under focus are constraints relevant for licensing-driven assimilation patterns.

First, patterns that show licensing effects involve violation of faithfulness constraints, which require identity between related input and output forms. Focusing on patterns that involve featural alternations or restrictions, the relevant constraint is from the IDENT-IO(F) family (McCarthy and Prince 1995).[10] In the formulation in (20), F stands for a given phonological feature such as [high] or [back].

(20) IDENT-IO(F): 'Corresponding input–output segments are identical in specification for [F]'
Let α be a segment in the input and β be any correspondent of α in the output. If α is [γF] then β is [γF].

If a licensing constraint for a feature F dominates IDENT-IO(F) in the constraint ranking, then licensing could be enforced for F.

Which licensing configurations occur in a pattern depend on the ranking of other constraints. Relevant to identity licensing is a constraint that prohibits correspondence among features within an output, elaborated below. Numerous studies support the existence of featural correspondence (e.g. Lamontagne and Rice 1995; McCarthy and Prince 1995; Pulleyblank 1996; Causley 1997; Ringen and Vago 1998; Lombardi 2001; Walker 2001a; Krämer 2003; Wolf 2007). Its assumption is warranted here because the chain over which feature licensing operates is a chain at the featural level of structure. I assume that GEN only produces candidate outputs in which featural correspondence occurs strictly between like feature specifications i.e. ones with the same feature and value (see Zoll 1998a; Wolf 2007; and Finley 2009 for related observations). This treats each feature as its own type, consistent with an autosegmental treatment; just as moras may correspond only with moras, roots with roots, etc.[11,12] Preservation of the relationship between segments and their features remains governed by IDENT(F) constraints.

The constraint pertinent to identity licensing prohibits related occurrences of the same feature in the output, that is, where a feature is duplicated in an output and stands in correspondence with its duplicant. To illustrate where duplication arises, (21) shows a word that presents identity licensing in Ascrea. Raising in the stressed syllable triggered by the final high vowel operates across an unaffected mid vowel in the penult. Recall that a single featural event may not skip an intervening segment (§3.3). The mid quality of the intervening vowel in

54   *Generalized licensing*

(21) signals that [+high] is not present during it, indicating that feature duplication is involved here. Structures on the left in (21) show the input and output segments and the feature specifications under focus, for which correspondence is indicated by subscript indices. On the right, a schematic of the relevant correspondence relations is provided.

(21)   *Input*   /t o r e ṵ u/
                   | | |
                   [–hi]$_i$ [–hi]$_j$ [+hi]$_k$ [–hi]$_i$ [–hi]$_j$ [+hi]$_k$
        Output   [t ú r e ṵ u]   ↑↓
                   | | |
                   [+hi]$_k$ [–hi]$_j$ [+hi]$_k$ [+hi]$_k$ [–hi]$_j$ [+hi]$_k$

The input [+high] specification in the final vowel has a correspondent in the same vowel in the output. That output specification has a corresponding duplicant in the vowel in the stressed syllable.

To prohibit duplication of this kind, I propose the constraint in (22), which penalizes feature chains with multiple members in an output.

(22)   *DUPLICATE(X)
        Let x and x' be variables ranging over occurrences of a given type of element (e.g. feature, tone, segment, etc.), and O be a candidate output.
        Then assign a violation to every pair <x, x'> such that the following holds
        x, x' ∈ O ∧ xℜx'

The constraint assigns a violation to pairs of corresponding elements within an output. It is violated in identity licensing configurations. Representations in which a single feature is shared across segments do not violate *DUPLICATE, because feature copy is not involved. A comparison of evaluations of feature copy and spreading is provided in tableaux later in this section. In conformity with proposals of Krämer (2003) and Hansson (2006, 2007a), I assume that constraints governing correspondence are assessed over local pairs within a chain of corresponding elements in an output. That is, in the chain [...F$_i$...F$_i$... F$_i$...], *DUPLICATE(F) evaluates the pair composed of the first and second F$_i$ and the pair composed of the second and third F$_i$, assigning a total of two violations. A non-local pair consisting of the first and third F$_i$ is not evaluated. For structures involving feature duplication, in this book I will assume monolithic *DUPLICATE(F), which penalizes any duplicated feature; however, I leave open the possibility of feature-specific versions of the constraint.

*DUPLICATE(F) is formulated as a markedness constraint, evaluating the form of the output without comparison to the input, so as to prohibit correspondence-based duplication regardless of the feature chain's origin. Thus, it penalizes feature duplication whether the duplicated feature already existed in the input or not. This avoids unwanted typological predictions under which the availability of identity licensing changes according to the origins of a duplicated feature.[13]

*DUPLICATE(F) is similar in effect to the INTEGRITY(F) constraint formulated by Krämer (2003: 93), but it has important differences. First, INTEGRITY(F) is a faithfulness constraint, whereas *DUPLICATE(F) is a markedness constraint. INTEGRITY(F) requires that no feature of S_1 have multiple correspondents in S_2. In feature correspondence configurations like the one in (21), Krämer characterizes a duplicate of the feature in the output as an 'indirect correspondent' of the feature in the input (p. 93),[14] and he counts these as correspondents for purposes of input–output INTEGRITY. The constraint therefore penalizes multiple-member feature chains that originate from a single input feature. To achieve this result, the assignment of violations departs from the usual treatment of duplication in the output, as implemented in the Basic Model of correspondence proposed for segment (re)duplication (McCarthy and Prince 1995). The Basic Model structure parallels the feature correspondence structure in (21), and it is interpreted such that only output elements that are in direct correspondence with the input are subject to IO faithfulness constraints. As *DUPLICATE(F) does not reference indirect correspondence relations, it does not present this issue.

If a licensing constraint dominates *DUPLICATE(F) and IDENT-IO(F), then identity licensing could be available. Further, if IDENT-IO(F) dominates *DUPLICATE(F), then IDENT will favor identity licensing across an intervening syllable rather than the intervening syllable undergoing assimilation to the licensed feature specification. The ranking for Ascrea is exemplified by the tableau in (23). Ascrea's licensing constraint is LICENSE([HEIGHT]/[+high], ó). Given the data presented thus far, LICENSE([+high], ó) would be sufficient; however, a fuller picture of the pattern that includes [−ATR] mid vowels, taken up in §6.4, supports licensing of all height features in a high vowel.[15] For reasons of space and succinctness, constraint names are sometimes abbreviated in tableaux. The winning candidate is (23a), with a duplicated feature in the licensing position. The faithful candidate in (c) – where [+high] lacks a correspondent in the stressed syllable – violates the licensing constraint. Notice that although [+high] and [−high] have distinct indices here, they could not correspond, because they have different values. Candidate (b) shows indirect licensing, but it incurs an extra violation of IDENT(high). For simplicity, the representation in (23b) shows linkage only between vowels, but there is reason to believe that propagated features in vowel harmony are present in intervening consonants as well (Gafos 1999; Ní Chiosáin and Padgett 2001). Only the feature [high] is shown in this tableau. In all candidates, [+ATR] and [−low] could be shared across all vowels without incurring violations of faithfulness.

(23)   Identity licensing in Ascrea
        LICENSE([HEIGHT]/[+high], ó́) >> IDENT-IO(high) >> *DUPLICATE(F)

/toreṵu/	LIC([HEIGHT]/[+hi], ó́)	IDENT-IO(high)	*DUPLICATE(F)

☞ a. túreṵu
   | |
   [+hi]ⱼ [+hi]ⱼ
		*	*

b. túriṵu
    \↓/
    [+hi]
		**!	

c. tóreṵu
   | |
   [−hi]ᵢ [+hi]ⱼ
	*!		

Despite the availability of identity licensing under this constraint ranking, when the licensor and vowel hosting the licensee are in adjacent syllables, indirect licensing is favored, because it minimizes violations of *DUPLICATE(F), as shown in (24).[16] All else being equal, *DUPLICATE(F) thus favors shared features over copied ones. This could be interpreted as a preference for a single gesture over a repeated one wherever possible, which could be considered to have a basis in minimizing complexity and effort in the articulatory plan and its execution.

(24)   Indirect licensing favored in adjacent syllables

/metessi/	LIC([HEIGHT]/[+hi], ó́)	IDENT-IO(high)	*DUPLICATE(F)

☞ a. metíʃʃi
       ⌐
       [+hi]
		*	

b. metíʃʃi
    | |
    [+hi]ⱼ[+hi]ⱼ
		*	*!

The metaphony of central Veneto is comparable to that of Ascrea in several respects. A chief way in which the patterns differ is that central Veneto raises a mid vowel that intervenes between the stressed syllable and the vowel whose height feature must be licensed, as in [órdeno]/[úrdini] 'order (1sg/2sg).' In other words, when the licensor and the vowel hosting the licensee are non-adjacent, central Veneto shows indirect licensing; identity licensing is not available. This pattern arises under a ranking where *DUPLICATE(F) has been promoted to dominate IDENT-IO(F), as illustrated in (25).

(25) Indirect licensing in central Veneto; identity licensing is not available
LICENSE([+high]/σ$_{post\text{-}tonic}$, ó), *DUPLICATE(F) >> IDENT-IO(high)

/ordeni/	LICENSE ([+high]/σ$_{post\text{-}tonic}$, ó)	*DUPLICATE(F)	IDENT-IO(high)

☞ a. úrdini
       ↘
   [+high]
			**

b. úrdeni │ │ [+hi]$_j$ [+hi]$_j$		*!	*

An issue in assimilatory licensing phenomena such as these is whether the prominent position or non-prominent position undergoes assimilation. Positional faithfulness constraints can preserve material originating in phonologically strong positions or with morphological roots or stems (McCarthy and Prince 1994a, 1995; Beckman 1997, 1999; Casali 1997, 1998; Lombardi 1999, 2001; Urbanczyk 2001, 2006). On the other hand, independent phonological markedness constraints may prevent a non-prominent position from assimilating or reducing (Walker 2005). These matters are addressed in the context of specific cases examined in following chapters and the predictions for licensing that arise from interactions with positional faithfulness constraints are taken up in chapter 4.

It is not hard to see that where identity or indirect licensing configurations are permitted by the constraint hierarchy, direct licensing will be too. For example, an Ascrea form like [mírʒa] 'spleen (f sg)' will satisfy the licensing constraint with a direct licensing structure while obeying faithfulness and *DUPLICATE(F).

Possible licensing configurations are narrowed to direct licensing alone when a crisp edge constraint comes into play that penalizes a chain for F that reports to more than one syllable. Its formal statement is given in (26), drawing on elements of precursors by Itô and Mester (1999), Walker (2001b), and Kawahara (2008). The formulation has been modified to incorporate feature chains, and it is expressed negatively to emphasize the locus of violation. The constraint prohibits any chain that contains feature specification occurrences (the same occurrence or different occurrences) that are dominated by different syllables, thus preventing indirect and identity licensing configurations. The constraint includes an optional restriction to a chain where F has a particular value α. The assignment of violations to a constituent dominated by multiple nodes follows Walker and Kawahara, as does the assessment of a single violation for each offending chain, whether it is dominated by two syllables, or more than two syllables. In practice, I will refer to the crisp edge constraint with the simplified label: CRISPEDGE([(α)F], σ). Crisp edge constraints for features that take a category other than the syllable as their second argument can be formulated along similar lines, and will be utilized later in this work where called for.

(26) *Crisp edge constraint schema for features and syllables:* CRISPEDGE([(α)F], σ)
  *C([F])/¬CRISPEDGE([(α)F], σ) ≡ $_{def}$
  Let
   [F] be a given feature,
   α be a given feature value,
   f$_j$ and f$_j$' be occurrences of [F] in a chain C$_j$([F]),
   s and s' be occurrences of σ, the prosodic category of syllables,
   [αF] mean that [F] has value α,
   and sδf mean that s dominates f.
  Then assign a violation to C$_j$([F]) if the following holds
   $\exists$ f$_j$, f$_j$', s, s' [sδf$_j$ ∧ s'δf$_j$' ∧ [s ≠ s']] (∧ [f$_j$ = αF ∧ f$_j$' = αF])

Note that as CRISPEDGE([F], σ) penalizes both indirect and identity licensing configurations, it does not alter the preference driven by *DUPLICATE(F) for indirect licensing over identity licensing for features belonging to adjacent constituents.

When a licensing constraint and CRISPEDGE([F], σ) together dominate IDENT-IO(F), the only licensing configuration permitted is direct licensing. This is illustrated in (27) for Ola Lamut, in which round non-high vowels occur only in the initial syllable. The licensing constraint is LICENSE([+round]/[−high], σ$_{Initial}$). The scenario shown here considers a hypothetical input that contains non-high round vowels in both the first and second syllable for the word [olək] 'lie, deception.' The output selected is one that alters the representation so that it no longer contains a non-initial non-high round vowel. Given the constraint ranking shown, this is accomplished by loss of rounding in the second vowel, although in the absence of alternations, other hypothetical repairs are also conceivable, such as vowel raising.

(27) Direct licensing in Ola Lamut
   LICENSE([+round]/[−high], σ$_{Initial}$), CRISPEDGE([round], σ) >> IDENT-IO(round)

/olok/	LICENSE ([+rd]/[−high], σ$_{Initial}$)	CRISPEDGE ([round], σ)	IDENT-IO (round)

☞ a. olək
    │ │
  [+rd]$_i$ [−rd]$_j$
			*

b. olok
   \ /
  [+rd]
		*!	

c. olok
   │ │
  [+rd]$_j$ [+rd]$_j$
		*!	

d. olok
   │ │
  [+rd]$_i$ [+rd]$_j$
	*!		

In this constraint hierarchy, the relative ranking of *DUPLICATE(F) will not alter the pattern, as indirect and identity licensing configurations (in [27b, c]) are prevented by the crisp edge constraint. Notice that the crisp edge constraint will not obviate *DUPLICATE(F) in patterns that present indirect licensing (e.g. central Veneto, above), because the crisp edge constraint will not discriminate between the acceptability of indirect licensing and identity licensing configurations, as *DUPLICATE(F) does in (25).

The rankings illustrated in this section demonstrate that conceptualizing prominence-based licensing as driven by an output-oriented constraint that penalizes chains wholly contained outside of a prominent position, as in (10), predicts the occurrence of the three licensing configurations. Generalized licensing therefore unites the motivation and analysis across the patterns that present these structures. Further, the set of constraints utilized in the analysis correctly predicts implications in the potential availability of these configurations: indirect and direct licensing are permitted in patterns that present identity licensing, and direct licensing is permitted in patterns with indirect licensing (barring any independent interfering effects). This is verified by the factorial typology in chapter 4.

The chapters that follow build on core interactions illustrated in this section. Chapter 4 investigates the typological effects that are obtained under factorial ranking of the basic constraints considered here together with certain positional faithfulness constraints. The next chapters each concentrate on patterns that are chiefly relevant to one of the licensing configurations: chapter 5 on indirect licensing, chapter 6 on identity licensing, and chapter 7 on direct licensing. In chapter 8, the scope of the investigation is expanded to include maximal licensing patterns, in which a licensee is driven to be associated with every vowel in a word. These patterns are shown to display shared feature associations, and in some cases, duplicated features as well, paralleling the occurrence of indirect licensing and identity licensing in prominence-based systems. First, the approach to morpheme-specific effects in licensing is introduced in the section that follows.

3.6   Morpheme-specific licensing

A number of licensing patterns show a measure of morphological conditioning. The restriction of metaphony patterns to specific high vowel suffixes in several Romance dialects of Italy is discussed by Maiden (1991a) (note also Savoia and Maiden 1997). At the same time, Maiden argues that such cases involve phonological assimilation. Morpheme specificity has largely arisen through diachronic changes that have obscured aspects of the phonological origins of metaphony in particular dialects. Although metaphony has become purely morphologically conditioned in some dialects or has even grown moribund, of chief interest here is the complement of patterns in which phonological conditioning remains, often with a simultaneous morphological component. For example, the dialect of Ragusa in Sicily exhibits metaphonic diphthongization in the stressed syllable triggered by particular high vowel suffixes only, e.g. [péṛi]/[pjéṛi] 'foot (m sg/pl)' (Maiden 1991a: 163). A similar effect seen in the dialect of Francavilla Fontana is taken up in §6.3.

Another pattern well known for its morphological conditioning is Germanic umlaut, which developed in the history of German from a general phonological assimilation into a phenomenon that occurred in specific morphological categories and eventually lost a consistent assimilatory character (§7.4) (Iverson and Salmons 1996; Holsinger and Salmons 1999). Historical developments like these suggest that it is not unusual for these kinds of patterns to originate as chiefly phonological but become partially or even fully morphologized in the course of language change.

To address morpheme-specific phonological licensing, I adopt the lexical indexation approach, applied to the licensing constraint. Pater (2009a) proposes that phonological processes that show morpheme-specific triggering can be caused by markedness constraints indexed to the triggering morphemes (see also Pater 2000; Flack 2007b; and Mahanta 2007, among others). Following Pater, the schema for a grammar that shows morpheme-specific triggering by a markedness constraint is given in (28). 'M' refers to the markedness constraint that drives the phonological process, 'Faith' to the faithfulness constraint that the process can cause to be violated, and 'L' is the lexical indexation.

(28)   Grammar: M_L >> Faith >> M
        Lexicon: /morpheme1/, /morpheme2$_L$/, /morpheme3/, …

In (28), M_L dominates Faith, allowing M_L to be active in relation to morphemes that are indexed to it; in this example that includes the item labeled 'morpheme2' in the lexicon. Since Faith dominates non-indexed M, when indexed morphemes are absent from the representation, the phonological process in question will be suppressed, for instance, when the representation contains only morphemes such as 'morpheme1' or 'morpheme3.' It is also possible for a grammar to assign different indices to different constraints, in which case, items in the lexicon could bear one or more indices or they could lack an index.

LICENSE(λ, π) takes two arguments, the constituent that is subject to the licensing restriction and the prominent position relevant for the contextual condition. It is only the λ argument that appears to show morpheme-specific effects in licensing. That is, licensing phenomena may penalize an element that constitutes the phonological exponence of a specific morpheme whose chain fails to coincide with a given prominent position. However, I am not aware of any licensing phenomenon where the morpheme specificity applies to π in the contextual condition on λ. For example, patterns in which an element is penalized for failing to coincide with a stressed syllable that belongs to the possessive morpheme seem to be unattested. Note that π might show morphological sensitivity in constraints where the licensing position is a morphological head, such as Root or Stem, but these general categories are broader than the specific morphemes to which indexation has the potential to be sensitive.[17] I therefore suggest that when a licensing constraint is lexically indexed, that is, $\text{LICENSE}_L(\lambda, \pi)$, the morphemes to which the constraint is indexed are referenced only with respect to λ. More generally, I hypothesize that in the case of context-sensitive markedness constraints, lexical indexation is relevant to the argument that constitutes the locus of violation and not the contextual restriction. This is consistent with the lexically indexed alignment constraint proposed by Pater (2009a) for Yine. In that instance, the constraint is formulated positively, but it is the constituent for which alignment is enforced, and whose misalignment is penalized, that is morpheme specific.

A lexically indexed licensing constraint for a feature F and a prominent position π is defined in (29).

(29)   *Morpheme-specific Prominence-based Licensing schema:* $\text{LICENSE}_L([F], \pi)$
        $*[F]_L/\neg\text{LICENSE}([F]_L, \pi) \equiv_{\text{def}}$
        Let
            any occurrence of [F], a given feature, in a chain $C_j([F])$ be $[F]_j$,
            p be an occurrence of π, a given type of prominent position,
            morph_L be an occurrence of Morph_L, a morpheme with index L,
            and $[F]/\text{Morph}_L$ mean that [F] is a phonological exponent for Morph_L.
        Then assign a violation to each $[F]_j$ if the following holds
        $\exists [F]_j [[F]_j/\text{morph}_L] \land \forall [F]_j [\neg\text{Coincide}([F]_j, p)]$

The phonological exponence of a morpheme is the phonological material that is identified with that morpheme in an output. See Walker and Feng (2004) for a formal means of representing this relation in the structure. Note that for a feature specification to qualify as the phonological exponence of a morpheme, it does not have to be that morpheme's sole phonological exponence (Pater 2009a). The morpheme in question could also be identified with other phonological material in the output, but only the content specified in the constraint – here, F – is in the scope of licensing. If there were further restrictions on F, for instance, that it have a particular value α, the constraint could be expanded along the lines described in §3.4.1.

The approach is illustrated with application to a morpheme-specific licensing pattern in Jaqaru (Aymaran). Romance metaphony and Germanic umlaut are addressed in later chapters. In Jaqaru, particular suffixes trigger complete harmony for all features in a preceding stressed vowel in the penultimate syllable, as shown in (30) (Cerrón-Palomino 2000; Cerrón-Palomino López 2003). Jaqaru's vowels are /i a u/. The language is purely suffixing; no prefixes occur (Hardman 1966).

(30)   ajʎú -ru   'to overflow'   ajʎi-   'to boil'
       nuná-ja   'to cause to rinse' nuni-   'to rinse'
       apí-ʃi   'to take along'   apa-   'to take'
       palí-ri   'eater'   palu-   'to eat'
       tʃimí-ni   'with belly'   tʃima   'belly'

The suffixes that trigger this harmony are: /–ru/ 'inductive,' /–ja/ 'causative,' /–ʃi / 'medial passive'/'reflexive,' /–ʃi / 'reciprocal,' /–ʃu / 'gerund,' /–ri/ 'agentive,' /–ni/ 'possessive,' /–ʎi / 'emphatic,' and /–ʃi / 'evoker.' Compare non-triggering [–sa] 'indefinite' and [–ni] 'translocative'; the latter is homophonous with the triggering possessive suffix.

(31)   kawkí-sa 'whoever (indef.)'
       mantá-ni 'to enter towards the speaker (transloc.)'

The triggering suffixes do not show any obvious phonological or morphological basis for their grouping to the exclusion of others (Cerrón-Palomino López 2003). Vowels of any quality can trigger harmony. Triggering suffixes may contain fricatives or sonorant consonants, but these are also found in non-triggering suffixes. Triggering suffixes are not restricted to a particular morphological subcategory; they include examples of derivational and inflectional suffixes from both verbal and nominal categories.

Following Cerrón-Palomino López, the suffix-induced harmony pattern is analyzed as driven by a licensing constraint where the licensee is any vowel feature and the licensor is the stressed syllable. The lexically indexed constraint posited here is LICENSE_L([V-FEATURE], ó). [V-FEATURE] refers to the class of vowel quality features. Triggering suffixes are marked in the lexicon with an index matching the licensing constraint. The morpheme-specific nature of the pattern is captured by the ranking: LICENSE_L([V-FEATURE], ó) >> IDENT-IO(V-FEATURE) >> LICENSE([V-FEATURE], ó). This causes only indexed morphemes to produce alternations, as illustrated in (32). I assume that lexical indices are immutable. They are shown in the input, where morphological constituency is indicated; for simplicity, they are not shown in candidate outputs. Also for simplicity, only a single violation is tallied for IDENT-IO(V-FEATURE) for each unfaithful vowel.

(32)   Morpheme-specific licensing

Input	Output	LICENSE$_L$ ([V-FEATURE], ó)	IDENT-IO (V-FEATURE)	LICENSE ([V-FEATURE], ó)
i. /tʃima-ni$_L$/	☞ a. tʃimíni		*	
	b. tʃimáni	*!		*
ii. /manta-ni/	☞ a. mantáni			*
	b. mantíni		*!	

The indexed constraint assigns a violation only to lexically indexed morphemes whose vowel features do not have membership in the stressed syllable. This compels harmony from the possessive suffix /-ni/. Lacking an index, translocative /-ni/ is not subject to the indexed constraint. IDENT-IO(V-FEATURE) prevents this suffix from triggering harmony. Further details of Jaqaru's data and analysis appear in §5.3.

3.7   Summary

This chapter has introduced a schema for a generalized prominence-based licensing constraint. The basic approach builds on previous treatments of licensing effects as positional markedness. An important aspect of the generalized constraint schema proposed here is that it is satisfied by direct, indirect, and identity licensing configurations, as well as by elimination of unlicensed material. It thereby supplies a common motivation for seemingly diverse vowel patterns, all of which share the common result of averting the realization of certain vowel qualities in a weak position only. Interactions of prominence-based licensing constraints with other constraints – governing feature identity, feature duplication, and crisp edges – were demonstrated to obtain the three licensing configurations under different rankings. Also introduced in this chapter were available restrictions on the element that is penalized if unlicensed. Substantive limitations on the constraints were also considered. Finally, morpheme-specific licensing constraints were motivated and introduced. The predictions and application of these formalisms are explored in the chapters that follow.

4 *Typological predictions*

4.1 Introduction

This chapter explores typological predictions made by the prominence-based licensing constraint in combination with other constraints relevant for a typology that includes licensing-driven assimilation. In OT, the typology of patterns predicted to be possible in language emerges from factorial ranking of the constraint set. In the classic conception of OT, constraints are the same across languages and there are no language-particular restrictions on inputs (Richness of the Base; Prince and Smolensky 2004). The language-particular part of grammar thus lies in the constraint ranking. Importantly, not every ranking necessarily produces a distinct pattern. In other words, multiple rankings may converge on the same outcome. As a basis for the investigation of typological predictions in this chapter, factorial typologies yielded by a particular constraint set applicable to prominence-based licensing were generated using OTSoft, Version 2.1 (Hayes *et al.* 2003). Licensing effects for input forms of different sizes are examined, as well as effects specific to an affix. Beyond the constraints and factorial typologies relevant for assimilation patterns, some main interactions of the prominence-based licensing constraint with other faithfulness constraints are also investigated.

The constraints considered in the factorial typologies for licensing are instantiations of the ones used in §3.5 to illustrate selection of the three licensing configurations: LICENSE, IDENT, *DUPLICATE, and CRISPEDGE. In addition, two positional faithfulness constraints are considered. Positional faithfulness constraints enforce identity of input–output mappings in particular positions deemed to be prominent. In §3.2 it was argued that positional faithfulness is not adequate to capture the range of vowel licensing effects. The common factor underlying direct, indirect, and identity licensing is captured by the positional markedness mode of licensing, as employed in the generalized licensing schema. However, this does not obviate the need for positional faithfulness constraints. They remain important for certain effects that involve position-sensitive preservation of content.[1] The positional faithfulness constraints included in the factorial typologies reference the stressed syllable and word-final syllable, as in (1–2).

(1)   IDENT-IO-ό(F)
       Let α be a segment in the stressed syllable in the output and β be a correspondent of α in the input. If α is [γF] then β is [γF].

(2)   IDENT-IO-σ$_{Final}$(F)
       Let α be a segment in the final syllable in the output and β be a correspondent of α in the input. If α is [γF] then β is [γF].

Positional faithfulness constraints can play a role in causing a vowel to resist licensing-driven neutralization and in deciding the trigger vowel for assimilations. It is pertinent to consider stressed syllable faithfulness (Beckman 1999), because in many prominence-based licensing patterns the stressed syllable is the licensing position. Faithfulness to another frequent licensing position, the initial syllable, could be substituted, because in the candidate set considered, the stressed syllable was also initial. Word-final faithfulness is relevant, because of the dual strength and weakness that word-final syllables may show in vowel patterns (see §2.4). Their weakness can cause them to be restricted by licensing effects, but their strength can cause them to control harmony and prevent their neutralization, as dictated by positional faithfulness (Hyman 1998; Cerrón-Palomino López 2003; Krämer 2003; Walker 2005; Sasa 2009).

In all, seven constraints were used in the factorial typology, given in (3). The feature was schematized as [F], with binary specification. Two licensing constraints were included, one that only penalized unlicensed occurrences of a feature value that serves as marked, arbitrarily assigned to [+F], and one that penalized both values of [F].

(3)   Constraints in factorial typology
       a. LICENSE([+F], ό)
       b. LICENSE([F], ό)
       c. *DUPLICATE(F)
       d. CRISPEDGE([F], σ)
       e. IDENT-IO(F)
       f. IDENT-IO-ό(F)
       g. IDENT-IO-σ$_{Final}$(F)

Factorial typologies were explored for input forms that are disyllabic (§4.2) and trisyllabic (§4.3), and, to explore non-local effects, results with trisyllabic affixed inputs were examined (§4.4). An overview of some primary interactions of the licensing constraint with some additional constraints is provided in §4.5.

4.2 Disyllables

A factorial typology was generated for disyllabic words. The file that formed the input to OTSoft for the factorial typology consisted of a table that contained inputs, the candidate outputs to be considered, the constraints, and the violations assigned to each candidate. Taking [F] as a vowel feature, such as [high] or [round], input forms were included for all combinations of [+F] and [–F]. These were /+ +/, /+ –/, /– +/, and /– –/, which are shorthand for input forms with the indicated specifications for [F] in vowels in a disyllabic word containing monophthongs. The same candidate outputs were considered for each input. They are given in schematic form in (4). Two identical feature values contained in a pair of square brackets represent a single feature linked across two syllables (e.g. [+ +]). Feature values in separate brackets represent distinct occurrences of feature specifications (e.g. [+][+]). Feature values with a matching index represent feature specifications in the same chain ([+]$_i$[+]$_i$). The absence of an index indicates that the feature specifications belong to separate chains. The first syllable was treated as stressed in all cases.

(4)   Candidate outputs in schematic form
     a. [–][+]
     b. [+ +]
     c. [+]$_i$[+]$_i$
     d. [+][+]
     e. [– –]
     f. [–]$_i$[–]$_i$
     g. [–][–]
     h. [+][–]

The number of possible rankings of seven constraints is 5,040. For the set of four inputs, ten different output sets were obtained, which I will term 'output patterns.' There were only six different patterns of output feature-value sequences generated because of covert structure, for example, shared versus separate occurrences of the same feature specification. As covert structure is not generally distinguished in linguistic transcriptions, output patterns were sorted into the six groups that are overtly distinct. The six vowel feature sequence patterns are described in (5). A fuller description of the output patterns is provided in the appendix (§4.7), including the full schematic forms of their outputs and the rankings that derive them.

(5)   *Overview of licensing typology for disyllabic words*

	Pattern description	Feature-value sequences	
i.	Full contrast: feature values remain identical in mapping from input to output.	Input − − − + + + + −	Output − − − + + + + −
ii.	Indirect licensing for [+F] alters feature specifications in stressed (initial) syllable.	Input − − − + + + + −	Output − − + + + + + −
iii.	Indirect licensing for [+F] and [−F] alters feature specifications in stressed (initial) syllable.	Input − − − + + + + −	Output − − + + + + − −
iv.	Indirect licensing for [+F] alters feature specifications in word-final syllable.	Input − − − + + + + −	Output − − − − + + + −
v.	Indirect licensing for [+F] and [−F] alters feature specifications in word-final syllable.	Input − − − + + + + −	Output − − − − + + + +
vi.	Direct licensing for [+F] causes neutralization in word-final position to [−F].	Input − − − + + + + −	Output − − − − + − + −

The typology encompasses a pattern of full contrast, in which no feature values are altered (5i), four patterns that alter input specifications to enforce indirect licensing, i.e. a shared feature specification, in some or all outputs (5ii–v), and a pattern that exhibits direct licensing only, where contrast for the feature values is maintained in the licensing position and there is neutralization to a single feature value in the non-licensing position (5vi). The following generalizations can be made about the typology.

(6)   Typological generalizations: disyllabic words
  i. Licensing for [−αF] implies licensing for [αF], where [αF] is a marked value for [F].
  ii. Direct and indirect licensing configurations may occur in a window of adjacent syllables, but not identity licensing.[2]
  iii. In asymmetrical licensing patterns – that is, patterns that show licensing for [+F] only – if indirect licensing configurations occur, so do direct licensing configurations.
  iv. Assimilation may operate in either direction.
  v. Neutralization to a single feature value may occur only in the non-licensing position.

The first result is that a licensing effect for [−F] implies a licensing effect for [+F], where [+F] is taken as the value with greater markedness in the schematic forms. This conforms with a prediction based on the hypothesized functional grounding for prominence-based licensing systems, discussed in chapter 2. It relies on a version of IDENT-IO(F) that is symmetrically violated by any change in value for [F] (McCarthy and Prince 1995). Value-sensitive versions of IDENT could subvert this result in the ranking IDENT-IO(+F) >> LICENSE([F], ó) >> IDENT-IO(−F). In that case, the licensing constraint would act on both feature values, but faithfulness to the value that serves as marked dominates to suppress an effect for [+F], producing an unwanted pattern of active licensing for [−F] only.

The second result is that where adjacent syllables are concerned, direct and indirect licensing configurations may occur but not identity licensing. This is driven by *DUPLICATE(F), which causes indirect licensing to harmonically bound identity licensing in adjacent contexts, as discussed in §3.5.

The third result is that in patterns that asymmetrically show licensing for [+F] only, the presence of indirect licensing configurations implies that direct licensing configurations are also present in that language. In other words, [+F] can occur shared across both syllables and it can occur in the stressed syllable alone.

The fourth result is that licensing-driven patterns that present assimilation can show either progressive or regressive directionality. This derives from the inclusion of positional faithfulness constraints for both the licensing position (stressed) and the non-licensing position (word-final). In the factorial typology, either positional faithfulness constraint may dominate, causing both positions to be potential triggers for licensing-driven assimilation. Note, however, that other factors besides positional faithfulness may also decide triggers in some licensing patterns, as will be discussed in §5.4.

Finally, the fifth result is that licensing-driven neutralization to a single feature value ([−F]) can happen only in the non-licensing position. This may transpire when licensing for [+F] is accomplished by eliminating this value in non-licensing positions and assimilation to the value in licensing position does not take place. Neutralization is not expected in the licensing position, since the licensing constraint would not drive [+F] to be eliminated in this context, consistent with the predictions following from aspects of speech perception and production. Other kinds of neutralization are possible when a larger range of scenarios is taken into consideration; for instance, neutralization to [ə] or another default vowel character.

Some examples of languages discussed in later chapters that display the general type of patterns identified in the typology for disyllables are listed in (7). A reminder about terminology: in this table, 'licensing position' refers to the prominent position identified in a licensing constraint, which was the stressed syllable in the factorial typology. The sample languages listed may show patterns with different licensing positions, such as word-initial syllables or roots. 'Non-licensing' position refers to any syllable that is not an active prominence-based licensing position in the language. In the factorial typology for disyllables, this was the word-final position, but there was a positional faithfulness constraint for this position. In some of the sample languages where the non-licensing position undergoes alteration, the non-licensing position is not the final position but another category of position that shows weakness, such as an affix or unstressed syllable. In all likelihood these other positions do not have a positional faithfulness constraint. As for the word-final faithfulness constraint, it is dominated by stressed syllable faithfulness and a prominence-based licensing constraint in the corresponding rankings in the factorial typology, so it is effectively neutralized when word-final syllables undergo change. In cases where asymmetric feature licensing occurs, the value was [+F] in all of the language examples listed, but this will not necessarily be the case for all features.

(7)   Sample licensing patterns

	Pattern description	Language and specifics
i.	Full contrast: feature values remain identical in mapping from input to output.	Any language without positional restrictions on vowels for the feature in question.
ii.	Indirect licensing for [+F] alters feature specifications in licensing position.	Central Veneto (§5.3) [F] = [high] Licensing position = σ́ Trigger = post-tonic σ
iii.	Indirect licensing for [+F] and [−F] alters feature specifications in licensing position.	Jaqaru (§5.3) [F] = [high], [back] Licensing position = σ́ Trigger = σ$_{Final}$

70 *Typological predictions*

	Pattern description	Language and specifics
iv.	Indirect licensing for [+F] alters feature specifications in non-licensing position.	Buchan Scots (§5.2.1) [F] = [high] Licensing position = ó Affected non-licensing position: post-tonic
v.	Indirect licensing for [+F] and [–F] alters feature specifications in non-licensing position.	Macuxi (§5.2.1) F = [back] Licensing position = Stem Affected non-licensing position: unaccented affix
vi.	Direct licensing for [+F] causes neutralization in non-licensing position to [–F].	Ola Lamut (§7.2.2) [F] = [round] Licensing position = σ$_{Initial}$ Affected non-licensing position: non-initial

Patterns of the type described in (7iv) break down into two types of scenarios detailed schematically in the corresponding row of the table in (19) in the appendix to this chapter. In both scenarios, /+ +/ maps to [+ +] and /+ –/ maps to [+][–]. They differ when the feature value in the first syllable is unmarked. Under one ranking, where the crisp edge constraint dominates LICENSE([F], ó), both vowels are realized as '–', without feature sharing (/– +/ and /– –/ map to [–][–]). Under the opposite ranking of these two constraints, these same inputs map to a shared feature specification [– –]. In other words, in the first case, there is neutralization to the unmarked value via feature insertion, without active assimilation, and in the second case, there is assimilation from the stressed syllable resulting in a shared feature structure. Whereas the second case is characterized as involving assimilation, the first is characterized in this work as a 'passive' licensing pattern. Because these two patterns involve covert structure – they both lead to the same vowel quality sequence in the output – identifying which representation is involved may depend on other subtleties of the system, or it may be ambiguous. These issues are explored with respect to specific cases in the next chapter.

4.3 Trisyllables

A factorial typology for the constraint set in (3) with application to trisyllabic words (with initial stress) was generated in order to examine implicational relationships between the licensing configurations, patterns with medial vowels, and the potential for 'majority rule' effects. Identity licensing effects are examined in trisyllabic forms with affixes, discussed in §4.4.

Eight inputs were considered, encompassing all possible combinations of binary feature values in three syllables: /– – –/, /– – +/, /– + –/, /– + +/, /+ + +/, /+ + –/, /+ – +/, /+ – –/. There were twenty-two output candidates, given in (8). The same output candidates were used for every input.

(8)   Candidate outputs in schematic form
    a. [– –][+]   l. [– – –]
    b. [–][–][+]   m. [–][–][–]
    c. [–]$_i$[–]$_i$[+]   n. [–]$_i$[–]$_i$[–]$_i$
    d. [–][+ +]   o. [+][– –]
    e. [–][+][+]   p. [+][–][–]
    f. [–][+]$_i$[+]$_i$ q. [+][–]$_i$[–]$_i$
    g. [+ + +]   r. [+ +][–]
    h. [+][+][+]   s. [+][+][–]
    i. [+]$_i$[+]$_i$[+]$_i$ t. [+]$_i$[+]$_i$[–]
    j. [+]$_i$[–][+]$_i$ u. [–]$_i$[+][–]$_i$
    k. [+][–][+]   v. [–][+][–]

There were thirty-five different output patterns. Because of covert structure, there were only twenty-two different feature-value sequences, which are listed in the appendix (§4.7). As summarized in (9), three noteworthy typological properties emerge, apart from ones already identified from the typology for disyllables.

(9)   Typological generalizations: trisyllabic words
    i. In asymmetrical licensing patterns (for [+F] only), if identity licensing configurations occur, so do indirect and direct licensing configurations. If indirect licensing configurations occur, so do direct licensing configurations.
    ii. Medial vowels can be singled out to undergo neutralization to a single feature value or undergo licensing-driven assimilation.
    iii. Unwanted majority-rule effects occur.

The first result is that in patterns that show licensing for [+F] only, the presence of identity licensing configurations implies that indirect and direct licensing configurations also occur in that pattern. Also, if indirect licensing occurs, so does direct licensing. The first implication arises because *DUPLICATE(F) favors indirect licensing over identity licensing when the licensor and licensee are adjacent. The second implication comes about because direct licensing for a feature value in a faithful licensing position does not incur violations with respect to the markedness constraints in the typology, whereas the other licensing configurations do: indirect licensing incurs a violation of CRISPEDGE([F], σ) and identity licensing incurs violations of CRISPEDGE([F], σ) and *DUPLICATE(F).

The second typological result is that medial vowels may be singled out to undergo neutralization to a single value for F or licensing-driven assimilation.

The special status of medial vowels arises because vowels in the trisyllabic forms used in this typology present a three-way distinction in strength. The initial vowel, which is stressed, occurs in a licensing position and is protected by a positional faithfulness constraint. The final vowel occurs in a non-licensing position but is protected by a positional faithfulness constraint. The medial vowel occurs in a non-licensing position and is not subject to positional faithfulness. Hence, it is the very weakest vowel that can be singled out for neutralization or targeted by assimilation, compatible with expectations deriving from perceptual difficulty. Interactions between the two stronger positions were investigated in the typology for disyllabic words. A sample predicted licensing pattern that affects vowels in a position that lacks positional faithfulness is given in (10). The vowel pattern in the dialect of Veroli supports both positional faithfulness constraints. It presents vowel neutralization in a post-tonic penult. Post-tonic final vowels do not undergo neutralization, nor do vowels in a stressed antepenult.

(10) Sample licensing pattern for vowels that lack positional faithfulness

Pattern description	Language and specifics
Neutralization: a non-licensing position that lacks positional faithfulness undergoes neutralization to a single feature value.	Veroli (§7.2.1) Only [ə] occurs in the penultimate syllable of words with antepenultimate stress.

An example of assimilation in weak position where there is evidence of ternary strength has not been found. For example, a post-tonic vowel in a penultimate syllable undergoes assimilation to a stressed vowel in the antepenultimate syllable, while the final vowel remains faithful (even in forms where stress is penultimate). As the pattern does not seem implausible, it is not necessarily a faulty prediction of the typology. Its apparent lack of attestation could be an accidental gap. Its occurrence requires several particular properties to converge in a language (e.g. antepenultimate stress in at least some words, active faithfulness to the word-final and stressed syllables, and licensing-driven harmony). Whereas such characteristics are present in a number of Romance languages, they must also interact in a very specific way to produce the pattern in question. Within Romance, words with antepenultimate stress are comparatively few, which further diminishes the opportunities for the pattern to emerge and be robustly sustained. Thus, the scarcity of such patterns is not surprising.

The third result of the factorial typology is that majority-rule effects are predicted. The problem of majority-rule effects in vowel harmony and other assimilations is discussed by Baković (2000) (see also Lombardi 1999). It arises in words that contain three or more vowels within the domain of a harmony process. The problem can be described as follows. When an assimilation-driving constraint for [F] is ranked high, then the candidate set is narrowed to candidates that best satisfy it. Candidates that show maximal assimilation for [+F] will tie with ones that show maximal assimilation for [–F]. If IDENT-IO(F) is situated in the constraint hierarchy so that it decides the competition between the tied candidates with maximal assimilation, it will select the candidate that incurs the fewest identity violations for [F]. That is, whichever value for [F] stands in the majority in the vowels of the input will decide the value for [F] that harmonizes: the majority value rules. This type of effect is predicted to arise in trisyllables when a licensing constraint is ranked high enough so as to be enforced and IDENT-IO(F) dominates the positional faithfulness constraints, as illustrated in (11). Recall that stress is assumed to be initial. In columns with multiple constraints, the constraint violated is notated in parentheses after the mark. The (c) and (d) candidates in (11i) and (11ii) are ruled out by the licensing constraint and *DUPLICATE(F), respectively. This narrows the field to the (a) and (b) candidates, which each satisfy licensing for [+F] through full assimilation to either [–F] (a) or [+F] (b). In (11i), (a) [– – –] is selected, because the input contains two [–F] specifications and only one [+F]. In (11ii), whose input contains two [+F] specifications and one [–F], candidate (b) [+ + +] is selected.

(11)   Majority-rule effects

Input	Output	LICENSE([+F], ó) *DUPLICATE(F)	IDENT-IO(F)	IDENT-IO-ó(F) IDENT-IO-σ$_{Final}$(F) CRISPEDGE([F], σ)
i. /– – +/	☞ a.[– – –]		*	*(IDENT-σ$_{Final}$) *(CRISP)
	b. [+ + +]		**!	*(IDENT-ó) *(CRISP)
	c. [–][–][+]	*!(LIC)		
	d. [+]$_i$[–][+]$_i$	*!(*DUP)	*	*(IDENT-ó) *(CRISP)
ii. /– + +/	a. [– – –]		**!	*(IDENT-σ$_{Final}$) *(CRISP)
	☞ b.[+ + +]		*	*(IDENT-ó) *(CRISP)
	c. [–][+ +]	*!(LIC)		*(CRISP)
	d. [–]$_i$[+][–]$_i$	*!(*DUP)	*	*(IDENT-σ$_{Final}$) *(CRISP)

As Baković points out, majority-rule effects are an unwanted prediction for phonological theory – no known pattern decides the value that assimilates by the majority count in the word. The prediction arises out of rankings in which IDENT-IO(F) dominates both positional faithfulness constraints. As Baković argues, there is reason to reject a solution that stipulates that the problematic ranking may not occur. He also argues against a solution that employs feature-value faithfulness, that is, IDENT constraints specific to [+] or [–] values for F. A further reason to reject the latter is that a value-symmetrical version of IDENT is integral to the typological result that licensing for [–αF] implies licensing for [αF], where [αF] serves as the marked value of [F] (§4.2).

I adopt Baković's solution to the majority-rule problem, which calls on local constraint conjunction (Smolensky 1993, 1997; Łubowicz 2002).[3] Baković (2000: 28) provides the following set of assumptions (adapted from Itô and Mester 1998).

(12)   Local conjunction theory
    a. Definition:
       If A and B are non-conjoined members of the universal constraint set CON, then their local conjunction A $\&_l$ B is also a member of CON.[4]
    b. Interpretation:
       A $\&_l$ B is violated if and only if both its conjuncts A and B are violated in the smallest domain evaluable by A and B.
    c. Ranking (universal): A $\&_l$ B >> {A, B}

The application of this construct to the majority-rule problem requires a local conjunction of markedness and faithfulness constraints pertinent to features, as in (13) (Baković 2000: 29).[5]

(13)   a. *[αF] $\&_l$ IDENT-IO(F)
       An output segment is not specified [αF] if its input correspondent is not specified [αF].
    b. *[αF, βG(, γH …)] $\&_l$ IDENT-IO(F)
       An output segment is not specified [αF, βG(, γH …)] if its input correspondent is not specified [αF].

The local conjunction *[+F] $\&_l$ IDENT-IO(F) assigns a violation to any [+F] segment in the output that was [–F] in the input, and it dominates its conjuncts *[+F] and IDENT-IO(F). Therefore, IDENT-IO(F) will not be in a position to dictate the outcome of harmony, ruling out the majority-rule effect, as illustrated in (14), which repeats the input and candidates from (11ii). In (11ii), the majority-rule candidate in (b) was selected. That candidate is eliminated in (14) by the local conjunction, resulting in the selection of (a).

(14) Preventing majority-rule effects

Input	Output	LICENSE([+F], ó) *DUPLICATE(F) *[+F] &$_l$ IDENT-IO(F)	IDENT-IO(F)	IDENT-IO-ó(F) IDENT-IO-σ$_{Final}$(F) CRISPEDGE([F], σ)
/−++/	☞ a. [− − −]		**	*(IDENT-σ$_{Final}$) *(CRISP)
	b. [+ + +]	*!(*[+F] &$_l$ ID-(F))	*	*(IDENT-ó) *(CRISP)
	c. [−][+ +]	*!(LIC)		*(CRISP)
	d. [−]$_i$[+][−]$_i$	*!(*DUP)	*	*(IDENT-σ$_{Final}$) *(CRISP)

The local conjunction *[+F] &$_l$ IDENT-IO(F) predicts the existence of a pattern in which assimilation must be to the feature value [−F], no matter what its position in the word. In the factorial typology schematization, the relatively marked feature value was arbitrarily assigned to [+F]. In cases where [αF] and [−αF] for a particular feature stand in a universal markedness hierarchy, where [αF] is more marked than [−αF], then their corresponding markedness constraints and local conjunctions would be ranked in like fashion, e.g. *[αF] &$_l$ IDENT-IO(F) >> *[−αF] &$_l$ IDENT-IO(F) (Baković 2000: 33). A harmony pattern where *[αF] &$_l$ IDENT-IO(F) dictates the value to which other vowels assimilate is an instance of what Baković terms "assimilation to the unmarked," as exemplified by dominant–recessive harmonies. An example of this type in a licensing-driven system occurs in Lango, discussed in §5.3. Local conjunction as a construct also has utility in deriving feature value control in licensing-driven harmony in central Veneto (§5.3).

Recall that a markedness asymmetry in the values for a feature is not always clear. While some feature values generally show a clear asymmetry across languages, e.g. [+round] is plausibly more marked than [−round], other features present more ambiguous evidence (see §2.6). [+high] and [−high] arguably fall in this second category. Further research on cases of the latter type is needed. If the ranking of the markedness constraints for a given feature's values was found to be unrestricted, each value could be expected to control assimilation in some language pattern.

4.4 Non-local effects

To explore non-local effects in licensing, a factorial typology was generated for trisyllables where the first syllable is the licensing stressed position, and the final syllable contains a vowel belonging to an affix to which a licensing constraint is indexed. (On indexation of licensing constraints to specific morphemes, see §3.6.) The second syllable of the forms under consideration contains a vowel with a fixed [−F] specification. This scenario is exemplified by instances of a licensing phenomenon where [+high] and [−low] in a final high suffix vowel show licensing by a prior stressed syllable, but an intervening syllable /a/ is unaltered (as in Lena, §6.4). The same constraints as those in (3) were used, except that the licensing constraints were indexed to a suffix represented by the final syllable of the input and output forms. There were four input forms, deriving from all combinations of feature values for the initial and final syllable: /+ − +$_L$/, /+ − ¬$_L$/, /− − +$_L$/, and /− − ¬$_L$/. The final feature value, representing the specification on a final suffix vowel, is indexed with 'L' to the licensing constraint. Eight output candidates were considered, schematized in (15). In adjacent syllables, identical feature values either belonged to separate chains or represented a single shared specification. The same set of candidate outputs was considered for each input.

(15)   Candidate outputs in schematic form
      a. [−][−][+$_L$]
      b. [− −][+$_L$]
      c. [+]$_i$[−][+$_L$]$_i$
      d. [+][−][+$_L$]
      e. [− − −$_L$]
      f. [−][−][−$_L$]
      g. [+][−][−$_L$]
      h. [+][− −$_L$]

There were sixteen different output patterns, but because of covert structure, there were just nine different feature-value sequences. Many of the sixteen patterns present sequences consistent with types already identified in the typology of disyllables and trisyllables above. These are (a) full contrast (four output patterns), (b) indirect licensing (three output patterns), and (c) direct licensing (two output patterns). One additional pattern shows a majority-rule effect, which will be ruled out by the local conjunction, discussed in §4.3. Of particular interest are patterns that show identity licensing with the capacity to alter feature specifications. Because the medial vowel in the candidate sets is fixed [−F], identity licensing is only evident for [+F]. Two scenarios for identity licensing emerge, one in which feature specifications are altered in licensing position and one in which they are altered in a non-licensing position. This could occur in combination with indirect licensing for [−F] conducted through the medial vowel, resulting in the four patterns of output feature values described in (16) (six output patterns). Schematic output forms and rankings for each pattern are provided in the appendix (§4.7).

Interactions with other faithfulness constraints 77

(16) Identity licensing patterns with fixed medial [−F] vowel

	Pattern description
i.	Identity licensing for [+F] in suffix alters feature specifications in licensing position.
ii.	Identity licensing for [+F] and indirect licensing for [−F] in suffix alters feature specifications in licensing position.
iii.	Identity licensing for [+F] in suffix alters feature specifications in a non-licensing position.
iv.	Identity licensing for [+F] and indirect licensing for [−F] in suffix alters feature specifications in a non-licensing position.

The two primary scenarios for non-local licensing effects are distinguished by the position in which licensing can alter features: licensing or non-licensing position. This distinction is distilled in (17) with sample languages that present the patterns.

	Pattern description	Language and specifics
i.	Identity licensing alters feature specifications in licensing position at a distance.	Ascrea (§6.4) [F] = members of class [HEIGHT] Licensing position = ó Trigger = ŏ [+high] (certain inflections)
ii.	Identity licensing alters feature specifications in a non-licensing position at a distance.	Eastern Meadow Mari (§6.2) [F] = [back] Licensing position = $\sigma_{Initial}$ Affected non-licensing position: σ_{Final}

(17) Sample indirect licensing patterns

An important aspect of these cases is that they fit with an expectation that assimilation could occur between a prominent position and a position at a distance whose material is subject to licensing, since the prominent position affords the critical exposure.

4.5 Interactions with other faithfulness constraints

The factorial typologies described above investigate interactions of licensing constraints with faithfulness and markedness constraints that are relevant to patterns that show assimilation. Particular rankings of these constraints produce direct licensing in a faithful licensing position, with neutralization to the less marked value of [F] in non-licensing positions. That solution occurs when IDENT-IO(F) is dominated by the licensing constraint for a marked value of [F] and by CRISPEDGE([F], σ), which prevents a shared feature chain. Yet there are several other conceivable ways of achieving direct licensing, each involving violation of at least one faithfulness constraint. This section introduces the chief constraint interactions involved in a sampling of these patterns, which are explored in depth in chapter 7. The faithfulness constraints referenced in what follows are drawn from the Correspondence Theory formalism of McCarthy and Prince (1995). Their definitions are provided, where relevant, in other chapters.

One cluster of solutions involves manipulations at the segmental level. For instance, an unlicensed feature can be prevented by deleting the vowel that contains it, which violates MAX-IO(Segment). This is exemplified by certain patterns that delete vowels with perceptually marked features in weak positions. High vowel deletion in northern dialects of Greek is an example. Another solution is to import the entire vowel whose feature would be unlicensed into the licensing position, producing a diphthong or a coalesced vowel. Patterns of this kind are found in northern dialects of Italy: a final unstressed consonant–vowel sequence undergoes apparent metathesis to shift the vowel into the immediately preceding stressed syllable. Because the unstressed vowel is a suffix, this pattern displays a kind of infixation, which violates MORPHOLOGICAL-O-CONTIGUITY (Landman 2003), a constraint that penalizes discontinuous morphemes. In some cases of infixation, the original final vowel and the stressed vowel coalesce, incurring a violation of UNIFORMITY-IO, which militates against segmental mergers.

Other solutions manipulate features and featural identity, while keeping segmental correspondence and sequencing intact. As already mentioned, direct licensing can cause neutralization to the less-marked value for [F] in a non-licensing position, as attested in Belarusian unstressed mid vowel lowering. Other patterns arise from mobile or floating features, which find their way to licensing positions independent of association to a sponsoring segment in a non-licensing position. One such case is found in Modern Standard German, in which a floating [−back] specification, introduced by particular suffixes, appears on a licensing stressed vowel.

Table (18) provides a sampling of direct licensing patterns. In each of these, a licensing constraint, and often also CRISPEDGE([F], σ), dominates some faithfulness constraint(s), indicated in the center column. A fuller range of direct licensing patterns is summarized in §7.5.

Interactions with other faithfulness constraints 79

(18)   Sample direct licensing patterns

	Pattern description	Faithfulness constraint(s) violated	Language and specifics
i.	Direct licensing causes vowel deletion in a non-licensing position.	MAX-IO(segment)	Northern dialects of Modern Greek (§7.2.3) Licensing position = σ́ Affected vowel: high, unstressed
ii.	Direct licensing causes infixation, which shifts a vowel into licensing position to form a coalesced vowel or diphthong.	UNIFORMITY-IO MORPH-O-CONTIGUITY	Dialects of Liguria (§7.3) Licensing position = σ́ Infixed vowel: final, unstressed /i/
iii.	Direct licensing causes vowels in non-licensing position to neutralize to a less-marked value for [F].	IDENT-IO(F)	Belarusian (§7.2.1) Licensing position = σ́ Affected vowel: mid, unstressed
iv.	Direct licensing causes floating [F] to associate to licensing position.	IDENT-IO(F)	Modern Standard German (§7.4) Licensing position = σ́ Floating feature: [−back]

Another primary faithfulness constraint is DEP-IO(segment), which penalizes segments in the output that lack an input correspondent. This constraint has the potential to come into play in assimilation-driven licensing patterns. If a markedness constraint prevents an existing vowel in licensing position from undergoing assimilation, an epenthetic vowel composing part of a diphthong in licensing position could serve as a licensor. A solution that is similar to this occurs in the dialect of Francavilla Fontana (§6.3). Avoidance of high [−ATR] vowels prevents mid [−ATR] vowels in stressed position from undergoing raising to license a [+high] feature. The language resolves the problem with diphthongization, where the [−ATR] vowel undergoes fission into two vowels in stressed position to supply a [+ATR] vowel to license [+high] while the other realizes the mid [−ATR] vowel quality (an approach building on insights of the analysis of Calabrese 1985, 1988). This structure involves multiple correspondents of a single input vowel, violating the faithfulness constraint INTEGRITY-IO.

A conceivable solution for prosodically based licensing that is notably absent is stress shift. That is, there appears to be no pattern in which the stressed syllable is the licensing position and stress shifts to a vowel that contains marked structure in order to license it (Walker 2005). This is part of a wider generalization regarding stress identified by Blumenfeld (2006): whereas quantity, sonority, and tone have the potential to condition stress assignment, segmental features do not. Blumenfeld has made a theoretical proposal on this topic, which I discuss in chapter 9.

4.6 Summary

The factorial typologies explored in this chapter provide a solid footing for the proposed set of constraints relevant for assimilation-driven licensing, and extend to include interactions with other faithfulness constraints. Under this theoretical approach, the manner in which unlicensed structure is resolved in a given language is determined by the language-particular constraint ranking. In this respect, utilizing the output-based framework of OT offers an essential insight for generalized licensing: what unites prominence-based licensing phenomena is what they accomplish, namely, preventing distinctive information from being expressed solely in a non-prominent position. This shared characteristic exists despite the plurality of processes and patterns.

This chapter has emphasized the core constraint interactions that produce the various licensing configurations, but there are further complexities. The description and analysis of prominence-based licensing patterns are explored in more detail in following chapters. Interactions with other phonological and morphological properties of linguistic systems are investigated, producing a rich set of typological and theoretical results.

4.7 Appendix

This appendix provides further details on the factorial typology for the licensing constraint and selected other constraints with which it interacts.

In all forms under consideration, the stressed syllable is the initial syllable. Table (19) provides a description of the six patterns of vowel feature sequences predicted by a factorial typology for disyllabic words. It includes full schematic forms of the candidate outputs as well as the rankings that derive the patterns. Where more than one output pattern is shown for a given set of feature-value sequences, language data is often ambiguous as to the particular representation involved.

(19) Full summary of factorial typology of disyllables

Pattern description	Summary	Output patterns		
Full contrast: feature values remain identical in both syllables in mapping from input to output.	Output pattern (a) presents no licensing. Output pattern (b) presents indirect licensing of word-final [+F] by the stressed (first) syllable where no identity violations are engendered. Output pattern (c) presents indirect licensing of word-final [+F] and [−F] by the stressed syllable where identity is respected. All output patterns show no alternations.	a. /−/−/ [−][−] /−+/ [−][+] /+ +/ [+][+] /+ −/ [+][−] <u>Stratum 1</u> IDENT-IO(F) IDENT-IO-σ́(F) IDENT-IO-σ$_{Final}$(F) *DUPLICATE(F) CRISPEDGE([F], σ) <u>Stratum 2</u> LICENSE([+F], σ́) LICENSE([F], σ́)	b. /−/−/ [−][−] /−+/ [−][+] /+ +/ [+][+] /+ −/ [+][−] <u>Stratum 1</u> IDENT-IO(F) IDENT-IO-σ́(F) IDENT-IO-σ$_{Final}$(F) *DUPLICATE(F) <u>Stratum 2</u> LICENSE([+F], σ́) <u>Stratum 3</u> CRISPEDGE([F], σ) <u>Stratum 4</u> LICENSE([F], σ́)	c. /−/−/ [−][−] /−+/ [−][+] /+ +/ [+][+] /+ −/ [+][−] <u>Stratum 1</u> IDENT-IO(F) IDENT-IO-σ́(F) IDENT-IO-σ$_{Final}$(F) *DUPLICATE(F) <u>Stratum 2</u> LICENSE([+F], σ́) LICENSE([F], σ́) <u>Stratum 3</u> CRISPEDGE([F], σ)
Indirect licensing for [+F] alters feature specifications in stressed syllable.	Output pattern (a) presents indirect licensing of word-final [+F] by the stressed syllable, altering specifications in the stressed syllable. Output pattern (b) presents indirect licensing of word-final [+F] and [−F] by the stressed syllable. Licensing for [+F] alters specifications in the stressed syllable, whereas licensing for [−F] occurs	a. /−/−/ [−][−] /−+/ [+ +] /+ +/ [+ +] /+ −/ [+][−] <u>Stratum 1</u> IDENT-IO-σ$_{Final}$(F) LICENSE([+F], σ́) *DUPLICATE(F) <u>Stratum 2</u> IDENT-IO(F) IDENT-IO-σ́(F) CRISPEDGE([F], σ)	b. /−/−/ [−−] /−+/ [+ +] /+ +/ [+ +] /+ −/ [+][−] <u>Stratum 1</u> IDENT-IO-σ$_{Final}$(F) LICENSE([+F], σ́) *DUPLICATE(F) <u>Stratum 2</u> IDENT-IO(F) IDENT-IO-σ́(F) <u>Stratum 3</u> LICENSE([F], σ́)	

Pattern description	Summary	Output patterns		
		Stratum 3		Stratum 4
		License([F], ό)		CrispEdge([F], σ)
Indirect licensing for [+F] and [−F] alters feature specifications in stressed syllable.	The output pattern presents indirect licensing of word-final [+F] and [−F] by the stressed syllable, altering specifications in the stressed syllable.	/−−/ [−−] /−+/ [++] /++/ [++] /+−/ [−−] Stratum 1 Ident-IO-σ$_{Final}$(F) License([+F], ό) License([F], ό) *Duplicate(F) Stratum 2 Ident-IO(F) Ident-IO-ό(F) CrispEdge([F], σ)		
Indirect licensing for [+F] alters feature specifications in word-final syllable.	Output pattern (a) presents indirect licensing of word-final [+F] by the stressed syllable, altering specifications in the word-final syllable. Specifically, a word-final [+F] is licensed if identity is respected in the stressed syllable or the word-final syllable becomes [−F]. Output pattern (b) presents indirect	a. /−−/ [−]|[−] /−+/ [−]|[−] /++/ [+]|[+] /+−/ [+]|[−] Stratum 1 Ident-IO-ό(F) License([+F], ό) *Duplicate(F) Stratum 2 Ident-IO(F) Ident-IO-σ$_{Final}$(F)		b. /−−/ [−−] /−+/ [−−] /++/ [++] /+−/ [+]|[−] Stratum 1 Ident-IO-ό(F) License([+F], ό) *Duplicate(F) Stratum 2 Ident-IO(F) Ident-IO-σ$_{Final}$(F)

	licensing of word-final [+F] and [−F] by the stressed syllable. Licensing for [+F] alters specifications in the word-final syllable by assimilation to the stressed syllable, but licensing for word-final [−F] in the input occurs only when identity in the word-final syllable is preserved.	Stratum 3 CRISPEDGE([F], σ́) Stratum 4 LICENSE([F], σ́)	Stratum 3 LICENSE([F], σ́) Stratum 4 CRISPEDGE([F], σ)
Indirect licensing for [+F] and [−F] alters feature specifications in word-final syllable.	The output pattern presents indirect licensing of word-final [+F] and [−F] by the stressed syllable, altering specifications in word-final position. In other words, a word-final syllable assimilates to the feature value of the stressed syllable.	/−−/ [−−] /−+/ [−−] /++/ [++] /+−/ [++] Stratum 1 IDENT-IO-σ́(F) LICENSE([+F], σ́) *DUPLICATE(F) Stratum 2 IDENT-IO(F) IDENT-IO-σ$_{Final}$(F) CRISPEDGE([F], σ)	

Pattern description	Summary	Output patterns	
Direct licensing for [+F] causes neutralization in word-final position to [−F].	The output pattern presents only direct licensing of [+F] by the stressed syllable. The word-final syllable is neutralized to [−F].	/−−/ [−][−] /−+/ [−][−] /++/ [+][−] /+−/ [+][−] **Stratum 1** IDENT-IO-σ́(F) LICENSE([+F], σ́) *DUPLICATE CRISPEDGE([F], σ) **Stratum 2** IDENT-IO(F) IDENT-IO-σ$_{Final}$(F) LICENSE([F], σ́)	

Table (20) provides a description of the feature-value patterns predicted by a factorial typology for trisyllabic words. Patterns (s–v), marked with an asterisk, show majority-rule effects. These are ruled out by the local conjunction discussed in §4.3.

(20) Summary of feature-value patterns for trisyllables

(a) Input	Output	(b) Input	Output	(c) Input	Output	(d) Input	Output	(e) Input	Output	(f) Input	Output
– – –	– – –	– – –	– – –	– – –	– – –	– – –	– – –	– – –	– – –	– – –	– – –
– – +	– – +	– – +	– – +	– – +	– – –	– – +	+ + +	– – +	+ + +	– – +	– – +
– + –	– + –	– + –	– – –	– + –	– – –	– + –	– – –	– + –	– – –	– + –	– – –
– + +	– + +	– + +	– + +	– + +	– + +	– + +	+ + +	– + +	+ + +	– + +	+ + +
+ – –	– + +	+ – –	+ + +	+ – –	+ + +	+ – –	+ + +	+ – –	+ + +	+ – –	+ + –
+ – +	+ + –	+ – +	+ + –	+ – +	+ + +	+ – +	+ + –	+ – +	+ + –	+ – +	+ – +
+ + –	+ – –	+ + –	+ – –	+ + –	+ – –	+ + –	+ – –	+ + –	+ – –	+ + –	+ – –
+ + +	+	+ + +	+	+ + +	+	+ + +	+	+ + +	+	+ + +	+

(g) Input	Output	(h) Input	Output	(i) Input	Output	(j) Input	Output	(k) Input	Output	(l) Input	Output
– – –	– – –	– – –	– – –	– – –	– – –	– – –	– – –	– – –	– – –	– – –	– – –
– – +	– + +	– – +	– – –	– – +	– – –	– – +	– – +	– – +	– – +	– – +	– – +
– + –	– + –	– + –	– – –	– + –	– – –	– + –	– + –	– + –	– + –	– + –	– – –
– + +	+ + +	– + +	+ + +	– + +	+ + +	– + +	+ + +	– + +	+ + +	– + +	+ + +
+ – –	+ + –	+ – –	+ + –	+ – –	+ + +	+ – –	+ – –	+ – –	+ + –	+ – –	+ + –
+ – +	+ – –	+ – +	+ + –	+ – +	+ + +	+ – +	+ – +	+ – +	+ + –	+ – +	+ – +
+ + –	+ – –	+ + –	+ – –	+ + –	+ – –	+ + –	+ – –	+ + –	+ – –	+ + –	+ – –
+ + +	+	+ + +	+	+ + +	+	+ + +	+	+ + +	+	+ + +	+

(m) Input	Output	(n) Input	Output	(o) Input	Output	(p) Input	Output	(q) Input	Output	(r) Input	Output
− − − −	− − − −	− − − −	− − − +	− − − −	− − − −	− − − −	− − − −	− − − −	− − − −	− − − −	− − − −
− − − +	− + + −	− − − +	+ − − +	− − − +	− − − −	− − − +	− − − −	− − − +	− − − −	− − − +	− − − −
− + − −	+ − − −	− + − −	+ − − +	− + − −	− − − −	− + − −	− − − −	− + − −	− − − +	− + − −	− − − −
+ + + −	+ + + −	+ + + −	+ + + −	+ + + −	+ + + −	+ + + −	+ + + −	+ + + −	+ + − +	+ + + −	+ − − +
+ + + −	+ + + −	+ + + −	+ + + −	+ + + −	+ + + −	+ + + −	+ + + −	+ + + −	+ + + −	+ + + −	+ + + −
+ + − −	+ + − −	+ + − −	− + − −	+ + − −	+ + − −	+ + − −	+ − + −	+ + − −	− + + −	+ + − −	− + − −
+ + − −	+ + − −	+ + − −	+ − − −	+ + − −	+ + − −	+ + − −	+ + − −	+ + − −	+ + − −	+ + − −	+ + − −
+ + − −	− + − +	+ + − −	+ − − +	+ + − −	− − − +	+ + − −	− − − +	+ + − −	+ − − +	+ + − −	− − − +

(s)* Input	Output	(t)* Input	Output	(u)* Input	Output	(v)* Input	Output
− − − −	− − − −	− − − −	− − − −	− − − −	− − − −	− − − −	− − − −
− − − +	− − − −	− − − +	− − − −	− − − +	− − − −	− − − +	− − − −
− + − −	− − − −	− + − −	+ + − −	− + − −	+ + − −	− + − −	+ + − −
+ + + −	+ + + −	+ + + −	+ + + −	+ + + −	+ + + +	+ + + −	+ + + +
+ + + −	+ + + −	+ + + −	+ + + −	+ + + −	+ + + −	+ + + −	+ + − −
+ + − −	+ + − +	+ + − −	+ + − +	+ + − −	+ + − −	+ + − −	− − − −
− + − −	− − − −	− + − −	− + − −	− + − −	− − − −	− + − −	− − − −
+ + − +	+ + − +	+ + − +	+ + − +	+ + − +	+ + − +	+ + − +	+ + − +

Appendix   87

Table (21) provides a description of the four vowel feature sequences for identity licensing predicted by a factorial typology for trisyllabic suffixed words with a fixed medial [−F] vowel. Full schematic forms of the candidate outputs are provided and also the rankings for each output pattern. Not included here are the one case of identity licensing that showed a majority-rule effect and the two cases of identity licensing that did not overtly alter feature specifications from the input because all faithfulness constraints belonged to the top stratum.

(21) Summary of identity licensing patterns in factorial typology of suffixed trisyllables

Pattern description	Summary	Output patterns	
Identity licensing for [+F] in suffix (indexed L) alters feature specifications in stressed syllable.	Output pattern (a) presents identity licensing of suffixal [+F] by the stressed syllable, causing alternations in the stressed syllable. Output pattern (b) presents identity licensing of suffixal [+F] and indirect licensing of suffixal [−F] by the stressed syllable. Licensing for [+F] causes alternations in the stressed syllable, whereas licensing for [−F] occurs only when identity in the stressed syllable is preserved.	a. /− − −$_L$/ [−][−][−] /− − +$_L$/ [+]$_i$[−][+]$_i$ /+ − +$_L$/ [+]$_i$[−][+]$_i$ /+ − −$_L$/ [+][−][−] Stratum 1 IDENT-IO-σ$_{Final}$(F) LICENSE$_L$([+F], ó) Stratum 2 IDENT-IO(F) IDENT-IO-ó(F) *DUPLICATE(F) CRISPEDGE([F], σ) Stratum 3 LICENSE$_L$([F], ó)	b. /− − −$_L$/ [− − −$_L$] /− − +$_L$/ [+]$_i$[−][+$_L$]$_i$ /+ − +$_L$/ [+]$_i$[−][+$_L$]$_i$ /+ − −$_L$/ [+][−][−$_L$] Stratum 1 IDENT-IO-σ$_{Final}$(F) LICENSE$_L$([+F], ó) Stratum 2 IDENT-IO(F) IDENT-IO-ó(F) *DUPLICATE(F) Stratum 3 LICENSE$_L$([F], ó) Stratum 4 CRISPEDGE([F], σ)
Identity licensing for [+F] and indirect licensing for [−F] in suffix (indexed L) alter feature specifications in stressed syllable.	The output pattern presents identity licensing of suffixal [+F] and indirect licensing of suffixal [−F], causing alternations in the stressed syllable.	/− − −$_L$/ [− − −$_L$] /− − +$_L$/ [+]$_i$[−][+$_L$]$_i$ /+ − +$_L$/ [+]$_i$[−][+$_L$]$_i$ /+ − −$_L$/ [− − −$_L$] Stratum 1 IDENT-IO-σ$_{Final}$(F) LICENSE$_L$([+F], ó) LICENSE$_L$([F], ó) Stratum 2 IDENT-IO(F) IDENT-IO-ó(F) *DUPLICATE(F) CRISPEDGE([F], σ)	

Pattern description	Summary	Output patterns	
Identity licensing for [+F] in suffix (indexed L) alters feature specifications in the suffix syllable.	Output pattern (a) presents identity licensing of suffixal [+F] by the stressed syllable, causing alternations in the suffix syllable. Specifically, suffixal [+F] is licensed if identity is respected in the stressed syllable or the word-final syllable becomes [−F]. Output pattern (b) presents identity licensing of suffixal [+F] and indirect licensing of suffixal [−F] by the stressed syllable. Licensing for [+F] causes alternations in the suffix syllable by assimilation to the stressed syllable, but licensing for [−F] occurs only when identity in the word-final syllable is preserved.	a. /−−−₋ₗ/ [−][−][−ₗ] /−−+ₗ/ [−][−][−ₗ] /+−+ₗ/ [+]ᵢ[−][+ₗ]ᵢ /+−−ₗ/ [+][−][−ₗ] Stratum 1 IDENT-IO-ó(F) LICENSE_L([+F], ó) Stratum 2 IDENT-IO(F) IDENT-IO-σ_Final(F) Stratum 3 *DUPLICATE(F) CRISPEDGE([F], σ) Stratum 4 LICENSE_L([F], ó)	b. /−−−₋ₗ/ [−−−ₗ] /−−+ₗ/ [−−−ₗ] /+−+ₗ/ [+]ᵢ[−][+ₗ]ᵢ /+−−ₗ/ [+][−][−ₗ] Stratum 1 IDENT-IO-ó(F) LICENSE_L([+F], ó) Stratum 2 IDENT-IO(F) IDENT-IO-σ_Final(F) Stratum 3 LICENSE_L([F], ó) *DUPLICATE(F) Stratum 4 CRISPEDGE([F], σ)
Identity licensing for [+F] and indirect licensing for [−F] in suffix (indexed L) alter feature specifications in the suffix syllable.	The output pattern presents identity licensing of suffixal [+F] and indirect licensing of suffixal [−F], causing alternations in the suffix syllable. In other words, a word-final suffix vowel assimilates to the feature value of the stressed syllable.	/−−−₋ₗ/ [−−−ₗ] /−−+ₗ/ [−−−ₗ] /+−+ₗ/ [+]ᵢ[−][+ₗ]ᵢ /+−−ₗ/ [+]ᵢ[−][+ₗ]ᵢ Stratum 1 IDENT-IO-ó(F) LICENSE_L([+F], ó) LICENSE_L([F], ó) Stratum 2 IDENT-IO(F) IDENT-IO-σ_Final(F) *DUPLICATE(F) CRISPEDGE([F], σ)	

5 *Indirect licensing*

5.1   Introduction

This chapter discusses vowel patterns that involve indirect licensing. According to the hypothesized functional underpinnings for these systems, indirect licensing serves to reduce perceptual difficulty by causing a vowel quality to be produced both in a prominent position and an adjacent non-prominent position or sequence of non-prominent positions. Where a feature subject to licensing is restricted to a particular value or context, that material is expected to have the capacity to serve as marked. Because the licensing position is prominent, patterns are anticipated to occur where the shared vowel quality issues from this site. In patterns where the shared property originates in a vowel external to the licensing position, it is expected either that this vowel occurs in a position serving as another locus of strength in the word or that some independent factor prevents it from capitulating to the original value of the licensing position. This chapter concentrates on patterns with indirect licensing that do not also present identity licensing, that is, it excludes cases where a given vowel quality is produced in prominent position and a non-adjacent non-prominent position through feature duplication. Characteristics that may be indicative of an indirect licensing pattern are the existence of blocking effects and licensing-driven assimilation that can cause more than one vowel to undergo harmony.[1]

The overarching formal properties of these systems under the proposed constraint-based analysis are previewed in what follows. Patterns that include indirect licensing structures but not identity licensing are characterized by the core ranking schematized in (1). Four constraints are considered here. Those in which [F] serves as a variable reference to the same feature. The licensing constraint could be for both values of [F] or narrowed to a specific value for [F]. Among these constraints, the licensing constraint and the constraint that prohibits feature duplication belong to a higher stratum and IDENT(F) and the crisp edge constraint belong to a lower stratum or strata. I have labeled the higher stratum here as *n*. In many cases, it will be the top stratum of the hierarchy, i.e.

stratum 1, but it could in principle be dominated by other constraints separate from those pertaining to the licensing pattern. The higher-ranked status of *DUPLICATE(F) reflects the absence of identity licensing configurations, which involve a duplicated feature. The dominance of the licensing constraint over IDENT reflects the existence of an active licensing pattern for [F] in the grammar, and its dominance over the crisp edge constraint reflects the occurrence of licensing-driven feature chains that span more than one syllable. Because of the enforcement of *DUPLICATE(F), such representations are only those in which a single feature is shared across syllables, as in indirect licensing. In some indirect licensing patterns, the ranking is elaborated such that *DUPLICATE(F) dominates the licensing constraint so that when indirect licensing is blocked, licensing can be violated.

(1)   Core ranking: indirect licensing
       Stratum n
       LICENSE([F], π), *DUPLICATE(F)
       Stratum > n
       CRISPEDGE([F], σ), IDENT-IO(F)

Because this core ranking structure is common across the indirect licensing patterns, some of these constraints will not be addressed in the context of every language under study, but they will be discussed where relevant to the properties under emphasis for a given system.

In this chapter the discussion centers on how each of the vowel patterns is compatible with a prominence-based licensing analysis. This theme is continued in chapters 6 and 7, which examine identity licensing and direct licensing, respectively. As all indirect licensing patterns show instances where a feature specification is shared across syllables, an issue alluded to above emerges concerning whether the licensing position or non-licensing position is faithful. The licensing constraint can drive vowel harmony, but it is silent on the direction of harmony and which vowel is the trigger or target. These properties emerge from the interaction of other constraints. If the vowel in the licensing position is faithful, it serves as the trigger for harmony or it is the anchor for licensing-based sequencing restrictions. If the non-licensing position is faithful, then the licensing position alternates, in which case the question arises of what causes the vowel in the non-licensing position to control an assimilation. In this situation, some constraint prevents the vowel in non-licensing position from being the target of harmony, which compels it to be the trigger. I will argue that in some patterns a vowel in non-licensing position is subject to a positional faithfulness constraint. In other cases examined here, a position-insensitive faithfulness constraint (sometimes in a local conjunction with a markedness constraint) causes a particular vowel quality to be preserved. Given the proposal that position-insensitive constraints can be the source of trigger control, a system is predicted that has forms in which the trigger vowel is in licensing position and other forms in which it is in non-licensing position. By the same token, it is expected that harmony could be progressive in some forms and regressive in others. These predictions are borne out in the case of Lango.

Various other issues cross-cut the patterns considered in this chapter. Sources of strength and control are examined for each system. In forms where indirect licensing does not succeed, the resolution of the unlicensed material is at issue. Related to this is the question of whether both values for a feature are subject to licensing or just one of the values. Interactions with the lexical status of material are examined where relevant. This includes morpheme-specific effects, the behavior of epenthetic vowels, and effects of lexical strata.

This chapter first deals with patterns of indirect licensing with control by the prominent licensing position. Buchan Scots, Macuxi, and Ticinese are cases where assimilation produces alternations in non-licensing position. Classical Mongolian and C'Lela present passive licensing, where indirect licensing for [αF] occurs without evidence of active assimilation from the licensing position. In these cases, indirect licensing can occur provided that it does not compel a violation of faithfulness in the licensing position. Otherwise, there is neutralization to [–αF] in the position whose content must be licensed. Next, licensing patterns that show assimilation in the licensing position are considered. The languages examined are Old High German, the dialect of central Veneto, and Jaqaru, where licensing occurs in a prosodically strong position, and Lango, where the strength of the licensing position has a morphological basis. A summary of sources of trigger control is provided, followed by discussion of some alternative approaches to the patterns at hand.

5.2 Control by the licensing position

This section examines indirect licensing patterns where the vowel in the licensing position does not alternate. That is, it controls active licensing-driven assimilation or it is the locus of strength in passive licensing patterns. These patterns of control can be accomplished with faithfulness constraints for the prominent position that serves as the licensor, such as the stressed syllable, a root or stem syllable, or the initial syllable of the word or root. Control by the vowel in the licensing position is compatible with the phonetic and/or psycholinguistic strength affiliated with these contexts.

5.2.1 Assimilation within non-licensing position

This section investigates three indirect licensing patterns that show assimilation in a non-licensing position. In Buchan Scots, licensing for [+high] by a stressed syllable is enforced, causing high vowels to assimilate for [high] to a preceding stressed vowel. Particular consonants block height assimilation, consistent with an indirect licensing structure. Macuxi provides a case where licensing operates over [round] and [back], and the licensing position is the stem. In Ticinese a licensing constraint is active that causes word-final unstressed low vowels to undergo total assimilation with the vowel in the stressed syllable.

BUCHAN SCOTS. In the Buchan dialect of northeast Scotland, a high unstressed front vowel assimilates in height to a preceding stressed non-high vowel (Paster 2004). Examples of harmony are provided with alternations involving the unstressed suffix /–i/. The suffix is realized as [–e] following a stressed non-high vowel (2a) and [–i] following a stressed high vowel (2b).

(2)   a. hér-e   'hairy'   b. míl-i   'mealie'
            més-e   'messy'   bík-i   'beakie'
            hɔ́l-e   'hilly'   dír-i   'dearie'
            hʌ́rt-e   'hurtie'   kúθ-i   'couthy'
            mán-e   'mannie'   snút-i   'snooty'
            bátʃ-e   'batchie'
            póst-e   'postie'
            rɔ́k-e   'rocky'

The pattern is also witnessed in monomorphemic forms, as in (3).

(3)   a. vére   'very'   b. píti   'pity'
            stánle   'Stanley'   bjúti   'beauty'
            kɔ́pe   'copy'

Paster describes the domain of harmony as a trochaic binary foot. Consistent with this description, only vowels that are adjacent to the stressed syllable undergo harmony. In (4), the final vowel in words with antepenultimate stress does not undergo lowering.

(4)   bʌ́təri   'buttery'
       snɔ́kəri   'snickery'

Height harmony in Buchan Scots can be analyzed as driven by a constraint that penalizes unlicensed [+high]. The stressed syllable is the licensing position: LICENSE([+high], ó). Licensing in this language is accomplished by harmony from the stressed syllable to the unstressed syllable, causing unstressed high vowels to lower to mid following a stressed non-high vowel. In functional terms, harmony serves to prevent [+high] from being expressed in the weak context of an unstressed syllable alone.

It is worth asking whether the non-high vowels in (2a) are the result of assimilation, that is, a [–high] specification that spreads from the stressed vowel, or are produced by a default lowering that satisfies licensing when [+high] cannot be shared with the stressed vowel. The data in (4) suggest that assimilation occurs. If default lowering occurred in vowels for which [+high] could not be licensed, the final vowels in the words in (4) would be expected to become mid.

Also relevant to the presence of feature sharing is that certain intervening consonants block harmony (5). In approximate terms, blockers are voiced obstruents; see Paster (2004) for further discussion on this point.

(5)   héz-i   'hazy'
      béd-i   'beddie'
      lád-i   'laddie'
      lʌ́v-i   'lovey'
      dɔ́dʒ-i   'dodgy'
      dóg-i   'doggie'

The blocking effect in (5) confirms that vowel lowering is caused by assimilation to a non-high vowel. It also signals that licensing in adjacent syllables is indirect. Under the assumption that indirect licensing causes a continuous featural occurrence to be present in harmonizing syllables (see §3.3), an intervening consonant is expected to block harmony when it cannot undergo the assimilation. Paster suggests that blocking by voiced obstruents originated in laryngeal lowering in these consonants, which lowered F1 in following vowels. This interfered with the lowering height harmony, which would have produced a higher F1 in the following vowel. Following Paster, I assume that blocking is caused by the constraint *D[–high], which penalizes voiced obstruents that are [–high]. The prevention of identity licensing configurations, which would allow licensing through a duplicated feature without association to an intervening voiced obstruent is handled by the ranking: *Duplicate(F), *D[–high] >> License([+high], ó) >> Ident-IO(high). A faithfulness constraint for the stressed syllable Ident-IO-ó(high) will ensure that it is the stressed syllable that controls harmony rather than the unstressed vowel. This constraint will cause the stressed vowel to be the trigger no matter where it is ranked with respect to the other constraints under consideration. As it is uniformly satisfied, I place it in the top stratum of the hierarchy.

The tableau in (6) illustrates the analysis. For the input /her–i/ (6i), the optimal output is (a), which only violates Ident(high). Candidate (b), which is faithful, violates licensing, and (c), in which the stressed vowel assimilates to the final vowel, violates stressed syllable faithfulness. For the input /hez–i/ (6ii), the optimal output is the faithful candidate (a). Candidate (b), which shows indirect licensing, violates *D[–high], and (c), which shows identity licensing, violates *DUPLICATE(F). IDENT(high) violations are shown not only for vowels, but also for consonants within the scope of an indirect licensing configuration. In general, IDENT violations for consonants will only be shown for patterns where consonants may affect the outcome.

(6) Height assimilation and blocking
IDENT-ǿ(high), *DUPLICATE(F), *D[–hi] >> LICENSE([+high], ǿ) >> IDENT(high)

Input	Output	IDENT-ǿ(high)	*DUPL(F)	*D[–hi]	LICENSE ([+high], ǿ)	IDENT(high)
i. /her-i/	☞ a. hére					**
	b. héri				*!	
	c. híri	*!				**
ii. /hez-i/	☞ a. hézi				*	
	b. héze |/ [–hi]			*!		**
	c. héze | | [–hi]ᵢ [–hi]ᵢ		*!			*

When licensing for the final high vowel fails, as in [hézi], it remains high, violating licensing, rather than undergoing lowering. This could be an effect of phonological faithfulness. Unlike the product of assimilation, where the final vowel becomes non-high by sharing an existing [–high] specification, lowering the vowel to [–high] in a blocking context would introduce a new feature specification to the representation.[2] This also bears on the occurrence of assimilation where possible. The licensing constraint must dominate CRISPEDGE([high], σ) to produce indirect licensing. In Buchan Scots, height harmony, incurring a violation of CRISPEDGE([high], σ), is preferred over non-assimilatory neutralization of a high vowel to a lower height by introducing a new feature.

Of course, when vowels within the same foot are both underlyingly [+high], and the intervening consonant is not one that blocks harmony, the analysis predicts that both vowels will surface faithfully, with [+high] shared across the syllables in question.

The restriction of harmony to vowels contained within the same trochaic foot is obtained by a crisp edge constraint: CRISPEDGE([high], Foot). Ranked above the licensing constraint, this constraint will prevent height harmony across a foot boundary, as shown in (7). Candidate (b) shows height harmony, but it violates the crisp edge constraint because assimilation spans a foot boundary. Three IDENT(high) violations are assessed for this candidate: one for the final vowel, and one each for [t] and [r], which are assumed to have become associated to [–high]. The winner is candidate (a), where crisp foot boundaries are maintained at the cost of licensing.

(7)   Harmony is restricted to vowels belonging to the same foot
      CRISPEDGE([high], Foot) >> LICENSE([+high], ó)

/bʌtəri/	CRISPEDGE ([high], Foot)	LICENSE ([+high], ó)	IDENT(high)
☞ a. (bʌ́tə)ri		*	
b. (bʌ́tə)re \\\| // [–hi]	*!		***

To sum up in broad strokes, height harmony in Buchan Scots presents a case where [+high] in a weak position is subject to licensing by a stressed syllable. Where possible, this drives assimilation of a high unstressed vowel to a neighboring stressed vowel, resulting in a height quality that is cued across both syllables.

MACUXI. In casual speech in Macuxi (Carib), /ɨ/ in certain unaccented affixes assimilates in backness to an adjacent syllable in the stem (Carson 1982; Odden 1991; Goad 1993). Syllables in the language may have high pitch (marked by '5' in [8]) or low pitch, or lack an accent. The data in (8) show alternations induced in a noun class prefix /pɨ-/, which also shows rounding assimilation.[3]

(8)   pɨ-riw5   'arrow (of someone)'
      pu-moi5   'egg (of someone)'
      pɨ-si5   'leg (of someone)'

The vowel transcribed as /ɨ/ is described as mid (Abbott 1991: 144) or mid high (Carson 1982: 51), suggesting that height can also be altered by this process (Goad 1993), but further study is needed to assess the specifics.

The pattern exemplified in (8) can be analyzed with LICENSE([COLOR]/ unaccented V, Stem).[4] COLOR refers to the class of vowel color features [round] and [back]. It is not entirely clear whether harmony affects /ɨ/ only (Carson 1982: 51), so I do not state that restriction in the licensing constraint, but the constraint could be augmented if appropriate. As a non-peripheral high vowel, /ɨ/ could be expected to serve as weak in comparison to other vowels. The licensing constraint will dominate IDENT-IO(round) and IDENT-IO(back), as shown in (9). The resulting system is one where backness and rounding properties in the unaccented affix are also realized in a stem vowel. It is not surprising that unaccented vowels are singled out by the licensing restriction, as they could be expected to be less salient than their accented counterparts.

(9) Licensing-driven color harmony
 License([Color]/unaccented V, Stem) >> Ident-IO(round), Ident-IO(back)

Input	Output	License ([Color]/unacc. V, Stem)	Ident (round)	Ident (back)
i. /pɨ-moiɔ̃/	☞ a. pumoiɔ̃		*	
	b. pɨmoiɔ̃	*!		
ii. /pɨ-siɔ̃/	☞ a. pisiɔ̃			*
	b. pɨsiɔ̃	*!		

Ident constraints for [round] and [back] in the stem will determine control of assimilation by the vowel in the licensing position in Macuxi.

Ticinese. A dialect spoken in the Ticino Canton shows a vowel harmony for all features that causes /a/ in a word-final suffix to assimilate to the stressed vowel (Salvioni 1894; Canalis 2007a, b). The harmony is exemplified in (10). The examples in (10a) show the realization of the imperative suffix, which is usually /–a/ in Lombard. The same phenomenon is seen in other suffixes with /a/. For example, although /a/ usually forms the feminine singular suffix, it shows harmony in Ticinese, as in (10b). Forms with the clitic that is /la/ 'her' in Lombard also show harmony (10c).

(10)   a. fíli   'off with you!'
             býty   'throw away!'
             skúzu   'sorry!' (lit. 'excuse!')
             léve su   'go away!'
             méndʒɛ   'eat!'
             lavørø   'work!'
             pɔ́tʃɔ   'rest!'
             pjáka   'keep quiet!'
     b. vívi   'alive (f)'
             kúrtu   'short (f)'
             polénte   'corn mush'
             fémne   'woman'
             mɔ́rtɔ   'dead (f)'
             váka   'cow'
     c. píkili   'beat her'
             véndele   'sell her'
             tʃápala   'catch her'

I propose to analyze this copy harmony as the effect of a prominence-based licensing constraint. As discussed in §2.6, a low vowel in an unstressed word-final syllable can present perceptual difficulty. The licensing constraint that drives the harmony penalizes any vowel feature in an unstressed word-final low vowel that is not licensed by the stressed syllable: LICENSE([V-FEATURE]/σ$_{Final}$[+low], ó).[5] This constraint will dominate non-positional IDENT constraints for all vowel features, which I collapse for convenience as IDENT-IO(V-FEATURE). Faithfulness constraints for vowel features in the stressed syllable, represented as IDENT-IO-ó(V-FEATURE), will be situated in the top stratum of the constraint hierarchy to produce control of harmony by the stressed vowel. Because the harmony generates indirect licensing configurations, the licensing constraint must dominate CRISPEDGE([V-FEATURE], σ).

The core of the ranking is illustrated in (11) with a case where /a/ undergoes copy harmony to [e]. I only consider output candidates that obey identity for vowel features in the stressed syllable. The selected output shows copy harmony with the stressed syllable, violating IDENT(V-FEATURE) and the crisp edge constraint. The faithful alternative in (b) is prevented by the licensing constraint. For simplicity, a single violation for each constraint is tallied here, even if more than one feature is involved.

(11)   Licensing-driven vowel copy harmony
       LICENSE([V-FEAT]/σ$_{Final}$[+low], ó) >> IDENT(V-FEAT), CRISPEDGE([V-FEAT], σ)

/lev-a/	LICENSE ([V-FEATURE]/σ$_{Final}$[+low], ó)	IDENT (V-FEATURE)	CRISPEDGE ([V-FEATURE], σ)
☞ a. léve		*	*
b. léva	*!		

Canalis interprets the forms in (12) as evidence that harmony can skip a post-tonic unstressed syllable in a word with antepenultimate stress.

(12)   kányla   'stick'
       trabákula   'fool'

I was unable to find any examples where there was evidence that /a/ had undergone feature-changing harmony with the stressed syllable across an intervening vowel that did not show the same harmonic quality. In the absence of such examples, I will tentatively assume that the harmony in Ticinese involves indirect licensing structures only. This is captured by placing *DUPLICATE(F) in the top stratum of the constraint ranking. Final [a] in forms like [kányla] and [trabákula] would thus violate the licensing constraint. As in Buchan Scots, I assume that the features of the vowel do not change when licensing-driven harmony is blocked because that would involve the addition of another feature to the representation. In other words, repairs to resolve licensing in this language can only make use of features that are already present in the form. This is also consistent with final /a/ undergoing harmony when possible rather than showing non-assimilatory neutralization to a fixed quality.

A final question is why the forms in (12) do not achieve satisfaction of the licensing constraint through assimilation of final /a/ to the vowel in the penultimate syllable, which would eliminate the offending final low vowel. This seems to be a consequence of the exceptional weakness of the penultimate syllable in these structures. Based on a study of vowel contrast neutralization, reduction, and harmony patterns, Canalis (2007b) suggests that Ticinese and various other dialects of Italy present a hierarchy of metrical strength as follows: stressed vowel > unstressed pretonic vowel > final unstressed vowel > penultimate vowel of proparoxytones. Proparoxytones are words that are assigned antepenultimate stress. The relative weakness of the penultimate syllable in proparoxytones of Ticinese is doubtless connected to their incapacity to trigger harmony in the forms in (12). Without further data, it would be premature to work out the specifics of the analysis for these items. In pursuing this topic, it would be valuable to investigate harmony patterns in proparoxytones and the vowel contrasts that are supported in the penultimate syllable of these forms.

OTHER PATTERNS. *Lango*. As will be discussed in §5.3, licensing for [ATR] by the morphological root in Lango causes harmony from a root vowel to suffix vowels under certain conditions.

Mazahua. Mazahua (Oto-Manguean) displays a vowel harmony for all features from the root to a category of suffixes labeled stem formatives (Spotts 1953). Following the analysis of Steriade (1995b: 160–1), the assimilation could be analyzed as driven by a constraint that penalizes vowel features in a stem formative affix that are not licensed by the root, resulting in indirect licensing. Consistent with expectations for a prominence-based licensing phenomenon, vowels in a weak position (affix) show dependence on the quality of vowels expressed in a privileged position (root). It is not always possible to achieve licensing through harmony. If a non-laryngeal consonant intervenes between a root vowel and the stem formative vowel, assimilation for [+round] does not occur. As a result, in such contexts, the stem formative vowel is realized as [ə] or [ə̃] after [u ũ o õ ɔ] in the root.[6] As Steriade observes, in these forms, direct licensing for [+round] is seen. If non-laryngeal consonants blocked assimilation for [+round] and identity licensing were unavailable because *DUPLICATE(F) dominates LICENSE([+round], Root), then the direct licensing outcome would be predicted for [+round] in this context.[7] The neutralization to [–round] when licensing cannot be satisfied would follow from assuming that [+round] is the marked specification, even if there is evidence that licensing effects for either specification of [round] are active in the system.

5.2.2   Passive licensing

This section examines 'passive' indirect licensing patterns in which the licensing position remains faithful, and when licensing for a particular vowel quality fails, the vowel is neutralized to the opposite value rather than undergoing active assimilation from the vowel in licensing position. The cases under study involve licensing for a particular feature value. Like assimilation patterns, they can result in vowel sequences where a quality that serves as marked survives in a non-licensing position only when it is shared with a vowel in the prominent licensing context, a specific circumstance where its opportunities for perception are increased. Classical Mongolian shows passive licensing for [+round] in non-high vowels by an initial syllable with neutralization to [–round] when a non-initial [+round] specification cannot be indirectly licensed. In C'Lela licensing by the root is enforced for [+high] in a word-final vowel. When the root vowel is [–high], licensing is satisfied by a word-final suffix vowel in an adjacent syllable becoming [–high]. This is also what transpires when licensing by the root is blocked by an intervening vowel with a value for [high] that is opposite to the root, a case that involves neutralization to [–high] in the word-final vowel rather than assimilation for [high] to the licensing position. In C'Lela, licensing shows morpheme specificity, and as expected, epenthetic vowels are exempted from the licensing restriction.

CLASSICAL MONGOLIAN. As introduced in chapter 1, Classical Mongolian presents a kind of sequencing restriction. The vowels of Classical Mongolian are [i y e ø a o u]. Non-high round vowels are permitted in non-initial syllables of the root only when all preceding syllables contain non-high round vowels (Svantesson 1985; Walker 2001b). Data in (13a) show the occurrence of [ø o] in non-initial syllables. A front/back vowel harmony is apparent in these forms. Whereas [ø o] are possible in non-initial syllables of the root, they never occur in suffixes. The examples in (13b) demonstrate that non-high unround vowels may follow syllables with a non-high round vowel. This indicates the absence of an active harmony for [+round] from the initial syllable. In other words, following a syllable with a non-high round vowel, rounding shows a contrastive distribution in a non-initial non-high vowel.

(13) a. nøkør   'friend'
          ølø   'gray'
          monɣol   'Mongol'
          qomoɣol   'horse dung'
      b. møren   'river'
          kømøske   'eyebrow(s)'
          bøgere   'kidney'
          qola   'far, distant'
          olan   'many'
          nomoɣodqa   'to tame'

High round vowels are not subject to the restriction. They occur freely in initial and non-initial syllables, as illustrated by examples in (14).

(14)   yne   'price'
        egyde   'door'
        sigesy   'piss'
        nidy-ji   'eye (acc.)'
        ydʒe-gyl   'see (caus.)'
        mede-gyl   'know (caus.)'
        bajiqu   'to be'
        ojimasu   'stocking'
        ɣaqai-luɣa   'pig (comitative)'
        ulus   'nation'
        qubi   'part'
        ulaɣan   'red'

I analyze Classical Mongolian's rounding distribution in roots as an effect of licensing that restricts the feature [+round] in non-high vowels, a perceptually disadvantaged context. The licensing position is the initial syllable. I conclude that indirect licensing is permitted but not identity licensing, because non-initial round non-high vowels must be part of an uninterrupted string of syllables with round vowels that leads from the initial syllable. The licensing constraint is LICENSE([+round]/[–high], σ$_{\text{Initial}}$). I classify the licensing pattern as passive, because it is compatible with an analysis where [+round] can be licensed provided the licensing position is faithful, and if licensing does not succeed, the non-prominent position neutralizes to [–round] rather than being the target of active assimilation initiated from the licensing position. That is, the pattern does not necessitate a solution of licensing by assimilation. Further, if the solution were assimilation from the licensing position, it would only be for [–round], which would occur when the input contained an unround vowel in the initial syllable and a round vowel in the following syllable. From a typological perspective, assimilation for [–round] only would be surprising.

The core ranking that causes non-high round vowels in roots to become unrounded in contexts where indirect licensing for [+round] is not available is LICENSE([+round]/[–high], σ_{Initial}), *DUPLICATE(F), IDENT-IO(high) >> IDENT-IO(round). Although the pattern does not present alternations, I assume that a hypothetical input with an unlicensed [+round] specification would map to an output that eliminates [+round]. An alternative repair that raises the vowel is an unlikely solution, given the history of vowel patterns in the language (see Svantesson 1985).

The tableaux in (15–16) illustrate the ranking. To demonstrate the constraint interactions, hypothetical inputs are considered that present non-high round vowels in contexts where rounding is eliminated. The input in (15) contains a non-high round vowel in a syllable following an initial non-high unround vowel. Candidate (b) makes no alteration to the input, but violates the licensing constraint. Candidate (c) raises the non-high round vowel so that it escapes being subject to licensing, but this solution is ruled out by IDENT(high). Candidate (a), which violates only IDENT(round), is selected. Not shown here is the candidate [mødøgyl] with round harmony from the peninitial vowel. This form will be ruled out by the initial syllable faithfulness constraint IDENT-σ_{Initial}-(round), which will cause this candidate to be suboptimal no matter where it is ranked.

(15) Loss of rounding in a peninitial vowel
      LICENSE([+round]/[–high], σ_{Initial}), IDENT-IO(high) >> IDENT-IO(round)

/medø-gyl/	LICENSE ([+rd]/[–hi], σ_{Initial})	*DUP(F)	IDENT (high)	IDENT (round)
☞ a. medegyl				*
b. medøgyl	*!			
c. medygyl			*!	

In sequences of non-high vowels, a peninitial syllable that contains a round vowel in the input always has a value for [round] in the output that conforms with that of the initial syllable. However, the output for an input that contains a round vowel in the third syllable does not necessarily show the same value for [round] as the initial syllable. A case where they could show different values is shown in (16). The input has round non-high vowels in the first syllable and third syllable but not the second. Like the output selected in (15), the winner loses rounding in the non-initial syllable. In this case, the initial syllable is round, but [+round] in the third syllable cannot be licensed through an indirect licensing structure, because of the intervening unround vowel. This output shows neutralization to [−round],[8] not assimilation to the vowel in the licensing position. A form in which licensing is satisfied by an identity licensing configuration, in (c), is prevented by *DUPLICATE(F). Candidate (b), in which the [+round] specifications belong to separate chains, violates the licensing constraint. Another candidate [bøgørø], which would tie with [bøgere] on the constraint hierarchy shown, is ruled out by a local conjunction that prevents majority-rule effects: *[+round] &$_l$ IDENT-IO(round) (see 4.3).[9]

(16) No identity licensing
      LICENSE([+round]/[−high], σ$_{Initial}$), *DUPLICATE(F), IDENT-IO(high) >> IDENT-IO(round)

/bøgerø/	LICENSE ([+rd]/[−hi], σ$_{Initial}$)	*DUPL(F)	IDENT (high)	IDENT (round)
☞ a. bøgere				*
b. bøgerø | | [+rd]$_i$ [+rd]$_j$	*!			
c. bøgerø | | [+rd]$_i$ [+rd]$_i$		*!		

The tableau in (17) shows a scenario in which a non-high round vowel in a non-initial syllable is preserved. Since indirect licensing causes a feature chain to span more than one syllable, IDENT-IO(round) must dominate CRISPEDGE([round], σ). The input here contains non-high round vowels in the first and second syllables. Candidate (a), with indirect licensing, is selected by the hierarchy. This output, which violates the crisp edge constraint, is superior to one that alters rounding, in (c), or one that contains an unlicensed [+round] specification, in (b).

(17) Indirect licensing
      LICENSE([+round]/[−high], σ$_{Initial}$) >> IDENT-IO(round) >> CRISPEDGE ([round], σ)

/moŋyol/	LICENSE ([+rd]/[-hi], σ$_{Initial}$)	IDENT (round)	CRISPEDGE ([round], σ)

☞ a. moŋyol
    \\ /
   [+round]
			*

b. moŋyol | | [+rd]$_i$ [+rd]$_j$	*!		
c. moŋyal		*!	

The result that comes out from (15–17) is that rounding in non-high vowels is retained only when licensing can be accomplished by sharing an existing [+round] feature specification that originates in the initial syllable. That active assimilation does not occur is suggested by the scenario in (16) where an unround vowel intervenes between a non-initial non-high round vowel and a round vowel in the initial syllable. For this input, the non-initial round vowel neutralizes to [–round].

A further detail remains: licensing of [+round] in non-high vowels is carried out only by vowels in a licensing position that are non-high. I attribute this to a constraint adapted from Kaun (1995, 2004) that I will refer to as GESTURAL UNIFORMITY([+round], [high]), defined in (18) (for related proposals see Cole and Kisseberth 1995, and Majors 1998). Kaun argues that production of a lip rounding gesture in vowels with different height requires different execution, an adjustment that is avoided for a single autosegment. The constraint assigns a penalty to each sequence of adjacent vowels that differ in height to which the same feature specification [+round] is linked.

(18) *Round/High Gestural Uniformity constraint*:
GESTURALUNIFORMITY([+round], [high])
*[+round]/¬GESTURALUNIFORMITY([+round], [high])
Let
    r be a variable ranging over occurrences of the feature specification [+round],
    v and v' be variables ranging over occurrences of vowels,
    |v| refer to the height of v,
    and vδr mean that v dominates r.
Then assign a violation to every pair <v, v'>, where v' occurs in an adjacent syllable following v, such that the following holds
∃r, v, v' [vδr ∧ v'δr ∧ [|v| ≠ |v'|]]

The gestural uniformity constraint dominates IDENT(round). The hierarchy favors a candidate that loses rounding in a non-initial non-high vowel (19a) over one that shares [+round] across high and non-high vowels (19b).

(19) [+round] is shared only across vowels of matching height
GESTURALUNIFORMITY([+round], [high]) >> IDENT-IO(round)

/ynø/	LICENSE ([+rd]/[–hi], $\sigma_{Initial}$)	GESTUNI ([+rd], [hi])	IDENT (round)
☞ a. yne			*
b. ynø \\ / [+round]		*!	

Here, articulatory markedness in the form of the gestural uniformity constraint prevents indirect licensing. Notice that if round vowels in the first and second syllable had separate [+round] specifications, GESTURALUNIFORMITY would be obeyed. The restriction of licensing to vowels with the same height is therefore suggestive that forms where round vowels survive in non-initial syllables must truly involve a shared [+round] specification.

C'LELA. C'Lela (Benue-Congo) presents a case of passive licensing where prominence of the licensing position has a morphological basis. The vowels of C'Lela are high [i ɨ u] and non-high [e ɛ a ɔ o]; vowel length is phonemic. Alternations in height are witnessed in specific final non-head morphemes that contain an underlying high vowel. A final vowel is realized as high when it occurs in a continuous sequence of syllables containing high vowels, including a syllable of the root; otherwise it is realized as non-high. Alternations in the direct object pronouns /mi/ and /vu/ and pronominal suffixes /–mi/, /–vu/ and /–u/ are shown in (20). The data are from Dettweiler (2000), and they are discussed by Pulleyblank (2002) and Archangeli and Pulleyblank (2007). The symbol [ᵊ] represents an excrescent non-phonemic vowel.[10] Following Dettweiler's transcriptions, tones are not represented.

(20) a. in-mi 'my mother' tʃet-me 'my father'
 b. sipkᵊ mi 'grabbed me' weɡaka me 'indicated me'
 buzᵊkᵊ mi 'chased me' ɛpkᵊ me 'bit me'
 fumtᵊkᵊ mi 'pulled me' batkᵊ me 'released me'
 c. in-vu 'your mother' tʃet-vo 'your father'
 d. sipkᵊ vu 'grabbed you' weɡaka vo 'indicated you'
 buzᵊkᵊ vu 'chased you' ɛpkᵊ vo 'bit you'
 fumtᵊkᵊ vu 'pulled you' batkᵊ vo 'released you'
 e. in-u 'her mother' tʃet-o 'her father'
 hɨn-u 'his sibling' waːr-o 'his child'

Following Pulleyblank (2002) and Archangeli and Pulleyblank (2007), I will refer to the morphemes that present height alternations as suffixes. Dettweiler characterizes the pronouns as clitics. Either way, I will assume that in C'Lela these morphemes are contained within a phonological word that contains the preceding lexical word. Given the existence of identical phonological forms with similar meanings such as –vo/–vu 'your' versus vo/vu 'you,' it is reasonable to suppose that these morphemes are drawn from at least a partially common set of lexical entries for dependent morphemes with the particular interpretation deriving from morphosyntactic structure.

Suffixes in adjectival constructions show the same kind of height alternation. When more than one of the potentially alternating suffixes is present, the suffix vowel in a non-final syllable is regularly realized as high, whereas the vowel in the final syllable is realized as high only if the root vowel is high, as seen in (21a–b) (CM = class marker, ADJM = adjectival suffix). Polysyllabic suffixes show the same generalization: height alternations occur only in final vowels (21c). If an intervening suffix contains a low vowel, such as the class marker /–a/, the vowel in the final syllable is realized as non-high (21d).[11]

(21)   a. i-zis-i   'CM-long-CM'   i-zis-i-ni   'CM-long-CM-ADJM'
            u-rim-u   'CM-black-CM'   u-rim-u-ni   'CM-black-CM-ADJM'
        b. i-rek-e   'CM-small-CM'   i-rek-i-ne   'CM-small-CM-ADJM'
            u-gʲɔz-o   'CM-red-CM'   u-gʲɔz-u-ne 'CM-red-CM-ADJM'
        c. sip-ini   'grab (perf.)'   ɛp-ine   'bite (perf.)'
        d. a-rim-a-ne   'CM-black-CM-ADJM' a-rek-a-ne   'CM-small-CM-ADJM'
            a-zis-a-ne   'CM-long-CM-ADJM'   a-gʲɔz-a-ne 'CM-red-CM-ADJM'

Pulleyblank (2002) argues that the alternating vowels are underlyingly high. His evidence comes from two classes of monosyllabic direct object pronouns. They either alternate in height, as in (20), or they are fixed in height, as in (22). All of those that do not alternate are non-high.[12] Pulleyblank observes that this distribution suggests that the alternating vowels are underlyingly high.[13] That vowels in alternating class markers are realized as high in non-final position – even when there is no neighboring high vowel (21b) – is also consistent with this supposition.

(22)   a. sipkᵊ o   'grabbed him'   wegaka o   'indicated him'
            buzᵊkᵊ no   'chased you'   batkᵊ no   'released you'
            buzᵊkᵊ tʃo   'chased us (excl.)' batkᵊ tʃo   'released us (excl.)'
        b. hinᵊkᵊ e   'uprooted them'   kedᵊkᵊ e   'picked them'
        c. sipkᵊ na   'grabbed us (incl.)' wegaka na   'indicated us (incl.)'

Although there is reason to suppose that alternating suffixes are underlyingly high, not all of the possessive pronominal suffixes with a high vowel show height alternations. As illustrated in (23), /–ri/ and /–ru/ remain high in final position even after a non-high vowel (Rikoto 2001).

(23)   wa-ri   'my husband'
       wa-ru   'her husband'

Given these forms, I will assume that the height alternations are specific to certain suffixes that are underlyingly high. Although these are the only /r/-initial pronominal suffixes with a high vowel, that does not seem likely to be the cause of their different behavior. First, it is not obvious that /r/ should block a shared feature among vowels to the exclusion of other consonants (and there are no reports of root-final /r/ producing blocking effects). Second, the final vowel in the suffixes in (23) remains high. If /r/ blocked feature sharing, the final vowel could be expected to become non-high, as is seen with the alternating suffixes when an intervening low vowel blocks feature sharing with a high root vowel (21d).

I propose to analyze C'Lela's apparent vowel height assimilation as a prominence-based licensing effect where [+high] in the final syllable of a phonological word is penalized if not licensed by the morphological root: LICENSE$_L$([+high]/σ$_{Final}$, Root). Because of examples like those in (23), I restrict the licensing constraint to particular affixes (or dependent morphemes); hence the constraint shows lexical indexation. Under this analysis, high suffix vowels are consistently realized as high in non-final syllables, because they are not restricted by the licensing constraint in this context. The restriction to final syllables is consistent with the propensity of final positions to manifest certain phonetic properties that can disadvantage perception. Notice that the vowels subject to licensing also occur in open syllables, a context where they are especially likely to present final weakening (see chapter 2).

High suffix vowels that are subject to licensing harmonize with a root vowel where possible. Feature sharing is prevented when the final vowel is separated from a high root vowel by an intervening low vowel, in which case the final vowel is neutralized to mid. That licensing for [+high] is blocked by a non-final low suffix vowel (e.g. [a-rim-a-ne]) points to a conclusion that only indirect licensing is permitted in C'Lela, not identity licensing, and active assimilation (at a distance or through the intervening syllable) does not seem to occur from the licensing position. Furthermore, a form like /ɛp-ini̱/ → [ɛp-ine̱] 'bite (perf.),' where the final vowel lowers even though the adjacent vowel is high, supports the conclusion that the final vowel undergoes neutralization to [–high] by feature substitution. Together, these circumstances are consistent with a pattern of passive licensing in C'Lela.

This pattern is captured by the core ranking: LICENSE$_L$([+high]/σ$_{Final}$, Root), *DUPLICATE(F) >> IDENT-IO(high), CRISPEDGE([high], σ). In addition, the positional faithfulness constraint, IDENT-Root(high) will guarantee control by the licensing position, and IDENT-IO(low) ranked in the top stratum will ensure that medial /a/ does not undergo raising. The manner in which the core ranking captures indirect licensing and prevents identity licensing is by now familiar, and will not be repeated in a tableau here. However, the interaction of the licensing constraint and IDENT with the realization of final vowels is explored below.

In C'Lela's system, epenthetic high vowels in word-final position are exempted from height alternations. A final closed syllable is avoided by epenthesis of [ɨ]. Unlike certain underlying high vowels, final epenthetic [ɨ] may occur after syllables containing non-high vowels, as seen in the examples on the right in (24).

(24) dᵊ-gʲɔz-dᵊ-ne   'CM-red-CM-ADJM'   dᵊ-gʲɔz-di̠   'CM-red-CM'
     dᵊ-ɾek-dᵊ-ne   'CM-small-CM-ADJM' dᵊ-ɾek-di̠   'CM-small-CM'

Dettweiler describes the phonetic height of [ɨ] as "near-close … a bit lower phonetically than [i] and [u]" (2000: 4, n. 3). There is evidence that [ɨ] is phonologically [+high] and is thus truly exempted from the final height alternations. Separate from the licensing effects involving high suffixes, roots show a height harmony that causes them to contain all [+high] vowels or all [–high] vowels. As seen in (25), [ɨ] groups with the high vowels.

(25) a. Roots with [+high] vowels
         dᵊtindi   'nest'
         tʃᵊɾinɨ   'charcoal'
         kᵊpiɾu   'flower'
         kumu   'get'
         dwiɾi   'hyena'
      b. Roots with [–high] vowels
         kwesa   'show'
         soma   'run'
         dᵊvɛso   'broom'
         tʃᵊgjɔmbo   'eyebrows'

Under a licensing account, the absence of alternations with the epenthetic high vowels is expected if the licensing constraint is restricted to [+high] in vowels of particular affixes, as proposed.

The selection of [ɨ] as the epenthetic vowel in the language is obtained by a constraint that minimizes the sonority of a syllable nucleus in a non-head position of the phonological word (de Lacy 2002, 2006, 2007a; cf. Crosswhite 2001, 2004). The constraint is expressed in (26) drawing on the formalism of de Lacy (2007a: 295). As a high non-peripheral vowel, [ɨ] is favored under epenthesis.

(26) *non-Hd$_\omega$/a,ɛ•ɔ,e•o,i•u
      Incur a violation for every non-head of a phonological word that contains either a high, mid or low peripheral vowel.

C'Lela has tones, but I found no mention of stress in Dettweiler (2000). Syllable structure points to the prosodic head being the first syllable of the root, because the 'heavy' syllable forms, CVC, CVV, and CVCC, are almost always restricted to this position (Dettweiler 2000: 5). This suggests that word-final syllables that contain a suffix are not a prosodic head.

IDENT constraints for vowel features dominate *non-Hd$_\omega$/a,ɛ•ɔ,e•o,i•u to prevent underlying peripheral vowels from neutralizing to [ɨ]. In an epenthetic vowel, where IDENT(F) is not at stake, the unmarked non-peripheral vowel quality will emerge. This is illustrated in (27). In (27i), IDENT protects the underlying non-high final vowel from becoming [ɨ]. In (27ii), the inserted final vowel does not have an input correspondent with which to be faithful, causing its realization to be determined by the markedness constraint.

(27)   Epenthetic vowel quality
        IDENT(VOWEL-FEATURE) >> *non-Hd$_\omega$/a,ɛ•ɔ,e•o,i•u

Input	Output	IDENT(V-FEATURE)	*non-Hd$_\omega$/a,ɛ•ɔ,e•o,i•u
i. /hink e/	☞ a. hinᵊkᵊ e		*
	b. hinᵊkᵊ ɨ	*!	
ii. /d-ɾek-d/	☞ a. dᵊ-ɾek-dɨ		
	b. dᵊ-ɾek-di		*!
	c. dᵊ-ɾek-de		*!

Although epenthetic vowels are high and central, word-final high vowels of certain suffixes become mid when they follow a syllable with a non-high vowel (21b, d). In this way they vacuously satisfy licensing when [+high] does not become licensed by association to the root. This result comes out of the combined effect of the rankings that have been proposed thus far for C'Lela, which include LICENSE$_L$([+high]/σ$_{Final}$, Root) >> IDENT-IO(high) and IDENT-IO(high) >> *non-Hd$_\omega$/a,ɛ•ɔ,e•o,i•u. When these are put together, epenthetic [ɨ] will remain favored, because licensing and faithfulness are not at stake. When a vowel that is in a suffix indexed to the licensing constraint has a [+high] feature that fails to be licensed, the licensing constraint and IDENT become relevant, which can prevent satisfaction of *non-Hd$_\omega$/a,ɛ•ɔ,e•o,i•u. In this circumstance, LICENSE$_L$([+high]/σ$_{Final}$, Root) is enforced at the cost of IDENT-IO(high), causing a final suffix vowel to be realized as non-high, the minimal change required to satisfy the licensing constraint.

Tableaux in (28–29) illustrate. In (28), the input contains a suffix with a high vowel that is indexed to the licensing constraint. The optimal output shows indirect licensing of [+high] in the final vowel by association to the root vowel. Candidate (b), with an unlicensed [+high] specification in the final affix vowel, violates the licensing constraint, and (c), which lowers the final vowel to mid, incurs a fatal violation of faithfulness. Violations for *non-Hd$_\omega$/a,ɛ•ɔ,e•o,i•u are tallied here for each non-root peripheral vowel. Note that candidates in which /u/ becomes [ɨ] would improve satisfaction of *non-Hd$_\omega$/a,ɛ•ɔ,e•o,i•u, but they will be prevented by other vowel feature IDENT constraints that dominate *non-Hd$_\omega$/a,ɛ•ɔ,e•o,i•u (see ranking in [27]).

(28)   Licensed [+high] in a final vowel

/u-rim-u$_L$/	LICENSE$_L$([+hi]/σ$_{Final}$, Rt)	IDENT-(high)	*non-Hd$_ω$/a,ɛ•ɔ,e•o,i•u

☞ a. uɾimu
   \ /
   [+high]
			**

b. uɾimu
  | |
  [+hi]$_i$[+hi]$_j$
	*!		**

c. uɾimo		*!	**

Tableau (29) illustrates two cases where licensing of a [+high] in a final affix vowel cannot be satisfied and the vowel lowers. Both of the suffixes here are indexed to the licensing constraint. In (29i), candidate (b) has an unlicensed [+high] specification in a final high suffix vowel. The low vowel that intervenes between final [i] and the high root vowel blocks indirect licensing. (Recall that *DUPLICATE(F) dominates IDENT(high) to prevent identity licensing.) The winner in (a) lowers the final high vowel to mid. In (29ii), a [+high] specification in a final suffix vowel cannot be licensed because the root vowel is non-high. Candidate (b), which preserves [+high] in the final vowel, violates the licensing constraint. The winner, in (a), lowers the final vowel to mid to vacuously satisfy licensing. The passive nature of licensing is evident here, because licensing is not resolved by feature spreading.

(29)   Loss of [+high] in a final vowel

Input	Output		LICENSE$_L$ ([+hi]/σ$_{Final}$, Rt)	IDENT (high)	*non-Hd$_ω$/ a,ɛ•ɔ,e•o,i•u
i. /a-ɾim-a-ni$_L$/	☞	a. aɾimane		*	***
		b. aɾimani	*!		***
ii. /ɛp-ini$_L$/	☞	a. ɛpine		*	**
		b. ɛpini	*!		**

To summarize, C'Lela's pattern is plausibly one that presents passive indirect licensing by the morphological root for [+high] in final vowels of specific suffixes, as evidenced by the patterns presented in forms with an intervening suffix vowel. This phenomenon conforms with expectations about possible positional strength asymmetries: the morphological root serves as prominent and final suffix vowels serve as weak. Unlike the final suffix vowels, high epenthetic vowels in final position do not show height alternations because they are not in the purview of C'Lela's licensing constraint. The general prediction of this approach is that if a licensing pattern shows morpheme-specific effects, epenthetic segments should pattern with the group that is not subject to licensing.

SUMMARY. In closing §5.2, let us review the main threads. This section has dealt with indirect licensing patterns where the vowel in the licensing position does not alternate. A common factor in these systems is the enforcement of faithfulness in the licensing position. Patterns that preserve material in this location are expected to be attested, given the privileged phonetic and/or psycholinguistic status of licensing positions. As a result of the prioritization of content originating in the licensing position, a feature specification that is targeted by a licensing constraint survives in non-licensing position only when that specification also occurs independently in the licensing position. When a targeted feature specification fails to become licensed and changes its value, two primary solutions have been highlighted. In one scenario, the opposite feature value spreads from the licensing position to produce active assimilation, and in the other, the vowel in non-licensing position shows neutralization to the opposite value without necessarily harmonizing with the feature value in licensing position, as in passive licensing patterns. The patterns examined above show evidence that points to one type of solution or the other. In some cases, feature substitution is necessary (i.e. altering a feature without assimilation), because feature sharing is blocked by an intervening segment (e.g. C'Lela). In chapter 4, the rankings and resulting representations were explored for adjacent syllables where a blocker does not intervene (see the table in [19] in §4.7). The situations of neutralization by feature insertion versus assimilation can be distinguished by the relative ranking of a crisp edge constraint and a licensing constraint that operates over both values of the feature. This effect is accomplished even though both of these constraints belong to a stratum below IDENT-IO(F). The existence of systems that show these different solutions thus bears out a typological prediction of the approach.

5.3 Assimilation within the licensing position

This section examines patterns with weak triggers, where indirect licensing causes the vowel in the licensing position to assimilate to a vowel quality in a non-licensing position. An interest of these systems is that control of assimilation is not attributable to the strength of the licensing position. Instead, a faithfulness constraint that is specific to the licensing position is dominated by the licensing constraint as well as some constraint that causes the vowel in non-licensing position to control harmony.

Sources of weak trigger control are various, but all of the cases examined in this chapter involve a faithfulness constraint, either alone or in a local conjunction with a markedness constraint. Four cases are studied. Old High German shows indirect licensing for [–back] in a high vowel by a stressed syllable. In this language, control of harmony by the unstressed vowel is attributed to a faithfulness constraint for high front unround vocoids, with a basis in the coarticulatory resistance that they present. The dialect of central Veneto exhibits indirect licensing for [+high] in a post-tonic vowel by a stressed syllable. Control of harmony by the prosodically weak vowel is attributed to a local conjunction of a faithfulness constraint and a markedness constraint that drives sonority minimization in an unstressed syllable, which prevents the unstressed high vowel from lowering to mid. In Lango, trigger control when high [+ATR] vowels are present is attributed to a local conjunction of markedness and faithfulness, obtaining dominance by high [+ATR] vowels whether they occur in a licensing position or non-licensing position. Finally, Jaqaru shows licensing by the stressed syllable for all vowel features and values in specific suffixes. Control of harmony by the suffix is proposed to be the effect of a word-final faithfulness constraint. The faithfulness constraint, or its conjunction, which produces trigger control in Jaqaru, Old High German, and central Veneto, is also responsible for the faithful realization of a vowel whose feature fails to be licensed, thereby playing a dual role in the system.

Additional features of interest are presented by each pattern under study. In support of indirect licensing representations, blocking effects are noted in Old High German, by certain consonants, and in central Veneto, by certain vowels. Lango's pattern of [+ATR, +high] dominance, in which harmony is progressive in some forms and regressive in others, lends credence to the proposed formal system, where directionality is an epiphenomenon of constraint interaction rather than stipulated in the harmony-driving constraint. Jaqaru shows differential licensing effects across the lexical strata of native words and loans, providing support for certain kinds of morpheme sensitivity in the system, and it interacts with vowel fission.

OLD HIGH GERMAN. Old High German (OHG) showed a pattern known as primary umlaut, which entered the grammar of early OHG starting about AD 750 and became established in records from the ninth century (Iverson and Salmons 1996: 70). It is distinct from non-primary umlaut, discussed in §6.4, which developed later in the language's history (Iverson and Salmons 1996; Howell and Salmons 1997). It is generally agreed that in primary umlaut, high front vocoids /i j/ caused short /a/ to front and raise to [e] in a preceding stressed syllable (Iverson and Salmons 1996), as in (30a). Stress in OHG was word-initial (Ellis 1953). Data are drawn from Ellis (1953), Iverson *et al.* (1994) (ID&S), Iverson and Salmons (1996) (I&S), and Holsinger and Salmons (1999) (H&S). For umlaut to occur, the high front vocoid must be in

112   *Indirect licensing*

an unstressed syllable.[14] If the vocoid is in a syllable with secondary stress, it does not trigger umlaut, as in (30b).

(30)   a.   gast   gesti   'guest (sg/pl)'   I&S
            lamb   lembir   'lamb (sg/pl)'   I&S
            anst   ensti   'mercy (sg/pl)'   ID&S
            faru   feris, ferit   'drive (1/2/3 sg)'   ID&S
            fasto   festi   'solid/fast (adv. and adj.)'   I&S
            walta   welita   'ruled/dominated'   H&S
       b.   kráftli:h   'strong'   Ellis

The effect of umlaut is to cause a front vowel quality in a high unstressed vocoid to become also expressed in a stressed syllable. I propose that primary umlaut is driven by a constraint that penalizes [–back] in a high vocoid when it is not licensed by a stressed syllable: LICENSE([–back]/[+high], ό). Further data reveal that licensing in this pattern is direct or indirect only. Umlaut is blocked by clusters composed of /x/ plus a consonant (<h> = /x/, possibly reduced to [h]) (31a) or a liquid plus a consonant (31b). These data suggest that when an intervening segment occurs that is prevented from undergoing the assimilation, it blocks umlaut. The existence of blocking thus points to identity licensing being unavailable.

(31)   a.   maht   mahti   'power (sg/pl)'   I&S
            naht   nahti   'night (sg/pl)'   ID&S
            wahsan   wahsit   'grow (inf./3 sg pres)'   ID&S
       b.   haltan   haltis, haltit 'hold (1/2/3 sg)'   ID&S
            waltan   waltit   'rule (inf./3 sg pres)'   Ellis
            chalb   chalbir   'calf (sg/pl)'   ID&S
            starch   starchiro   'strong/stronger'   I&S

The core ranking for primary umlaut as indirect licensing is *DUPLICATE(F) >> LICENSE([–back]/[+high], ό) >> IDENT-IO(back), CRISPEDGE([back], σ). Top-ranked *DUPLICATE(F) will prevent identity licensing when blockers are present. Why particular clusters cause blocking requires something further. It has been noted that blocking by /xC/ was widespread in most of OHG, but blocking by liquid+C happened in only some dialects (Iverson and Salmons 1996: 70). Iverson *et al.* (1994) propose that blocking by liquids occurred where they were reduced to vocalic segments in codas. They also suggest that coda realizations of /x/ that block umlaut share a V-place specification with the preceding vowel. Building on those claims, Howell and Salmons (1997) characterize blockers as an intervening coda that contains V-place. The particular formal means by which this generalization is obtained are not crucial to the issues under focus here. I will refer to it with a cover constraint labeled *UMLAUT/xC,LC, which dominates the licensing constraint.

Assimilation within the licensing position   113

The primary constraint interactions are demonstrated in (32). The evaluation in (32i) shows that the licensing constraint drives umlaut in a non-blocking context. Two violations of IDENT(back) are notated for (a), one for the stressed vowel and one for the intervening consonant. The evaluation in (32ii) illustrates a blocking scenario. Candidate (c) accomplishes licensing by feature copy, violating *DUPLICATE(F), and (b) spreads [−back] through the intervening consonants, violating *UMLAUT/xC,LC. The winner in (a) obeys both of these constraints, at the cost of the lower-ranked licensing constraint.

(32)   Umlaut and blocking of umlaut
        *DUPLICATE(F), *UMLAUT/xC,LC >> LICENSE([−back]/[+high], σ́) >> IDENT-IO(back)

Input	Output	*DUP(F)	*UMLAUT /xC,LC	LICENSE ([−bk]/[+hi], σ́)	IDENT- (back)
i. /faris/	☞ a. féris				**
	b. fáris			*!	

ii. /chalbir/	☞ a. c h á l b i r
	       |
	      [−bk]
				*	

	b. c h é l b i r
	       ↘
	      [−bk]
			*!		***

	c. c h é l b i r
	      | |
	   [−bk]$_i$ [−bk]$_i$
		*!			*

Another characteristic to be addressed is the control of assimilation by a vocoid in an unstressed syllable. This could be linked to plausible ties of the pattern to coarticulation.[15] Iverson and Salmons (2003) point out that /i/ in German exerts the greatest coarticulatory influence in vowel-to-vowel coarticulation (Butcher and Weiher 1976); /i/ also tends to show the weakest coarticulatory effects from other vowels. They speculate that umlaut as a sound change has origins in coarticulation. This would also be consistent with the restriction of primary umlaut to indirect licensing, which causes a single [−back] feature to become extended. Nevertheless, as umlaut consistently issues from an unstressed vowel, the pattern seems to have a true perceptually based licensing component as well. As discussed in chapter 2, it has been shown that certain unstressed vowels, including /i/, undergo more vowel-to-vowel coarticulation than their stressed counterparts. If coarticulation was the only force involved in the pattern's emergence, we might not expect the lack of fronting in forms like [tágalì:h] *[tágelì:h] 'daily,' [fírstantnìssi] *[fírstentnìssi] 'understanding' (Ellis 1953). The role of perceptual licensing notwithstanding, it is reasonable to assume that the coarticulatory strength of /i/ is relevant in OHG umlaut. I propose to reflect this strength in the grammar using a faithfulness constraint for high front unrounded vocoids: IDENT-IO(+high, –back, –round), defined in (33). More generally, I speculate that context-sensitive faithfulness constraints that are specific to a segment type may exist for segments that show resistance to coarticulatory effects from other segments.[16]

(33)   IDENT-IO(+high, –back, –round)
       Let α be a segment in the input and β be any correspondent of α in the output. If α is [+high, –back, –round], then β is [+high, –back, –round].

In OHG, IDENT-IO(+high, –back, –round) dominates the licensing constraint, IDENT(back), and faithfulness to the stressed syllable, causing /i j/ to control assimilation in umlaut and to remain unaltered when licensing does not succeed. The effect is shown in (34). A case where licensing is satisfied is shown in (34i). The umlauted candidate (a) wins, incurring violations of IDENT(back). An alternative, in (b), that lowers the high front vowel to mid to satisfy licensing is prevented by IDENT(+high, –back, –round). The input in (34ii) contains a consonant cluster that blocks umlaut. The winner in (a) leaves the final /i/ intact, violating licensing. Candidate (b) lowers the final vowel to [e], but it is ruled out by the top-ranked faithfulness constraint.

(34)   Faithfulness is enforced for high front vocoids
       IDENT-IO(+high, –back, –round) >> LICENSE([–back]/[+hi], ó) >> IDENT(back), IDENT-ó(back)

Input	Output	IDENT (+hi, –bk, –rd)	LICENSE ([–bk]/[+hi], ó)	IDENT (back)	IDENT-ó- (back)
i. /faris/	☞ a. féris			**	*
	b. fáres	*!			
ii. /chalbir/	☞ a. chálbir		*		
	b. chálber	*!			

As mentioned above, the target of primary umlaut is reported to be short /a/ only. Later developments of umlaut caused fronting, and sometimes raising, of a larger set of vowels. I will assume that fronting of non-low stressed vowels was blocked by an avoidance of front round vowels, which tend to be marked. This system specifically avoids deriving these vowels, as obtained by a local conjunction of markedness and faithfulness: *[+round, –back] &$_l$ IDENT-IO(back), which is ranked above the licensing constraint. This approach to averting derived marked structure in a licensing system is discussed in more detail in the cases of central Veneto and Lango below. I attribute the failure of long /a/ to undergo umlaut to a faithfulness constraint for long vowels, IDENT-V:-IO(back). This constraint reflects the greater strength of long vowels in comparison to their short counterparts. In functional terms, we could expect long vowels to show more resistance to change than short vowels because their increased duration supplies longer cues and they are less susceptible to articulatory undershoot.

There is debate about whether primary umlaut occurs only when the triggering vocoid is in a syllable immediately adjacent to the stressed syllable (Klein 1995; Iverson and Salmons 1996). Forms such as that in (35a) suggest that umlaut was not triggered by a non-adjacent syllable, while those in (35b) suggest the opposite (Braune 1987: 29).

(35) a. magad   magadi   'maiden (sg/pl)'
      b. apful   epfili   'apple (sg/pl)'
          nagal   negili   'nail (sg/pl)'

The data in (35) are suggestive that long-distance umlaut existed but was variable; possibly it was emerging. In future research on this question, it would be valuable to establish a timeline for these forms. The examples in (35b) are complicated by the unstressed penultimate vowels, whose fronting (and raising in *negili*) departs from the primary umlaut pattern of fronting short /a/ to [e]. It is difficult to ascertain the quality of these vowels with certainty, as they were likely reduced (see n. 14). As the question of long-distance umlaut remains unclear, I leave its analysis open here. If fronting of the stressed vowel and medial vowel occurred, the licensing account would not require further augmentation, excepting the problem of the particular qualities of the medial vowels. If umlaut was prevented when the trigger vocoid did not occur adjacent to the stressed syllable, then the domain could be restricted by a crisp edge constraint that restricts associations of [–back] to segments within the same foot (compare Buchan Scots in §5.2.1, and see Flemming 1993).

CENTRAL VENETO. The metaphony pattern in the Romance dialect of central Veneto is a case where a combination of faithfulness and phonological markedness causes the non-prominent position to be the trigger of assimilation rather than the target. The vowels of central Veneto are [i e ɛ a ɔ o u]. In unstressed syllables these are reduced to [i e a o u]. Metaphony in this language causes stressed /e/ and /o/ to raise to [i] and [u] when they are followed by an unstressed high vowel (Rizzi 1989; Belloni 1991; Maiden 1991a; Marcato and Ursini 1998; Brunelli 2000a, b, 2001; Walker 2005, 2010; see also Calabrese 1988, 1998; Kaze 1989). Following Calabrese, I assume that [i e o u] are

116 *Indirect licensing*

[+ATR] and [ɛ a ɔ] are [–ATR]. Raising is triggered by any post-tonic high vowel whether it belongs to a suffix or stem and whether it is word final or word medial, as shown in (36). Also, the stressed vowels that undergo raising may belong to the root or an inflectional suffix. Alternative forms given in (36) are ones that are available for speakers for whom metaphony is optional. In central Veneto, /i/ is the only high inflectional vowel. No examples were found with /u/ in a stem in a context to trigger metaphony.

(36)   bév-o   bív-i   'drink (1sg/2sg pres. ind.)'
       kant-é-se   kant-í-si-mo   'sing (1sg/1pl impf. subj.)'
       fas-é-a   fas-í-vi-mo   'do (3sg/1pl impf. ind.)'
       kals-ét-o   kals-ít-i   'sock (m sg/pl)'
                     (/-et-/ dim., lexicalized in this form)
                     víndit-a   'sale, shop (f sg)'
                     (cf. alternative *véndita*)
       skólt-o   skúlt-i   'listen (1sg/2sg pres. ind.)'
       kantór   kantúr-i   'choir singer (m sg/pl)'
                     gúm(b)i-o   'elbow (m sg)'
                     (cf. alternative *góm(b)io*)
       órden-o   úrdin-i   'order (1sg/2sg pres. ind.)'

These data indicate that the harmony is not morphologically conditioned, that is, triggers are not restricted to high vowels that belong to (particular) inflectional suffixes. Also, targets are not restricted to vowels belonging to a particular prominent morphological category, such as the root. The final example in (36) shows that the harmony can affect more than one vowel, as it can cause raising in the stressed syllable and an intervening unstressed mid vowel. On the other hand, metaphony is bounded in that raising terminates at the stressed syllable, as seen in (37).

(37)   trasmét-o   trasmet-í-v-i   'transmit (1sg pres. ind./2sg impf. ind.)'
       botón   botún-i   'button (m sg/pl)'

Central Veneto also shows a pattern where a post-tonic high vowel causes stressed and pretonic [e o] to raise, but the attestation of pretonic raising is much more variable than metaphonic raising of the stressed syllable. As argued in Walker (2005), I assume that raising of pretonic vowels is driven by a constraint separate from the one that drives metaphony, and I will not consider those instances of raising here.

Although metaphony can trigger raising of an unstressed mid vowel in the penult, it only does so when the stressed vowel also undergoes raising. [–ATR] vowels do not undergo raising in a stressed syllable (38a). In words with antepenultimate stress assigned to a [–ATR] vowel, a high vowel does not trigger raising of an intervening mid vowel (38b). It is not the case that high vowels are generally excluded in an unstressed penult after a [–ATR] vowel, e.g. [ezérsito] 'army (m sg),' [másimo] 'maximum (m sg)' (Brunelli 2006), so the absence of raising in (38b) is not due to a general well-formedness constraint. The contrast between the lack of raising in (38b) and the occurrence of raising in the penult in a form like [úrdini] in (36) thus shows that raising of an unstressed mid penult vowel happens only as a by-product of harmony that proceeds to the stressed syllable.

(38)   a.   gát-i   'cat (m pl)'
               vétʃ-i   'old man (m pl)'
               tǫk-i   'piece (m pl)'
    b.   pérseg-o   pérseg-i   'peach (fruit) (m sg/pl)'
               ángol-o   ángol-i   'angle (m sg/pl)'

Finally, if a low vowel intervenes between a mid [+ATR] stressed vowel and a post-tonic high vowel, it blocks raising.

(39)   la(v)ór-a-v-a   la(v)ór-a-v-i   'work (1sg/2sg impf. ind.)'

The bounded character of metaphony in central Veneto follows if it is driven by a licensing constraint: LICENSE([+high]/σ$_{\text{post-tonic}}$, ó), as do the circumstances under which it affects an intervening mid vowel. The imperative for harmony drives a feature in a post-tonic (weak) position to find realization in a stressed syllable. An intervening non-prominent vowel only undergoes harmony when a preceding prominent vowel does, because assimilation by the intervening vowel alone does not achieve the positional licensing requirement. The blocking of raising when a [–ATR] vowel intervenes between a target and trigger (in [39]) indicates that central Veneto does not permit identity licensing; the examples of harmony are restricted to indirect licensing configurations. This conclusion is also supported by a form like [úrdini], where an unstressed syllable that is not otherwise targeted by raising undergoes harmony to satisfy continuous feature extension.

When the stressed vowel and a post-tonic high vowel disagree in height, assimilation is triggered by the unstressed vowel rather than it being the target of a height harmony from the stressed vowel, as in Buchan Scots, or undergoing neutralization by substituting [–high] for [+high], as in C'Lela (where the licensing position is the root). An appeal to word-final faithfulness for control by the unstressed vowel would not be successful for central Veneto since word-medial vowels may also trigger harmony. Typological evidence within Romance gives reason to believe that the coarticulatory-based faithfulness constraint, IDENT-IO(+high, –back, –round), is also not the source of trigger control here. Background on this issue was discussed in §2.6. Metaphony patterns across Romance are triggered by high vowels, but unlike umlaut in OHG, they are not consistently triggered exclusively by high front vocoids. Across languages, it is [i] that tends to show the weakest coarticulatory effects from other vowels. However, in a number of Romance dialects both /i/ and /u/ trigger metaphonic raising, and in some, /u/ serves as the only trigger. Cross-Romance patterns thus do not point to a conclusion that weak triggers in metaphony have a basis in coarticulation. As proposed in Walker 2005, I instead assume that post-tonic /i/ does not lower to [e] because of a markedness constraint that minimizes sonority in unstressed syllables. As part of this, I employ the constraint in (40), formulated along similar lines to the constraint that is responsible for minimizing sonority in epenthetic vowels in C'Lela.[17]

(40)   *ŏ/a,e•o
       Incur a violation for every unstressed syllable that contains either a low or mid vowel.

While non-high vowels are permitted in unstressed syllables of central Veneto when they derive from an underlying non-high vowel, the language does not derive unstressed non-high vowels through vowel lowering. This pattern is analyzed using a local conjunction of markedness and faithfulness: *ŏ/a,e•o &$_l$ IDENT-IO(high).

The ranking for the pattern will place the local conjunction, IDENT-IO(ATR) and *DUPLICATE(F) in the top tier. These will dominate the licensing constraint, which will in turn dominate IDENT-IO(high) and stressed syllable faithfulness. The ranking is illustrated by tableaux in (41–43).

The tableau in (41) shows a case where metaphony in a word with a final high vowel and antepenultimate stress causes two vowels to harmonize. The winning output in (a) satisfies licensing through an indirect licensing configuration, incurring two violations of IDENT(high) and a violation of IDENT-IO-ó(high). Candidate (b) incurs only a single violation of IDENT(high) and IDENT-IO-ó(high) by passing over the intervening vowel with an identity licensing configuration. This is ruled out by *DUPLICATE(F). The faithful candidate in (c) is eliminated by the licensing constraint. In candidate (d) the licensing constraint is satisfied by lowering the post-tonic high vowel. This is ruled out by the local conjunction. If the same ranking were applied to a word like /boton-i/ → [botúni], the bounded nature of the harmony would emerge from the licensing constraint's reference to the stressed syllable. This constraint does not promote assimilation that progresses to the pretonic syllable.

Assimilation within the licensing position 119

(41)   Raising that affects multiple vowels

/orden-i/	*ŏ/a,e•o &_l IDENT(high)	IDENT (ATR)	*DUP(F)	LICENSE ([+hi]/σ_post-tonic, ó)	IDENT(hi) IDENT-ó(high)
☞ a. úrdini					**(IDENT) *(IDENT-ó)
b. úrdeni			*!		*(IDENT) *(IDENT-ó)
c. órdeni				*!	
d. órdene	*!				*(IDENT)

The tableau in (42) deals with a form where harmony does not affect an adjacent mid vowel because the non-adjacent stressed vowel cannot undergo harmony. For simplicity, the positional faithfulness constraint is not shown here. The winner is the faithful form in (a), which violates the licensing constraint. The alternative in (b) satisfies licensing through harmony that proceeds to the stressed syllable, but it is ruled out by IDENT(ATR). I assume that an undominated constraint *I,U rules out a candidate like [písrigi], which raises the stressed vowel without altering its [–ATR] specification. Candidate (c) raises the unstressed penult vowel only, incurring a violation of faithfulness that does not cause it to improve its satisfaction of the licensing constraint. Candidate (d) lowers the post-tonic high vowel to mid. The suboptimality of this form indicates that the local conjunction must dominate the licensing constraint, since a post-tonic high vowel remains high even if its [+high] feature is not licensed.

(42)   No harmony when the stressed syllable does not raise

/pɛrseg-i/	*ŏ/a,e•o &_l IDENT-(high)	IDENT (ATR)	*DUP(F)	LICENSE ([+high]/σ_post-tonic, ó)	IDENT (high)
☞ a. pɛ́rsegi				*	
b. písrigi		*!			**
c. pɛ́rsigi				*	*!
d. pɛ́rsege	*!				*

The tableau in (43) deals with a form where harmony is blocked by an intervening vowel, which verifies that identity licensing is unavailable. In the input, the post-tonic high vowel is separated by /a/ from a mid vowel that is assigned stress. The winner is the faithful candidate in (a), which violates the licensing constraint. Raising that proceeds through the penult in (b) is ruled out by IDENT(ATR), because of /a/ → [i], and raising that passes over the intervening vowel in (c) through feature duplication is prevented by *DUPLICATE(F).

(43) Blocking of harmony

/lavor-a-v-i/	*ŏ/a,e•o &$_l$ IDENT-(high)	IDENT (ATR)	*DUP(F)	LICENSE ([+high]/σ$_{post\text{-}tonic}$, ó)	IDENT (high)
☞ a. lavóravi				*	
b. lavúrivi		*!			**
c. lavúravi			*!		*

The pattern of central Veneto provides persuasive evidence that harmony-driving constraints that reference a specific position are needed in the theory. For some vowel harmony patterns with a specific target, those effects can be realized using a constraint with the capacity to drive unbounded harmony in interaction with markedness constraints and/or faithfulness constraints that prevent certain vowels from undergoing harmony (e.g. Kaun 1995; Beckman 1997; Baković 2000). In central Veneto, vowels with a particular quality in a stressed syllable serve as targets of harmony, while vowels with the same quality in an unstressed syllable are not targeted except as a by-product of harmony that arrives at the stressed syllable. These characteristics are problematic for an account lacking a position-centered harmony-driving constraint. Because vowels in stressed and unstressed syllables with the same quality can show different behavior as targets, the difference cannot be attributed to context-free markedness constraints or non-positional IDENT(F) constraints. Also, since vowels in a stressed syllable are regularly targeted, the difference is not predicted by positional faithfulness, which could be expected to protect stressed syllables, not unstressed ones. Markedness that proceeds from metrical prominence is unlikely to help. Metaphony causes raising in a stressed syllable, which reduces sonority in a prominent syllable, something that metrical prominence constraints are expected to penalize. Further, such constraints are unlikely to inhibit raising in an unstressed syllable where needed, because raising would reduce sonority-based prominence in a non-prominent context. On the other hand, the relevant characteristics of central Veneto metaphony are predicted by a prominence-based licensing analysis.

To summarize, that central Veneto's harmony is driven by prominence-based licensing is supported both by its failure to persist past the stressed syllable and the absence of raising in an unstressed intervening mid penult when the stressed vowel cannot raise. These properties are consistent with the proposed organization of the system around achieving realization of [+high] in a robust (stressed) position when it appears in a weak (post-tonic) position. The exclusion of identity licensing representations is supported by the blocking of harmony by intervening low vowels and the occurrence of harmony that proceeds through an intervening mid penult when the stressed vowel undergoes raising. The source of control by the high unstressed vowel is proposed to be a conjunction of a constraint that minimizes the prominence of unstressed syllables with a faithfulness constraint. This prevents high unstressed vowels from lowering as a means of satisfying the licensing constraint.

LANGO. Lango shows ATR harmony between suffix vowels and roots (Woock and Noonan 1979; Poser 1982; Archangeli and Pulleyblank 1994; Smolensky 2006; Kaplan 2008a). Prior studies have demonstrated that the harmony is quite complex, and a comprehensive treatment would go beyond the focus of this work. I will concentrate on aspects of the pattern that bear on two pertinent theoretical matters. One is that the system is driven by a prominence-based licensing constraint in which the morphological root is the licensing position (Kaplan 2008a, b), and the other is that it shows a type of [+ATR] dominant system in which high [+ATR] vowels control harmony when they are present.

Lango has five [+ATR] vowels [i e ə o u] and five [−ATR] vowels [ɪ ɛ a ɔ ʊ]. In the majority of contexts, disharmonic vowel sequences are resolved by [+ATR] harmony. The examples in (44) show assimilation of a root-final vowel to a [+ATR] suffix vowel. Notice that in stems that contain more than one [−ATR] vowel, ATR harmony does not progress beyond the root-final syllable. (Recall that numbers mark tones.)

(44)   Regressive [+ATR] harmony
       jɪb5̄   'tail'   jib5̄-i5̄   'your (sg) tail'
       dɛk1   'stew'   dek1-ki5̄   'your (sg) stew'
       kɔm1   'chair'   kom1-mi5̄   'your (sg) chair'
       mac1   'fire'   mec1-ci5̄   'your (sg) fire'
       a1mʊk5̄   'shoe'   a1muk5̄-ki5̄   'your (sg) shoe'
       cɔ1ŋɔ1   'beer'   cɔ1ŋo1-ni5̄   'your (sg) beer'
       ɪ1maɲ5̄   'liver'   ɪ1meɲ5̄-i5̄   'your (sg) liver'
       pɪ5̄   'for'   pi1-wu5̄   'for you'
       lʊt1   'stick'   lut1-wu5̄   'your (pl) stick'
       lɛ1   'axe'   le1-wu5̄   'your (pl) axe'
       bɔ5̄   'net'   bo5̄-wu5̄   'your (pl) net'

lɛlm'ʊn	'orange'	lɛlm'ʊn-wu5	'your (pl) orange'
olkwe'ɔcɛ5	'bitch'	olkwe'ɔcɛ5-wu5	'your (pl) bitch'
pallal	'knife'	pallal-wu5	'your (pl) knife'
ɪldɪ5kɛl	'leech'	ɪldi5lk-e5l	'leeches'
mɔltɔlkal	'car'	mɔltɔlkal-e5l	'cars'
dakltall	'doctor'	dakltall-e5l	'doctors'

In some plural nouns formed with a vowel-initial suffix, the suffixation causes deletion of a root-final vowel. In these instances, harmony from the suffix proceeds to the closest remaining root vowel, as in (45a) (and see the form meaning 'leeches' in [44]). Comparison with formations composed of the same roots plus /–wu5/[18] in (45b) shows that these earlier root vowels do not undergo harmony when the root-final vowel does not delete. Poser (1982) points out that the termination of harmony at the final root vowel thus does not seem to be due to lexical opacity of the other root vowels, as otherwise they would be expected to resist harmony in the forms in (45a).

(45) a. bɔlŋɔ5 'dress' bolŋ-i5 'dresses'
         rɔlmɔl 'sheep' rolm-i5 'sheep (pl)'
      b. bɔlŋɔ5-wu5 'your (pl) dress'
         rɔlmɔl-wu5 'your (pl) sheep'

While the data in (44–45) show harmony that operates from the suffix to the stem, a high [+ATR] vowel in the root will trigger progressive ATR harmony in [–ATR] suffix vowels (46). The underlying suffix forms follow Kaplan (2008a). Evidence that the vowels in these suffixes are underlyingly [–ATR] is discussed later in this section. The example in (46b) shows that [+ATR] harmony can affect more than one suffix vowel.

(46) Progressive [+ATR] harmony
      a. /buk5-Ca5/ → [buk5-ka5] 'my book'
         /pig5-Ca5/ → [pig5-ga5] 'my juice'
      b. /wulc-ɛ5rɛ5l/ → [wulc-e5re5l] 'throw'

The data thus far reveal two key elements of the Lango harmony system. First, it does not show a fixed directionality, and second it is both 'iterative' and 'non-iterative.' It is iterative in the respect that progressive harmony from the root can affect more than one suffix vowel, but it is non-iterative and bounded in the respect that regressive harmony from a suffix affects only the vowel in the last syllable of the root.

Kaplan analyzes the harmony as driven by a licensing constraint that requires [ATR] specifications to be linked to a root segment. Using the formalism assumed in this work, the constraint is LICENSE([ATR], Root). This constraint will dominate IDENT-IO(ATR). Given that the harmonized forms are compatible with indirect licensing and there are no forms that require an identity licensing structure, I assume the latter representations are not employed in the system. As Kaplan points out, the licensing analysis captures both the lack of iterativity of harmony in (44–45), where harmony affects only the last vowel of the root, and the progression of harmony through all suffix vowels in (46). The licensing constraint makes no stipulation about a trigger for harmony, so it will fall to other constraints to determine the trigger and direction of harmony. In other words, what the progressive and regressive harmony forms have in common is that they cause the ATR value realized in the suffix vowels to be the same as that in the closest root vowel, a locus of prominence.

Where high [+ATR] vowels are concerned, the trigger and direction for assimilation show a pattern of [+ATR] dominance. As introduced in §4.3, Baković (2000) has proposed to analyze dominance as 'assimilation to the unmarked.' He uses a local conjunction of the kind *[αF] &$_l$ IDENT-IO(F) to drive assimilation to [–αF], where [αF] is more marked than [–αF]. For particular cases, Baković narrows the markedness constraint in the conjunction to refer to multiple features, i.e. *[αF, βG]. That schema is applicable to a local conjunction that Smolensky (2006: 88) has proposed for Lango: *[–ATR, +high] &$_l$ IDENT(ATR). This conjunction penalizes the marked vowels [ɪ] and [ʊ] when they are derived from a [+ATR] vowel. When a disharmonic input containing /i/ or /u/ is repaired by ATR harmony, the conjunction will cause these vowels to be the trigger of [+ATR] harmony rather than the target of [–ATR] assimilation.

The tableau in (47) shows the workings of the licensing and [+ATR] dominance analysis in regressive harmony. The input contains a root with [–ATR] vowels and a suffix with a high [+ATR] vowel. The winner in (a) shows [+ATR] harmony from the suffix to the final root vowel. This satisfies licensing by causing the suffix [+ATR] specification to become associated to the root, and it incurs a minimal violation of faithfulness by altering only a single vowel. Candidate (b) shows [+ATR] harmony from the suffix to both root vowels. This too satisfies the licensing constraint, but it incurs an extra faithfulness violation. The licensing constraint rules out candidate (c), which is faithful to the input. Candidate (d) satisfies licensing by [–ATR] harmony from the root to the suffix vowel. This solution is ruled out by the local conjunction, which penalizes the mapping from /i/ → [ɪ]. Notice that since the winning candidate violates faithfulness in a root vowel, whereas candidates (c) and (d) respect root faithfulness, the local conjunction and the licensing constraint must also dominate root faithfulness for [ATR] (on root faithfulness, see McCarthy and Prince 1994a, 1995).

(47) Regressive harmony from a high [+ATR] vowel
*[–ATR, +high] &$_l$ IDENT(ATR), LICENSE([ATR], Root) >> IDENT-IO(ATR)

/cɔlŋɔl-ni5/	*[–ATR, +high] &$_l$ IDENT(ATR)	LICENSE([ATR], Root)	IDENT(ATR)
☞ a. cɔlŋol-ni5			*
b. colŋol-ni5			**!
c. cɔlŋɔl-ni5		*!	
d. cɔlŋɔl-nɪ5	*!		*

The tableau in (48) illustrates progressive harmony. The input contains a high [+ATR] vowel in the root and a sequence of [–ATR] vowels in the suffix. The winning output (a) shows iterative assimilation of both suffix vowels to [+ATR] in the root. This satisfies the licensing constraint, because a single [+ATR] specification is shared across the suffix vowels and a root vowel. Candidate (b) has harmony to the root-adjacent suffix syllable only. This candidate is suboptimal, because the suffix-final [–ATR] vowel violates the licensing constraint. The licensing constraint also rules out the faithful candidate in (c). I have marked a single violation of licensing here, assuming that a single [–ATR] specification is shared across the two suffix vowels. Candidate (d) shows regressive [–ATR] assimilation. This fares better on faithfulness than (a), but it incurs a fatal violation of the local conjunction.

(48) Progressive harmony from a high [+ATR] vowel

/wulc-ɛ5rɛ51/	*[–ATR, +high] &$_l$ IDENT(ATR)	LICENSE([ATR], Root)	IDENT(ATR)
☞ a. wulc-e5re51			**
b. wulc-e5rɛ51		*!	*
c. wulc-ɛ5rɛ51		*!	
d. wʊlc-ɛ5rɛ51	*!		*

The overall pattern bears out the prediction noted in chapter 2 that the licensing solution may be altered when it would produce a marked vowel. Given that a positional faithfulness constraint for the root exists, harmony could be expected to issue from the root if all else were equal. However, regressive harmony from the suffix transpires when a high [–ATR] vowel would have been derived by progressive harmony.

Smolensky's proposal that *[–ATR, +high] &$_l$ IDENT(ATR) is active in Lango is part of his more comprehensive analysis of its ATR harmony system.

As mentioned above, Lango's ATR harmony is complex. Even though assimilation for [+ATR] is the most common resolution of vowel sequences that show disharmony for [ATR], particular sequence types remain disharmonic or show [−ATR] harmony from the root to a suffix. Based on the outputs predicted by the rules that Archangeli and Pulleyblank propose for Lango's harmony, Smolensky proposes six constraints that dominate the harmony-driving constraint, for which his descriptive definitions are provided in (49). I have substituted [±back] for [±front] in these definitions. (See Smolensky 2006: 86–91 for formal statements of the constraints.) The local conjunction employed above is one of these constraints. In Smolensky's analysis, ATR harmony only occurs in the output for a disharmonic input if all of these constraints can be satisfied; otherwise it remains disharmonic. Apart from the local conjunction, I will not deal with the formal statement of the other constraints and their motivation here, and simply assume that constraints with the described effects dominate the licensing constraint.[19] (/–e5̄1/ in (44) is an apparent exception to C_2.) These constraints serve to describe aspects of Lango's harmony system, and in this regard they will be relevant to some following discussion.

(49)   a. [−ATR] constraints
         $\mathbb{C}_X$: "No regressive [−ATR] spread."
         $\mathbb{C}_Y$: "No [−ATR] spread from a [−back] vowel."
         $\mathbb{C}_Z$: *[−ATR, +high] &$_l$ IDENT(ATR)
    b. [+ATR] constraints
         $\mathbb{C}_1$: "No [+ATR] spread from a [−high] source in a closed syllable."
         $\mathbb{C}_2$: "No regressive [+ATR] spread from [−high] source."
         $\mathbb{C}_3$: "No regressive [+ATR] spread from a [+back] source onto a [−high] vowel in a closed syllable."

The constraints in (49) bear on the underlying [ATR] value for the vowels in the suffixes in (46). Kaplan (2008a) gives these as [−ATR]. In the case of /–Ca/, this is confirmed by the disharmonic form [gwen1-na5̄] 'my chicken.' In this word, the [+ATR] root vowel cannot be the trigger for harmony, because of $\mathbb{C}_1$. The [−ATR] suffix vowel also cannot be the trigger for harmony, because of $\mathbb{C}_X$. If the suffix instead had a [+ATR] vowel in its underlying representation, the output would be expected to be *[gwen1-nə5̄]. For /–ɛ5̄rɛ5̄1/, the underlying form is verified by the word [mɛ1-ɛ1rɛ5̄1] 'intoxicate.' Here, the root and suffix vowels are posited to be [−ATR] in the input and output. If the suffix vowels were instead /e/, the output predicted by Smolensky's constraints would be disharmonic *[mɛ1-e1rɛ5̄1]. Harmony for [−ATR] from the root is not predicted because of $\mathbb{C}_Y$ and [+ATR] harmony from a suffix is not predicted because of $\mathbb{C}_2$. Under the assumption that these constraints are descriptively accurate, they therefore confirm that progressive [+ATR] harmony from a high vowel occurs in the system, and it can cause multiple suffix vowels to assimilate, as demonstrated in (48).

We have seen that ATR harmony in Lango can show progressive and regressive [+ATR] harmony. In certain vowel sequences, progressive [−ATR] harmony can also occur. For example, the infinitive suffix /–Co/ cannot trigger [+ATR] harmony because of $\mathbb{C}_2$. If the root contains a [−ATR] back vowel, [−ATR] harmony ensues, as seen in (50a). If the root vowel is a front [−ATR] vowel, the output is disharmonic (50b) consistent with $\mathbb{C}_Y$.

(50)   a. Progressive [−ATR] harmony
           Root   Infinitive
           lwɔk   'wash' lwɔk-kɔ
           lʊb   'follow' lʊb-bɔ
       b. Disharmony
           Root   Infinitive
           lɪm   'visit' lɪm-mo
           nɛn   'see'   nɛn-no

ATR harmony in Lango can thus show assimilation for [+ATR] and [−ATR]. This indicates that the licensing constraint that drives harmony operates over both values of [ATR]. Smolensky observes that there is no evidence for prioritizing assimilation for [+ATR] or [−ATR] in the system. The disharmonic cases where licensing cannot be satisfied do not show neutralization in the suffix vowels' specification for [ATR], rather they remain faithful to whatever the underlying value for [ATR] was, e.g. [ol-cell-gɪ5] 'she hit them,' [lɪm-mo] 'to visit.' This indicates that IDENT-IO(ATR) dominates any markedness constraints that would promote neutralization to a vowel that lacks any [ATR] specification. It also will dominate any licensing constraint that singles out a particular value for [ATR]. For example, a constraint that penalizes an unlicensed [−ATR] specification in a high vowel, LICENSE([−ATR]/[+high], Root), would promote a change from /ɪ/ → [i] in a suffix when harmony with the root cannot occur. As /ɪ/ remains faithful in this situation, IDENT(ATR) must dominate this constraint.

To sum up, like central Veneto, the bounded nature of harmony in Lango supports its analysis as a pattern that is driven by prominence-based licensing, as do the circumstances under which it affects more than one vowel. With respect to high [+ATR] vowels, triggers are not restricted to a weak or strong position but rather trigger control is an effect that emerges from avoidance of generating marked high [−ATR] vowels. The availability of this non-positional trigger control is tied to the enforcement of licensing for both values of [ATR], which promotes repair whenever suffix vowels and the root-final syllable are disharmonic for [ATR]. The case of Lango is important for the output constraint-oriented approach advanced in this work, because it shows that the direction and control for harmony emerge from the conjunction of independently motivated markedness and faithfulness constraints. An account in a process-oriented framework, such as the rule-based analysis of Archangeli and Pulleyblank (1994), must posit separate rules for progressive and regressive harmony from high [+ATR] vowels. This misses the common factor of the licensing configuration that results from spreading in either direction. In addition, the markedness of deriving high [–ATR] vowels need be stated only once in the constraint hierarchy, whereas trigger control by high [+ATR] vowels must be listed separately for each rule.

JAQARU. As introduced in §3.6, the final unstressed vowel of certain suffixes in Jaqaru causes harmony for all features in a stressed vowel, as shown in (51). Notice that harmony does not progress beyond the stressed syllable. The description of this pattern owes to Cerrón-Palomino (2000) and personal communication with Rodolfo Cerrón-Palomino. Certain of these data have been analyzed by Cerrón-Palomino López (2003).

(51)   a. i-final

tʃimí-ni	'with belly'	tʃima	'belly'
hajní-ni	'with husband'	hajnu	'husband'
paki-ʃí-ʃi	'to break oneself'	paki-ʃu-	'to break'
was-mí-ʎi	'hey, be careful'	wasa-ma	'be careful'

      b. a-final

nará-ja	'to make someone laugh'	naru-	'to laugh'
tʃuqá-ja	'to make someone pull'	tʃuqu-	'to pull'
nuná-ja	'to cause to rinse'	nuni-	'to rinse'
tʃ'ipá-ja	'to cause to shine'	tʃ'ipi-	'to shine'

      c. u-final

ajú-ru	'to introduce the hand'	aja-	'to give the hand'
ajʎú-ru	'to overflow'	ajʎi-	'to boil'
im-kú-ʃu	'sewing'	ima-ka-	'to sew (durative)'
pal-ʃú-ʃu-	'eating'	palu-ʃi-	'to eat (med. pass.)'

The Jaqaru pattern is one where all vowel features and all values must be licensed. The triggering vowels occur in morphologically weak contexts, i.e. affixes; however, the phenomenon seems to be idiosyncratic to particular affixes, not reducible to any generalized weak morphological category (see §3.6).

Distinct positions present strength along different dimensions in this system: the stressed syllable serves as licensor and the final syllable controls harmony. This pattern conforms with the observation of Barnes (2006) that final syllables do not tend to serve as the only prominent syllable in the words of a language (see §2.7). The morpheme-specific constraint that was established for this pattern is LICENSE_L([V-FEATURE], ó), which is indexed to the suffixes that trigger harmony.[20] This constraint dominates IDENT-IO(V-FEATURE). The analysis in terms of licensing is supported by harmony halting at the stressed syllable, a prominent position. Cerrón-Palomino López proposes that control of assimilation by the final syllable is due to a word-final faithfulness constraint. Since indirect licensing is permitted and harmony is initiated by the word-final vowel, the licensing constraint and word-final faithfulness (IDENT-IO-σ_Final[V-FEATURE]) will dominate CRISPEDGE([V-FEATURE], σ) and stressed syllable faithfulness (IDENT-IO-ó[V-FEATURE]). There are no forms that point to the availability of identity licensing, so I will assume that such configurations do not occur in the language.

In what follows, I investigate the interaction of this pattern with vowels that are added in loanwords. These vowels usually replicate the quality of a root vowel in unaffixed forms and otherwise undergo licensing-driven harmony with a suffix. Word contraction may also occur, and we will see that the added vowels resist licensing-driven harmony just when they serve as the sole realization for a distinctive quality of a root vowel.

Evidence for a ranking between word-final faithfulness and the licensing constraint comes from borrowings. Although stress in Jaqaru is usually penultimate, antepenultimate stress occurs in borrowings that were consonant-final and stressed on the penultimate syllable in the original word, as shown in (52). A final vowel is added to avoid a consonant-final root. Stress remains on the original vowel, which becomes antepenultimate. The final vowel is usually a copy of the preceding one.[21]

(52) áxusu < ajos (Spanish) 'garlic'
     ríluxu < reloj (Spanish) 'watch'
     híkuʃu < higos (Spanish XVI c.) 'figs'
     lúnisi < lunes (Spanish) 'Monday'
     mártisi < martes (Spanish) 'Tuesday'
     qántsiʃi < qantsiʃ (Quechua) 'seven'
     púsaqa < pusaq (Quechua) 'eight'
     húpasa < uvas (Spanish) 'grapes'
     qáʎaja < qaʎaj (Quechua) 'to begin'

When a harmony-triggering suffix occurs with these loans, stress shifts to the penultimate syllable, as in (53). If the trisyllabic base of affixation is retained, the stressed vowel shows harmony with the suffix vowel. An alternative form is available in which the second vowel of the base is omitted. This contraction may occur when the word exceeds three syllables. In this circumstance, the final vowel of the base retains the quality of the original vowel in the last root syllable rather than harmonizing to the suffix. These alternative forms reveal an instance where licensing is violated in Jaqaru and word-final faithfulness causes the final vowel to retain its original quality at the cost of licensing.

(53)   Affixed form   Contracted alternate
       axusí-ni   ~   axsú-ni   'garlic (poss.)'
       riluxí-ni   ~   rilxú-ni   'watch (poss.)'

First, I address the vowels in the root. I attribute the avoidance of consonant-final roots to the anchoring constraint ANCHOR(Root$_O$, V$_I$, R), which requires that any element at the right edge of a root in the output have a correspondent with some vowel in the input (extending the ANCHOR formalism of McCarthy 2003).[22] In Aymaran languages in general, roots must not end in a consonant, but words can. The 'inserted' vowel must actually be an exponent of the root in order to satisfy the anchoring constraint. I propose that the root-final vowel stands in a correspondence relation with the vowel to which it is identical. Since the copied vowel can occur even under deletion of the original root vowel to which it harmonizes, I postulate that the correspondence relation in question exists between the input root vowel and the added vowel (Karabay 2004; note also Lamontagne and Rice 1995; Struijke 2002). The situation is illustrated in (54). In (54a), the second root vowel stands in correspondence both with the vowel in the same position in the output and with the inserted final vowel, i.e. it displays vowel fission. Correspondence among segments is indicated with subscript numerals. In (54b), the base is reduced to two syllables, and the root vowel of the second syllable is realized only in root-final position, amounting to consonant–vowel metathesis.

(54)   Input   Output
       a.   /axu$_1$s$_{Root}$/   [axu$_1$su$_1$]$_{Root}$
       b.   /axu$_1$s$_{Root}$-ni$_{Af}$/   [[axsu$_1$]$_{Root}$-ni$_{Af}$]

Cases involving multiple segment correspondence spur a refinement of faithfulness constraints in existential terms. Struijke (2002) conceptualizes input–output faithfulness as regulating *preservation* of properties of the input rather than demanding identity of input–output strings. In other words, they require that characteristics of the input be preserved somewhere in the output. She accomplishes this using existential quantification in input–output faithfulness constraints. For example, ∃-LINEARITY-IO requires that the input's precedence structure be preserved somewhere in the output, i.e. if a segment precedes

130   *Indirect licensing*

another in the input, *some* output correspondent of each segment must respect that ordering (Struijke 2002: 33). If there are other output correspondents of those segments that do not respect the ordering, they do not interfere with satisfaction of the constraint.

(55)   ∃-LINEARITY-IO
Let α and β be segments ∈ input in the domain of a correspondence relation ℜ, such that α precedes β; then there is some segment α' ∈ output such that αℜα' which precedes some segment β' ∈ output such that βℜβ'.

The output in (54a) satisfies ∃-LINEARITY-IO because it contains the sequence [axu₁s], which is consistent with the precedence of the input correspondents. The output in (54b) is assigned a violation, because it contains the sequence [su₁], which is not consistent with the input's precedence structure, without preserving the sequence [u₁s] elsewhere in the string.

INTEGRITY-IO, which penalizes mappings where an element of the input has multiple output correspondents (Lamontagne and Rice 1995; McCarthy and Prince 1995), is violated by the output in (54a), with vowel fission.[23] This necessitates its domination by ANCHOR(Root$_O$, V$_I$, R) and ∃-LINEARITY-IO, as shown in (56). The winning candidate violates INTEGRITY because /u/ has two correspondents in the output. Candidate (b) falls out of the running because its root is not vowel final, whereas (c) is ruled out by failing to preserve the precedence of /u/ before /s/ somewhere in the output.[24]

(56)   Vowel fission in consonant-final roots
       ANCHOR(Root$_O$, V$_I$, R), ∃-LINEARITY-IO >> INTEGRITY-IO

/axu₁s$_{Rt}$/	ANCHOR-R	∃-LINEARITY	INTEGRITY-IO
☞ a. [áxu₁su₁]$_{Rt}$			*
b. [áxu₁s]$_{Rt}$	*!		
c. [áxsu₁]$_{Rt}$		*!	

Because the output in (54b) violates ∃-LINEARITY-IO, ANCHOR(Root$_O$, V$_I$, R) dominates this constraint to compel the sole correspondent of the second root vowel to appear out of sequence when a vowel in the base of affixation is omitted. Also outranking ∃-LINEARITY-IO will be the constraint or combination of constraints that drive contraction of words with more than three syllables, which I refer to by the cover constraint *[σσσσ]$_ω$. The particulars of this phenomenon and its optionality await further analysis. The constraint interactions are demonstrated in (57). Candidate (a) is selected despite its violation of ∃-LINEARITY. The alternative in (b) preserves precedence structure and obeys the root anchoring constraint through vowel duplication, but it is eliminated by *[σσσσ]$_ω$. Candidate (c) is faithful to the input but violates anchoring.

(57)   CV metathesis under word contraction

/axu$_1$s$_{Rt}$-ni$_{Af}$/	*[σσσσ]$_ω$	ANCHOR-R	∃-LINEARITY	INTEGRITY-IO
☞ a. [[axsú$_1$]$_{Rt}$-ni$_{Af}$]			*	
b. [[axu$_1$sú$_1$]$_{Rt}$-ni$_{Af}$]	*!			*
c. [[axú$_1$s]$_{Rt}$-ni$_{Af}$]		*!		

*[σσσσ]$_ω$, ANCHOR(Root$_O$, V$_I$, R) >> ∃-LINEARITY-IO >> INTEGRITY-IO

There still is a problem that concerns licensing. When the base is contracted, and only then, the vowel features of the suffix are not licensed. I propose that this is caused by a faithfulness constraint indexed to roots in the loan stratum of the lexicon: IDENT-IO(F)$_{L2}$. L2 is the index that I will use for loan roots, and L1 is henceforth the index used for harmony-triggering suffixes, for which the licensing constraint is marked. This approach is consistent with Pater's (2009a) observation that lexically indexed faithfulness constraints can cause morpheme-specific blocking, and lexically indexed markedness constraints can cause morpheme-specific triggering, an issue that is also taken up in the analysis of a licensing pattern in the dialect of Ascrea in §6.4.

Again, as we are dealing with multiple correspondence of segments, an existential interpretation of faithfulness is relevant. ∃-IDENT-IO(F) requires that for an input segment with correspondent output segment(s), there is *some* output correspondent with identical specification for [F], as framed in (58) (adapted from Struijke 2002: 33).

(58)   ∃-IDENT-IO(F)
       Let α be a segment ∈ input in the domain of a correspondence relation ℜ and α have a correspondent segment in the output. If α is [γF], then there is some segment α' ∈ output such that αℜα' and α' is [γF].

When a vowel undergoes fission and has two output correspondents, ∃–IDENT-IO(F) will be satisfied provided at least one of those correspondents is identical to the input vowel. This makes one of the two correspondents of a fissioned vowel receptive to a phonological process that alters it. If there is only a single output correspondent of an input vowel, it could resist alteration, since that would entail violation of ∃-IDENT-IO(F).

∃-IDENT-IO(V-FEATURE)$_{L2}$ dominates LICENSE$_{L1}$([V-FEATURE], ó) to prevent a repair for unlicensed structure that causes the root-final vowel quality to be altered when it is the sole correspondent of a root vowel in the input. When the suffix vowel's features are unlicensed, it nevertheless maps faithfully in final position rather than undergoing deletion or harmony to the stressed vowel. This indicates that MAX-IO(segment) and word-final IDENT also dominate the licensing constraint, as illustrated in (59). MAX-IO(seg) prohibits segment deletion by requiring that every segment in the input have some correspondent in the output (McCarthy and Prince 1995). As already demonstrated in §3.6, LICENSE$_{L1}$([V-FEATURE], ó) dominates the general IDENT-IO(V-FEATURE) constraint, i.e. one that is not lexically indexed, to guarantee that harmony occurs in the usual case, when a loan root is not involved. This constraint could be characterized as ∃-IDENT-IO(V-FEATURE), but because there is only a single output correspondent for each vowel, it would not affect the outcome. As before, a single mark is indicated for IDENT(V-FEATURE) for each unfaithful vowel to simplify the presentation.

The inputs in (59i) and (59ii) are identical, each containing a loan-based root, indexed L2, and a harmony-triggering suffix, indexed L1. In (59i), the input maps to an output with a trisyllabic root, whereas in (59ii) it maps to the alternant with a disyllabic root. Both are well-formed outputs in the language. What determines the choice of variant is a separate issue, not addressed here.[25] In (59i), the second root vowel in the input has two correspondents in the optimal output. This enables the root-final vowel to undergo licensing-driven harmony, in (a), without incurring a violation of ∃-IDENT(V-FEATURE)$_{L2}$, because some correspondent of the root vowel exists in the output that is faithful to its features in the input. Candidate (b) is suboptimal because of its violation of the licensing constraint. The word-final faithfulness constraint ensures that the final vowel controls harmony rather than undergoing harmony itself, as in (c). In (59ii), the alternative form where the second root vowel has only one output correspondent is considered. In the winning output in (a), harmony does not operate; regressive harmony is prevented by ∃-IDENT(V-FEATURE)$_{L2}$ (b). Candidates that seek to satisfy the licensing constraint by deletion of the suffix vowel (c), or harmony issuing from the stressed vowel (d), are prevented by MAX and word-final faithfulness, respectively.

(59)　　Harmony and lack of harmony in borrowings with consonant final roots
∃-IDENT(V-F)$_{L2}$, MAX-IO, IDENT-σ$_{Final}$(V-F) >> LICENSE$_{L1}$([V-F], σ́) >> IDENT(V-F)

Input	Output	∃-IDENT (V-F)$_{L2}$	MAX-IO	IDENT-σ$_{Final}$(V-F)	LIC$_{L1}$ ([V-F], σ́)	IDENT (V-F)
i. /axu$_1$s$_{L2}$-ni$_{L1}$/	☞ a. axu$_1$sí$_1$-ni					*
	b. axu$_1$sú$_1$-ni				*!	
	c. axu$_1$sú$_1$-nu			*!		*
ii. /axu$_1$s$_{L2}$-ni$_{L1}$/	☞ a. axsú$_1$-ni				*	
	b. axsí$_1$-ni	*!				*
	c. axsú$_1$-n		*!			
	d. axsú$_1$-nu			*!		*

In sum, licensing-driven harmony in Jaqaru shows triggering and blocking effects that are morpheme sensitive, and it shows a complex interaction with another morphophonological process causing vowel duplication.[26] Word-final faithfulness plays a dual role in the system: it causes the suffix vowel to control harmony and causes it to remain faithful under conditions where satisfaction of the licensing constraint by harmony from the final vowel is blocked. An overview of some basic constraint interactions that give rise to these effects in the vowel patterns of Jaqaru is given in (60).

(60)　　Some basic constraint interactions in Jaqaru

　　a. IDENT-σ$_{Final}$(V-FEATURE), LICENSE$_{L1}$([V-FEATURE], σ́) >> IDENT (V-FEATURE)
　　　Licensing-driven harmony in the stressed syllable is triggered by particular morphemes (in the set L1) and is controlled by the vowel in the word-final syllable.

　　b. ANCHOR(Root$_O$, V$_1$, R), ∃-LINEARITY-IO >> INTEGRITY-IO
　　　Vowel fission can occur to guarantee vowel-final roots.

　　c. *[σσσσ]$_ω$, ANCHOR(Root$_O$, V$_1$, R) >> ∃-LINEARITY-IO
　　　Metathesis can occur to guarantee vowel-final roots in contracted forms.

　　d. ∃-IDENT(V-FEATURE)$_{L2}$ >> LICENSE$_{L1}$([V-FEATURE], σ́) >> IDENT (V-FEATURE)
　　　Licensing-driven harmony is blocked by particular morphemes (in the set L2) when vowel fission in that morpheme does not occur.

　　e. IDENT-σ$_{Final}$(V-FEATURE) >> LICENSE$_{L1}$([V-FEATURE], σ́)
　　　When licensing-driven harmony is blocked, a vowel in a word-final syllable remains faithful.

The analysis developed here posits that the copied vowel in borrowings is the result of vowel fission, i.e. a second occurrence of an input vowel, rather than the product of epenthesis, where a vowel without an input correspondent is inserted. Likewise, in contracted forms, the final root vowel is analyzed as the outcome of metathesis, not epenthesis. If the vowel were instead treated as epenthetic, certain properties of the system would become more complex or not be predicted. First, contracted forms like [axsúni] would seem to present a counterbleeding opacity, whereby vowel epenthesis and harmony in the root must precede vowel deletion, as in the derivational sequence: /axus-ni/ → (epenthesis) axusV-ni → (harmony in root) axusu-ni → (deletion) [axsúni]; otherwise, vowel deletion would bleed harmony with the appropriate vowel for the inserted vowel. Counterbleeding opacity can lend complexity to the analysis and for the learner, and its modeling presents problems for the assumptions of 'classic' OT (e.g. McCarthy 1999, 2007b). A second problem with an epenthesis analysis is that it does not predict that harmony from the suffix in the contracted form will be blocked (e.g. [axsúni]), while harmony operates in the uncontracted form e.g. [axusíni]). In both cases, the penultimate vowel would be epenthetic, and there is no reason to expect it to resist harmony in the contracted form only.

On the other hand, these properties of the system are handled without difficulty by the fission analysis. The occurrence of 'copy harmony' among root vowels in contracted forms and non-contracted roots is straightforward: there is in fact no harmony within roots, the 'added' vowel is actually a realization of a root vowel. Therefore, no sequencing is needed for the operations of 'insertion,' harmony, and deletion in contracted forms. Further, the blocking of harmony from the suffix only in contracted forms is predicted as a possibility by the existential formulation of faithfulness. In circumstances of fission, an existential IDENT(F) constraint will be satisfied provided one of the output correspondents of an input vowel is faithful. This leaves the other correspondent free to undergo licensing-driven harmony with the suffix vowel. However, when there is only a single output correspondent, as in contracted forms, harmony from the suffix can be blocked in order to satisfy existential IDENT(F). Licensing-driven harmony is thus prevented in contracted words by a demand for there to be some realization of distinctive vowel qualities in roots belonging to the loan vocabulary.

In closing, a remark on faithfulness is in order. The analysis of Jaqaru employs existentially quantified definitions of faithfulness to make precise the assignment of violations in cases involving multiple correspondence of input segments. Elsewhere in this work, in analyses where multiple correspondence of input segments is not involved, I will assume the more familiar definitions of correspondence constraints proposed by McCarthy and Prince (1995), unless otherwise noted.

In these cases, the quantification of segmental faithfulness as enforcing existential or universal faithfulness in the output will not distinguish the outcome.[27]

OTHER PATTERNS. *Chamorro*. Chamorro shows an umlaut pattern in which a front vowel in a prefix or particle triggers fronting of a stressed vowel in the first syllable of the stem (for data, see Kaplan 2008a and references therein). Kaplan analyzes Chamorro umlaut as driven by a prominence-based licensing constraint. In his terms, the licensing constraint requires [–back] in an immediate pretonic syllable to be linked to a root segment. In the formalism used here, this would be characterized by the constraint LICENSE([–back]/$\sigma_{Immed.pretonic}$, Root). Kaplan argues that the immediate pretonic syllable is weaker than other syllables in the language, which explains its being singled out in this phenomenon. As Kaplan demonstrates, a positive result of the licensing approach to Chamorro umlaut is that it obtains non-iterativity in the pattern as an emergent property of the system.

SUMMARY. This section has examined several patterns of harmony that improve the exposure of weak material through indirect licensing where the vowel in licensing position undergoes assimilation. Each of the languages under study shows a pattern that is plausibly driven by a licensing constraint. This is supported by harmony in central Veneto, Lango, and Jaqaru that is bounded by a prominent position, and by the particular circumstances under which harmony proceeds through multiple syllables in central Veneto and Lango. The availability of an indirect licensing structure but not identity licensing is consistent with blocking by certain consonants in OHG and certain vowels in central Veneto, and it is also compatible with the distributions seen in Lango and Jaqaru. Trigger control in each of these systems is independent of the prominence of the licensing position and is proposed to arise from the activity of a faithfulness constraint, in some cases in a local conjunction with a markedness constraint. The constraint that is responsible for trigger control also causes the vowels in question to resist undergoing change when licensing fails, performing double duty in these systems.

5.4 Sources of trigger control

In summation to the preceding sections on vowel patterns with indirect licensing, this section provides an overview of the sources of trigger control. At issue is which vowel or position is faithful in the enforcement of licensing patterns. In some cases the vowel in licensing position is the one that it consistently faithful. In that circumstance, I have proposed that the ranking structure in (61) is active. Here the higher stratum contains the licensing constraint and an IDENT constraint for [F] that is specific to the licensing position. ([F] refers to the same feature and π the same position in these constraints.) Thus, preserving material that originates in a prominent position π and a licensing effect associated with

136 *Indirect licensing*

that position are both granted priority. Because positional faithfulness and the non-position-sensitive IDENT constraint stand in a specific-to-general relation, it is not crucial that the positional IDENT constraint actually dominate its non-positional counterpart, but the outcome is compatible with the hierarchical structure shown here.

(61) Control by vowel in the licensing position
Stratum n
LICENSE([F], π), IDENT-IO-π(F)
Stratum $> n$
IDENT-IO(F)

The table in (62) presents a synthesis of the patterns of control by a vowel in the licensing position discussed in this chapter. Note that the faithful vowel in the licensing position does not necessarily trigger assimilation. Active assimilation is observed in Buchan Scots, Macuxi, and Ticinese. In Classical Mongolian and C'Lela, indirect licensing can generate representations where a feature is shared across vowels in licensing and non-licensing position, but evidence points to a passive licensing pattern rather than one of active assimilation. (The same notation as that used in constraints is used here for restrictions on features subject to licensing.)

(62) Indirect licensing: patterns of control by a vowel in licensing position

	Pattern specifics	Positional faithfulness constraint	Language(s)
i.	Licensing position = ó [F] = [+high] (Buchan Scots) [F] = all vowel features/ σ$_{Final}$[+low] (Ticinese) The vowel in the stressed syllable is faithful.	IDENT-IO-ó(F)	Buchan Scots Ticinese
ii.	Licensing position = σ$_{Initial}$ [F] = [+round]/[−high] The vowel in the word-initial syllable is faithful.	IDENT-IO-σ$_{Initial}$(F)	Classical Mongolian
iii.	Licensing position = Root or Stem [F] = [+high]/σ$_{Final}$ (in specific suffixes) (C'Lela) [F] = [COLOR]/unaccented V (Macuxi) Vowels in the root or stem syllable are faithful.	IDENT-IO-Root(F) IDENT-IO-Stem(F)	C'Lela Macuxi

In other licensing patterns, faithfulness to a vowel that is in non-licensing position is enforced at the cost of faithfulness in the licensing position, in some or all circumstances. Here positional privilege in the form of a site serving as a licensor where certain material must be realized is distinct from preservation of material originating in that position. In this case the faithfulness constraint for the licensing position is on a par with non-positional IDENT in a lower-ranked stratum. Some faithfulness constraint other than faithfulness specific to the licensing position determines which vowel is faithful in the licensing pattern by taking its place in the higher stratum. I refer to this constraint by the cover label 'TRIGGER-FAITH.' As we have seen, this may consist of a faithfulness constraint alone or a local conjunction of faithfulness and markedness. As above, [F] and π each refer to the same feature or position across constraints.

(63)　Control by vowel that may be in non-licensing position
　　　 Stratum n
　　　 LICENSE([F], π), TRIGGER-FAITH
　　　 Stratum $> n$
　　　 IDENT-IO(F), IDENT-IO-π(F)

Further detail in the hierarchy in (63) will determine the outcome in circumstances where licensing does not succeed. If in that instance the vowel in non-licensing position is subject to the TRIGGER-FAITH constraint, and TRIGGER-FAITH dominates the licensing constraint, then the vowel will remain faithful at the cost of licensing. On the other hand, if the licensing constraint dominates TRIGGER-FAITH, then the vowel with an unlicensed feature might alter its value for the feature to satisfy the licensing constraint. This situation requires an active licensing constraint that singles out a specific value for [F]. If it operates over both values for [F], no gain is achieved by altering the unlicensed feature specification.

The cases studied in this chapter where a vowel in non-licensing position shows the capacity for control in indirect licensing are summarized in the table in (64). In each case, the TRIGGER-FAITH constraint causes particular vowels to be faithful. These constraints have a basis in inherent or positional strength or markedness. In OHG, faithfulness to high front unround vocoids is proposed to have origins in the coarticulatory strength of these segments. In Jaqaru, the strength of word-final position causes faithfulness to be enforced for vowels in this position. In each of these languages, the trigger vowel shows characteristics that are a mix of weak and strong. For example, in Jaqaru, the trigger vowel is weak by virtue of being affixal and unstressed. It is also in final position, which may produce certain phonetic weakening effects (see §2.4).

The trigger vowel's weakness is consistent with its features being subject to licensing by the stressed syllable. At the same time, final syllables can show some increased prominence, which is characterized by positional faithfulness for the final syllable. Phonological strength and weakness are therefore not always fully complementary. In central Veneto, the TRIGGER-FAITH constraint has a basis in prominence-based markedness, specifically the marked representation that ensues from generating a non-high unstressed vowel. For Lango, the TRIGGER-FAITH constraint is applicable to forms that contain a high [+ATR] vowel. In this case, the marked representation that is avoided is high [−ATR] vowels, a context-insensitive segmental restriction.

(64)   Indirect licensing: patterns of control by a vowel that may be in non-licensing position

	Pattern specifics	TRIGGER-FAITH	Language
i.	Licensing position = σ́ [F] = [−back] Vocoids [i j] are faithful.	IDENT(+high, −back, −round)	Old High German
ii.	Licensing position = σ́ [F] = All vowel features (in specific suffixes) The vowel in the word-final syllable is faithful.	IDENT-IO-σ$_{Final}$(F)	Jaqaru
iii.	Licensing position = σ́ [F] = [+high]/σ$_{post\text{-}tonic}$ High unstressed vowels are faithful.	*ŏ/a,e•o &$_l$ IDENT-IO(high)	Dialect of central Veneto
iv.	Licensing position = Root [F] = [ATR] High [+ATR] vowels are faithful.	*[−ATR, +high] &$_l$ IDENT(ATR)	Lango

This approach to TRIGGER-FAITH does not involve a faithfulness constraint that directly singles out non-licensing positions. Indeed, given that non-licensing positions could have a weaker phonetic and psycholinguistic status, we would not expect them to be identified as a class where distinctive properties were preserved to the exclusion of others. Where positional faith is active, as in Jaqaru, there is cross-linguistic evidence for some form of strength in that position. Faithfulness constraints are not posited for positions that are called out as weak by virtue of being non-heads in prosodic terms (e.g. unstressed syllable) or morphological terms (e.g. affix, clitic) (see Smith 2005 for arguments against such constraints). As a result, in circumstances where a vowel in non-licensing position triggers licensing-driven assimilation in the vowel in licensing position, control by the non-licensing vowel is treated as an epiphenomenon of other factors that govern faithfulness, and in some cases also markedness. This approach predicts the possibility that where a vowel in non-licensing position controls harmony because of particular properties that it has, it could also control harmony if it presented those properties when it occurred in licensing position. Lango bears out this prediction, with high [+ATR] vowels triggering licensing-driven harmony when they occur in licensing and non-licensing positions alike.

Notice that trigger control by a vowel in a non-licensing position does not necessarily have to involve the activity of a faithfulness constraint, although each of the cases in (64) does. It is conceivable that trigger control could be achieved by a markedness constraint that blocks the vowel quality that would be derived if the vowel in non-licensing position were to be a target rather than a trigger. For instance, markedness constraints like *ŏ/a,e•o or *[–ATR, +high], used in conjunction with a faithfulness constraint in central Veneto and Lango, respectively, could yield trigger control on their own in some language. An example of this kind is seen in the dialect of Francavilla Fontana, taken up in §6.3.

It is worth considering whether the hypothesized sources of trigger control could be exchanged across the systems under study. In fact, they cannot be readily substituted, either because they would fail to make the correct predictions or for other theoretical reasons. For example, a word-final faithfulness constraint, postulated for Jaqaru, cannot be used in OHG, central Veneto, or Lango, because the triggers in these languages are not consistently in the final syllable. Faithfulness to a specific group of features, employed for OHG, would not be successful for Jaqaru, because vowels with the same qualities as the triggers can serve as targets of harmony. It could be possible to devise an approach for control by /i/ in central Veneto that involved faithfulness specific to this vowel, but this would miss the generalization that /u/ can trigger harmony in many related patterns of Romance metaphony, and it is high *front* vocoids in particular that are suggested to show coarticulatory strength. Likewise, for Lango, one could conceive of a faithfulness constraint specific to high [+ATR] vowels, but this overlooks a connection with the well-established markedness of high [–ATR] vowels, which are not generated by the harmony system. The metrical prominence approach to trigger control in central Veneto, which prevents lowering of a high vowel in an unstressed syllable, is not a solution for the other patterns, because they do not involve harmony for [+high],

140 *Indirect licensing*

or at least not for [+high] alone. Finally, the conjunction of faith and a feature cooccurrence constraint, as employed for Lango, is either not viable or not suitable for the other patterns. It is not viable for Jaqaru, where vowels of all qualities can be triggers or targets of harmony. For OHG, it would be necessary to postulate a constraint that penalizes a derived [+back] high vocoid, but it is not clear that these segments are marked. For central Veneto, a constraint would be needed that penalizes derived non-high vowels (independent of context). While this could be a possible approach to pursue, it misses the connection with the preference for vowels with lower sonority in unstressed syllables within many Romance languages, an effect independently evidenced in central Veneto (Walker 2005). For these reasons, I conclude that the sources of weak trigger control are diverse.

5.5 Alternatives

This section considers some alternative approaches to the phenomena under study or particular aspects of them.

POSITIONAL FAITHFULNESS AND FEATURE-DRIVEN MARKEDNESS. Positional faithfulness constraints (Casali 1997, 1998; Beckman 1997, 1999; Lombardi 1999, 2001) have been used in alternative analyses of certain positional licensing phenomena, including passive licensing. Beckman posits the ranking schema, IDENT-*Position*(F) >> C >> IDENT-IO(F), where C is a constraint or constraints that favor alternations for feature *F*. In Walker 2001b, I apply this to passive licensing in Classical Mongolian as follows: IDENT-IO-σ_{Initial}(round) >> *[+round, –high] >> IDENT-IO(round). This approach assumes the principle of Feature-Driven Markedness (Beckman 1997, 1999), wherein featural markedness constraints are assessed at the level of the autosegment rather than the segment. A specification for [+round, –high] linked across two or more syllables is interpreted as incurring a single violation with respect to *[+round, –high], whereas separate tokens of [+round, –high] incur distinct violations. Specification for [+round, –high] in a non-initial syllable that also extends to an initial syllable will therefore not incur violations with respect to *[+round, –high] beyond the violation incurred by the initial syllable. The presence of [+round, –high] in an initial syllable is protected by initial syllable faithfulness.

While this account is capable of obtaining the Classical Mongolian pattern, the principle of Feature-Driven Markedness on which it relies is questionable when considered in the context of other patterns addressed in this work. If the lack of marked features or feature combinations in non-prominent positions is driven by markedness constraints assessed at the autosegmental level, then the identity licensing configuration is not predicted as a possible type of positional licensing. This is because identity licensing involves the presence of separate feature specifications in the licensing position and non-prominent position (see §3.3). When a feature specification [αF] has a duplicate in a prominent position, it incurs more violations with respect to *[αF] than a representation in which [αF] occurs in the prominent position alone. As a result, an approach to positional licensing effects that is driven by positional faithfulness and feature-driven markedness fails to capture effects of licensing at a distance, i.e. identity licensing. Yet patterns that involve indirect licensing alone versus those with identity licensing are closely related, as seen, for example, in Romance metaphony patterns across dialects and in the historical development of umlaut in Germanic, discussed in this chapter and the next two chapters. This connection is lost if feature-driven markedness drives the avoidance of features that are associated solely to a non-prominent position.

Moreover, the full range of licensing effects studied here cannot be modeled using positional faithfulness constraints. Many prominence-based licensing phenomena produce alternations in the prominent position, as seen in §5.3, §6.4 and §7.4, violating positional faithfulness rather than enforcing it. Positional faithfulness therefore fails to unite the basis for prominence-based licensing phenomena.

The generalized prominence-based licensing approach finds a common impetus for such patterns. Critical to this result is that the constraint which drives licensing penalizes particular constituents occurring solely in non-prominent position, a type of positional markedness constraint. In other words, it is essential that feature markedness constraints that are sensitive to positional prominence exist (see also Zoll 1998b; de Lacy 2007a). At the same time, positional faithfulness constraints still play a role in characterizing certain kinds of position-sensitive effects. For example, positional faithfulness constraints obtain control by the strong position in licensing patterns that enforce alternations in weak positions, as discussed in §5.2 and in later chapters, and they obtain position-sensitive trigger control in certain strong positions that do not serve as licensors, as in Jaqaru. Positional faithfulness constraints therefore characterize preservation of content in strong positions, but they are not suitable for a comprehensive account of patterns that revolve around avoidance of certain content in a non-prominent position alone.

PRIMARY VOWEL FAITHFULNESS. Mahanta (2007) rejects the claim that high vowels may serve as triggers by virtue of their perceptual weakness. She proposes that these vowels can control harmony when they occur in a weak position because they are phonologically 'primary' (Stevens and Keyser 1989). High vowels are suggested to resist alternation because of their primary nature.

A drawback of this account is that it does not predict that high vowels in a non-prominent position would be singled out as targets for harmony, as is the case in Buchan Scots; also, in C'Lela, high vowels undergo neutralization when their height feature is not shared with the root. On the other hand, if high vowels whose qualities are expressed solely in a non-prominent syllable can serve as 'marked', as hypothesized in this work, phenomena are predicted that would eliminate or augment them, as is indeed attested.

Utilizing faithfulness to particular vowel qualities is not necessarily without merit. In the analysis of umlaut in OHG, it was proposed that faithfulness to vowels that are specified [+high, –back, –round] is what causes control of harmony by high front vocoids. However, rather than being based in primary qualities, this was attributed to the coarticulatory strength of these vocoids, which directly supports their resistance to coarticulatory effects from neighboring vowels. Whereas this approach is applicable to OHG, it is not a solution to the problem of weak trigger control in all harmony patterns, as discussed in §2.6 and §5.4.

Mahanta makes the interesting claim that there are no patterns in which non-peripheral vowels control harmony from an unstressed position (2007: 265). This seems to be largely true, although in Eastern Andalusian, high, mid, and low unstressed vowels participate in triggering harmony for [–ATR] in a stressed syllable (see §6.4). It is not clear what the cause is for the rarity of unstressed non-peripheral triggers for harmony. It could be tied to the finding of Mielke (2008) that high vowels are more active than mid vowels as a natural class in phonology in general. Genealogical factors could also contribute to the number of weak trigger patterns controlled by high vowels, with metaphony attested in many related Romance languages, and likewise for umlaut in Germanic. Nevertheless, the tendency for mid vowels to be less active as triggers deserves fuller investigation.

CONSTITUENT-DELIMITED SPREADING. In order to address the bounded nature of harmony in patterns such as metaphony and umlaut, Flemming (1993) proposes an analysis where harmony occurs within the bounds of a prosodic constituent, such as the metrical foot. Within this domain, assimilation proceeds blindly, without sensitivity to the relative prominence of positions. A problem with this approach is that it fails to extend to several of the patterns studied in this chapter where the bounds on assimilation do not coincide with the boundary of a prosodic constituent. One such example is regressive [+ATR] harmony in Lango, where harmony ceases after affecting a single vowel in the root, e.g. /bɔ1ŋɔ́-wú/ → [bɔ1ŋó-wú] 'your (pl) dress.' According to Noonan (1992), stress is assigned to the first syllable of the root. The second and third syllables in [bɔ1ŋó-wú] would thus not be expected to form a metrical constituent. Further, it would be difficult to reconcile a prosodically based domain for harmony in [bɔ1ŋó-wú] with forms where [+ATR] harmony operates progressively from the root through *two* suffix syllables: /wu1c-ɛ́rɛ́1/ → [wu1c-é̱ré̱1] 'throw.'

Given its sensitivity to stress, metaphony in the central Veneto dialect might seem to be a good candidate for a foot-delimited analysis, but it too presents problems for this approach. In proparoxytones with a final high vowel and a mid vowel in the penult, the penult vowel undergoes raising only when the stressed vowel raises, as in /orden-i/ → [úrdi̱ni], but /pɛrseg-i/ → [pérse̱gi]. There is no reason to expect that these two words would have a different metrical structure, so it is hard to see how assimilation could be blocked in the second form and not the first if spreading is indeed blind to syllable prominence. Patterns such as these lead me to conclude that constituent-delimited harmony is not suitable as a general solution to the phenomena under study. Nevertheless, the concept of constituent-delimited boundaries shares some commonalities with crisp edge constraints. These can operate to restrict the maximal bounds of a feature chain to a particular constituent type, such as the foot, as was suggested to be active in the vowel pattern in Buchan Scots. However, a prominence-based licensing constraint still serves as a shared harmony-driving factor for the systems examined here.

5.6   Conclusion

This chapter has explored vowel patterns that present indirect licensing without evidence of identity licensing configurations. These systems are organized around outcomes where a vowel quality in a position that functions as non-prominent or weak comes to also find expression in a prominent position. The property in question spans the licensing and non-licensing positions without interruption. The phenomena examined include vowel harmony as well as passive licensing, where neutralization occurs without active assimilation. The licensing positions for the systems discussed in this chapter are the stressed syllable, initial syllable, and root or stem syllables, falling in line with what could be expected on the basis of phonetic and psycholinguistic strength. In cases where the feature(s) subject to licensing are restricted to a particular value or context, they are not unambiguously less marked or more perceptually robust than their unrestricted counterpart, compatible with what is predicted. Further, as predicted by the formal approach, direct licensing – where a restricted quality belongs to the licensing position alone – also occurs where applicable in systems with indirect licensing. For instance, in Classical Mongolian, round non-high vowels can occur in initial syllables even when rounding is not shared with a non-initial syllable.

A dimension across which systems can differ is whether there is control by a vowel in the licensing position or by one that may be in a non-licensing position. In the former cases, control is attributed to a faithfulness constraint that references a prominent position that is also the licensing position. Here, there is convergence of the strong position whose underlying material is preserved and the strong position where certain material must be realized. Sources of control by a vowel that may be in a non-licensing position are found to be more diverse, arising from the activity of a faithfulness constraint or a conjunction of faithfulness and markedness constraints (and in chapter 6 by markedness alone). In these systems, the bounded nature of the pattern is in accordance with what is expected for prominence-based licensing, that is, harmony operates to reach the privileged position and is not driven to proceed further. Furthermore, an important contribution of the prominence-based licensing analysis is that it unifies the imperative behind harmony and passive licensing in strong trigger and weak trigger systems; in functional terms, it causes vowel qualities to coincide with a position where perception is facilitated.

6 *Identity licensing*

6.1 Introduction

This chapter deals with vowel patterns that include identity licensing configurations. Like indirect licensing, such configurations cause a vowel quality in a non-prominent position to also be produced in a prominent position. Unlike patterns with indirect licensing alone, these systems can manifest non-local interactions, where a licensed feature is absent during segments that intervene between the vowel that displays the feature in the licensing position and a vowel that displays the feature in a non-licensing position. Patterns that involve identity licensing can thus be signaled by transparency effects. As discussed in chapter 4, these systems could be expected to include indirect licensing in forms where transparency effects are not applicable. With respect to the vowel whose quality controls assimilation, systems with identity licensing are expected to show similar effects to ones that display only indirect licensing. Patterns where the vowel in licensing position is in control are anticipated to exist by virtue of the strength of this position. Where the controlling vowel is in a non-licensing position, that position is itself expected to be strong in some aspect or an independent factor is expected to be responsible for the vowel's control.

In an identity licensing structure, a vowel quality in a non-prominent position is licensed by a duplicate of the feature in a prominent position. Aspects of the formal approach to these systems are highlighted in what follows. They are characterized by the core ranking in (1). Where [F] is a variable, the constraints are considered to reference the same feature. A given stratum in the hierarchy contains the licensing constraint, and the other three constraints belong to lower strata. The licensing constraint dominates IDENT-IO(F) to actively enforce a licensing distribution, and it dominates the crisp edge constraint to permit licensing configurations where a feature chain spans more than one syllable. A key difference from the patterns examined in chapter 5, which show indirect licensing but not identity licensing, is that *DUPLICATE(F) is situated lower in the hierarchy. *DUPLICATE(F) is dominated by the licensing constraint, because licensing can be achieved by feature duplication.

(1) Core ranking: identity licensing
Stratum *n*
LICENSE([F], π)
Stratum > *n*
CRISPEDGE([F], σ), IDENT-IO(F), *DUPLICATE(F)

In addition to the core ranking structure in (1), *DUPLICATE(F) will be dominated by at least one other constraint that prevents indirect licensing in place of identity licensing in a particular circumstance. For example, as illustrated in §3.5 for Ascrea, if IDENT-IO(F) dominates *DUPLICATE(F), licensing-driven harmony for [αF] via indirect licensing can be prevented when an intervening vowel is [−αF]. This ranking favors duplication of [αF] across the intervening vowel rather than local assimilation through it. In the patterns examined in this chapter, this is the ranking structure seen most often.

In another possible scenario, a markedness constraint dominates *DUPLICATE(F) to render a vowel transparent. This is seen in the dialect of Francavilla Fontana, where a markedness constraint prevents vowels with particular qualities in the licensing position from undergoing licensing-driven harmony. In that circumstance, the vowel that is prevented from undergoing harmony behaves as transparent, with the result that a more distant vocoid that shares membership in the licensing position displays harmony instead in an identity licensing configuration. In this case, a markedness constraint dominates *DUPLICATE(F) to prevent local assimilation. Faithfulness also plays a role in driving this pattern. An IDENT constraint dominates *DUPLICATE(F) to rule out other alternatives.

Because identity licensing can be signaled by transparent segments, diagnosing whether assimilation is local or non-local is an important issue. In local assimilation, a single occurrence of a feature is shared across a sequence of segments that are articulatorily adjacent. This is the representation involved in indirect licensing. In non-local assimilation that involves identity licensing, separate occurrences of [αF] in the same chain belong to vowels in the licensing position and non-licensing position with intervening transparent segment(s) that lack [αF]. As discussed in §3.3, I assume that a single feature occurrence (or 'event') must be continuous. Forms with licensing-driven harmony for [αF] and intervening transparent segments that display [−αF] thus motivate a structure with a duplicated feature.[1] In each of the patterns discussed in this chapter, attention is paid to the nature of transparency effects in the system.

Preserving properties in the licensing position   147

   This chapter deals first with patterns of identity licensing that drive alternations in the non-licensing position. Two patterns of this kind are considered in Eastern Meadow Mari. Next, the pattern in the dialect of Francavilla Fontana is examined, where vowel properties can be preserved in both the licensing position and the non-licensing position. This occurs with licensing-driven diphthongization of certain vowels in the licensing position. The focus then shifts to identity licensing patterns that show assimilation in the licensing position. The languages under study are Lena, Ascrea, Eastern Andalusian, and Old High German. In the majority of these languages, control of harmony by the non-licensing position is attributed to a faithfulness constraint for the word-final syllable.

   In the course of this chapter, the patterns under study intersect with a number of additional theoretical topics. General themes involve the role of context-free markedness constraints involving vowels, which can block licensing-driven harmony or alter its effect, and the attestation of morpheme-specific effects, which can cause triggering and blocking effects in licensing. Other issues include evidence for prioritizing one licensing effect over another in the same language (in Eastern Meadow Mari), segmental fission and the emergence of the unmarked (in Francavilla Fontana), sensitivity to the role of contrast (in Lena), and the occurrence of variation in the attestation of identity versus indirect licensing structures (in Eastern Andalusian). Following the individual case studies, a summary is provided of identity licensing systems and their non-locality effects. Alternative approaches to these patterns are then discussed.

6.2   Preservation of vowel properties in the licensing position

This section examines identity licensing patterns where the vowel in the licensing position preserves its character. In the scenarios under study, a vowel in the licensing position controls licensing-driven alternations in a non-licensing position; hence, strength in terms of licensing and positional faithfulness converge on the same site. Two patterns in Eastern Meadow Mari are considered, as well as their interaction. Where the feature [back] is concerned, harmony is controlled by the word-initial syllable, whereas for [+round], harmony is controlled by the stressed syllable. In both cases, the vowel that undergoes alternations occurs in the word-final syllable. Licensing by assimilation or agreement can operate over intervening syllables that do not display the harmonizing feature, pointing to the availability of identity licensing. Control by the vowel in the licensing position is attributed to faithfulness constraints for the word-initial and stressed syllables.

EASTERN MEADOW MARI. The Eastern Meadow dialect of Mari (Uralic) presents two types of harmony that target vowels in a word-final syllable, one for backness and one for rounding (Vaysman 2009). Although I will refer to both of these vowel distributions as 'harmony,' I will analyze the pattern for rounding as a case of passive licensing, which does not involve active assimilation. The vowels of Eastern Meadow Mari are [i y e ø æ ə a o u]. [æ] occurs only in non-initial syllables and is possibly non-phonemic.[2] Vaysman characterizes [ə] as 'reduced' whereas the other vowels are 'full,' but she finds evidence for [ə] in underlying representations. Back and round harmony cause alternations in suffixes that display a full vowel. All of the suffix vowels that Vaysman describes in her study are non-high (2009: 61).[3]

I focus first on back harmony. Vowels in the word-final syllable assimilate in backness to the vowel in the initial syllable. The product of harmony is illustrated by the suffix alternations in (2). Vowels that intervene between the initial vowel and the final one can be transparent. An intervening transparent vowel is frequently [ə], which can occur between harmonizing front vowels and back vowels alike. Suffix harmony with disharmonic stems [uβér] 'news' and [meráŋ] 'hare' show that harmony from the initial syllable for either value of [back] can operate across an intervening full vowel with the opposite specification. As will be discussed later in this section, the vowel /e/ does not undergo back harmony and the vowels [a] and [ə] do not trigger it. In view of these facts, the underlying quality of the suffix vowels in (2a–b) can be inferred to be /a/, because this is the vowel quality that occurs when the vowel in the word-initial syllable is [ə]. This is also consistent with the possibility that [æ] is not a phoneme of the language.

(2)   a. Nominative singular 2 pl possessive
        ém-dæ̱   'your (pl) medicine'[4]
        tʃødrǽ-tæ̱   'your (pl) forest'
        tʃijǽ-tæ̱   'your (pl) paint'
        tyrə-tǽ̱   'your (pl) edge'
        uβér-ta̱   'your (pl) news'
        kutkó-ta̱   'your (pl) ant'
        olək-tá̱   'your (pl) meadow'
        rəwəʒ-tá̱   'your (pl) fox'
   b. Dative
        imɲə-lǽ̱n   'horse (dat.)'
        kyzə-lǽ̱n   'knife (dat.)'
        meráŋ-læn 'hare (dat.)'
        keŋéʒ-læn 'summer (dat.)'
        olmá-la̱n   'apple (dat.)'

munə-lán   'egg (dat.)'
təlzə-lán   'moon (dat.)'

Back harmony in Eastern Meadow Mari has hallmarks that are consistent with a licensing-driven pattern. A vowel that can show asymmetric weakness – here a vowel in the word-final syllable – undergoes assimilation to a vowel in a prominent position, namely, the word-initial syllable. I analyze these alternations as driven by the constraint License([back]/σ_{Final}, $\sigma_{Initial}$), that is, the pattern enforces licensing by the initial syllable for [back] in a word-final vowel. The data thus far are compatible with a licensing constraint for [+back] alone or for both values of [back]. In the absence of positive evidence to the contrary, I will assume that a licensing effect is symmetric for both values of a feature rather than asymmetric. Furthermore, we will see presently that there is evidence in Mari that points to an active licensing constraint for [back] that is applicable to both feature values.

Licensing for [back] in Mari is achieved by assimilation for [back] across the initial and word-final vowels. Where the vowels in these positions disagree in the input, the vowel in the initial syllable controls assimilation, as driven by initial syllable faithfulness: Ident-IO-$\sigma_{Initial}$(back). I situate this constraint in the top stratum of the hierarchy, as there is no evidence that it is dominated in this pattern. The licensing constraint must dominate non-positional Ident-IO(back) to drive alternations. The occurrence of assimilation, which causes a feature chain to span more than one syllable, necessitates ranking the licensing constraint over CrispEdge([back], σ).

Thus far we have established the ranking: Ident-$\sigma_{Initial}$(back), License([back]/σ_{Final}, $\sigma_{Initial}$) >> CrispEdge([back], σ), Ident-IO(back). Because assimilation can operate across intervening vowels that do not display the harmonizing feature value, I posit that identity licensing structures are permitted. These become a possibility when the licensing constraint dominates *Duplicate(F). Where an intervening vowel is concerned, identity licensing structures can be favored over indirect licensing by the enforcement of a constraint pertaining to the intervening vowel. For Mari, I posit that Ident-IO(back) outranks *Duplicate(F).

The rankings are demonstrated by tableaux in (3–4). The form in (3) shows licensing-driven harmony for [−back] across a back vowel. The winner is candidate (a), which satisfies licensing by duplicating the [back] specification of the word-initial syllable in the vowel of the word-final syllable. This incurs a violation of the crisp edge constraint, Ident(back) and *Duplicate(F). Candidate (b) is faithful, but it earns a fatal violation of the licensing constraint.

Satisfaction of licensing by regressive assimilation from the word-final vowel in (c) is ruled out by the initial syllable faithfulness constraint. Finally, candidate (d), which shows progressive assimilation that alters the intervening medial vowel is ruled out by its second violation of IDENT(back). The ranking of IDENT(back) over *DUPLICATE(F) thus prevents medial vowels from undergoing licensing-driven assimilation. Notice that the crisp edge constraint does not crucially dominate *DUPLICATE(F), but the pattern is consistent with the constraint strata shown here.

(3)   Identity licensing for [back]
       IDENT-$\sigma_{Initial}$(bk), LICENSE([back]/σ_{Final}, $\sigma_{Initial}$) >> CRISPEDGE([bk], σ),
       IDENT-IO(back) >> *DUPLICATE(F)

/meraŋ-lan/	IDENT-$\sigma_{Initial}$(bk)	LICENSE ([bk]/σ_{Fin}, σ_{Init})	CRISPEDGE ([bk], σ)	IDENT(bk)	*DUPL(F)
☞ a. meráŋlæn | | [–bk]$_i$ [–bk]$_i$			*	*	*
b. meráŋlan | | [–bk] [+bk]		*!			

c. maráŋlan
    |/
  [+bk]
	*!		*	*	

d. meræŋlæn
    |/
  [–bk]
			*	**!	

The tableau in (4) illustrates a case where an indirect licensing representation is hypothesized, applicable where medial vowels in the input have the same value for [back] as the vowel in the word-initial syllable. The input contains back vowels in all syllables. The optimal candidate, in (a), shares a [+back] specification across all syllables, violating only the crisp edge constraint. Candidate (b) has an identity licensing structure, where the vowel in the word-final syllable has a duplicate of a feature in the word-initial syllable. This likewise violates the crisp edge constraint but it also earns a violation of *DUPLICATE(F). The comparison of these candidates thus shows a preference for indirect licensing structures over identity licensing, when harmony is not prevented from proceeding locally. In other words, where no interruption occurs, a single autosegment is favored over a duplicated one. Candidate (c) has separate and non-duplicated [+back] specifications in every vowel. This obeys the crisp edge constraint but violates the higher-ranked licensing constraint.

(4)   Indirect licensing for [back]

/kutko-ta/	IDENT-σ_{Initial}(bk)	LICENSE ([bk]/$\sigma_{\text{Fin}}, \sigma_{\text{Init}}$)	CRISPEDGE ([bk], σ)	IDENT(bk)	*DUPL(F)
☞ a. kutkóta \\/ [+bk]			*		
b. kutkóta /|\\ [+bk]$_i$ [+bk]$_j$ [+bk]$_i$			*		*!
c. kutkóta /|\\ [+bk]$_i$ [+bk]$_j$ [+bk]$_k$		*!			

Whereas the controlling position for licensing-driven back harmony in Eastern Meadow Mari is the word-initial syllable, in round harmony it is the stressed syllable. Like back harmony, vowels in the word-final syllable undergo alternations. Examples of rounding harmony are given in (5). Alternations are demonstrated with the 3rd singular possessive suffix, which presents the vowel [e] when the vowel of the stressed syllable is [–round] and [ø] or [o] when it is [+round]. We will see presently that there is reason to believe the vowel in this suffix is underlyingly round. The examples in (5a), where the stressed vowel and word-initial vowel differ in rounding, reveal that it is the stressed vowel that controls the occurrence of rounding in the final vowel. By contrast, a form from (2) such as [uβérta] demonstrates that the word-initial vowel and not the stressed one controls back harmony. The data in (5b) show that syllables that contain [ə] are transparent in round harmony between the stressed and final vowels.

(5)   a. pykʃermé-ʃe̱   'his/her/its walnut tree'
            tʃødrǽ-ʃe̱   'his/her/its forest'
            ʃyzǽr-ʃe̱   'his/her/its sister'
            køgørtʃén-ʃe̱   'his/her/its dove'
            kəʎmó-ʃø̱   'his/her/its shovel'⁵
        b. kíndə-ʃe̱   'his/her/its bread'
            érgə-ʃe̱   'his/her/its boy'
            yrémə-ʃe̱   'his/her/its street'
            ʃóʃə-ʃo̱   'his/her/its spring'
            ʃýrə-ʃø̱   'his/her/its soup'
            kýrtɲə-ʃø̱   'his/her/its iron'

Round harmony does not affect suffixes with underlying /e/ or /a/, as shown in (6).

(6) a. jýksə-ge 'swan (commitative)'
     sør-ge   'milk (commitative)'
  b. lúm-lan   'snow (dat.)'
     kornó-lan 'road (dat.)'

Data bearing on the interaction of round and back harmony are introduced later in this section.

Like back harmony, round harmony in Eastern Meadow Mari shows characteristics compatible with a licensing effect: a word-final syllable, which plausibly serves as weak, undergoes assimilation to a stressed syllable, which is prominent. I propose that round harmony is driven by LICENSE([+round]/σ_{Final}, ó), which penalizes [+round] in a word-final vowel when it is not licensed by the stressed syllable. I posit that the underlying representation of the suffix in (5) is [–ʃo] with a specification for [+round]. Because /e/ and /a/ are unround, they do not participate in the licensing-driven round harmony in word-final position. The round licensing pattern in Eastern Meadow Mari is like that of Classical Mongolian (§5.2.2) in that it can be regarded as a passive licensing system. In passive licensing for [+round], a vowel whose [+round] specification fails to be licensed by a round vowel in licensing position undergoes neutralization to [–round] rather than active assimilation to [–round]. Although treatments as neutralization and active assimilation are both possible, typological trends give reason to suspect that [–round] does not assimilate alone (if ever).

Round licensing seems to have the capacity to operate at a distance because a [+round] specification in a word-final vowel can be licensed by a vowel in a stressed syllable despite an intervening [ə] that does not appear to be rounded. I found no examples in the source where a full vowel occurred between the suffix and a stressed round vowel. I will analyze the representation for [+round] licensing across [ə] as identity licensing. It is also conceivable that [ə] could be analyzed as [+round] in harmony contexts but that it is not perceived as such because of its reduced nature.[6] In the case of back harmony, there is stronger evidence for identity licensing. For purposes of uniformity, I adopt the same strategy for round harmony. The constraint ranking for round harmony in Eastern Meadow Mari will thus be parallel to that for back harmony. The top tier will include the licensing constraint and a positional faithfulness constraint, in this case for the stressed syllable: IDENT-IO-ó(round). The second tier will contain the crisp edge constraint for [round] and IDENT-IO(round). *DUPLICATE(F) will belong in the third tier to allow the possibility of identity licensing across an intervening vowel. The dynamics of these rankings should be clear from the illustrations of back harmony above.

In addition to the circumstances where back and round harmony in Eastern Meadow Mari cause alternations in suffixes, there are situations where harmony between a word-final vowel and the relevant prominent position does not occur. Some of these arise from the nature of the vowel in the licensing position and some depend on the word-final vowel.

Backness harmony is not triggered by [ə] and [a]. In words with one of these vowels in the initial syllable, a non-low suffix vowel can be realized as [e]. Examples are provided in (7a). The examples in (7b) show that the same suffix otherwise shows backness alternations as expected.

(7) a. óʃkəl-ʃk<u>e</u>   'step (illative sg non-poss.)'
        wástər-ʃk<u>e</u>   'maple (illative sg non-poss.)'
     b. kíndə-ʃk<u>e</u>   'bread (illative sg non-poss.)'
        ʃýʃpək-əʃk<u>ø</u> 'nightingale (illative sg non-poss.)'[7]
        kornó-ʃk<u>o</u>   'road (illative sg non-poss.)'

We could wonder whether the reason that backness harmony fails in a form like [wástərʃke] is because there is no mid back unround vowel [ɤ] and [–ʃko] cannot occur in this form because [+round] cannot be licensed in the suffix. However, we will see later that when backness harmony and round licensing conflict, it is backness harmony that is enforced. The vowels in the initial syllable in the forms in (7a) thus seem to be truly inactive as triggers for back harmony.

In agreement with Vaysman (2009), I assume that [ə] lacks features in this language.[8] This will prevent words with [ə] in the initial syllable from satisfying licensing, because the initial syllable has no [back] specification with which the vowel in the final syllable can assimilate. I will assume that the failure of initial syllables containing /a/ to license [+back] in a word-final vowel is a frozen property of the system that stems from the weak contrastive status of [back] in the low vowels. Recall that [æ] might be non-phonemic in the language and it does not occur in word-initial syllables – the very position where [a] does not show activity in back harmony. I will not develop a formal analysis of the non-trigger status of /a/ here, as it would go beyond the primary issues under attention. Nevertheless, a fuller investigation is warranted on the status of a contrast among the low vowels and its implications for their representation.

The realization of the mid suffix vowel as [e] in (7a) can be attributed to the activity of the licensing constraint for [+round]. Let us suppose that the underlying form of the suffix is /–ʃko/. If the suffix's [back] specification cannot be licensed when the initial syllable contains [ə] or [a], then the licensing constraint for [back] will be violated no matter what the realization of the suffix. If the suffix were realized as [–ʃko] or [–ʃkø] and the stressed vowel was unrounded, as in the forms in (7a), it would also violate the [+round] licensing constraint. However, if the suffix were realized as [–ʃke], it would obey the licensing constraint for [+round]. This realization is captured by the ranking LICENSE([+round]/σ$_{Final}$, ó) >> IDENT-IO(back), IDENT-IO(round), illustrated in (8). The back licensing constraint is included here to show that it is violated by any of the suffix realizations when the initial vowel is [ə], so it does not influence the output form of the suffix. The winning candidate in (a) obeys the round licensing constraint at the cost of faithfulness to [round] and [back]. Alternative realizations of the suffix that preserve its rounding are ruled out by the licensing constraint for [+round]. I assume that undominated constraints not shown in this tableau prevent the final full vowel from being realized as back unrounded [ɤ] or from being reduced to featureless [ə].

(8)   Front realization of a mid back suffix vowel when back licensing cannot be satisfied and stressed vowel is unround

/əʃkəl-ʃko/	LICENSE ([bk]/σ$_{Final}$, σ$_{Initial}$)	LICENSE ([+round]/σ$_{Final}$, ó)	IDENT (back)	IDENT (round)
☞ a. óʃkəlʃke	*		*	*
b. óʃkəlʃko	*	*!		
c. óʃkəlʃkø	*	*!	*	

This analysis predicts that when the vowel in the initial syllable does not trigger back harmony, the suffix vowel will be realized as back and round if the stressed vowel is round. This prediction is borne out by the example in (9) with /a/ in the initial syllable and /u/ in the stressed syllable.

(9)   kaβún-əʃko 'pumpkin (illative sg non-poss.)'

The application of the constraint hierarchy to the form in (9) is demonstrated in (10). Note that [ə] in this form is epenthetic. As in (8), all realizations for the full suffix vowel violate the licensing constraint for [back] because the initial syllable contains a vowel that does not license [back] in a vowel in the final syllable. Unlike the form in (8), licensing for [+round] can be achieved in this word, because the stressed vowel is round. This leaves the selection to the IDENT constraints, even though they are at the bottom of the hierarchy of constraints under consideration. These favor the faithful output in (a) over unfaithful forms with front suffix vowels in (b) and (c).

(10) Back realization of a mid back suffix vowel when stressed vowel is round

/kaβun-ʃko/	LICENSE ([bk]/σ_Final, σ_Initial)	LICENSE ([+round]/ σ_Final, ó)	IDENT (back)	IDENT (round)
☞ a. kaβún-əʃko	*			
b. kaβún-əʃke	*		*(!)	*(!)
c. kaβún-əʃkø	*		*!	

An example like that in (9) points to the activity of a licensing effect for both values of [back]. If [−back] in a word-final syllable were not subject to an initial syllable licensing restriction, attested suffix vowel [o] would be less harmonic than [ø] or [e], because the latter two vowels would obey licensing for [+back].

Whereas /a/ and /ə/ in the initial syllable fail to trigger back harmony, /e/ in a final syllable fails to undergo licensing-driven back harmony. This is illustrated by the forms in (11).

(11) a. lúm-ge 'snow (commitative)' cf. íj-ge 'year (commitative)'
olmá-ge 'apple (commitative)' keŋéʒ-ge 'summer (commitative)'
b. ʃudó-de 'hay (caritive sg)' cf. ímnə-de⁹ 'horse (caritive sg)'
óləк-de 'meadow (caritive sg)' jýk-te¹⁰ 'voice (caritive sg)'

I suggest that the undominated markedness constraint *ɤ prevents suffix /e/ from alternating in licensing-driven back harmony. This constraint must dominate the licensing constraint for [back]. In addition, an underlying unround vowel cannot become round to satisfy the back licensing constraint. This is prevented by the local conjunction *[+round] &_l IDENT-IO(round), which penalizes derived round vowels. The conjunction also dominates the back licensing constraint. The ranking is demonstrated in (12). Candidate (b) satisfies the back licensing constraint by displaying back harmony with the vowel in the initial syllable, but it is ruled out by *ɤ. Candidate (c) shows back and round harmony with the stem vowel, but it violates the local conjunction because the suffix vowel acquires a [+round] specification. The winner is (a), which is faithful but violates the back licensing constraint. The failure of /e/ to undergo back harmony is thus a circumstance where licensing is blocked when the resulting vowel quality would be marked, a way in which the comparative markedness of vowel qualities is expected to potentially interact with licensing.

156 *Identity licensing*

(12)   Absence of back harmony for suffix /e/

/lum-ge/	*[+round] &$_l$ IDENT(round)	*ɤ	LICENSE ([bk]/σ$_{Final}$, σ$_{Initial}$)	IDENT (back)	IDENT (round)
☞ a. lúm-ge			*		
b. lúm-gɤ		*!		*	
c. lúm-go	*!			*	*

Notice that the local conjunction in (12) will not interfere with the round harmony pattern, because the round licensing constraint is for [+round] only and the suffixes in which it produces alternations are underlyingly round. Round licensing can thus drive suffix vowels that are round to become unround, but not the reverse, in conformity with the conjunction.

A final matter of interest is that when the back and round licensing constraints conflict, the back licensing constraint wins. The situation for a conflict arises when an underlying mid round suffix vowel is affixed to a stem with a back vowel in the initial syllable and an unround vowel in the stressed syllable. If both licensing constraints were satisfied, the resulting suffix vowel would be [ɤ], a vowel that does not occur in Eastern Meadow Mari. In this situation, the suffix vowel is realized as [o] in compliance with the back licensing constraint, rather than [e] in compliance with the round licensing constraint. Examples are shown in (13a). The example in (13b) with a front round vowel in the initial syllable and a front unround suffix confirms that the rounding in the suffix vowel in (13a) is present because of the [+back] quality of the vowel in the initial syllable, not its rounding. Other examples of licensing-driven back and round alternations in this suffix were provided in (7b).

(13)   a. ojləmáʃ-əʃk<u>o</u>   'story (illative sg non-poss.)'
          kuguʒán-əʃk<u>o</u>   'princess (illative sg non-poss.)'
       b. køgørtʃén-əʃk<u>e</u> 'dove (illative sg non-poss.)'

The tableau in (14) shows the workings of the constraint hierarchy when a conflict exists between the two licensing constraints. The hierarchy has been elaborated so that the back licensing constraint dominates the licensing constraint for [+round]. The input considered in (14) has a back vowel in the initial syllable, an unround vowel in the syllable that is assigned stress, and a round suffix vowel. The second [ə] is epenthetic. Candidate (c) satisfies both licensing constraints by showing harmony with the stressed vowel for [round] and with the initial syllable for [back], but it violates *ɤ. In candidate (b) the suffix

Preserving properties in the licensing position 157

vowel is realized as [e], which conforms with the round licensing constraint but violates the higher-ranked back licensing constraint. The winner is candidate (a), which satisfies the back licensing constraint at the cost of the licensing constraint for [+round].

(14)   Back harmony wins out over round harmony

/ojləmaʃ-ʃko/	*[+rd]&$_l$ ID-(rd)	*ɤ	LICENSE ([bk]/σ$_{Fin}$, σ$_{Init}$)	LICENSE ([+rd]/σ$_{Fin}$, ó)	IDENT (back)	IDENT (round)
☞ a. ojləmáʃəʃko				*		
b. ojləmáʃəʃke		*!			*	*
c. ojləmáʃəʃkɤ		*!				*

A summary of some basic rankings for the analysis of Eastern Meadow Mari is given in (15).

(15)   Some main constraint interactions in Eastern Meadow Mari
   a. IDENT-σ$_{Initial}$(back), LICENSE([back]/σ$_{Final}$, σ$_{Initial}$) >> CRISPEDGE([back], σ), IDENT-IO(back)
       Licensing for [back] in the final syllable by the initial syllable drives harmony that is controlled by the initial syllable.
   b. IDENT-ó(round), LICENSE([+round]/σ$_{Final}$, ó) >> CRISPEDGE([round], σ), IDENT-IO(round)
       Licensing harmony for [+round] in the final syllable by the stressed syllable drives harmony that is controlled by the stressed syllable.
   c. LICENSE([back]/σ$_{Final}$, σ$_{Initial}$) >> IDENT-IO(back) >> *DUPLICATE(F)
       Identity licensing for [back] occurs across word-medial syllables with a value for [back] that is opposite to the harmonizing value. (An analogous ranking structure is posited to obtain identity licensing for [+round].)
   d. *[+round] &$_l$ IDENT-IO(round), *ɤ >> LICENSE([back]/σ$_{Final}$, σ$_{Initial}$)
       Suffix /e/ does not undergo back harmony.
   e. LICENSE([back]/σ$_{Final}$, σ$_{Initial}$) >> LICENSE([+round]/σ$_{Final}$, ó)
       In case of a conflict, back harmony wins out over round harmony.
   f. LICENSE([+round]/σ$_{Final}$, ó) >> IDENT-IO(back), IDENT-IO(round)
       A mid back suffix is realized as front when the stressed vowel is unround (provided that back licensing cannot be satisfied).

To conclude, the analysis developed here posits that the Eastern Meadow Mari vowel harmony patterns under study are driven by prominence-based licensing. This offers a natural explanation of the assimilation at a distance between a strong trigger and a weak target. Back harmony in Eastern Meadow Mari shows evidence of identity licensing across intervening full and reduced vowels. The operation of licensing for [+round] across reduced vowels is also suggestive that identity licensing is available for [+round]. The licensing position is the initial syllable for [back] and the stressed syllable for [+round]. This indicates that different patterns within the same language can have distinct positions that serve as prominent. In each of the harmony patterns, the licensing position is the same as the position that controls assimilation.

The absence of a back vowel counterpart of /e/ in the vowel inventory causes effects whereby the system avoids generating marked [ɤ]. When the initial syllable cannot license the [back] specification for word-final /o/ (for example, because the vowel in the initial syllable itself lacks a [back] specification), then the suffix vowel shows the most faithful realization that satisfies the round licensing constraint and *ɤ. Thus, it is realized as [o] if the stressed syllable is round, but [e] if it is unround. The constraint *ɤ also blocks underlying /e/ from alternating in back harmony. In addition, the absence of [ɤ] creates a situation where the licensing constraints for [back] and [+round] conflict. When the initial syllable contains a back vowel and the stressed vowel is unround, *ɤ blocks simultaneous satisfaction of both licensing constraints. In this circumstance, the back licensing constraint causes an underlying /o/ suffix vowel to be realized as [o], rather than as [e] in compliance with round licensing. The complexities of the system are thus addressed within a licensing account sensitive to vowel markedness and positional prominence, and the pattern shows evidence that licensing for one feature can be prioritized over another.

6.3 Preservation of vowel properties in the licensing position and non-licensing position

This section examines an identity licensing pattern where properties of the vowel in the licensing position and the non-licensing position are preserved. The case under study is a metaphony in the dialect of Francavilla Fontana where the [+high] quality of certain unstressed vowels comes to also be expressed in a stressed syllable. Of interest in this system is how the combined demands of licensing, vowel markedness, and preservation of [ATR] specifications are solved by fission of underlying [−ATR] mid vowels in the licensing position to form a diphthong. The diphthong supplies two vowels in the stressed syllable to realize characteristics of the original vowel in that position and satisfy licensing for [+high]. Identity licensing is evidenced by assimilation for [+high] across an intervening non-high vowel in the diphthong. The failure of the non-licensing position to capitulate is caused by an independent phenomenon of raising in unstressed syllables, which prevents a high unstressed vowel from lowering.

FRANCAVILLA FONTANA. The Romance dialect spoken in Francavilla Fontana displays a metaphony pattern that is comprehensively studied by Calabrese (1985, 1988), and also examined in work by Sluyters (1988). The data are drawn from these sources, who rely on Ribezzo (1912), Jaberg and Jud (1928–1940) (AIS), Rohlfs (1956–1961, 1966), and Mancarella (1974). According to Calabrese, the language contrasts seven vowels underlyingly /i e ɛ a ɔ o u/. However, he reports that there is no 'superficial distinction' for [ATR] among the mid vowels, with there being neutralization of surface mid vowels to [ɛ] and [ɔ] (1985: 133f.). Sluyters concurs that oppositions between e/ɛ and o/ɔ are relevant for this dialect (1988: 162). I follow these analysts in the assumption that seven vowels contrast underlyingly. In the context of this analysis, this means that the grammar is sensitive to the value of the [ATR] specification of mid vowels in the input and that speakers acquire lexical representations that encode distinctive [ATR] values for mid vowels.

The dialect of Francavilla Fontana shows a metaphony that raises stressed /e o/ to [i u] preceding a high vowel, as illustrated in (16a). When an underlying [−ATR] mid vowel occupies the syllable that is assigned stress, a diphthong of rising sonority is formed in metaphonic contexts: /ɛ/ → [ié], /ɔ/ → [ué], as in (16b). These cases indicate preservation of the [−ATR] quality in the stressed syllable in metaphony. Although mid vowels are given as [−ATR] in all surface forms here, the underlying quality of stressed mid vowels is notated at the left for clarity. These values are based on those given by Calabrese and Sluyters, who actually represent the ATR contrast in mid vowels in the forms as they provide them.

(16)   Fem. sg   Masc. sg   Masc pl
     a. /e/   frédd-a   frídd-u   frídd-i   'cold (adj.)'
     /o/   pilós-a   pilús-u   pilús-i   'hairy (adj.)'
     b. /ɛ/[11]   lént-a   liént-u   liént-i   'slow (adj.)'
     /ɔ/   gróss-a   gruéss-u   gruéss-i   'big (adj.)'

The low vowel /a/ is not affected by metaphony, as seen in (17a). Compare the form in (17b), which shows metaphonic diphthongization conditioned by the same suffix in a similar structure.

(17)   a. /andʒil-i/   [ándʒili]   'angel (pl)'
        b. /mɛtik-i/   [miétitʃi]   'physician (pl)'

Metaphony in Francavilla Fontana is restricted to specific morphemes, all of which contain high vowels. Certain other inflections with a high vowel, such as the feminine plural (18a) and high post-tonic stem vowels (18b), do not trigger metaphony (Sluyters 1988, cf. Calabrese 1985).[12]

(18) a. Fem. pl
    /e/   frédd-i   'cold (adj)'
    /o/   pilós-i   'hairy (adj)'
    /ɛ/   lɛ́nt-i   'slow (adj)'
    /ɔ/   grɔ́ss-i   'big (adj)'
  b. High post-tonic stem vowels
    /e/   fémmin-a   'woman'
    /e/   dumɛ́nik-a 'Sunday'
    /ɛ/   pɛ́rsik-a   'peach'
    /ɔ/   tɔ́lik-a   'bean'

In this pattern, the high quality of an unstressed vowel finds realization in a stressed syllable either by assimilation or the formation of a diphthong with a high vocoid component. Like other cases of metaphony considered earlier, I postulate that the metaphony of Francavilla Fontana is driven by a prominence-based licensing constraint, in this case lexically indexed to specific morphemes. The licensing constraint for this dialect is LICENSE$_L$([+high], σ́).

I will argue that identity licensing is involved in forms that show diphthongization, but I deal first with the raising of underlying mid [+ATR] vowels /e o/ to [i u]. It is reasonable to suppose that these vowels show indirect licensing of [+high]. As is by now familiar, this is achieved by ranking LICENSE$_L$([+high], σ́) over IDENT-IO(high) and CRISPEDGE([high], σ).

The control of assimilation by the unstressed vowel finds an explanation in a general unstressed vowel raising phenomenon in the language, which raises all mid vowels to high, as illustrated by alternations in (19). Note that the first person singular suffix is not one that triggers metaphony. The second example in (19) shows that unstressed /a/ does not undergo raising.

(19)   1sg pres. ind.   1pl pres. ind.
    /e/   kréu   kritiámu   'believe'
    /o/   kanósku   kanuʃʃímu   'know'
    /ɛ/   sɛ́ntu   sintímu   'feel'
    /ɔ/   trɔ́u   truámu   'find'

Unstressed vowel raising can be attributed to a constraint that minimizes the sonority of a syllable nucleus in an unstressed syllable, as assumed for central Veneto in §5.3. The active constraint in Francavilla Fontana penalizes a syllable nucleus whose sonority exceeds that of a high vowel: *σ̆/a,ɛ•ɔ,e•o. This constraint dominates IDENT-IO(high) and IDENT-IO(ATR) to induce raising. The ranking *[−ATR, +high] >> IDENT-IO(ATR) prevents /ɛ ɔ/ from raising to [ɪ ʊ]. To prevent unstressed /a/ from raising, I assume that IDENT-IO(low) dominates *σ̆/a,ɛ•ɔ,e•o. The workings of the hierarchy with a [−ATR] mid vowel is demonstrated in (20). Candidate (c), with a mid unstressed vowel, is ruled out by the sonority minimization constraint. Candidate (b), which raises /ɔ/ to [ʊ], violates *[−ATR, +high]. The winner is (a), which obeys the two markedness constraints at the cost of faithfulness for [high] and [ATR].

(20) Raising of unstressed mid vowels
*[−ATR, +high], *ŏ/a,ɛ•ɔ,e•o >> IDENT-IO(high), IDENT-IO(ATR)

/trɔamu/	*[−ATR, +high]	*ŏ/a,ɛ•ɔ,e•o	IDENT(high)	IDENT(ATR)
☞ a. truámu			*	*
b. trʊámu	*!		*	
c. trɔámu		*!		

The satisfaction of the licensing constraint by assimilation of the stressed vowel to an unstressed high vowel is obtained by ranking the licensing constraint and the sonority minimization constraint for unstressed syllables over the positional faithfulness constraint IDENT-IO-ó(high), as shown in (21). The input in this tableau includes a morpheme that contains [+high] and is indexed to the licensing constraint. Candidate (b) is faithful to specifications for [high], but it violates the licensing constraint. Candidate (c) solves the licensing problem by eliminating [+high] in the unstressed vowel; however, this incurs a violation of the sonority minimization constraint, which prohibits non-high unstressed vowels. In candidates (b) and (c), the output neutralization of surface mid vowels to [−ATR] is shown, although its analysis is not included here.[13] The selected output is (a), which shows raising in the stressed syllable, the result of assimilation from the high unstressed vowel to produce an indirect licensing configuration.

(21) Licensing achieved by assimilation of the stressed syllable to an unstressed syllable
LICENSE$_L$([+high], ó), *ŏ/a,ɛ•ɔ,e•o >> IDENT-IO-ó(high)

/fredd-u$_L$/	LICENSE$_L$([+high], ó)	*ŏ/a,ɛ•ɔ,e•o	IDENT-ó(high)	IDENT(high)
☞ a. fríddu			*	*
b. frɛ́ddu	*!			
c. frɛ́ddɔ		*!		*

The control of assimilation by an unstressed syllable in Francavilla Fontana is thus similar to the treatment of central Veneto: it is caused by avoidance of unstressed non-high vowels. In Francavilla Fontana, the avoidance is also evidenced in the raising of mid vowels to high in unstressed syllables, whereas in central Veneto, the avoidance is restricted to unstressed non-high vowels that are derived through lowering. Importantly, this strategy for control does not single out an unstressed syllable as a position of prominence, rather it singles out this context for prominence reduction.

I turn now to the formation of diphthongs in metaphony of [−ATR] mid vowels. Calabrese (1985, 1988) has argued that the diphthongization is caused by avoidance of [−ATR] high vowels, using the constraint *[−ATR, +high]. Diphthongization permits [+high] in an unstressed vowel to be licensed by the stressed syllable while preserving the [−ATR] feature of the original stressed vowel. Of particular interest for our purposes is that the resulting licensing configuration involves identity licensing: [+high] is not present during the mid vowel that intervenes between the high vowel in the diphthong and the final high vowel.

The correspondence relations that I assume for prominence-based licensing involving diphthongs in Francavilla Fontana are shown in (22). Only the segments concerned are shown here. With inspiration from Calabrese's analysis (but differences in specifics), I assume that the diphthong is produced by fission of the vowel in the stressed syllable. In the fission structure there is not vowel insertion, rather both vowels in the diphthong in the output are correspondents of the mid [−ATR] vowel in the input. Both output correspondents belong to the stressed syllable. The high vowel in the diphthong satisfies licensing through duplication of the [+high] specification in the following unstressed syllable. The mid vowel in the diphthong realizes the [−high] and [−ATR] values of the underlying mid [−ATR] vowel. Because the input vowel for the stressed syllable has multiple correspondents in the output, the existential statement of faithfulness for features, $\exists$-IDENT-IO(F), becomes relevant, as discussed in the analysis of Jaqaru in §5.3. $\exists$-IDENT-IO(ATR) requires that the specification for [ATR] for an input segment be identical in *some* output correspondent of that segment. [ɛ] in the diphthongs in (22) satisfies this constraint for input /ɛ/ and /ɔ/. Likewise for [−high]. I will deal later in this section with the realization of vowel color features for /ɔ/ in the high vowel in the diphthong and the preference for diphthongs that are rising in sonority.

(22)   Diphthong licensing structure

        Input: /ɛ$_1$ - i$_2$/   /ɔ$_1$ - i$_2$/

        Output: [i$_1$ɛ́$_1$ - i$_2$]   [u$_1$ɛ́$_1$ - i$_2$]
                      | | | | | |
                [+hi]$_i$ [−hi] [+hi]$_i$ [+hi]$_i$ [−hi] [+hi]$_i$

The constraints that drive the diphthongization structure in (22) are LICENSE$_L$([+high], ó), *[−ATR, +high], and ∃-IDENT-IO(ATR). Together, these constraints will dominate a constraint that prohibits diphthongs, *DIPHTHONG. Rosenthall (1997a, b) defines this constraint as prohibiting tautosyllabic moras that dominate separate vocalic root nodes. Fission of the mid vowel violates INTEGRITY-IO (see §5.3), which must be dominated by the same constraints that dominate *DIPHTHONG. These constraints also dominate *DUPLICATE(F), which is violated in the diphthong licensing structure.

The ranking is illustrated for metaphony with /ɛ/ in (23). The candidate in (b) is faithful but violates the licensing constraint. Candidate (c) achieves licensing by raising /ɛ/ to [ɪ], which violates *[−ATR, +high]. Candidate (d) instead achieves licensing by raising /ɛ/ to [i], which incurs a violation of ∃-IDENT(ATR). The optimal form, in (a), satisfies each of these constraints, at the cost of feature duplication, introducing a diphthong, and multiple segment correspondence. The representation assumed for this form is along the lines shown in (22).

(23) Diphthongization in metaphony with /ɛ/
      LICENSE$_L$([+high], ó), *[−ATR, +high], ∃-IDENT(ATR) >> *DUPL(F),
      *DIPH, INTEGRITY

/lɛnt-u$_L$/	LIC$_L$([+hi], ó)	*[−ATR, +hi]	∃-ID(ATR)	*DUPL(F)	*DIPH	INTEG
☞ a. liéntu				*	*	*
b. lɛ́ntu	*!					
c. lɪ́ntu		*!				
d. líntu			*!			

Note that ∃-IDENT(ATR) is intended to be the same identity constraint for [ATR] as the one shown in the tableau in (20): IDENT(ATR). The existential characterization of the constraint did not figure there, because none of the vowels had undergone fission – each had only a single output correspondent. It was established in (20) that *[−ATR, +high] dominates ∃-IDENT(ATR), which is represented in (23) with a solid line separating the columns for these constraints; however, there is no evidence that ∃-IDENT(ATR) is dominated by the licensing constraint. The tableau in (20) also established that *ŏ/a,ɛ •ɔ,e•o dominates ∃-IDENT(ATR). The posited ranking of ∃-IDENT(ATR) over *DIPH in (23) does not interfere with the prior results with respect to raising of unstressed vowels, because diphthongization of a non-high unstressed vowel would not serve to avoid a violation of *ŏ/a,ɛ•ɔ,e•o.

The diphthongization solution for licensing is only invoked for underlying mid [−ATR] vowels. In the case of /e/ or /o/, there is instead raising at the cost of IDENT-IO-ó(high). This indicates that IDENT-IO-ó(high) is dominated by at least one of the constraints violated by the diphthong licensing structure: *DUPLICATE(F), *DIPHTHONG or INTEGRITY-IO. Thus, diphthongization is driven strictly by avoidance of a high [−ATR] vowel and preservation of identity for [ATR], problems that arise just with raising of /ɛ/ or /ɔ/. This case is consistent with the prediction (§2.7) that where a particular marked vowel could result (here [−ATR, +high]), a licensing-driven phenomenon may show a departure from the regular pattern to circumvent it, i.e. diphthongization instead of the usual monophthongal raising.

We may wonder why the diphthong that is formed is one that is rising in sonority rather than one that is falling. For example, a diphthong [ɛ́i] could satisfy licensing without necessitating identity licensing, because the high vowel in the diphthong could be considered articulatorily adjacent to an unstressed high vowel in the following syllable. The reason seems to be part of a wider tendency in Francavilla Fontana to avoid diphthongs that are falling in sonority. Sluyters (1988: 178) observes that all derived diphthongs in Francavilla Fontana are rising in sonority, including ones derived through vocalization of [l]. This suggests that a constraint (or set of constraints) that prohibits falling diphthongs dominates *DUPLICATE(F) in the hierarchy for this language.[14]

The last issue that I address in the metaphony of Francavilla Fontana is the formation of the diphthong [uɛ́] for /ɔ/. A diphthong that we might have expected in this circumstance is [iɔ́], which is otherwise attested in the language, e.g. [iɔ́nnula] 'catapult'. However, a diphthong that is the output of metaphony could show different characteristics from an underlying diphthong, because it is composed of two vowels that are each in correspondence with the same mid [−ATR] vowel of the input. Given the assumption of existential faithfulness, realization for the features of /ɔ/ could be satisfied by either of its output correspondents. As Struijke's study of existential faithfulness effects has shown, this opens the possibility of an emergence of the unmarked effect (McCarthy and Prince 1994b) in an output correspondent through 'distributing diphthongization,' where the input vowel divides its features among the vowels in the diphthong. I propose that this is what happens in the realization of a diphthong that results from metaphony. Specifically, it avoids violation of *[+round, −high], a constraint that reflects the markedness of non-high round vowels. The effect is illustrated in (24). The optimal candidate in (a) does not display a non-high round vowel. Observe that ∃-IDENT(round) and ∃-IDENT(back) are satisfied in this form, because the [+round] and [+back] qualities of /ɔ/ are realized in its output correspondent [u]. The output correspondent [ɛ] for /ɔ/ will satisfy the IDENT constraints for [ATR] and [high]. An alternative form, in (b), in which the diphthong contains [ɔ], violates *[+round, −high]. Notice that the formation of [ué] rather than [ió] in metaphony affecting /ɔ/ supports a fission analysis of diphthongization. Because the high vocoid in the diphthong is a correspondent of /ɔ/, its realization of the round quality of /ɔ/ has a natural explanation that would be missing if the high vowel were instead epenthetic.

(24) The emergence of the unmarked in [ué]

/grɔ₁ss-i_L/	∃-IDENT(round)	∃-IDENT(back)	*[+round, −high]
☞ a. gru₁ɛ́₁ssi			
b. gri₁ɔ́₁ssi			*!

In Struijke's approach to distributing diphthongization, the breaking of the qualities of /ɔ/ over two segments violates 'surface faithfulness' constraints which require that fissioned segments be identical (IDENT[F]_ΣΣ). The constraints in question, for [back] and [round], would be dominated by *[+round, −high] in the grammar of Francavilla Fontana. The diphthongs [iɛ] and [uɛ] will also violate surface faithfulness constraints for [high] and [ATR] as a result of the constraints that drive diphthongization in licensing (see [23]), which must dominate them.

To review, some main constraint interactions are given in (25).

(25) Some main constraint interactions in the dialect of Francavilla Fontana
  a. *[−ATR, +high], *ŏ/a,ɛ•ɔ,e•o >> IDENT-IO(high), IDENT-IO(ATR)
      Unstressed mid vowels raise to high [+ATR] vowels.
  b. LICENSE_L([+high], ó), *ŏ/a,ɛ•ɔ,e•o >> IDENT-IO-ó(high)
      Licensing-driven height harmony is resolved by raising in the stressed syllable that is controlled by the unstressed syllable.
  c. LICENSE_L([+high], ó), *[−ATR, +high], ∃-IDENT(ATR) >> INTEGRITY-IO, *DIPHTHONG
      Metaphony of [−ATR] target vowels causes diphthongization.
  d. LICENSE_L([+high], ó), *[−ATR, +high], ∃-IDENT(ATR) >> *DUPLICATE(F)
      An identity licensing configuration can occur when metaphonic diphthongs are formed.

To summarize, diphthongization in the metaphony of Francavilla Fontana presents a striking resolution of the tension between satisfying licensing, faithfulness, and segmental markedness. Rather than the simple raising seen with

/e, o/, this scenario arises when the stressed syllable contains underlying mid [−ATR] vowels, because high [−ATR] vowels are avoided. The formation of a diphthong through vowel fission causes the height features of a mid [−ATR] vowel to be preserved while also allowing [+high] in an unstressed syllable to be licensed by its expression in the stressed syllable. This solution is implemented using an identity licensing configuration. In the case of /ɔ/, the fission structure opens an opportunity for reduction of vocalic markedness, which results in a distribution of features in the diphthong that avoids a non-high round vowel.

6.4 Assimilation at a distance in the licensing position

This section continues on the theme of licensing-driven harmony patterns that can show assimilation at a distance through identity licensing configurations. The focus here is on systems where the licensing position undergoes assimilation. Additional topics are addressed in the context of individual patterns.

In several of the patterns under study in this section, identity licensing effects are seen in proparoxytones, that is, words where stress is assigned to the antepenultimate syllable. When the licensing position is the stressed syllable and the vowel that is subject to licensing is in a word-final syllable, the medial post-tonic vowel presents an opportunity for transparency effects. Three cases of this kind are examined. In Lena, licensing-driven harmony from a final high vowel for height features, [+high] and [−low], can operate across a transparent low vowel in the penultimate syllable of a proparoxytone. In Ascrea, harmony for height features of a final high vowel can operate across a transparent mid vowel in the penultimate syllable of a proparoxytone. Eastern Andalusian is a case where variation is seen between identity licensing and indirect licensing in proparoxytones. In Eastern Andalusian, harmony for [−ATR] can optionally operate across a transparent [+ATR] mid vowel in the penult of a proparoxytone. A variant form is attested with a [−ATR] mid vowel in the penult.

The case of non-primary umlaut in Old High German is also discussed in this section. This pattern has been considered a phonological extension of primary umlaut in OHG, which was discussed in chapter 5. For non-primary umlaut, identity licensing is motivated for licensing-driven assimilation for [−back] across consonant clusters that blocked primary umlaut.

A characteristic common to the systems discussed in this section is that some constraint that produces control of assimilation by the vowel in non-licensing position dominates positional faithfulness for the licensing position. In some of the language patterns examined here, trigger control is produced by faithfulness to the word-final syllable. This is the case for Lena, Ascrea, and Eastern Andalusian. Like Jaqaru, discussed in chapter 5, these systems show some form of strength in two distinct positions: one position shows faithfulness and the other serves as prominent for licensing. In the case of trigger control for non-primary umlaut in OHG, an identity constraint for high front unround vocoids is employed, following the approach for primary umlaut in §5.3.

LENA. The metaphony pattern of the central Asturian variety of Lena was introduced in §3.4.2, where the restriction of triggers to vowels that show a height contrast in inflectional suffixes was discussed. I return to this pattern here to focus on the capacity of the pattern to show assimilation at a distance (Neira Martínez 1955, 1983; Hualde 1989, 1998).

In Lena's metaphony system, a high vowel in an inflectional suffix causes raising of stressed /e o/ to [i u] respectively (26a) and /a/ to [e] (26b). Unsurprisingly, if the stressed vowel is high outside of a raising environment, it undergoes no change when followed by a high vowel suffix (26c). The high vowel trigger for raising in the examples in (26) is /u/ for reasons identified in §3.4.2. These will be recalled presently.

(26) a. féa   fíu   'ugly (f sg/m sg)'
       kabéθos   kabíθu   'head (m pl/m sg)'
       fondéro   fondíru   'lower (mass/m sg)'
       néna   nínu   'child (f sg/m sg)'
       reónda   reúndu   'round (f sg/m sg)'
       kókos   kúku   'worm (m pl/m sg)'
       tsóbos   tsúbu   'wolf (m pl/m sg)'
       flóʃo   flúʃu   'lazy, loose (mass/m sg)'
       kóʃa   kúʃu   'cripple (f sg/m sg)'
     b. tsamárga   tsamérgu   'muddy lake (f sg/m sg)'
        blánko   blénku   'white (mass/m sg)'
        gátos   gétu   'cat (m pl/m sg)'
        ʃána   ʃénu   'diligent worker (f sg/m sg)'
     c. kúbos   kúbu   'pail (m pl/m sg)'
        kabríta   kabrítu   'kid, young goat (f sg/m sg)'

Of particular interest is that in Lena proparoxytones, a non-high vowel in the penult is transparent to metaphony, i.e. it does not undergo raising but does not prevent raising in the stressed syllable, as shown in (27).[15] Observe that for these examples, the expected quality for the intervening vowel /a/ is [e] if it underwent stepwise raising as it does in metaphony or [i] if it displayed the full set of height features that transmitted to the stressed syllable in the first two examples. Both of these vowel qualities are attested in unstressed syllables of Lena stems. This suggests that the reported absence of raising in these vowels is not a transcription error.[16] These cases are therefore consistent with an identity licensing configuration.

(27)   trwébanos   trwíbanu   'beehive (m pl/m sg)'
       burwébanos burwíbanu   'wild strawberry (m pl/m sg)'
       kándanos   kéndanu   'dry branch (m pl/m sg)'
       páʃara   péʃaru   'bird (f sg/m sg)'

The role of morphology in Lena's metaphony merits further attention. That raising is triggered only by vowels in inflectional suffixes is confirmed by the examples in (28).

(28)   a. silikútiku / silikótikos / silikótika   'suffering from silicosis (m sg/m pl/f sg)'
       b. abáxu   'down'
       c. fjéru   'iron'   (cf. Castilian [jero])
       d. jélsu   'plaster'   (cf. Castilian [jeso])

In the triplet in (28a), /i/ in the penultimate syllable belongs to the stem. It does not trigger raising in the stressed vowel, as seen in the masculine plural and feminine singular forms; however, it does not interfere with raising triggered by a high vowel suffix in the masculine singular form. Examples in (28b–d) present a high vowel in the final syllable but lack an inflectional suffix (Campos-Astorkiza 2009). These high vowels also do not trigger harmony. Castilian counterparts of (28c–d) suggest that the stressed vowel in these forms has not raised from /a/ to [e].

Further data indicate that raising is not purely morphologically induced by a (masculine) singular count inflection. Masculine singular count forms that end in non-high vowels do not show raising, as seen in (29) (Hualde 1992). Phonological conditioning is therefore evidenced by the occurrence of raising only in the presence of a high vowel.

(29)   fére   'a type of hawk (m sg)'
       tóro   'bull (m sg)'
       boldrégo 'worthless person (m sg)'

Despite the phonological component of Lena's metaphony, the licensing phenomenon is restricted to inflectional suffixes, as demonstrated above. In addition, apparent exceptions exist where a high vowel suffix in a particular form does not trigger raising, e.g. [aseméju] 'resemblance' (cf. [asémejos] pl) (Neira Martínez 1955; Finley 2009). To address these properties of the system, the analysis calls upon a licensing constraint that is indexed to the category of inflectional suffixes. For stems that exceptionally resist harmony, lexically indexed faithfulness constraints will block alteration of height features, following the general strategy of Pater (2009a) (see also Finley 2009: 488). For more on this type of approach, see the analysis of Ascrea later in this section (and see the analysis of Jaqaru in §5.3).

The metaphony system of Lena shows asymmetries that fall in line with a prominence-based licensing phenomenon: the height features of a high vowel ([+high], [−low]) in inflectional suffixes come to also be realized in a stressed vowel. The licensing constraint active in Lena is LICENSE$_L$([HEIGHT]/V$_h$[+high], ǿ). As discussed in §3.4.2, this constraint restricts the scope of licensing to height in high vowels that are minimally contrastive for height. I briefly review some background on this point for Lena. The minimal contrast restriction in the licensing constraint is motivated by the failure of vowels that are non-contrastively high to trigger harmony. Whereas stems show a five-way vowel contrast /i e a o u/, Lena's inflectional suffixes only contrast the vowels /e a o u/. Front /e/ is realized as [i] in some circumstances, but [i] in suffixes does not trigger productive metaphony, while contrastively high [u] does trigger the process. The failure of suffixal /i/ to trigger harmony is illustrated in (30). The form on the right verifies that the stem vowel is underlyingly /e/ – not /a/ raised to [e] by height harmony.

(30)   bént-i 'twenty' cf. bentidós 'twenty-two'

It is not surprising that licensing phenomena could show restrictions to material that is minimally contrastive, since it represents distinctive information that is important for the listener to perceive accurately.

The core ranking for Lena's metaphony is LICENSE$_L$([HEIGHT]/V$_h$[+high], ǿ) >> IDENT-IO(high), IDENT-IO(low) >> *DUPLICATE(F). Because satisfaction of the licensing constraint can cause a feature chain to span more than one syllable, CRISPEDGE([F], σ) constraints for height features will also be dominated by the licensing constraint in Lena. Preservation of height in the suffix vowel rather than the stressed syllable could be attributed to word-final faithfulness, similar to the analysis of Jaqaru (§5.3). The word-final faithfulness constraint and the licensing constraint dominate faithfulness constraints for height features in the stressed syllable.

The tableau in (31) illustrates the core ranking with a form that shows licensing at a distance. The input contains a suffix [−u] indexed to the licensing constraint. Because /u/ is minimally contrastive for height among inflectional morphemes, this vowel is indexed with a subscript 'h' to encode its contrastive status for the height dimension. For illustration of the procedure by which this index is assigned, which occurs prior to candidates' submission to EVAL, see §3.4.2.[17] The winning candidate, in (a), licenses the [−low] specification on the final high vowel through correspondence with a feature in the stressed syllable. This leaves the intervening low vowel unaltered, incurring only one violation of IDENT(low). Multiple correspondence for [−low] causes a violation to be assigned for *DUPLICATE(F). The [+high] specification on the suffix vowel does not become licensed on a stressed vowel that was underlyingly /a/ because of the stepwise raising effect in Lena. This can be analyzed using a local conjunction of IDENT(high) and IDENT(low) that dominates the licensing constraint (Walker 2005; see also §8.3). As a result, the licensing constraint will incur a violation for unlicensed [+high] in the winning candidate. The alternative in (b) satisfies the licensing constraint with respect to [−low] by spreading through the penultimate syllable. Although this avoids a violation of *DUPLICATE(F), the candidate is ruled out by its additional violation of IDENT(low). Candidate (c) loses in the competition because it contains unlicensed instances of both [−low] and [+high].

(31)   Identity licensing in Lena

[−hi] [−hi] [+hi]
  | | |
/paʃ ar- u_L/
  | | |
[+lo] [+lo] [−lo]
	LICENSE$_L$
	([HEIGHT]/V_h[+hi], σ́)
		IDENT(high)
		IDENT(low)
			*DUPLICATE(F)

☞ a. [−hi] [−hi] [+hi]
    | | |
  p é ʃ a r u_h
    | | |
  [−lo]$_i$ [+lo] [−lo]$_i$
	*	*(low)	*

b. [−hi][−hi][+hi]
    | | |
  p é ʃ e r u_h
         ↘↙
         [−lo]
	*	**!(low)	

c. [−hi][−hi][+hi]
    | | |
  p á ʃ a r u_h
    | | |
  [+lo] [+lo] [−lo]
	**!		

The constraint hierarchy for Lena will produce an indirect licensing configuration when stress falls on the penultimate syllable, as in a mapping from /gat–u/ → [getu]. Because a form with penultimate stress lacks a medial post-tonic vowel, satisfaction of *DUPLICATE(F) will favor indirect over identity licensing. See §3.5 for a demonstration with a similar form from the dialect of Ascrea.

Metaphony is not triggered by high suffix vowels that are not minimally contrastive for height or by stem vowels. The application of the analysis to these forms is illustrated in (32). In (32i), /i/ in the penultimate syllable has an index encoding that it is minimally contrastive for height, because it is a stem vowel. However, because the licensing constraint is indexed to inflectional suffixes, this vowel is not subject to licensing. Therefore, the candidate that shows raising in (32ib) incurs a gratuitous violation of faithfulness, and the faithful output in (a) is selected. In (32ii), the final /i/ belongs to an inflectional suffix, and is thereby lexically-indexed to the licensing constraint. However, because inflectional /i/ is not minimally contrastive for height, it is not restricted by licensing, and the selected output is the faithful one.

(32)   Morpheme-specific licensing
In summary, licensing-driven harmony in Lena shows evidence of identity

Input	Output	LICENSE$_L$ ([HEIGHT]/ V_h[+hi], ó)	IDENT(high) IDENT(low)	*DUPL(F)
i. /silikotik-os/	☞ a. silikóti$_h$kos			
	b. silikúti$_h$kos		*!(high)	
ii. /bent-i$_L$/	☞ a. bénti			
	b. bínti		*!(high)	

licensing in assimilation across a transparent /a/ in proparoxytones. It also shows evidence of a licensing pattern whose effects are restricted by morpheme specificity and contrast. The existence of patterns that limit prominence-based licensing to material that functions as contrastive fits with a view of these phenomena as largely perceptually driven.

ASCREA. The Romance dialect of Ascrea displays a pattern of metaphony in which stressed /e o/ raise to [i u] (33a) and stressed /ɛ ɔ/ raise to [e o] (33b) preceding a high suffix vowel (Fanti 1938–1940; Maiden 1991a). Apart from metaphony, Fanti shows the following vowel qualities in stressed syllables [i e ɛ a ɔ o u]. The examples in (33c) show that high vowels can occur in the stressed syllable independent of metaphony.

(33) a. metésse   metíʃʃi   'reap (1sg/2sg impf. subj.)'
          véʃte   víʃtu   'this (f pl/m sg)'
          aésse   aíʃʃi   'have (1sg/2sg impf. subj.)'
          sórda   súrdi   'deaf (f sg/m pl)'
          fjóre   fjúri   'flower (m sg/m pl)'
          prefónna   prefúnnu   'profound (f sg/m sg)'
      b. méto   métu   'reap (1sg/3pl pres. ind.)'
          bbélle   bbélli   'beautiful (f pl/m pl)'
          kapɔ́to   kapóti   'overturn (1sg/2sg pres. ind.)'
          ɔ́ssa   óssu   'bone (pl/sg)'
          mɔ́rtse   mórtsi   'die (3sg/1sg perf.)'
      c. mírʒa   'spleen (f sg)'
          fúme   'smoke (m sg)'

The low vowel does not undergo raising in metaphony, as seen in (34).

(34) mánno   mánni   'send (1sg/2sg pres. ind.)'
      sállo   sállu   'climb (1sg/3pl pres. ind.)'
      krápa   krápi   'goat (f sg/f pl)'

In proparoxytones, a final high vowel can cause raising in the stressed syllable. As shown in (35), a medial post-tonic mid vowel does not hinder metaphonic raising of a mid [−ATR] vowel. The medial vowel does not raise to high in this context as it does in a stressed syllable. Fanti lists further examples of this kind: /ɛ / → [é], mḗdeku, lḗu̯etu, ḗtteru, ʃtḗtteru (1938: 213), /ɔ/ → [ó], sọ́kkoli, nọ́nnetu, ọ́mmenu, kọ́reu̯u, addọ́rmenu, pọ́zzenu (1938: 215). Note that only [i e a o u] occur in unstressed syllables. The status of /a/ in the penult of a proparoxytone is discussed later in this section.

(35) mɔ́rtse   mɔ́rtseru   'die (3sg/3pl perf.)'
      mɔ́re   mɔ́renu   'die (3sg/3pl pres. subj.)'
      pɔ́tte   pɔ́tteru   'to be powerful (3sg/3pl perf.)'

In forms with an underlying mid [+ATR] vowel in a stressed antepenult, a non-high vowel in the penult is transparent to metaphony, as shown in (36). Additional forms of this kind that Fanti characterizes as displaying metaphony are /e/ → [í], domíneku (1938: 211), /o/ → [ú], súreku (1938: 216).

(36) tóreu̯a   túreu̯u   'cloudy (f sg/m sg)'
      fósse   fússeru   'be (3sg/3pl imperf. subj.)'

The failure of the intervening vowel to raise in these forms is not due to a general prohibition on high vowels in a word-medial post-tonic syllable. Numerous forms of this kind are listed by Fanti, e.g. ápi̯le, kírika, móru̯idu,[18] ratíku̯la, štróppu̯le, štítiku, tríi̯ći.

Fanti also provides the pair u̯édoa/u̯ídu̯u 'widow (f)/widower' (1938: 211). These forms suggest that although unstressed /e/ does not raise to [i] (in [36]), an intervening unstressed /o/ could raise to [u] when harmony for [+high] occurs in the stressed syllable. However, given this single pair, it is not clear whether the hiatus between the two unstressed vowels could be relevant. It is possible that unstressed [ou] sequences are independently dispreferred in the language. Further data are needed to assess whether /o/ in the penult of a proparoxytone systematically undergoes raising in metaphony. If it does, then it could be fruitful to consider whether unstressed /o/ raising is driven by an avoidance of non-high round vowels (*[+round, −high]; see e.g. §6.3), whose effect emerges in licensing-driven metaphony.

The examples in (37) show a post-tonic high vowel in the stem that does not trigger raising in a mid vowel in the stressed syllable. On the basis of these forms, I infer that metaphony is only triggered by high vowels that belong to an affix.

(37) mǫ́nika   'nun (f sg)'
      dǫ́mino si fa bbiʃku 'the Lord be with you'

I analyze metaphony in Ascrea as driven by the constraint LICENSE_L([HEIGHT]/[+high], ó), indexed to affixes. Later in this section we will see reason to further distinguish indices for different affixes. As mentioned in §3.4.2, the feature class [HEIGHT] is taken to include [ATR]. This will motivate the raising of mid [−ATR] vowels to [+ATR], even though they do not become [+high]. On the treatment of stepwise raising, see §8.3 where a similar pattern in the Servigliano dialect is analyzed using a conjunction of identity constraints for [high] and [ATR].

Examples like those in (35–36), where mid vowels in an unstressed penult do not raise to high, show the need for material in a weak position to be realized specifically in a prominent position, which enhances it in a robust way. The core analysis for Ascrea was sketched in the illustration of identity licensing in chapter 3. An identity licensing configuration is motivated for examples like those in (36), where assimilation for [+high] bypasses an intervening unstressed mid vowel. The possibility for licensing at a distance arises under the ranking: LICENSE_L([HEIGHT]/[+high], ó) >> IDENT-IO(high) >> *DUPLICATE(F). See §3.5 for tableaux that show the workings of this ranking. Because indirect and identity licensing can occur in Ascrea, CRISPEDGE([HEIGHT], σ) will also be dominated by the licensing constraint. Control of height assimilation by the final vowel could be handled by a word-final faithfulness constraint, IDENT-IO-σ_{Final}(high), that dominates faithfulness for the stressed syllable, adopting a strategy like that employed for Jaqaru in §5.3, and Lena, above.[19]

The metaphony pattern of Ascrea is complicated by morpheme-particular resistance to raising triggered by particular morphemes. Consider the examples in (38). Each of these stems shows metaphony that is caused by high vowels in some metaphony-triggering affixes but they resist metaphony from high vowels in other affixes that were shown to trigger metaphony in other words in (33) and (35–36).

(38) kapǫ́tenu   'overturn (3pl pres. subj.)'   cf. kapóti (2sg pres. subj.)
      mę́tenu   'reap (3pl pres. subj.)'   cf. mę́ti (2sg pres. subj.)
      ųę́denu   'see (3pl pres. subj.)'   cf. ųídi (2sg pres. subj.)

aétti	'have (1sg perf.)'	cf. aíʃti (2sg perf.)
aésseru	'have (3pl imperf. subj.)'	cf. aíʃʃi (2sg imperf. subj.)

These data point to a dual kind of morpheme specificity. Following Pater (2009a), I assume that morpheme-specific blockers can be induced by lexically indexed faithfulness constraints and morpheme-specific triggers can be caused by lexically indexed markedness constraints (see §5.3). For the pattern under study in Ascrea, the faithfulness constraints will be identity constraints for height features and the markedness constraints will be licensing constraints.

I will first illustrate morpheme-specific blocking. Consider the stem /kapɔt-/, which blocks metaphony from the formation [–enu]. An IDENT-IO(ATR) constraint that is lexically indexed to /kapɔt-/, and other stems that behave like it, will dominate the licensing constraint that drives metaphony. The licensing constraint will in turn dominate an IDENT-IO(ATR) constraint that is not lexically indexed to cause licensing-driven harmony from [–enu] for [+ATR] in other stems.

The ranking is illustrated in (39). Recall that the licensing constraint is also lexically indexed. Indices on separate constraints are numbered to indicate that they refer to different sets of morphemes. Both of the inputs in (39) contain a suffix formation that is indexed to the licensing constraint. The formation [–enu] could perhaps be broken down into separate morphological components, but for simplicity, I will not do so here. What is essential is that the element containing the high vowel is indexed to the licensing constraint. The input in (39i) contains a stem that is indexed to the identity constraint for [ATR] that dominates the licensing constraint. This constraint prevents selection of candidate (b), which shows a change from /ɔ/ to [o] in the stressed vowel. The winning output, in (a), is therefore the faithful form. This output incurs two violations with respect to the licensing constraint, one for each of its unlicensed specifications for [+high] and [+ATR] in the high affix vowel. The input in (39ii) differs critically from that in (39i) in that the stem is not indexed to the faithfulness constraint for [ATR] that dominates the licensing constraint. As a result, the licensing constraint holds sway in this form, and the selected output is the one in (39iia), with harmony for [+ATR], rather than the faithful form in (b). As mentioned above, I assume that other constraints not shown here prevent raising of /ɔ/ all the way to [u], so only licensing-driven assimilation for [+ATR] occurs in a vowel that is underlyingly [–ATR].

(39) Morpheme-specific blocking of metaphony (for [ATR])
IDENT-IO(ATR)$_{L1}$ >> LICENSE$_{L2}$([HEIGHT]/[+high], ó) >> IDENT-IO(ATR)

Input	Output	IDENT IO(ATR)$_{L1}$	LICENSE$_{L2}$ ([HEIGHT]/[+hi], ó)	IDENT IO(ATR)
i. /kapɔt$_{L1}$-enu$_{L2}$/	☞ a. kapótenu		**	
	b. kapótenu	*!	*	*
ii. /mɔr-enu$_{L2}$/	☞ a. mórenu		*	*
	b. mɔ́renu		**!	

I turn now to the different 'strengths' of affixes in triggering metaphony. For instance, although the stem /kapɔt-/ blocks metaphony from the third person plural present subjunctive formation [–enu], it undergoes metaphony from the second person singular present subjunctive suffix [–i]. This difference is attributed to separately indexed licensing constraints. The licensing constraint indexed to the set of affixes that includes [–i] dominates the IDENT-IO(ATR) constraint to which [kapɔt-] is indexed. However, this faithfulness constraint dominates the licensing constraint to which [–enu] is indexed.

The hierarchy is illustrated in (40). Both inputs here contain the stem [kapɔt-] indexed to the [ATR] identity constraint that is shown. The identity constraint is ranked between two licensing constraints for height features in a high vowel. The suffix in (40i) is indexed to the higher-ranked licensing constraint, and the suffix in (40ii) is indexed to the lower-ranked one (consistent with the ranking for this constraint below IDENT-IO[ATR]$_{L1}$ in [39]). In (40i), the indexation of the suffix to the higher-ranked licensing constraint drives harmony for [+ATR] in this form. This results in selection of the output in (a), which better satisfies the licensing constraint, rather than the faithful candidate in (b). In (40ii), the suffix is indexed to the lower-ranked licensing constraint. Here, the identity constraint for [ATR] blocks metaphony, resulting in selection of the faithful candidate in (a).

(40) Morpheme-specific triggering of metaphony (for [ATR])
LICENSE$_{L3}$([HEIGHT]/[+high], ó) >> IDENT-IO(ATR) >>
LICENSE$_{L2}$([HEIGHT]/[+high], ó)

Input	Output	LIC$_{L3}$([HEIGHT]/ [+hi], ó)	IDENT-IO (ATR)$_{L1}$	LIC$_{L2}$([HEIGHT]/ [+hi], ó)
i. /kapɔt$_{L1}$-i$_{L3}$/	☞ a. kapóti	*	*	
	b. kapɔ́ti	**!		
ii. /kapɔt$_{L1}$-enu$_{L2}$/	☞ a. kapótenu			**
	b. kapótenu		*!	*

In the case of the stem in /mɔr-enu/, all metaphony-triggering suffixes are expected to cause [ATR] harmony when there is a final high vowel and an underlying mid vowel is assigned stress. As shown in (39), this stem is subject only to the general identity constraint for [ATR].

This approach to morpheme-specific triggering predicts that the hierarchy of relative triggering strengths of suffixes will remain constant across all forms. For example, if [–enu] '3pl pres. subj.' triggers metaphony in a stem, that implies that [–i] '2sg pres. subj.' would as well. The forms that I examined were consistent with this prediction, but a full-scale investigation remains to be undertaken. If there were exceptions to this prediction, it would necessitate complicating the analysis, possibly with lexically listed affixed forms.

Another issue that merits further investigation in the metaphony of Ascrea is whether a systematic relation exists between the strength for triggering metaphony and the phonological structure of a suffix formation. In particular, suffix formations that display an unstressed vowel in the penult might be weaker triggers, as there seem to be more stems that resist metaphony from them. If research on this question establishes that this is indeed a generalization and that it should be considered part of the grammar for this dialect, then there would be reason to account for a preference for harmony in adjacent syllables in the metaphony of Ascrea. In that case, a possibility would be to engage a strategy like that applied to Buchan Scots (§5.2.1) where a crisp edge constraint is employed for a constituent composed of the stressed syllable and an unstressed syllable that immediately follows it. This would be compatible with a foot structure postulated by Flemming (1993), who links metaphony in dialects of Italy to a bisyllabic trochee structure for the primary stress foot. Whether this foot structure is appropriate for the Ascrea dialect would need to be examined.

The last matter for Ascrea that I consider concerns the behavior of proparoxytones with /a/ in the penult. The metaphony pattern in this circumstance is not clear. A suffix formation /–anu/ does not trigger metaphony, e.g. [kapɔ́tanu] (3pl pres. ind.). Given that triggering of metaphony shows morpheme-specific effects in Ascrea, this suffix could be inactive simply because it is not indexed to a licensing constraint that is ranked sufficiently high to cause metaphony. On the other hand, another way to construe the inactivity of /–anu/ is that an intervening /a/ blocks metaphony. Further study of the issue is needed. If /a/ were determined to block harmony, then the prevention of identity licensing across this vowel could perhaps be tied to its greater duration compared to the non-low vowels. Rose (2004) and Rose and Walker (2004) have proposed proximity constraints that restrict the material that can intervene between corresponding elements in an output.[20] Identity licensing across /a/ could be blocked by a proximity constraint that prohibits correspondence across a vowel with the greatest inherent length, namely /a/ (or any intervening material that exceeds /a/).[21]

In closing, licensing-driven harmony in Ascrea shows assimilation for [+high] in the stressed syllable across a transparent mid vowel. If the mid vowel had undergone assimilation for [+high], it would have been expected to be perceived, because high vowels are attested in post-tonic medial position in the language. This supports the availability of identity licensing in the pattern, where a feature in a weak position also finds expression in a prominent position without the participation of an intervening non-prominent vowel. The system in Ascrea offers rich morpheme-specific interactions. These include both morpheme-specific triggering effects and morpheme-specific blocking effects, which point to lexical indexation of markedness and faithfulness constraints in the grammar.

EASTERN ANDALUSIAN. Eastern Andalusian varieties spoken in the province of Granada and neighboring areas display a vowel harmony with a capacity for action-at-a-distance that has been analyzed in terms of prominence-based licensing by Jiménez and Lloret (2007). The analysis discussed in what follows recapitulates their account in the essentials. The data and description are also drawn from Jiménez and Lloret, whose sources were mainly educated people from Granada. For a list of prior studies of the phenomenon, see Jiménez and Lloret (2007) and Hualde (2005: 130, n. 10).

Vowel harmony in Eastern Andalusian involves [−ATR] ([RTR] for Jiménez and Lloret). A final vowel that is [−ATR] causes a stressed non-high vowel to become [−ATR], as shown in (41a). A stressed high vowel does not assimilate for [−ATR] (41b). The vowel phonemes of Eastern Andalusian are /i e a o u/. [−ATR] allophones [i̞ ɛ æ̞ ɔ u̞] occur in final position when a word-final /s/ aspirates and generally deletes (aspiration may be retained in emphatic pronunciations).[22] The transcription of the [−ATR] allophones follows Jiménez and Lloret. These vowels are characterized as more open than their [+ATR] counterparts. [−ATR] high vowels open to a lesser degree relative to their [+ATR] counterparts than non-high vowels. The low vowel also fronts in its /s/-aspiration induced [−ATR] form, but fronting does not occur in low [−ATR] vowels that are the product of harmony.

(41) a. lɛ́ʃɛ 'milks' *leches*
pɛ́sɔ 'weights' *pesos*
mɔ́nɔ 'monkeys' *monos*
bɔ́kæ̞ 'mouths' *bocas*
ǽsæ̞ 'handles' *asas*
tési̞ 'thesis' *tesis*

b. mío 'mine (pl)' *mios*
múʃɔ 'many' *muchos*

Whereas harmony for [−ATR] must proceed to a non-high stressed vowel, pretonic vowels are only optionally affected, as shown in (42).

(42) te̞némɔ ~ te̞némɔ 'we have' *tenemos*
mo̞méntɔ ~ mɔméntɔ 'instants' *momentos*

Of particular interest for the topic under focus is that in a proparoxytone, a non-high stressed vowel undergoes harmony but a medial post-tonic vowel is optionally affected, as shown in (43).

(43) tréβo̞lɛ ~ tréβɔlɛ 'clovers' *tréboles*

The report that both forms in (43) are attested reveals that listeners can perceive whether a medial post-tonic vowel is [−ATR]. The form with a transparent vowel would thus truly seem to be [+ATR], because it is perceptibly distinct from a [−ATR] allophone. Following Jiménez and Lloret, forms like this motivate an identity licensing configuration. That the system is licensing-driven is supported by the targeting of a prominent syllable, which serves to improve the perception of the harmonizing quality.

Although the phenomenon of /s/-aspiration induced [−ATR] allophones of final vowels has intrinsic interest of its own, it is peripheral to the themes under attention here. Jiménez and Lloret analyze the source of [−ATR] as a [spread glottis] feature in /s/. Given findings that phonation types can affect formant frequencies (Gordon and Ladefoged 2001), Jiménez and Lloret propose that [−ATR] essentially serves to realize [spread glottis], that is, it provides a cue for the laryngeal feature.[23] Under this approach, [−ATR] is taken as a means of satisfying faithfulness for the [spread glottis] feature. Jiménez and Lloret analyze this using a Max(LaryngealF) constraint (Gordon 2001).[24] Although further research is needed on the formalization of cue preservation, the same basic idea could be implemented using IDENT-IO-C(LaryngealF) if it were assumed that /s/ and the final vowel coalesce. In that case, the final vowel is in correspondence with both the vowel and /s/, and it can realize features that originate in either segment. In the spirit of Jiménez and Lloret's approach, IDENT-IO-C(LaryngealF) is interpreted as satisfied if a consonant that is [+spread glottis] in the input has an output correspondent that is [−ATR], which serves to cue [+spread glottis]. The restriction to consonants in this constraint could perhaps be obviated if laryngeal features were assumed to be privative (e.g. Lombardi 1994), but that entails shifts in the formalization of featural faithfulness that go beyond the scope of this investigation. I will assume a coalescence representation. It is also compatible with the proposal of Jiménez and Lloret that fronting of the low vowel serves to preserve the coronal feature of /s/. They suggest that fronting of round vowels does not occur because of a constraint that prohibits front round vowels.

In this system, [−ATR] serves as a marked value. This is compatible with the observation of Rice (1999) that the markedness of values correlated with an advanced-versus-retracted tongue root opposition can be variable across languages (independent of context). Notice that the participation of [−ATR] low vowels in this pattern is consistent with the prediction that if material that is less marked is subject to a restriction (i.e. [−ATR] low vowels), its more-marked counterpart will be too ([−ATR] non-low vowels) (see chapter 2). That [−ATR] is singled out in this pattern may be tied to the hypothesized connection between [−ATR] and the realization of a laryngeal feature in this language. Furthermore, the inclusion of low vowels among the triggers for this harmony might be tied to their fronting under /s/-aspiration, which could render them more marked than their non-fronted counterparts.

Jiménez and Lloret propose that [−ATR] harmony that targets the stressed syllable is driven by the licensing constraint, LICENSE([−ATR], ó). They analyze the optional harmony that persists to pretonic vowels in Eastern Andalusian using a harmony-driving constraint that is separate from the stressed syllable licensing constraint. I will not consider that aspect of the pattern here (although I return briefly to the issue in §8.2). The ranking that allows [−ATR] non-high vowels to be derived by licensing-driven harmony but not serve as phonemes is LICENSE([−ATR], ó) >> *[−ATR, −high] >> IDENT-IO(ATR). *[−ATR, +high] dominates the licensing constraint to prevent high vowels from undergoing harmony. Both *[−ATR, +high] and *[−ATR, −high] dominate the [ATR] identity constraint to prevent [−ATR] vowels from surviving in the output in general. [−ATR] vowels of any height can arise through /s/-aspiration in Eastern Andalusian, so the constraints that drive that phenomenon must dominate *[−ATR, +high] and *[−ATR, −high], as Jiménez and Lloret have shown (although with some different specific constraint formulations). I assume that faithfulness for laryngeal features in the correspondent of a final consonant, IDENT-IO-σ_{Final}-C(LaryngealF), is what causes [−ATR] to be retained in the output at the cost of faithfulness in the stressed syllable. This constraint will dominate IDENT-IO-ó(ATR). Because licensing can cause feature chains to span a syllable, the licensing constraint will dominate CRISPEDGE ([−ATR], σ).

Variation in the occurrence of identity licensing versus indirect licensing in the face of a medial post-tonic vowel, as seen in (43), can be analyzed with

180   *Identity licensing*

variable rankings of IDENT-IO(ATR) and *DUPLICATE(F). Selection of variant forms is illustrated in (44–45). In (44), *DUPLICATE(F) dominates IDENT(ATR) to favor indirect licensing in a proparoxytone. The reverse ranking in (45) results in an identity licensing pattern.

(44)   Indirect licensing with a medial post-tonic vowel
        LICENSE([–ATR], ó) >> *DUPLICATE(F) >> IDENT-IO(ATR)

/treβol-es/	LICENSE([–ATR], ó)	*DUPLICATE(F)	IDENT-IO(ATR)
☞ a. trɛ́βɔlɛ			***
b. trɛ́βolɛ		*!	**
c. tré βolɛ	*!		*

(45)   Identity licensing across a medial post-tonic vowel
        LICENSE([–ATR], ó) >> IDENT-IO(ATR) >> *DUPLICATE(F)

/treβol-es/	LICENSE([–ATR], ó)	IDENT-IO(ATR)	*DUPLICATE(F)
☞ a. trɛ́βolɛ		**	*
b. trɛ́βɔlɛ		***!	
c. tré βolɛ	*!	*	

Although their account is slightly different in the specifics, Jiménez and Lloret point out that an approach to variation like this – which uses different rankings – predicts that if there are multiple post-tonic medial vowels, either all of them will undergo [–ATR] harmony or none of them will. They observe that this is borne out, as seen in (46).

(46)   kɔ́mɛtɛlɔ ~ kɔ́mɛtɛlɔ   'eat them (for you)!'   *cómetelos*
        *kɔ́mɛtɛlɔ, kɔ́mɛtɛlɔ

In summary, the Eastern Andalusian case provides important evidence for identity licensing, where harmony operates at a distance between a prominent position and a non-prominent vowel of a particular type. That licensing-driven harmony in this system can skip medial post-tonic vowels is confirmed by the attestation of variants in which the vowels in question undergo the harmony. It therefore shows variation between identity licensing and indirect licensing. Both solutions serve to realize [–ATR] in the stressed vowel, signaling that assimilation by intervening vowels is incidental to the driving force behind the phenomenon, if it occurs at all.

OLD HIGH GERMAN. Distinct from primary umlaut (§5.3), OHG showed a pattern known as non-primary umlaut or secondary umlaut. Non-primary umlaut developed later than primary umlaut, beginning in the middle of the OHG period

(Iverson and Salmons 1996). Iverson and Salmons (2003) consider it to be a generalization or phonological extension of primary umlaut. Non-primary umlaut fronted long and short back vowels in a syllable preceding a high front vocoid. It affected more vowels than primary umlaut, which only caused short /a/ to become [e], and unlike primary umlaut, it did not cause raising together with fronting; thus /a/ fronted to [æ]. Intervening consonant clusters that blocked primary umlaut of /a/ (<hC>, <lC>, <rC>) did not generally block non-primary umlaut (Iverson *et al.* 1994; Iverson and Salmons 1996). Examples of non-primary umlaut in Middle High German (MHG), when it was marked more consistently in the orthography, are given in (47). Recall that stress in OHG was assigned to the word-initial syllable. Data are from Iverson *et al.* (1994) (ID&S), Iverson and Salmons (1996) (I&S) and Holsinger and Salmons (1999) (H&S). Fronted vowels are provided in (47) in the orthography of the sources, but Iverson and Salmons state that non-primary umlaut produced long and short versions of [y ø æ] (1996: 83). In some of the forms in (47) the high vowel has been lost in the development of the word. Presumably this occurred after the stage at which it was present and triggered umlaut (cf. OHG forms). Iverson and Salmons (1996) note that non-primary umlaut appears to be restricted to certain morphological contexts and was somewhat variable in its application. At a later stage of MHG, primary and non-primary umlaut developed into a single morphologically restricted phenomenon.

(47)
	MHG	OHG		Source
	mähti	mahti	'powers'	I&S
	geslähte	gislahti	'race, tribe'	ID&S
	gärwen	garwin or garwen	'prepare (inf.)'	ID&S
	mänlich		'masculine, manly'	I&S
	zähere	zahari	'tears'	I&S
	grüene	gruoni	'green'	H&S
	schœn(e)	skoni	'beautiful'	H&S

Recall from §5.3 that Iverson and Salmons (2003) hypothesized a source of primary umlaut in vowel-to-vowel coarticulation. Blocking environments were analyzed as ones in which an intervening consonant had a vocalic component in its articulation, which prevented extension of the fronting feature (Howell and Salmons 1997). The occurrence of non-primary umlaut across consonant clusters that blocked primary umlaut therefore points to duplication of [−back] – i.e. identity licensing – across such consonants.[25] The licensing constraint is LICENSE([−back]/[+high], ό). Identity licensing is made available by the ranking: LICENSE([−back]/[+high], ό) >> IDENT-IO(back) >> *DUPLICATE(F). The licensing constraint will also dominate CRISPEDGE([back], σ). Control of licensing-driven assimilation by the high vowel can be captured in the same way as for primary umlaut in §5.3. The constraint, IDENT-IO(+high, −back,

–round), reflects the coarticulatory resistance of high, front, unround vowels. It will dominate IDENT-IO-ó(back).

The workings of a licensing ranking of this type were illustrated in discussion of other languages earlier in this section, and will not be repeated here. The non-primary umlaut data are of interest not only because they provide an additional example of identity licensing, where content in a non-prominent position is enhanced by expression in a prominent position across transparent material, but also because they bear on the evolution of a prominence-based licensing pattern. In the earlier primary umlaut stage of OHG, umlaut was restricted to indirect licensing configurations for [−back]. In non-primary umlaut, the pattern had developed so as to permit non-local interactions with identity licensing. In chapter 7 we will see that umlaut in Modern Standard German has evolved so that only direct licensing representations are permitted.

6.5 Non-local effects in review

The preceding sections have centered on licensing-driven patterns that show identity licensing. In each case, evidence has been discussed for an interaction at a distance between a prominent position and a non-prominent one across transparent segment(s). The table in (48) provides a summary of patterns with a faithful vowel in the licensing position and their non-locality effects. Control of harmony in these systems is attributed to a positional faithfulness constraint that references the licensing position. (As before, the notation in constraints for restrictions on features subject to licensing is used here.)

(48)   Identity licensing: Patterns with faithful vowel in licensing position

	Pattern specifics	Non-locality effect	Positional faithfulness constraint	Language
i.	Licensing position = $\sigma_{Initial}$ [F] = [back]/σ_{Final} The vowel in the initial syllable is faithful.	Harmony for [back] across transparent medial vowels, e.g. harmony for [+back] across [e] and for [−back] across [a].	IDENT-IO-$\sigma_{Initial}$(F)	Eastern Meadow Mari
ii.	Licensing position = ǿ [F] = [+round]/σ_{Final} The vowel in the stressed syllable is faithful.	Harmony for [+round] across transparent medial vowels, e.g. [ə]	IDENT-IO-ó(F)	Eastern Meadow Mari

Non-local effects in review   183

The table in (49) summarizes patterns that show a faithful vowel in non-licensing position. As in chapter 5, TRIGGER-FAITH refers to the constraint that determines which vowel is faithful in the system, although notice that it is not always a faithfulness constraint. The pattern seen in Francavilla Fontana is included here because the vowel in the stressed syllable can undergo some metaphony-triggered changes.

(49)   Identity licensing: patterns with faithful vowel in non-licensing position

	Pattern specifics	Non-locality effect	TRIGGER-FAITH	Language
i.	Licensing position = ó [F] = [+high] (in specific inflectional suffixes). The vowel in the unstressed syllable triggers harmony. The vowel in the stressed syllable is faithful for [ATR]. A mid [−ATR] vowel in the stressed syllable undergoes fission into a diphthong.	When diphthongization occurs, assimilation for [+high] occurs across a transparent stressed mid [−ATR] vowel, e.g. [ɛ], [ɔ].	*ă/a,ɛ•ɔ,e•o	Dialect of Francavilla Fontana
ii.	Licensing position = ó [F] = [HEIGHT]/ V_h[+high] (in inflectional suffixes). The vowel in the word-final syllable is faithful.	Harmony for [+high] and [−low] across transparent post-tonic vowels in a non-final syllable, e.g. [a].	IDENT-IO-σ_Final(F)	Dialect of Lena
iii.	Licensing position = ó [F] = [HEIGHT]/[+high] (in specific inflectional suffixes). The vowel in the word-final syllable is faithful.	Harmony for [+high] across transparent post-tonic vowels in a non-final syllable, e.g. [e].	IDENT-IO-σ_Final(high)	Dialect of Ascrea
iv.	Licensing position = ó [F] = [−ATR] The vocalic correspondent of a word-final consonant is faithful.	Harmony for [−ATR] across transparent post-tonic vowels in a non-final syllable, e.g. [o].	IDENT-IO-σ_Final-C(LaryngealF)	Eastern Andalusian dialect
v.	Licensing position = ó [F] = [−back] Vocoids [i j] are faithful.	Harmony for [−back] across transparent consonant clusters with a hypothesized vocalic component, e.g. <hC>, <rC>.	IDENT-IO(+high, −back, −round)	Old High German

As outlined in (48–49), it has been established that identity licensing patterns are attested that involve assimilation with control by the licensing position and assimilation with control by a non-licensing position. For most of the patterns examined in this chapter, the licensing position is the stressed syllable. For [back] licensing in Eastern Meadow Mari, the licensing position is the word-initial syllable.

No cases were discussed with licensing by the root or stem. However, I suspect that these do not constitute significant gaps. It is more probable that the patterns with identity licensing identified thus far are less diverse than those with indirect licensing without identity licensing, because identity licensing patterns are generally less frequent. For instance, whereas all cases of canonical phonological metaphony in Romance include indirect licensing configurations, only some of these also display identity licensing. (By 'canonical phonological metaphony' I mean metaphony patterns in which an overt high vowel trigger is present in the output form.) Various factors may contribute to identity licensing being less common. First, in many languages the forms that could cue an identity licensing configuration are fewer than ones that could cue indirect licensing. For example, in Romance languages, which are members of a family that is rich in licensing-driven assimilation, proparoxytones (words with antepenultimate stress) are usually much less frequent than paroxytones (words with penultimate stress). For example, in Italian, penultimate word stress occurs in about 70–80 percent of lexical items, antepenultimate stress in about 20 percent, and final stress in about 2 percent (Krämer 2009: 161). Since the licensing position in these languages tends to be the stressed syllable, and the content subject to licensing is frequently restricted to post-tonic syllables or inflectional suffixes, proparoxytones are often the forms that provide evidence about whether identity licensing is available. Because words with penultimate stress are informative about indirect licensing, there are more forms to cue the pattern. Not only are proparoxytones less frequent, but also, in some cases only certain intervening vowels are informative about identity licensing. For instance, in a licensing pattern for [+high] in a post-tonic syllable that causes assimilation in the stressed syllable, a proparoxytone with two post-tonic high vowels is compatible with an indirect licensing configuration. Only forms with a [+high] vowel in the final syllable, an underlying non-high vowel in the penult, and a vowel that can undergo raising in the stressed syllable will be revealing about whether identity licensing occurs.

It is possible that patterns that are actively reinforced by fewer words could be more at risk of loss in language change. Of course, many factors can contribute to whether or not a pattern is sustained in the history of a language, but stronger reinforcement could be a factor that supports a pattern's retention. It is also possible that interactions between segments at a distance in a word could be less stable; for instance, they could be harder to learn or sustain. Whether these speculations are supported requires further study. Nevertheless, it is noteworthy that identity licensing in non-primary umlaut of OHG has since evolved into a direct licensing pattern in Modern German (§7.4).

In contrast to patterns that restrict licensing configurations to direct and indirect licensing, systems with identity licensing incur violations of *Duplicate(F) and they may incur violations of proximity constraints for corresponding elements within the output, as mentioned in §6.4 in the analysis of Ascrea. On the other hand, patterns that display indirect licensing but not identity licensing could incur more violations of faithfulness if intervening segments undergo assimilation as a by-product of licensing-driven harmony. If non-local assimilations were less stable, with interactions at a greater distance at higher risk of attrition and loss, that could tend to cause a promotion of some or all proximity constraints in the constraint ranking. This is possibly a common path for language change. Proximity constraints could be independently important in that they will favor licensing by the closest licensor where more than one potential licensor is available. For instance, if a language were to show licensing-driven assimilation for a vowel property by the root, and it displayed identity licensing, then in a polysyllabic root, proximity constraints will select the syllable that is nearest to the vowel that undergoes or triggers assimilation.

6.6 Alternatives

Some alternative approaches to the patterns studied in this chapter, relating to non-local assimilations and morpheme-specific effects, are considered in what follows.

Metrical theories. A metrical approach to metaphony has been proposed for Lena by Hualde (1989). Under this approach, the assimilating feature percolates through metrical foot structure. The metrical mode of spreading is suggested to be available as a parameter setting for a feature-spreading rule, and it offers a possible treatment of non-local metaphony. The rule for Lena involves a metrical operation of spreading within the stress foot. In this account, the last syllable is considered to be extrametrical in proparoxytones but it becomes adjoined to a preceding metrical foot. Metaphony occurs across an intervening vowel because the target parameter setting for the rule is the head, i.e. the stressed syllable. The representation that results from the operation of metaphony is shown in (50) for [trwíbanu] 'beehive (m sg)', with feature association gapped across the intervening syllable.

(50)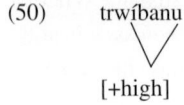

[+high]

By calling upon a gapped representation for feature associations, this approach to non-local interactions is open to the objections raised about such representations in work advocating that shared features or gestures must respect articulatory locality (or feature sharing conceived of as constrained by 'strict segmental locality') (Gafos 1999; Walker 2000a; Ní Chiosáin and Padgett 2001; note also Flemming 1995). Typological arguments have been adduced in support of this stricter view of locality. In addition, it is compatible with a representation of each feature specification as a unitary, continuous element, achieving a closer connection with insights of gesture-based models of speech production (Browman and Goldstein 1986, 1989, 1990). Whereas the feature duplication structure postulated under the generalized prominence-based licensing approach is consistent with that perspective, the assumption of the gapped configuration under the metrical approach is not.

A second point of departure between the metrical approach and the generalized licensing approach concerns assimilation patterns that involve prominent positions other than stressed syllables. The metrical approach handles patterns in which feature spreading is organized around a prosodic head, but it does not address local or non-local assimilation patterns organized around other prominent positions, such as the word-initial syllable or the morphological root or stem (attested in Classical Mongolian, C'Lela, Macuxi, Eastern Meadow Mari, etc.). On the other hand, the licensing approach is capable of handling assimilation patterns that revolve around prominent syllables of various kinds, not just metrically prominent positions, and it treats them as formally similar.

Yet another difference between the metrical and generalized licensing approaches involves addressing processes that involve vowels beyond assimilation alone. The prominence-based licensing approach postulates a common basis for phenomena that circumvent perceptually difficult content that lacks expression in a prominent position. It accommodates processes that accomplish various repairs that achieve direct, indirect and identity licensing, as well as cases of vowel deletion and neutralization (the latter phenomena are discussed chiefly in the next chapter). On the other hand, the metrical approach deals with assimilation phenomena in particular. These points indicate that the theoretical approach of generalized prominence-based licensing is more successful in terms of empirical coverage and explanatory scope.

SEGMENT CORRESPONDENCE. Another approach to assimilation at a distance posits that the harmonizing segments stand in correspondence. This differs from the proposal in this work, where individual features correspond in harmonizing segments at a distance. Analyses of this type for certain vowel harmony patterns have been advanced by Kitto and de Lacy (1999), Krämer (2003), Rhodes (2008), and Walker (2009), involving correspondence between segments in the output. Also, Struijke (2002) has studied phenomena where two or more segments in an output are in correspondence with the same segment in the input – a type of fission. Like feature duplication, representations where harmonizing segments stand in correspondence offer a possible means of obtaining harmony among vowels in non-adjacent syllables.

Whereas segmental correspondence could be appropriate for the phenomena studied in the aforementioned research, it makes faulty predictions for prominence-based licensing phenomena. First, corresponding segments could be expected to assimilate for every property, not just those restricted by the licensing constraint. For example, let us suppose that a language enforces licensing for [−ATR] by the stressed syllable (as in Eastern Andalusian). In circumstances where licensing-driven harmony operates among corresponding segments, a pattern is predicted to be possible where assimilation for other features would occur as well (e.g. for [round] or [high]). Harmony for the other features would be motivated by the IDENT(F) constraints applicable to the correspondence relation between the segments.[26] In other words, once a correspondence relation existed between two vowels in an output, there would be two harmony-driving pressures: the licensing constraint and IDENT(F) constraints enforcing identity between the segments. This predicts that prominence-based licensing patterns could be attested for arbitrary combinations of features, which does not seem to be borne out.

If segment correspondence structures were favored just in the case of identity licensing, along the same lines that feature correspondence is, then a second unwanted prediction arises. Identity licensing is expected to show a greater capacity for assimilation than indirect licensing. This is because in indirect licensing configurations, the only harmony-driving source would be the licensing constraint, which operates over the feature(s) restricted by licensing. In identity licensing, both the licensing constraint and IDENT(F) constraints would be applicable, motivating harmony for all features. I am unaware of any language that shows licensing-driven harmony for more features when assimilation occurs at a distance than when it operates in adjacent syllables.

Bypassing these problematic predictions, the assumption made in this work is that identity licensing is accomplished via correspondence among the feature(s) that are restricted by licensing. Correspondence at the featural level will favor identity for the corresponding features alone, not other features belonging to the same segment. *Duplicate(F) will serve to inhibit correspondence among features, so these relations will only arise when driven by the need to satisfy other constraints, such as licensing. Thus, non-local harmony that is driven by prominence-based licensing is expected to produce assimilation only for the feature(s) that licensing restricts. For these reasons, I conclude that correspondence at the level of features is preferable to segment-level correspondence for licensing-driven harmony.

Morphemic Harmony and morpheme realization. I consider next the morphemic harmony approach (Finley 2009) as it relates to morpheme-specific effects and non-local assimilation in metaphony phenomena. I also touch on another kind of morpheme realization account.

Finley's morphemic harmony analysis of Lena's vowel harmony makes use of morpheme-specific feature correspondence constraints that enforce the realization of a feature in particular positions in the output. Correspondence constraints posited for Lena's pattern enforce correspondence between [αF] of a given morpheme and vowels in two positions: the right edge of the word (R-Anchor-[αF]-Morph) and the stressed vowel (V́-[αF]-Morph). The underlying representation for the masculine singular morpheme is assumed to consist of a suffix vowel and floating features [+high] and [−low]. R-Anchor-[αF]-Morph and V́-[αF]-Morph dominate Ident-IO constraints for [high] and [low] to cause the floating features to be realized through correspondence in the stressed vowel and final vowel (within the parameters of stepwise raising). The Ident constraints dominate O-Contiguity-[αF]-Morph, a constraint that requires the correspondents of [αF] to form a contiguous string. This ranking prevents the penultimate vowel in a proparoxytone from undergoing raising.

The morphemic harmony account is well equipped to handle Lena's morpheme-specific triggering, and it predicts that this morpheme specificity will be limited to the feature(s) that trigger harmony rather than the target position(s) of harmony, as seems to be borne out by attested languages. However, the morphemic feature approach presents drawbacks when considered in the context of the cross-linguistic typology of metaphonic patterns and the theoretical treatment of morpheme-specific phonological phenomena.

Because the constraints that drive metaphony are morpheme-specific correspondence constraints, this approach fails to predict the ubiquitous occurrence of metaphony phenomena elsewhere in Romance where high suffix vowels of multiple morphemes in the language trigger raising in the stressed vowel. For example, in dialects of Italy a metaphonic alternant often occurs (or once occurred) in the masculine singular and plural of Class One nouns and adjectives, the plural of Class Two, the singular of Class Three nouns, and the second singular inflection of verbs, all characterized (in some cases historically) by suffixes with high vowels (Savoia and Maiden 1997). Because morphemic harmony is analyzed as the product of a correspondence relation between particular phonological features of a morpheme and segments in certain positions, it necessitates positing morphemic height features and morpheme-specific feature correspondence constraints for each suffix that triggers harmony. That all of the suffixes in question are [+high] would be an accident in this account.[27]

Another issue concerns the relation between patterns that show morpheme sensitivity and those that do not. Although morphemic harmony has the capacity to handle patterns triggered by the presence of specific morphemes, it is not designed to capture harmonies that are purely phonologically conditioned. The metaphony of central Veneto presents an example of the latter (§5.3). It is triggered by any post-tonic vowel, regardless of its morphological affiliation. A theory that adopts a morphemic feature approach for Lena would be compelled to analyze the metaphony pattern of central Veneto as arising from the activity of different constraints, i.e. not morpheme-specific feature correspondence, and possibly as involving different types of representations, i.e. not floating features. This would treat metaphony in central Veneto as distinct in its driving mechanism and structure from metaphonies that show morpheme sensitivity, which misses an opportunity for generalization.

As an aside, despite the issues presented by a morphemic harmony analysis, floating features as a construct do not necessitate that particular approach, and they show utility in certain other vowel patterns. Floating features can be appropriate, for example, when productive feature change in a prominent position occurs in the presence of certain morphemes or allomorphs without evidence of a segmental origin. Umlaut in Modern Standard German is one such case: floating [−back] feature specifications, present in the representation of particular morphemes, are associated to a stressed vowel in the output. This is analyzed in §7.4 as driven by a single prominence-based licensing constraint that is morpheme specific.[28]

Returning to the different treatment of systems that do not show morpheme sensitivity, notice that this issue would likewise arise for an analysis of Lena that analyzes the driving force as a morpheme realization constraint that requires an affixed stem to be phonologically distinct (in certain ways) from the base stem (Dillon 2004).[29] Indeed, any account that attributes the cause of harmony to the triggering morpheme, rather than analyzing it as a morpheme-specific phonological phenomenon, fails to extend to vowel patterns where the triggering material or trigger control are purely phonologically conditioned (metaphony in central Veneto, [+ATR]-dominant harmony in Lango, etc.).

By comparison, the licensing approach finds a common phonological motivation for metaphonic harmony patterns, regardless of whether they also show morphological conditioning or are purely phonologically conditioned. In addition, together with the lexical indexation approach to morpheme-specific triggering (Pater 2000, 2009a), a single licensing constraint can be responsible for metaphonic harmony triggered by a single morpheme, by several specific morphemes, or by all morphemes, providing a unified analysis for the attested patterns.

Beyond the featural phenomena considered in this work, lexical indexation of constraints captures a wider range of morpheme-specific phonology than morphemic feature correspondence. For example, Pater (2009a) discusses its application to morpheme-specific triggering of syncope in Yine, a phenomenon unlikely to submit to analysis by feature correspondence. Other morpheme-specific triggering that involves constituents other than features are discussed by Pater (2000) and Flack (2007b). There is no reason to expect that morpheme-specific triggering should be tied to featural phenomena alone. If a general approach is already necessary in the theory, another explanation that is particular to features is obviated. Furthermore, lexical indexation of constraints also accommodates phenomena that show morpheme-specific blocking (Pater 2009a, and see analyses of Lena and Ascrea in §6.4).

A final issue to consider is the representations involved in the treatment of harmony among vowels in non-adjacent syllables. The generalized licensing approach and morphemic feature correspondence both obtain harmony across transparent segments by employing a correspondence relation that involves the harmonizing feature(s). In licensing, correspondence is between features in the output, whereas in the case of morphemic features, the correspondence relation is between a morphemic feature in the input and segments in the output. The existence of correspondence between elements at distinct levels of structure (e.g. segments in correspondence with features) does not find significant utility beyond phenomena that involve the association of floating features, and an alternative has been proposed that compels preservation of floating features through input–output correspondence of features (Wolf 2007). This suggests that an account that does without correspondence between separate structural levels is desirable. The generalized licensing approach conceptualizes corresponding elements in an output as an entity known as a *chain*. While applications of this construct are restricted to features in the present work, a concept of 'correspondence chains' for corresponding segments in an output is vital in analyses of consonant harmony (Hansson 2006, 2007a), providing independent motivation.

6.7 Conclusion

This chapter has examined vowel patterns that involve identity licensing configurations. Like systems that show indirect licensing alone, these patterns produce results where a vowel quality in a non-prominent position is also realized in a prominent position. In patterns with identity licensing, vowels can interact at a distance, across transparent material. Such outcomes are expected to be possible within some prominence-based licensing systems, because the licensing requirement centers on expressing a property in a privileged position, without reference to whether that property is realized in a continuous fashion. The licensing positions for patterns discussed in this chapter are the stressed syllable and the word-initial syllable, both of which are expected to have the capacity to serve as prominent. It is predicted that systems that display identity licensing will also have forms with indirect and direct licensing configurations, where applicable, for the material that is subject to licensing, and this is borne out in the patterns examined here. In addition, in cases where a feature specification is subject to licensing in a less marked context (e.g. [−ATR] in low vowels of Eastern Andalusian), this specification is also restricted by licensing in the more marked context ([−ATR] in non-low vowels), as expected.

The phenomena explored include systems that show control by a vowel in the licensing position and ones where a vowel in a non-licensing position wields control. The former systems show the activity of positional faithfulness in the strong licensing position. In the majority of the latter systems studied here, control is due to faithfulness to the final position, which serves as a second context that shows aspects of strength in the word. In OHG, faithfulness with a grounding in coarticulatory strength is responsible for trigger control. In addition, a system in the dialect of Francavilla Fontana was studied where both the licensing and non-licensing positions show active preservation of vowel qualities in certain circumstances, resulting in vowel fission in the licensing position. Markedness in the form of prominence reduction in metrically weak syllables plays a part in trigger control in this language. In none of these cases was faithfulness to the class of non-licensing positions employed, compatible with what could be expected on the basis of their possible weak status.

Another interesting aspect of the Francavilla Fontana case is that it shows how the relative markedness of vowels can influence the solution for licensing. Although prominence-based licensing causes the stressed syllable to raise in the usual case, licensing is achieved by diphthongization instead just when raising would have yielded a particular marked vowel. Another situation is found in Eastern Meadow Mari, where licensing of a vowel quality can be blocked when it would otherwise have generated a marked vowel. This falls in line with the expectation that licensing patterns could show avoidance for forming marked vowel qualities.

A central issue in this chapter concerns non-locality effects in phenomena that present identity licensing. Case studies in this chapter found evidence of harmony across transparent consonants in non-primary umlaut of OHG, across transparent full and reduced vowels in Eastern Meadow Mari, and across posttonic non-high vowels in Lena, Ascrea, and Eastern Andalusian. Each of these last dialects can display the vowel quality that would be expected if the intervening vowel had actually undergone harmony, giving reason to doubt that reports of transparent intervening vowels were due to misperception. Although instrumental studies of the languages in question would be valuable, all of the information available strongly points to the occurrence of non-local harmony in these systems. Eastern Andalusian even shows detectable variation in the quality of an intervening vowel, with variants displaying a transparent vowel or a harmonizing intervening vowel, which lends credence to distinguishing local and non-local harmony in phonological representations.

7 *Direct licensing*

7.1 Introduction

This chapter considers the description and analysis of several prominence-based licensing patterns that involve strictly direct licensing. The solution that direct licensing offers to minimize perceptual difficulty for restricted elements is to realize them only in a prominent licensing position and prevent their appearance elsewhere. This is the key respect in which it differs from indirect and identity licensing, where the material subject to licensing is expressed in both the licensing position and a non-licensing position. Many of the patterns under study in this chapter preserve restricted feature specifications when they arise in a prominent licensing context and eliminate them elsewhere. This is what is expected if faithfulness is enforced for the strong position that serves as the licensor. In other patterns, the features in question, or segments that bear those features, migrate to the licensing position. Here it is expected that some other factor can be identified that is responsible for preserving the material subject to licensing.

From a formal standpoint, a common thread that runs through patterns that show solely direct licensing is the containment of feature chains that are subject to licensing entirely within the licensing position, entailing satisfaction of CRISPEDGE([F], σ). This constraint thus plays an essential role in the majority of analyses in this chapter. The core ranking structure for systems with direct licensing alone is given in (1). The higher stratum contains the licensing constraint, the crisp edge constraint, and the constraint that prohibits feature duplication. In constraints where [F] is a variable, they are assumed to reference the same feature here. Each of the constraints in the higher-ranked stratum is obeyed in a direct licensing configuration. A lower stratum contains some faithfulness constraint.

(1) Core ranking: direct licensing
Stratum n
LICENSE([F], π), CRISPEDGE([F], σ), *DUPLICATE(F)
Stratum $> n$
FAITH

It is not crucial that all of the stratum *n* constraints dominate the faithfulness constraint in question. As discussed in §3.5, strict enforcement of CRISPEDGE([F], σ) will imply satisfaction of *DUPLICATE(F), at least pertaining to vowels in separate syllables. For this reason, the ranking of *DUPLICATE(F) will not figure in the analysis of most of the patterns studied in this chapter. Because direct licensing does not permit elements that are restricted by licensing to occur outside of the licensing position, it presents the opportunity for more diverse interactions with faithfulness constraints than are seen in systems with indirect and identity licensing, where chains span more than one syllable. In the cases studied here, these effects play out in patterns where the licensing constraint dominates one or more of MAX(segment), IDENT(F),[1] UNIFORMITY, and MORPHOLOGICAL-O-CONTIGUITY. The FAITH constraint in the lower-ranked stratum in (1) could be any of these, or possibly another.

Several of the systems studied in this chapter show active effacement of unlicensed material or a static absence of it. Patterns of this kind are examined first. Examples include neutralization in unstressed syllables (in Belarusian and dialects of Italy), static lack of contrast in non-initial syllables or suffixes (in Ola Lamut and Western Asturian dialects), and segment deletion in unstressed syllables (in northern dialects of Modern Greek). Next I turn to systems where elements that are subject to licensing migrate to the licensing position, producing some change in that context. Two scenarios are presented in this chapter. One scenario involves infixation, which shifts a vowel in a weak position into the licensing position, where it forms a diphthong or coalesces with another vowel (in dialects of northern Italy). In another scenario, floating features with values that are subject to licensing become associated with the licensing position (in Modern Standard German and Esimbi). A summary of direct licensing patterns and the domination of a faithfulness constraint in these systems is provided. This is followed by a discussion of alternative approaches to the patterns under study.

7.2 Effacement or deficiency of vowel properties in a non-licensing position

This section deals with direct licensing patterns where properties of the vowel in the licensing position are preserved and a vowel in non-licensing position undergoes effacement or is statically deficient, so that an asymmetric absence of certain contrasts is displayed in a weak context. These patterns are achieved using a core ranking structure like that in (1) where the dominated faithfulness constraint is IDENT(F) or MAX(segment). Where IDENT is dominated, patterns with neutralization of vowel quality in non-licensing position are obtained, either in a static pattern or showing alternations. In systems where MAX(seg) is dominated, vowel deletion occurs.

7.2.1   Vowel neutralization with alternations
This section examines direct licensing patterns that drive neutralization of vowel properties in a non-licensing position without assimilation to a vowel quality in licensing position. The cases under study show evidence of alternations. In Belarusian, licensing for [−high] in a mid vowel by a stressed syllable causes unstressed mid vowels to undergo lowering. Certain dialects of Italy manifest neutralization of post-tonic vowels to [ə]. The dialect of Nova Siri shows reduction of post-tonic vowels in all positions, whereas the dialect of Veroli shows reduction only in post-tonic non-final syllables, exhibiting evidence of word-final faithfulness. The systems under study are obtained by a core ranking structure in which a licensing constraint and a crisp edge constraint dominate one or more IDENT(F) constraints.

BELARUSIAN. Certain patterns of unstressed vowel neutralization have a basis in prominence-based licensing. An example is found in Belarusian (Slavic). Five vowels contrast in stressed syllables [i e a o u]. In unstressed syllables /e o/ lower to [a], as shown in (2) (Krivitskii and Podluzhnyi 1994; Crosswhite 2001, 2004).[2]

(2)   ʃépt   'whisper'   ʃaptátsʲ   'to whisper'
      réki   'rivers'   raká   'river'
      klʲéj   'glue'   klʲajónka   'oil-cloth'
      mʲót   'honey'   mʲadóvi   'honey (adj.)'
      nóɣi   'legs'   naɣá   'leg'
      kól   'pole (nom.)'   kalá   'pole (gen.)'
      vʲósni   'spring (gen.)'   vʲasná   'spring (nom.)'

Crosswhite argues that patterns like this are contrast enhancing, because the resulting inventory in unstressed syllables is well dispersed, consisting of the 'corner' vowels [i a u] (2001: 21). She suggests that the pattern is driven by a constraint requiring that non-peripheral vowels be licensed in stressed positions, which serves to prevent these qualities in unstressed (weak) contexts. Building on her analysis, I propose the following constraint in generalized licensing formalism: LICENSE([−high]/[−low], σ́). This constraint penalizes an unlicensed [−high] specification in a mid vowel.[3] The licensing constraint and IDENT-IO(high) will dominate IDENT-IO(low), IDENT-IO(round), and IDENT-IO(back) to produce the appropriate alternations when stress shifts. This recapitulates Crosswhite's account in the essentials.

196 *Direct licensing*

The tableau in (3) illustrates the ranking. The winning candidates show the mid vowels lowering to /a/ in an unstressed syllable, at the cost of IDENT(low) and IDENT(round) for /o/ in (3i), and IDENT(low) and IDENT(back) for /e/ in (3ii). Alternatives that raise the vowel to high are prevented by IDENT(high), and the faithful candidates are ruled out by the licensing constraint.

(3) Direct licensing causes lowering of mid vowels in an unstressed syllable
LICENSE([–high]/[–low], ó), IDENT(high) >> IDENT(low), IDENT(round), IDENT(back)

Input	Output	LICENSE ([–high]/[–low], ó)	IDENT (high)	IDENT (low)	IDENT (round)	IDENT (back)
i. /kola/	☞ a. kalá			*	*	
	b. kolá	*!				
	c. kulá		*!			
ii. /reka/	☞ a. raká			*		*
	b. reká	*!				
	c. riká		*!			

The failure of unstressed mid vowels to be rescued by sharing [–high] with the stressed syllable is achieved by CRISPEDGE([HEIGHT], σ), which penalizes height features that span a syllable boundary. The crisp edge constraint dominates IDENT(low), IDENT(back) and IDENT(round). The prevention of feature sharing is demonstrated in (4). Both candidates here obey licensing. Candidate (b) obeys all IDENT(F) constraints by sharing [–high] across the mid stressed and unstressed vowels, but it incurs a fatal violation of the crisp edge constraint. The winner satisfies this constraint, but undergoes lowering.

(4) Undominated crisp edge constraint prevents indirect licensing

/mʲodovi/	LICENSE ([–high]/[–low], ó)	CRISPEDGE ([HEIGHT], σ)	IDENT (low)	IDENT (round)	IDENT (back)
☞a. mʲadóvi | [–hi]			*	*	
b. mʲodóvi \ / [–hi]		*!			

As discussed in §2.6, high and mid vowels seem to each present perceptual challenges in unstressed syllables, and there appears to be variable markedness of high and mid vowels across prominence-based licensing vowel patterns. Belarusian is a case that emphasizes avoidance of mid vowel height expressed solely in unstressed syllables. We have seen that it achieves this through direct licensing of [−high] in a mid vowel, with neutralization by lowering in unstressed syllables.

DIALECTS OF ITALY. Several Romance varieties show particularly aggressive reduction of contrast in post-tonic syllables. In the southern Lucanian dialect of Nova Siri, post-tonic vowels generally merge to [ə] (5a), whereas pretonic vowels distinguish /a u ə/ (5b) (Lausberg 1939; Maiden 1995). Vulgar Latin distinguished five vowels in unstressed syllables. Postulated historic forms show the hypothesized diachronic mergers in atonic vowels.

(5) a. fíkətə   < *fíkatu   'liver'
        fúmə   < *fúma   'he smokes'
        préβətə < *prébete   'priest'
     b. natá   < *natáre   'to swim'
        məsurá   < *mesuráre   'to measure'
        suɲɲá   < *soɲɲáre   'to dream'

Stress shift under affixation produces alternations in vowel quality, as illustrated for reduced pretonic vowels in Nova Siri forms in (6).

(6) Infinitive   2sg
     məná   tu mínəsə   'throw'
     ləβá   tu léβəsə   'take away'
     skupá   tu skópəsə   'sweep'

In some cases, contrast reduction specifically affects non-final post-tonic vowels. In the southern Lazio dialect of Veroli, [ə] is the only vowel that may occur in the penultimate syllable of proparoxytones (Vignoli 1925; Canalis 2009). This can produce alternations, as illustrated by the Veroli forms in (7).

(7) máɲɲətə 'eat yourself!'   maɲɲatéllu 'eat it yourself!'

Post-tonic syllables in Romance tend to be phonologically weaker than pretonic syllables. A review of the evidence for this is provided in §8.3. For the Romance dialects described above, I propose that contrast reduction in post-tonic contexts is caused by a constraint that penalizes unlicensed vowel features in post-tonic syllables. The constraint in question is LICENSE([V-FEATURE]/σ$_{\text{post-tonic}}$, ó). I will make the assumption that unstressed [ə] lacks vowel features in these dialects (see also §6.2 on [ə] in Eastern Meadow Mari). Post-tonic vowels thus respond to the licensing constraint by eliminating all vowel features in weak position. This is captured by the ranking: CRISPEDGE([V-FEATURE], σ), LICENSE([V-FEATURE]/σ$_{\text{post-tonic}}$, ó) >> IDENT-IO(V-FEATURE). As in Belarusian, the crisp edge constraint prevents a solution that involves sharing features with the stressed syllable.

The patterns in Nova Siri and Veroli are distinguished by their sensitivity to word-final faithfulness. In Nova Siri, vowel quality is neutralized in unstressed final syllables, indicating that IDENT-IO-σ_{Final}(V-FEATURE) is situated in the ranking alongside non-positional IDENT-IO(V-FEATURE). Veroli, however, shows reduction to [ə] in post-tonic penultimate syllables only. This conforms with a typological prediction made by the constraint set explored in chapter 4 (§4.3). In a pattern where the stressed syllable serves as the licensing position, it is possible that positional faithfulness could be displayed by both a stressed antepenultimate syllable and the word-final syllable (a non-licensing position), while an unstressed penultimate syllable undergoes neutralization. In other words, only the weakest of the post-tonic syllables undergoes effacement. In the Veroli pattern, word-final faithfulness dominates the licensing constraint.

The rankings are contrasted in (8–9). The tableau in (8) illustrates the case of Nova Siri, where all post-tonic vowels are reduced to [ə]. The input given here is the hypothesized historical form. This might not be the underlying form in the present-day language, but it serves to demonstrate the effect of the constraint ranking. Candidate (d) represents a form in which the post-tonic vowels have undergone harmony with the stressed syllable, which violates the top-ranked crisp edge constraint. For this particular input, the undominated status of the crisp edge constraint is not essential, but it would matter if the stressed vowel and a post-tonic vowel were identical in the input, as in (9). Candidates (b) and (c) are ruled out because they each fail to license features in at least one post-tonic vowel. The winner is (a), which satisfies the markedness constraints and violates only the dominated faithfulness constraints. Although vowel reduction incurs multiple marks with respect to IDENT(V-FEATURE), only a single mark is notated for each reduced vowel in the tableaux for ease of interpretation. Likewise, just one mark per offending vowel is notated for the licensing constraint and one for the crisp edge constraint to cover all cross-syllable feature chains.

(8) Nova Siri: word-final faithfulness is not active in the licensing pattern

/fikatu/	CRISPEDGE ([V-FEATURE], σ)	LICENSE ([V-F]/$\sigma_{post-tonic}$, σ́)	IDENT-σ_{Final} (V-FEATURE)	IDENT (V-FEATURE)
☞ a. fíkətə			*	**
b. fíkatu		*!*		
c. fikətu		*!		*
d. fíkiti	*!		*	**

The case of Veroli is shown in (9), where word-final faith is promoted to dominate the licensing constraint. Candidate (b), which neutralizes all posttonic vowels, obeys licensing, but it violates higher-ranked word-final IDENT. Candidates (c–d) obey IDENT constraints, but with different structures. In (d), the second [a] shares its features, represented by '[F]', with the stressed syllable. This violates the crisp edge constraint. In Veroli, the crisp edge constraint need only dominate non-positional IDENT, but the pattern is consistent with it being ranked in the top stratum. In (c), the first and second [a]'s do not share features and the features belong to separate chains. This causes (c) to incur a fatal second violation of the licensing constraint. The winner, in (a), shows reduction just in the penult, resulting in a violation of licensing by features in the final vowel only, as compelled by satisfaction of word-final faithfulness.

(9)   Veroli: word-final faithfulness protects final syllable from reduction

/maɲɲate/	CRISPEDGE ([V-F], σ)	IDENT-σ_{Final} (V-FEATURE)	LICENSE ([V-F]/$\sigma_{post\text{-}tonic}$, ό)	IDENT (V-FEATURE)
☞ a. máɲɲəte			*	*
b. máɲɲətə		*!		**

c. máɲɲate
   | |
  [F]$_i$ [F]$_j$
			**!	

d. máɲɲate
    \ /
    [F]
	*!		*	

The vowel patterns in the Nova Siri and Veroli dialects are thus consistent with a treatment in which all post-tonic syllables are regarded as prosodically weak, as witnessed in many Romance languages. Nevertheless, privilege for the final syllable in the form of word-final faithfulness can intervene to protect vowels in the last syllable from neutralization, as seen in Veroli.

OTHER PATTERNS. *Northern Mantuan dialect.* The northern Mantuan dialect of Italy displays a comparatively rich inventory of vowels in a stressed syllable: [i ɪ y e ø ɛ a ʌ ɔ o u] (Miglio 2005).[4] This inventory is reduced to [i y e a u] in unstressed syllables. In an unstressed syllable, mid vowels raise to high, except for mid unround [−ATR] vowels /ɛ ʌ/, which become [+ATR] [e]. Like Belarusian, the raising suggests the activity of a constraint that penalizes mid vowels that are not licensed by a stressed syllable: LICENSE([−high]/[−low], ό). A different ranking of IDENT(F) constraints for northern Mantuan will obtain the raising outcome rather than lowering of mid vowels seen in Belarusian. As Miglio observes, northern Mantuan unstressed vowel reduction shows a chain shift, which she analyzes in terms of a conjunction of faithfulness constraints (see also §8.3). In concert with the other constraints that she assumes, this prevents raising of mid unround [−ATR] /ɛ ʌ/ to high. The shift of these vowels to [+ATR] points to the activity of a licensing constraint for [−ATR] in non-low vowels: LICENSE([−ATR]/[−low], ó). Another aspect of the vowel distribution in northern Mantuan that involves licensing in multiple contexts will be taken up in §9.2.3.

7.2.2 Static lack of contrast

This section centers on direct licensing patterns that show a static lack of contrast for certain vowel properties in a non-licensing position, without alternations. These systems conform with predictions following from the functional underpinnings for prominence-based licensing, because contrasts are absent in non-prominent positions, that is, contexts expected to present greater perceptual difficulty. In Ola Lamut, prominence-based licensing causes non-high round vowels to be absent in non-initial syllables. In Western Asturian dialects, non-low suffix vowels lack a contrast for height that is found in roots. Like the patterns examined in the preceding section, these systems are analyzed with a ranking in which IDENT(F) is dominated by the licensing and crisp edge constraints. In the case of Western Asturian, the interaction with a Dispersion Theoretic constraint on contrast is also considered.

OLA LAMUT. As introduced in chapter 1, Ola Lamut displays a case of static lack of contrast for rounding. Non-high round vowels [o oː ɔ ɔː] can occur in word-initial syllables, as shown in (10) (Li 1996); however, words with a non-high round vowel in a non-initial syllable are absent.

(10) olək   'lie, deception'   ɔran   'reindeer'
      komərə   'oblong'   bɔlanı   'autumn'
      oːlə-   'to become weak'   ɔːta   'sea wave'
      toːnɲə   'to believe'   ŋɔːmbatı   'white'

Ola Lamut belongs to the Altaic family, which is suffixing. The word-initial syllable is also the root-initial syllable, so no alternations occur in the pattern. The system can be analyzed as involving prominence-based licensing by the initial syllable, a position expected to have the capacity to serve as prominent. The markedness of rounding in non-high vowels is well established. The constraint ranking was demonstrated in §3.5: LICENSE([+round]/[−high], σ$_{Initial}$), CRISPEDGE([round], σ) >> IDENT-IO[round], which causes [+round] in non-high vowels of non-initial syllables to be eliminated.

WESTERN ASTURIAN. Western Asturian dialects (Romance) show an asymmetry in contrast in roots versus inflectional suffixes (Granda: Gutiérrez 1960;

Dyck 1995; Campos-Astorkiza 2009). Whereas roots distinguish five vowels /i e a o u/, only three vowels contrast in inflectional suffixes known as 'desinences.' The three desinential vowels are a front unround non-low vowel, a back round non-low vowel, and /a/. Dyck presents a detailed study supporting the lack of contrast between high and mid vowels in desinences. I review some of the evidence here.

The pronunciation of non-low vowels in suffixes shows considerable variation in the region, ranging from close-mid to open-high. In some locales, the rounded vowel also presents a front open-high rounded variant or a centralized mid back or close-mid back variant. The particular realization often depends on the dialect or phonological context. Some forms are idiosyncratically produced with a particular non-high variant or choice of variants. Individual speakers may vary in their usage of a more open or close vowel. In (11–12), I use the following symbols to represent the subtleties of the vocalic variants characterized by Granda Gutiérrez and Dyck: [i̞ y u̞] represent lowered or 'open' high vowels, [y] being characterized as a 'fronted' variant of the back vowel, [e̝ o̝] represent raised or 'close' mid vowels, and [ö ö̞] represent centralized mid back variants.

The data in (11) illustrate the variable realization of the front vowel. Pronominal and nominal forms in (a–b) show the possibility of variation between a raised mid and lowered high front vowel. Examples in (c) show that certain verbal suffixes from the same region may be realized with a raised mid or lowered high vowel, but without any apparent basis in the phonological context.

(11)   a. Pronominal forms   Locale
            est[i̞]/est[e̝]   'this (m sg)'   General
            es[i̞]/es[e̝]   'that (m sg)'   General
       b. Nominal forms
            [-i̞] ~ [-e̝]   General
       c. Verbal forms (in orthography)
            perdisti   'you (sg) lost'   Salas, Labio
            partiste   'you (sg) left'   Salas, Labio
            perdiestes   'you (pl) lost'   Soto de los Infantes
            partiestis   'you (pl) left'   Soto de los Infantes

Examples of variant pronunciations of the round (and usually back) vowel in desinences for nouns and adjectives are given in (12) from the municipalities of Cangas del Narcea and Salas. Some forms are reported to show variation between a raised mid and lowered high vowel. Others show one of these variants or a fronted or centralized variant. Locales for which particular forms are reported are noted. Glosses are not provided by Granda Gutiérrez. He indicates that these suffixes are masculine, and I infer them to be singular, as his practice is to explicitly indicate plural forms when he provides them, and those forms end in /s/.

(12) a. Cangas del Narcea   Locale
      [u̞]/[o̞] rouc[u̞]/rouc[o̞]   Cibuyo
               chen[u̞]/chen[o̞]   Viliella
               toup[u̞]/toup[o̞]   Villaoril, Jarceley
               muit[u̞]/muit[o̞]   Jarceley, Viliella
      [u̞]   cuerp[u̞]   Jarceley
               ʃueg[u̞]   Jarceley
      [o̞]   pin[o̞]   Villaoril
      [ö̞]   sin[ö̞]   Villaoril
               mal[ö̞]   Viliella
      [y̞]   cordeir[y̞]   Villaoril, Viliella
               corder[y̞]   Jarceley
               cuerp[y̞]   Cibuyo
               friesn[y̞]   Villaoril
      b. Salas
      [u̞]/[o̞] fulech[u̞]/fulech[o̞] Labio, Previdal
               gots[u̞]/gots[o̞]   Previdal
               goch[u̞]/goch[o̞]   Arbodas, Labio, Idarga
               sagart[u̞]/sagart[o̞] Arbodas
      [u̞]   viey[u̞]   Labio
               much[u̞]   Labio
      [o̞]   tod[o̞]   Silvota
               carbay[o̞]   Labio
      [ö̞]   poy[ö̞]   Silvota, Labio
               tod[ö̞]   Labio
               f[ö̞]   Arbodas
      [y̞]   viey[y̞]   Arbodas, Silvota, Idarga
               tod[y̞]   Arbodas
               muit[y̞]   Previdal
               cuerp[y̞]   Previdal

In forms for which there is variation in pronunciation between [i̞]/[e̞] or [u̞]/[o̞], it is possible that there is no [high] specification. These vowels could simply be specified [−low] and lack a mid or high target.[5] Other realizations, which may be conditioned by neighboring segments or otherwise contextually conditioned, or may be idiosyncratic and lexically listed, might have a [−high] or [+high] value specified. However, the distribution of these variants is not contrastive. Thus, like Ola Lamut, this pattern shows a position-sensitive static lack of contrast. In this case, the contrast neutralization is in inflectional affixes.

In analyzing this pattern, I propose that a licensing constraint LICENSE$_L$([+high]/V$_h$, ó) is active in Western Asturian dialects, where the constraint is indexed to the set of desinences. Although the data are compatible with the stem as licensing context, this particular formulation is chosen – with licensing by the stressed syllable – because of its conformity with licensing constraints that are active in other Asturian dialects that show metaphony, for typological reasons discussed below.[6] As discussed in §3.4.2, V$_h$ refers to vowels that bear a contrast coindex for height, that is, vowels that minimally contrast for the dimension of height.

According to the contrast-coindexing algorithm of Campos-Astorkiza (2009), inflectional vowels in Western Asturian dialects will lack an index for the dimension of height. Assuming a systemic approach to contrast, contrast coindexation takes place in candidate outputs (which are candidate languages) to assign indices to segments that minimally contrast along a particular dimension. This function operates on the output of GEN prior to the submission of candidates to EVAL. Assignment of contrast coindices is thus not affected by the language-particular constraint rankings. See the illustration of contrast coindexation for the example of non-contrastive [i] versus [e] in the inflections of Lena in chapter 3.

Assuming that only direct licensing is available, the licensing constraint will drive the lack of a mid-versus-high distinction in desinences of Western Asturian dialects. If a [+high] specification were to produce a contrastive distribution in an unstressed inflection, it would be in violation of this constraint. The lack of a height contrast in the non-low vowels correlates with the lack of metaphony in Western Asturian dialects. Typological studies of Asturian vowel patterns by Dyck (1995) and Campos-Astorkiza (2009) point to a connection between the occurrence of metaphony and the presence of a mid-versus-high height contrast in inflectional vowels. Three patterns are identified, as summarized in (13).

(13)   Inflectional vowel contrasts and presence/absence of metaphony in Asturian varieties

Asturian variety	Inflectional mid/high contrasts	Trigger(s) of metaphony	Examples
Aller (Central Asturian)	/i/-/e/, /u/-/o/	/i/, /u/	Metaphony kúri/kóre 'run (imp./pres.)' kaldíru/kaldéros 'pot (m sg/pl)'

Asturian variety	Inflectional mid/high contrasts	Trigger(s) of metaphony	Examples
Lena (Central Asturian)	/u/-/o/ Not /i/-/e/	/u/	Metaphony tsúbu/tsóbos 'wolf (m sg/pl)' No metaphony matéstis/matémos 'you (pl) killed/we kill'
Western Asturian and Eastern Asturian dialects	None Not /i/-/e/ or /u/-/o/	None	No metaphony est[i]/est[e] 'this (m sg)' chen[u]/chen[o] No gloss (m sg) (examples from Western Asturian)

To obtain this typology, Campos-Astorkiza proposes that metaphony in Asturian dialects is driven by licensing constraints that specifically license height features in vowels that are minimally contrastive for the dimension of height, as already introduced in the analysis of Lena (§3.4.2, §6.4). This predicts exactly the distribution seen in (13): metaphony is triggered by high vowels only when they stand in a minimal contrast with a mid vowel. It thus serves to realize [+high] in a prominent position when this specification is distinctive in nature, a circumstance where its accurate perception by the listener is important.

The licensing constraint will dominate IDENT-IO(high) and a Dispersion Theoretic constraint for height, *MERGE (Padgett 2003), to prevent distinctive [high] specifications in the inflectional vowels of Western Asturian (for background on Dispersion Theory, see Padgett 1997, 2003; Ní Chiosáin and Padgett 2001, 2009; Flemming 2002, 2004; Sanders 2003). Padgett (2003: 57) defines *MERGE as requiring that no word in the output have multiple correspondents in the input. Because we are dealing with contrasts in roots versus inflections, I will consider *MERGE as penalizing any morpheme in the output whose phonological form has multiple correspondents in the input. *MERGE will penalize the merger of height contrasts within a hypothetical input in the output. The ranking, $\text{LICENSE}_\text{L}([+\text{high}]/V_h, \acute{\sigma})$, CRISPEDGE([high], σ) >> IDENT-IO(high), *MERGE, will handle the absence of harmony between the stressed vowel and the inflectional vowel as well as the neutralization of a height contrast in non-low inflectional vowels in Western Asturian. The ranking is illustrated in (14). For purposes of illustration, it is demonstrated with application to a system that contains just mid and high vowels.

In accordance with the assumption that a systemic approach to contrast involves evaluation of candidate languages, each candidate here consists of a set of words. In order to facilitate assessment of violations with respect to *MERGE, input–output correspondence among the phonological forms of morphemes is tracked using numeric indices. The phonological form of each morpheme is assigned a single index in the input, even if it contains multiple segments. Where two numerals are assigned to a root or affix, that segment or string has merged two morphemes from the input. Contrast coindices, represented by alphabetic indices, are present in outputs. These signify the existence of segmental contrasts for particular dimensions (e.g. vowel height, notated by the index 'h'). The outputs considered here consist of languages that contrast up to four inflectional vowels. In order to facilitate focus on the contrasts in inflections, there are just two roots /ped/ and /pid/. To avoid clutter in the candidates, the 'h' index is only marked – where applicable – on suffix vowels. Vowels /e/ and /i/ in roots are contrastive for height in all of the candidates considered, but their contrast coindex is not shown.

In candidate (14a) the input is mapped to a language in which height contrasts among the desinential non-low vowels are absent. In this particular case, the inflectional inventory is realized as [e u], with [e] merging /e/ and /i/, and [u] merging /o/ and /u/. In (14a), [i] could be substituted for [e] and/or [o] for [u] with the same result. Candidate (a) satisfies the licensing constraint, because there are no specifications for [high] in a desinential vowel that minimally contrasts for height; hence the index 'h' is absent in the final vowels in this candidate language. This candidate violates IDENT(high) four times, because of the four output vowels that each have two correspondents in the input with different height. *MERGE is likewise violated four times, twice each for the front vowel suffix and the back vowel suffix.[7,8] Candidates (b) and (c) maintain a two-way height contrast in desinences, but (b) violates the licensing constraint by having unlicensed [+high] in inflectional vowels that minimally contrast for height (in four words), and (c) violates the crisp edge constraint by showing height harmony from a suffix vowel to a stressed stem vowel (in two words). Candidate (c) also incurs two violations of IDENT(high) and *MERGE as a result of the height harmony.

(14) Neutralization of a height contrast in non-low vowels (hypothetical forms)
    LICENSE$_L$([+high]/V$_h$, ó), CRISPEDGE([high], σ) >> IDENT-IO(high), *MERGE

/ped$_1$/, /pid$_2$/ /-i$_3$/, /-e$_4$/, /-u$_5$/, /-o$_6$/	LICENSE$_L$ ([+high]/V$_h$, ó)	CRISPEDGE ([high], σ)	IDENT (high)	*MERGE
☞ a. péd$_1$-u$_{5,6}$ píd$_2$-u$_{5,6}$ péd$_1$-e$_{3,4}$ píd$_2$-e$_{3,4}$			****	****
b. péd$_1$-i$_{3h}$ píd$_2$-i$_{3h}$ péd$_1$-e$_{4h}$ píd$_2$-e$_{4h}$ péd$_1$-u$_{5h}$ píd$_2$-u$_{5h}$ péd$_1$-o$_{6h}$ píd$_2$-o$_{6h}$	*!***			
c. píd$_{1,2}$-i$_{3h}$ péd$_1$-e$_{4h}$ píd$_2$-e$_{4h}$ píd$_{1,2}$-u$_{5h}$ péd$_1$-o$_{6h}$ píd$_2$-o$_{6h}$		*!*	**	**

The specific realization of non-low vowels in the absence of a high-versus-mid contrast will be determined by constraint interaction and possibly non-distinctive lexical specifications for [±high] in some cases. However, a [+high] specification in an inflectional vowel would not be restricted by the licensing constraint, because the vowel does not stand in a minimally contrastive distribution for height, as in (14a). Observe that if the licensing constraint were not restricted to vowels that are minimally contrastive for height, candidate (a) would also violate the licensing constraint (twice), as would any candidate with [+high] realizations of the suffix vowels. This candidate would then be harmonically bounded by one with mid realizations of all suffix vowels. However, the licensing constraint that is sensitive to the contrastive status of [high] instead predicts that suffix vowels may be realized as [+high], provided they do not stand in a contrastive distribution for height. This is compatible with the vowel realizations in Western Asturian dialects. As mentioned above, this constraint is also consistent with the observed correlation between the existence of contrastive height among non-low vowels in suffixes and the occurrence of metaphony in Asturian dialects.

There is much more to be explored in the relation between licensing and contrast. Whether constraints that penalize unlicensed contrastive features in affixes are sufficient to obtain the range of effects involving contrast neutralization within affixes remains to be seen. Also, there are other conceivable ways to drive contrast neutralization in affixes, such as prioritizing root faithfulness. Predictions that come out of the interaction of root faithfulness with contrast-driving constraints versus licensing constraints have yet to be investigated. Despite these unanswered questions, the typology of metaphony and contrast in Asturian points to a relation between contrast and licensing that deserves to be more fully explored in phonological theory.

OTHER PATTERNS. *Modern German*. In German, a wide range of distinctive vowel qualities occurs in roots, but only [ə] and non-distinctive variants occur in monophthongs in inflectional suffixes (Bach 1968; Beckman 1999). This is a pattern that could plausibly be handled by a root-based licensing constraint for vowel features in a pattern that displays direct licensing only.

Valencian dialects. In certain Valencian Catalan varieties, final unstressed /a/ undergoes neutralization to a fixed vowel quality (Jiménez 1998). In the locality of Sueca, final unstressed /a/ is regularly realized as [ɛ]. In Xaló, the same phenomenon is observed with neutralization to [ɔ]. Some examples are as follows, with comparison to the variety spoken in the city of València, where final /a/ is preserved: Sueca: [míɾɛ], [téɾɛ], [kɔ́zɛ]; Xaló: [míɾɔ], [téɾɔ], [kɔ́zɔ]; València: [míɾa] 's/he looks', [téɾa] 'land', [kɔ́za] 'thing'. It is not clear whether this phenomenon produces alternations. It is interesting that [ɛ] and [ɔ] do not otherwise occur in unstressed syllables in these varieties, which indicates that the constraint that causes these vowels to be avoided in an unstressed syllable is overridden by other constraint(s) in this context. I suggest that an overriding constraint is a licensing constraint. The markedness of /a/ in a final unstressed syllable was discussed in §2.6. The final raising could be analyzed as driven by a licensing constraint that penalizes [+low] in a final syllable when it is not realized in a stressed syllable.

Tamil. In Tamil, short round vowels are restricted to the initial stressed syllable. The facts in question are drawn from Beckman (1999), who relies chiefly on the description of Christdas (1988) of a dialect spoken in the Kanniyakumari district. In the initial syllable, short vowel allophones are [i ɛ a ɔ u]. In non-initial syllables /a/ is realized as [ɜ], /i/ as [ɪ], and /u/ as [ʊ]. (Underlying short mid vowels do not occur outside of the initial syllable.) The absence of round short vowels in a non-initial syllable could be considered as a direct licensing pattern that penalizes a [+round] specification in a short vowel that is not licensed by a stressed syllable (or, alternatively, an initial syllable) (cf. Barnes 2006).

Chumash. In Chumash, roots display the vowels [i ɨ u e o a], but prefixes usually contain only peripheral vowels [i a u] (Applegate 1971; Steriade 1995b). Following Steriade, this distribution could be attributed to the effect of a licensing constraint that penalizes non-peripheral vowels that are not licensed by the root. She suggests that non-peripheral vowels are perceptually disadvantaged because they are not well dispersed. Consistent with a licensing-based analysis – as Steriade points out – non-peripheral vowels in Chumash can occur in prefixes just when they are the product of harmony from the root, i.e. when they are licensed by the root. Whether a licensing constraint is also what drives harmony with the root requires further consideration, but either way, the licensing constraint would provide an account for the lack of non-peripheral vowels in prefixes in the absence of harmony.

7.2.3 Vowel deletion

In this section, I turn to a pattern in which prominence-based licensing drives deletion. In northern dialects of Modern Greek, a vowel that would otherwise bear unlicensed material is deleted in an unstressed syllable. This offers a solution to reducing perceptual difficulty that eliminates the offending segment rather than altering its content or augmenting its exposure. This pattern is obtained with a ranking structure in which a licensing constraint dominates MAX(segment).

NORTHERN DIALECTS OF MODERN GREEK. In northern dialects of Modern Greek, underlying high vowels delete when they are unstressed and occur between consonants or between a consonant and a word boundary (Joseph 1990, cf. Sakellariades 1985). Examples from the dialect of northern Euboea are given in (15) (from Sakellariades). Notice that /i/ becomes [j] when adjacent to a vowel.

(15) /mi̱sos/   [msós]   'half'
      /mi̱kros/   [mkrós]   'small'
      /eti̱ma/   [étma]   'ready'
      /psi̱xi/   [psxí]   'soul'
      /xeri̱/   [xér]   'hand'
      /alevri̱/   [alévr]   'flour'
      /sku̱likia/ [sklíkja] 'worms'
      /ku̱dunia/   [kdúnja]   'bells'
      /du̱lia/   [dljá]   'work'

Joseph (1990: 5, n. 3) notes that the underlying forms that Sakellariades posits are either based on historical antecedent forms or a comparison with the standard variety. He confirms the existence of synchronic alternations, illustrated by the pair in (16). As a separate issue, notice that the final vowel fails to delete in the first form. This is addressed later in this section.

(16) Northern dialects   Standard Modern Greek
      pí̱n-a-mi   'we were drinking'   píname
      é-pṉ-a   'I was drinking'   épina

Deletion is blocked when it would form a consonant cluster that is illicit in the language (17) (Sakellariades 1985: 112, n. 2).

(17) /skifta/   [skiftá]   *[skftá]   'stoopingly'
      /pnigmena/   [pnigména] *[pngména]   'drowned'

This pattern of vowel deletion can be handled by prominence-based licensing. It eliminates material that can serve as marked (a high vowel) in a non-prominent position. The constraint is LICENSE([+high], ǿ). Unlike cases that satisfy licensing by altering feature specifications, the constraint is enforced in the northern dialects of Greek by deleting segments that contain a [+high] specification that would not be licensed. The ranking that drives deletion is CRISPEDGE([high], σ), IDENT-IO(high), LICENSE([+high], ǿ) >> MAX-IO(segment).

The licensing analysis is illustrated in (18). The hypothesized input contains two high vowels. In the winning candidate, (a), the unstressed high vowel is deleted, violating MAX(seg). Candidate (d), which lowers the unstressed vowel from [+high] to [–high], is ruled out by IDENT(high). Candidates (b) and (c) obey IDENT(high). In (c), [+high] is not shared across the two syllables and the [+high] features belong to separate chains. This incurs a fatal violation of the licensing constraint. Candidate (b) displays indirect licensing for [+high], but this outcome is ruled out by the crisp edge constraint.

(18) Licensing-driven vowel deletion
      CRISPEDGE([high], σ), IDENT-IO(high), LICENSE([+high], ǿ) >> MAX-IO(segment)

/psixi/	CRISPEDGE ([high], σ)	IDENT (high)	LICENSE ([+high], ǿ)	MAX(seg)
☞ a. psxí				*
b. psixí \\/ [+hi]	*!			
c. psixí | | [+hi]$_i$ [+hi]$_j$			*!	
d. psexí		*!		

Deletion is blocked when it would cause an unsyllabifiable consonant cluster. I will refer to the constraint(s) that govern possible consonant clusters in the language with the cover constraint 'SYLLSTRUC.' When deletion does not occur, licensing is violated. This indicates that SYLLSTRUC, IDENT(high) and CRISPEDGE([high], σ) dominate the licensing constraint. The cumulative ranking is shown in (19). The winning output is the faithful candidate in (a), which violates licensing. Constraints in the top stratum of the hierarchy prevent alternatives that obey licensing. Candidate (b) deletes the unstressed high vowel, but forms a cluster that violates SYLLSTRUC. Candidate (c) retains the vowel but lowers it to mid, violating IDENT(high). Candidate (d) displays indirect licensing by the unstressed vowel undergoing harmony with the stressed vowel. This violates both the crisp edge constraint and IDENT(high). Notice that harmony with the stressed vowel can be prevented by IDENT(high) alone in this particular form. However, indirect licensing in words where the unstressed and stressed vowel are both underlyingly [+high] would not violate IDENT(high), e.g. hypothetical /skifti/ → [skiftí], and see (18). In such cases, the crisp edge constraint will be crucial to prevent indirect licensing, i.e. shared [+high] across vowels.

(19)   Vowel deletion is blocked when it would create a cluster that cannot be syllabified
        SYLLSTRUC, CRISPEDGE([high], σ), IDENT(high) >> LIC([+high], ó), >> MAX(seg)

/skifta/	SYLLSTRUC	CRISPEDGE ([high], σ)	IDENT (high)	LICENSE ([+high], ó)	MAX(seg)
☞ a. skiftá				*	
b. skftá	*!				*
c. skeftá			*!		
d. skaftá		*(!)	*(!)		

Another candidate [stá] that satisfies licensing and SYLLSTRUC by deleting the high vowel as well as neighboring consonants could be prevented by a MAX constraint for consonants that dominates the licensing constraint (MAX-C, e.g. McCarthy 1999).

In addition to deletion being blocked by constraints on syllable structure, deletion does not occur for a set of high vowels that Sakellariades analyzes as underlying mid vowels that raise to high in unstressed syllables. This is illustrated in (20) along with Sakellariades' hypothesized underlying forms. The final vowel that fails to delete in the first form in (16) [pínami] also falls in this category. Note that it is produced as a mid vowel in the standard variety [píname].

(20)   /kremidia/   [krimídja]   'onions'
        /mesimeri/   [mismér]   'noon'
        /xorafi/   [xuráf]   'farm'
        /foni/   [funí]   'voice'

Given that the underlying forms that Sakellariades assumes appear to be based on historical and comparative evidence, it is not clear whether there is any synchronic evidence that the vowels that resist deletion in (20) are actually mid in northern dialects of Greek. If there were, then the absence of raising in these forms would constitute a case of counterfeeding derivational opacity. It could be handled by a theoretical mechanism designed to encompass such phenomena (see e.g. McCarthy 2007b for discussion). Alternatively, if direct evidence for underlying mid vowels in these cases were lacking, they could be analyzed as segmental exceptions (e.g. Temkin Martinez 2010), where the segments in question are indexed to a faithfulness constraint that dominates the licensing constraint responsible for deletion. Which approach is most suitable for these dialects is left open for further research.

OTHER PATTERNS. *Awajún*. The Jivaroan language, Awajún, also known as Aguaruna, shows a pattern of deletion of unstressed vowels (Payne 1990; McCarthy 2008a). McCarthy proposes that the deletion is driven by a constraint *V-PLACE$_{weak}$, which is violated by a place-bearing vowel that occurs in a metrically weak position. McCarthy identifies such contexts as the non-head syllable of a disyllabic foot and a syllable that is immediately dominated by the word node. This constraint could be recast as a licensing constraint that penalizes unlicensed vowel features that occur in metrically weak contexts. If the licensing constraint dominated MAX-IO(seg), it would drive vowel deletion. See McCarthy (2008a) for a complete description and analysis of the pattern.

SUMMARY. In closing §7.2, let us recall the primary results. The direct licensing patterns examined to this point resolve unlicensed elements by eliminating them in a weak position, either as witnessed in alternating forms or as a static generalization over the structure of the lexicon. Two scenarios have been considered. In one, a vowel that bears an unlicensed feature (sometimes hypothetically) undergoes a change in identity so that the licensing constraint is obeyed. In some cases, the pattern is actively neutralizing, e.g. showing alternations under stress shift, and in others a simple lack of contrast results, e.g. in affix vowels. This type of pattern arises under the domination of IDENT in the core ranking structure. In a second scenario, a vowel containing a feature that would be penalized by the licensing constraint undergoes deletion. This resolution comes about in a situation where MAX(seg) is the faithfulness constraint that is dominated in the core ranking structure. A uniting outcome in these systems is that certain material is absent in non-prominent contexts, and the preserved material is that which originates in the prominent licensing position.

Ligurian infixation causes the final high vowel to belong not just to the stressed syllable, but to its head nuclear mora, thus attracting the marked structure in question to a locus of prominence within a stressed syllable. It coalesces to form a monophthong ([ɛ e]) or it forms a diphthong with nuclear [i] ([u̯í]). I suggest that this is driven by a licensing constraint like that for Piedmontese dialects but with the licensing position being μ́, which is the head mora of the stressed syllable.

When coalescence occurs, it violates UNIFORMITY-IO, in (26) (McCarthy and Prince 1995). In addition, identity constraints for height features in the stressed syllable are violated. The licensing constraint must therefore dominate these constraints.

(26) UNIFORMITY-IO:
 'No element of the output has multiple correspondents in the input.'
 Let x, y ∈ Input and z ∈ Output
 If x is in correspondence with z and y is in correspondence with z, then x = y.

CRISPEDGE([V-FEATURE], σ) will prevent a harmony solution for licensing. I assume it is in the top stratum of the hierarchy.

The hierarchy for infixing coalescence in Ligurian dialects is shown in (27). The input considered here consists of a stem and suffix /–i/. Subscript numerals are used to track the correspondence relations for the vowels. Candidate (b), the faithful form, and candidate (c), which shows harmony, are ruled out by licensing and crisp edge constraints, respectively. Three violations of IDENT-IO-σ́ (HEIGHT) are tallied for candidate (c) for changes in specification for [high], [low], and [ATR] in the mapping from /a/ → [i]. (On the class of height features, see §3.4.2.) Candidate (d), which forms the diphthong [ai̯], also violates the licensing constraint, because the inflectional high vowel is not dominated by the head mora of the stressed syllable. The winner is candidate (a), which coalesces the stem vowel and the inflectional vowel in the stressed syllable to achieve direct licensing. This incurs a violation of UNIFORMITY. It also incurs three violations of IDENT-σ́(HEIGHT), two for high /i/ mapping to non-high [–ATR] [ɛ] and one for low /a/ mapping to non-low [ɛ]. I assume that MAX(segment), not shown here, is situated in the top stratum to prevent vowel deletion, e.g. /ka₁n-i₂/ → *[ka₁n]. Likewise in this stratum, the local conjunction *ŏ/a,e•o &$_l$ IDENT-IO(high), which penalizes high vowels that lower to [–high] in an unstressed syllable, will block /kan-i/ → [kán-e] (see §5.3 on central Veneto for application).

(27)   Licensing-driven vowel coalescence
         LICENSE$_L$([V-F]/[+high], ή), CRISPEDGE([V-F], σ) >> UNIFORMITY, IDENT-
         IO-ό(HEIGHT)

/ka$_1$n-i$_2$/	LICENSE$_L$ ([V-FEATURE]/ [+hi], ή)	CRISPEDGE ([V-Feature], σ)	UNIFORMITY	IDENT-ό (HEIGHT)
☞ a. kɛ$_{12}$ŋ			*	***
b. ka$_1$ni$_2$	*!			
c. ki$_1$ni$_2$		*!		***
d. ka$_1$i̯$_2$ŋ	*!			

The coalesced vowel's realization as a mid vowel will come about through the rankings IDENT-IO-ό(high) >> *[+high] >> *[−high], and IDENT-IO-ό(low) >> *[+low] >> *[−low]. Because the identity constraints dominate the featural markedness constraints, vowels with either feature value will normally be preserved when they occur in the stressed syllable in the output. When a high and low vowel coalesce, it is not possible to obey the IDENT constraints, so the markedness constraints *[+high] and *[+low] will decide the coalesced vowel's height.[13]

When the stem vowel is [u], the licensing constraint can be obeyed by forming the diphthong [u̯i], which obeys UNIFORMITY, favoring it over a coalesced form [y]. This kind of option is not available when the stem vowel is /a/, since diphthongs in which the low vowel forms a glide are dispreferred (*[a̯i]). Because Ligurian dialects have the capacity to form diphthongs in infixation for particular vowel combinations, MORPH-O-CONTIG will also be dominated by the licensing constraint and the crisp edge constraint in the hierarchy, as in the Piedmontese dialects.

OTHER PATTERNS. Similar patterns of metathesis are discussed by Blevins and Garrett (1998, 2004). They label such phenomena "compensatory metathesis" and hypothesize a diachronic phonetic origin: "a vowel at the edge of the phonological domain undergoes phonetic weakening in quality or duration, with compensation for this weakening by anticipatory or perseverative coarticulation of the original vowel quality in stressed position" (1998: 527). Examples that Blevins and Garrett discuss include Rotuman and Kwara'ae (both Oceanic). It is plausible that patterns of this kind could be analyzed as driven by prominence-based licensing that is resolved with a direct licensing structure. The reader is referred to the work of Blevins and Garrett for specifics on the patterns in these languages.

Finally, Féry notes that some words with a final syllabic sonorant show umlaut in the stressed syllable, as in (30). She speculates that in these forms the syllabic sonorant does not constitute a syllable peak, and as a result the whole stem counts as a single heavy syllable.

(30)   Diminutive
        M[áu̯]er   'wall'   M[ɔ́y̆]er-chen
        K[úː]gel   'ball'   K[ýː]gel-chen

In sum, the relevant generalizations about productive umlaut in MSG for this analysis are (a) that it causes a stem-final stressed syllable to become front if it is not already so, and (b) it occurs with suffixes *–chen* and *–lein*.

I follow several prior researchers in positing a floating feature as part of the underlying representation of umlaut-triggering suffixes (Lieber 1987; Lodge 1989; Féry 1994; Klein 1995). I will assume that the feature is [–back] (Lieber 1987, among others). The feature is floating because the phenomenon cannot consistently be attributed to an overt front vowel in the triggering suffix: *–chen* lacks a front vowel; *–lein* contains a front glide that is separated from the stem by an intervening back vowel.

I propose that licensing drives the attraction of the floating feature to the stem. Analyzing umlaut in MSG in these terms is inspired by Klein (1995). However, he makes use of an ANCHOR constraint rather than a licensing constraint, and he interprets certain generalizations regarding the pattern differently. Umlaut causes the floating features to be realized in a position with heightened salience. The licensing constraint is $\text{LICENSE}_L([-\text{back}], \acute{\sigma})$ indexed to the diminutive suffixes *–chen* and *–lein*. I assume that the licensing constraint is not applicable to [–back] specifications in consonants. Therefore, if [ç] is specified [–back], it does not violate the constraint. This could be accomplished by restricting the marked structure in the constraint to [–back] in vowels, i.e. segments in which the feature is a primary articulator. The status of the front glide in *–lein* is addressed below.

Since umlaut involves licensing-driven association of floating [–back] to a stressed syllable, $\text{IDENT-IO-}\acute{\sigma}(\text{back})$ and non-positional IDENT-IO(back) are dominated by the licensing constraint and a constraint that enforces preservation of the floating feature. The latter constraint is given in (31), as defined by Wolf (2007). It requires all floating features in the input to have an output correspondent (for a related proposal, see Zoll 1998a).[16]

(31)   MAX-IO(FLOAT)
        (I = input, O = output)
        $\forall F \in I$, where F is a feature:
        [¬[∃ S ∈ I such that S is a segment and F is associated to S]] → [∃ F' ∈ O such that FℜF']

Alternating properties in licensing position 219

The ranking is supported by the tableau in (32). The input contains the suffix *–chen* with a floating [–back] feature. The segments of this suffix and its floating feature are indexed to the licensing constraint. Candidate (a), with direct licensing, is the winner. It satisfies the licensing constraint by docking the floating [–back] feature in the stressed syllable, which incurs single violations of IDENT(back) and IDENT-σ́(back). Candidate (b), which shows indirect licensing by associating [–back] to both the stressed syllable and the suffix, is ruled out by a second violation of IDENT(back). Candidate (c) docks the floating feature only in the unstressed suffix, incurring a fatal violation of the licensing constraint. Candidate (d), which deletes the floating feature, is prevented by MAX(FLOAT).[17]

(32) Direct licensing of [–back]
       LICENSE$_L$([–back], σ́), MAX(FLOAT) >> IDENT-IO-σ́(back), IDENT-IO(back)

/nʊs-çən$_L$/ [–back]$_L$	LICENSE$_L$ ([–back], σ́)	MAX (FLOAT)	IDENT-IO- σ́(back)	IDENT- IO(back)
☞ a. nýsçən | [–back]			*	*
b. nýsçen \ / [–back]			*	**!
c. nʊ́sçen | [–back]	*!			*
d. nʊ́sçən		*!		

In (32) the ranking of the licensing constraint over IDENT-IO(back) is not essential. This ranking would be necessary, however, if a floating [–back] feature were to associate to the front glide in *–lein*.

Thus far the MSG umlaut pattern is compatible with a hierarchy in which CRISPEDGE([back], σ) is ranked in the top stratum. That ranking is not essential to prevent indirect licensing here, since IDENT-IO(back) can also prevent this outcome, as seen in (32b). This effect of IDENT-IO(back) is a consequence of the floating status of [–back] in the input and the fact that the suffix vowel is not [–back]. We will see evidence to support ranking the crisp edge constraint in the upper stratum presently.

When the stem-final syllable is not stressed, umlaut does not productively occur. I attribute this to the combined activity of the licensing constraint and a version of MORPHOLOGICAL-O-CONTIGUITY that restricts the distance between the site to which the floating feature docks and the remainder of the phonological content in its morpheme, the suffix string *–chen*. Whether umlaut has the capacity to produce a structure in which the exponence of

222 *Direct licensing*

affixed. Back and round qualities of a prefix vowel remain fixed. The data in (35) illustrate alternations in an infinitive prefix, which contains a back round vowel, and alternations in a singular class 9 prefix, which contains a front unround vowel.[19] Following Stallcup and Hyman, /ɛ ɔ/ are interpreted as [+low] vowels in these prefixes (see also Odden 1991; Goad 1993, cf. Clements 1991). Stems consist of the root plus suffixes. Stem vowels are limited to high [i ɨ u], and all vowels in a stem are realized as identical in quality. (Numbers mark tones.)

(35)

		Infinitive		Sg class 9	
a.	High	u̱-ri	'eat'	i̱1-bi1	'goat'
		u̱-bini	'dance'	i̱1-dʒi1mi1	'back'
		u̱-mu	'drink'	i̱1-su1	'fish'
		u̱-suhuru	'crouch'	i̱1-su1mu	'thorn'
b.	Mid	o-si	'laugh'	e1-gbi1	'bushfowl'
		o-jihiri	'learn'	e1-ki1bi1	'antelope'
		o-mu	'go up'	e1-su1	'hoe'
		o-juwuru	'hear'	e1-nu1nu1	'bird'
		o-dzɨ	'steal'	e1-bɨ	'cane rat'
		o-tinɨ	'refuse'	e1-kpɨ1sɨ1	'rock'
c.	Low	ɔ-rini	'be poor'	ɛ1-nji1mi1	'animal'
		ɔ-njihiri	'chew'	ɛ1-ji1si	'hole'
		ɔ5-mu	'sit'	ɛ1-zu1	'snake'
		ɔ-zumulu	'wither'	ɛ1-fumu1	'hippo'
		ɔ-bɨ	'come'	ɛ1-tlɨ1	'place'
		ɔ-nimi	'bite'	ɛ1-kɨ1rɨ1	'headpad'

My focus here is on the realization of vowel height contrasts in the initial syllable, because I suggest that this pattern is an effect of prominence-based licensing. Although it offers intrinsic interest of its own, I will not analyze the color harmony seen in non-initial vowels. This could be treated as a pattern of vowel harmony in weak syllables, a case of which is analyzed in §8.3.[20]

Stallcup and Hyman argue that height features are transferred from the stem to the prefix. Hyman provides diachronic evidence that vowel height contrasts formerly appeared in the root. The examples in (36) provide a comparison of Proto-Bantu stems and their corresponding forms in present-day Esimbi. In each of the cases shown, low vowels in Proto-Bantu correspond with a high stem vowel in Esimbi, and the prefix form that the Esimbi stem selects contains a low vowel.

(36)

	Proto-Bantu	Esimbi	
	*baɔ-	ɔ5-mɨ	'to be'
	*gabl-	ɔ-gɨbɨ	'to divide'
	*bamɔbaɔ	ɔ-hɨmbɨ	'cowry'
	*gaŋ1gaɔ	ɔ-ɣɨɔŋgɨ1	'root'

Synchronic feature transfer is supported by the generalization that a given stem occurs with prefix vowels of the same height tier across different prefixes, as shown in (37).

(37)   Sg class 7/8   Pl class 7/8
   a. High   kí-kú   bí-kú   'bone'
   b. Mid   ke-hɨ   be-hɨ   'bundle'
   c. Low   kɛ̀l-sìl   bɛ̀l-sìl   'comb'

Because stems control height alternations in prefixes but stem vowels themselves do not alternate in height, I assume that the stem height features are floating in the underlying representation, a possibility noted by Hyman and adopted by Goad (1993).[21] In the output, these features are associated with the prefix vowel, at least if they include [−high]. This gives the underlying forms and outputs in (38) for a near-minimal pair from (35). The vowels are given as 'U' in these inputs to represent that they are specified [+back] and [+round] but lack associated height features. The floating height features are interpreted as part of the phonological material of the root; hence there is a 'transfer' in the sense that height features introduced by the root become associated to the prefix vowel. In the output forms in (38), only the height specifications linked to the prefix vowel are shown. A third (near-)minimal contrast is presented by the form [u-mu] 'drink', with floating features [+high] and [−low]. Since the prefix and stem vowels are both realized as [+high] in the output of this form, the locus of association of the floating features in this case will demand further consideration.

(38)   Input   Output
   a. /U – mU/   'go up'   →   [o m u]
                                           ∧
         [−hi][−lo]   [−hi][−lo]

   b. /U – mU/   'sit'   →   [ɔ́ m u]
                                           ∧
         [−hi][+lo]   [−hi][+lo]

Because height features are floating in the input, the eight vowel phonemes listed earlier are actually shorthand for underlying stem vowels with floating height features. Note that /ə/, representing a central vowel in a stem with floating [−high] and [−low] in the input, never occurs in the output, since mid prefix vowels are only [e] and [o]. In the stem, central vowels are neutralized to /ɨ/ in the output.[22]

I propose a licensing approach for the height transfer, where height features in combination with the specification [−high] are penalized if not associated with the word-initial syllable (Walker 2001a). Transfer phenomena where restricted feature(s) that originate elsewhere become realized solely in a privileged position are predicted as a possible effect of prominence-based licensing (see also MSG above). The markedness of the features that are restricted in this phenomenon are best understood in the context of Esimbi's vowel inventory. As mentioned in §2.6, although low vowels in languages where /a/ is the only vowel are not expected to serve as comparatively marked on the basis of perceptual difficulty, when it comes to vowel color contrasts (i.e. F2), higher vowels typically show greater perceptual distance. Esimbi displays three low vowels and front and back mid vowels, so non-high vowels in this system are expected to have the capacity to serve as marked in comparison to high vowels. As a result of this effect, F2 contrasts in non-initial syllables will generally be realized only in high vowels (and they will be further augmented by color harmony in the stem).

The constraint that drives the height transfer in Esimbi is LICENSE([HEIGHT]/ [−high], $\sigma_{Initial}$). This constraint dominates IDENT-IO(HEIGHT). An identity constraint for height features in a word-initial syllable will be situated in the same stratum as non-positional IDENT(HEIGHT). The licensing configuration is direct, because non-high vowels do not usually occur in non-initial syllables. This is driven by a crisp edge constraint that prevents vowel height features from spanning a syllable: CRISPEDGE([HEIGHT], σ). Because the representations with which we are concerned contain floating features, MAX(FLOAT) will be relevant (see [31]). We will see below that floating features of the root in particular are preserved, so the constraint will be an instantiation of root faithfulness. MAX-IO-ROOT(FLOAT) will dominate IDENT-IO(HEIGHT).

The application of the constraint hierarchy is illustrated in (39). Some preliminary orientation is in order. The input in (39) contains two floating features that are part of the phonological content of the root, as notated by the subscript 'R'. I assume that the morphological affiliation is not altered in the candidate outputs, so the 'R' is not repeated there. Only height feature specifications for non-high vowels are shown in the candidate outputs. High vowels will be associated with [+high, −low]. IDENT-IO(HEIGHT) is violated not only when a vowel that is specified for a height feature value in the input has a different value for that feature in the output, but also when a vowel that is unspecified for a height feature in the input becomes specified for that feature in the output. The vowels in the input considered in (39) have no height features specified, so each candidate incurs four violations for two vowels that each acquire two height specifications. Each candidate likewise incurs two violations with respect to IDENT-IO-$\sigma_{Initial}$(HEIGHT) for the vowel in the initial syllable. I assume that a top-stratum constraint HAVEHEIGHT, not shown here, enforces specification for height features in outputs (see Itô and Mester 1993, and Padgett 1995, 2002 for a similar constraint for place features; note also Smith 2005: 59, n. 22 on HaveVPlace). Since all of the candidates in (39) tie on violations of Ident-IO(Height) and Ident-IO-σ$_{Initial}$(Height), this tableau serves only to show how the crisp edge constraint, Max-Root(Float), and the licensing constraint rule out candidates that compete with the winner. The necessity for ranking these constraints over height identity constraints is shown later, in (40).

Turning now to the competition in (39), candidate (d) deletes the floating features [–high] and [+low]. This incurs two violations of Max-Root(Float), the first of which is fatal. Candidate (c) shows indirect licensing for [–high] and [+low]: these features are shared across the prefix and stem vowels. This outcome is ruled out by the crisp edge constraint, for which a violation is incurred for each height feature that spans a syllable. Candidate (b) associates the floating features to the stem vowel only. This incurs two violations of the licensing constraint. The winner in (a) satisfies all three constraints in the top stratum of this tableau. The realization of the vowel in the non-initial syllable as high in (a) supports the claim that the first argument in the licensing constraint is non-high vowel height features. If the constraint instead operated over height features in high vowels as well as non-high vowels, candidates (a) and (b) would tie with respect to the hierarchy shown. In that case, (a) could be expected to lose on the basis of a constraint which requires that morphemic contents be disjoint (MorphDis, McCarthy and Prince 1995), because (a) combines features from separate morphemes within the initial vowel. The crisp edge constraint is also important in achieving the high realization of the root vowels, because it prevents a non-high vowel from surviving in a root vowel through indirect licensing.

(39)   Realization of non-high vowel height in the word-initial syllable
        CrispEdge([Height], σ), Max-Root(Float), License([Height]/[-high], σ$_{Initial}$) >> Ident-IO(Height), Ident-IO-σ$_{Initial}$(Height)

/U-mU/ [–hi]$_R$[+lo]$_R$	CrispEdge ([Ht], σ)	Max-Rt (Float)	License ([Ht]/[–hi], σ$_{Initial}$)	Ident [Height]	Ident-σ$_{Initial}$ [Height]
☞ a. ɔ̃mu /\ [–hi][+lo]				****	**
b. ũmɔ /\ [–hi][+lo]			*!	****	**
c. [–hi] / \ ɔ̃mɔ \ / [+lo]	*!			****	**
d. ũmu		*!*		****	**

Evidence that IDENT-IO(HEIGHT) and IDENT-IO-σ_{Initial}(HEIGHT) are situated in a stratum below the other constraints under consideration comes from hypothetical inputs that contain floating features as well as vowels that are specified for height. The input in (40) is a hypothetical input that maps to the same output as the one in (39a). The difference is that in this case the input contains a high vowel in the prefix, specified [+high] and [−low], and a low vowel in the stem, specified [−high] and [+low]. Like the input in (39), there are also floating root features [−high] and [+low]. These features are numerically indexed here to track their realization in the output distinct from the features in the input that are not floating. The same array of output candidates from (39) are considered in (40). Violations differ from the candidates in (40) only with respect to height identity constraints for (b–d). Candidate (a) incurs four violations of IDENT(HEIGHT) and two for IDENT-σ_{Initial}(HEIGHT), because each vowel has different specifications for two height features. Candidate (b) incurs no violations of the height identity constraints, because the vowel qualities are the same as in the input, even though the features that were associated to the stem vowel in the input have been replaced with the features that were floating. Candidate (c) incurs two violations of each height identity constraint for the change in height in the prefix vowel, and candidate (d) incurs two violations of IDENT(HEIGHT) for the change in height in the stem vowel. Candidate (a) incurs more violations of IDENT-IO(HEIGHT) than each of the other candidates, but it obeys the constraints in the top stratum of this tableau. The other candidates each violate a top-stratum constraint. Therefore, the top-stratum constraints must dominate IDENT-IO(HEIGHT). IDENT-σ_{Initial}(HEIGHT) must be dominated by the licensing constraint and MAX-ROOT(FLOAT).

(40) Evidence that height identity constraints are dominated

/u - mɔ/ /\ /\ [+hi][−lo] [−hi][+lo] [−hi]$_{R1}$[+lo]$_{R2}$	CRISPEDGE ([HT], σ)	MAX-RT (FLOAT)	LICENSE ([HT]/[−hi], σ_{Init})	IDENT [HEIGHT]	IDENT-σ_{Initial} [HEIGHT]
☞ a. ɔ̃mu /\ [−hi]$_1$[+lo]$_2$				****	**
b. ũmɔ /\ [−hi]$_1$[+lo]$_2$			*!*		
c. [−hi]$_1$ / \ ɔ̃mɔ \ / [+lo]$_2$	*!*			**	**
d. ũmu		*!*		**	

As I mentioned earlier, the floating features are interpreted as part of the root material. This is because the presence of non-high vowel height features in an output is attributable to the root. The preservation of non-high vowel height features of the root only is enforced by the ranking MAX-ROOT(FLOAT) >> *[−high] >> IDENT-IO(HEIGHT), IDENT-IO-σ$_{\text{Initial}}$(HEIGHT), MAX(FLOAT). The ranking of *[−high] over IDENT-IO(HEIGHT), IDENT-IO-σ$_{\text{Initial}}$(HEIGHT), and MAXFLOAT prevents the occurrence of non-high vowels in general, whether they originate with features already associated to a segment or via attachment of floating features. The ranking of MAX-ROOT(FLOAT) over *[−high] will produce non-high vowels when they derive from the association of floating root features.

The effects of this ranking are illustrated in (41). CRISPEDGE([HEIGHT], σ) is included here in the same stratum as MAX-ROOT(FLOAT), as before. In (41i), there is a hypothetical input for [u-mu] 'drink' in which the root has floating features [+high] and [−low] and the prefix has associated features [−high] and [+low]. Candidate (41ib) retains the non-high vowel features of the prefix and realizes the floating features on the stem vowel. This result is ruled out by *[−high]. The remaining two candidates both contain only high vowels. Candidate (c) shares the specifications across both syllables, while candidate (a) has separate specifications for [+high] and [−low] in each vowel. (Alphabetic indices show the absence of feature duplication here.) Given the hierarchy that has been established, CRISPEDGE([HEIGHT], σ) will rule in favor of the representation shown in candidate (a). Note that the licensing constraint would not favor (c) over (a), because it is applicable to non-high vowel features only. The evaluation in (41ii) verifies the need for MAX-ROOT(FLOAT) >> *[−high], based on the hypothesized input for [ɔ́mu] 'sit'. When non-high vowel features derive from root material, they are retained in the output at the cost of *[−high]. Their realization in the prefix syllable is due to the licensing constraint, as was shown in (39).

228 *Direct licensing*

(41) Non-high vowel height that does not originate in floating root features is not preserved

Input	Output	CRISPEDGE ([HT], σ)	MAX-RT (FLOAT)	*[–hi]	ID [HT]	ID-σ$_{Init}$ [HT]
i. /ɔ - mU/ /\ [–hi][+lo] [+hi]$_{R1}$[–lo]$_{R2}$	☞ a. ũ mu /\ /\ [+hi]$_i$ [–lo]$_j$ [+hi]$_{1k}$[–lo]$_{2m}$				****	**
	b. ɔ̃ mu /\ /\ [–hi][+lo][+hi]$_1$[–lo]$_2$			*!	**	
	c. [+hi]$_1$ / \ ũmu \ / [–lo]$_2$	*!*			****	**
ii. /U - mU/ [–hi]$_{R1}$[+lo]$_{R2}$	☞ a. ɔ̃mu /\ [–hi]$_1$ [+lo]$_2$			*	****	**
	b. ũ mu /\ /\ [+hi]$_i$ [–lo]$_j$[+hi]$_{1k}$ [–lo]$_{2m}$		*!*		****	**

In summary, the Esimbi vowel height pattern shows a prominence-based licensing effect where non-high vowel features are penalized when not directly licensed by the initial syllable. From a historical vantage point, it is noteworthy that research on Esimbi's vowel height patterns has hypothesized that height harmony from the root to prefix occurred prior to the present stage where non-high qualities are transferred to the prefix (Stallcup 1980a, b). This would entail a progression from indirect licensing to direct licensing in the language. That course of evolution would be similar to what was seen for umlaut in the history of German, although in German there was plausibly an intermediate stage that displayed identity licensing.

Before closing the discussion of Esimbi, I consider the theoretical implications of some possible exceptional forms. The word-initial licensing analysis postulates that it is not prefixes but word-initial syllables that present a capacity to license stress. Unprefixed roots are not common in Esimbi, which makes this prediction difficult to explore fully. The data that are available show different phenomena in verbs and nouns. A few nouns exist in the native vocabulary that exceptionally lack a singular prefix, as in (42). These forms are consistent with the licensing approach in that they show the capacity of the initial syllable to present vowel height contrasts in the absence of prefixation. Nouns that occur exceptionally without a prefix are not fully understood as they behave in unusual ways in other inflectional classes. Nevertheless, if the realization of non-high vowel heights were dependent on prefixes, the existence of non-high vowels in these forms would be unexpected.

(42) Sg class 1/2
      bami5   'lake'
      gɔgu   'duck'

Verb roots appear without a prefix in the second person singular imperative. In these forms, the verbs present the same vowels as they do in a prefixed stem: all vowels are identical and drawn from [i ɨ u]. The pair in (43c) shows that these verbs can nevertheless condition prefixes with non-high vowels.

(43) a. ki5li5   'trap (2sg imp.)'
      b. sɨm1bɨ1rɨ1   'scatter (2sg imp.)'
      c. gumu5   'pay (2sg imp.)'   mɛ1-gu1mu1   'I paid'

The failure of the floating height features of the root to associate to the verb stem in (43c) could be attributed to a paradigm uniformity effect that causes corresponding vowels in instances of a given verb stem to present the same quality across a paradigm. Effects of this kind could be captured using output–output correspondence among morphologically related forms, or a related approach (e.g. Burzio 1997; Benua 2000; McCarthy 2000).[23]

Apart from loans, there are a handful of cases in Esimbi that display apparently exceptional non-high vowel height in a non-initial syllable. For example, a prefix [kɨna1-] and post-stem nominalizer [-(n)anɨ] are both unusual in that they are disyllabic and they present [a] in a non-initial syllable. [kɨna1-] is also unusual in that it occurs with only a small number of irregular nouns. The disyllabicity of these morphemes points to the possibility that they form some kind of morphological head, and perhaps a compound structure is involved (for related research in Bantu, see Mpiranya and Walker 2005; Downing 2006). This could be related to the exceptional occurrence of non-initial [a]. Reduplicative structures also show the potential for non-high prefix vowels in non-initial syllables. For example, the reduplicated progressive (first person singular) with the root /dzu5/ 'pound' is formed as: [mi5-dzu-e-dzu5-nu5] 'I'm pounding,' with the secondary person marker prefix [e-] occurring before the root and after the reduplicant that copies the root syllable. Like the disyllabic morphemes, this construction plausibly involves a compounding of morphological heads, where the first member of the compound consists of a prefix plus reduplicant and the second member consists of a prefix plus stem. This might be related to the two occurrences of first person singular prefixes in the word: the 'primary' person marker [mi-] and the 'secondary' person marker [e-] (Koenig et al. 2007: 19–20).[24] Further investigation of these forms might reveal that the licensing position in Esimbi should be adjusted to reference the initial syllable of some yet to be identified major morphological category in the language that can be smaller than the word.

SUMMARY. In closing §7.4, let us review the chief points of analysis common to the patterns. We have examined two systems that show the activity of licensing in determining the site at which floating features dock in the word. As expected on the basis of the hypothesized functional grounding for licensing, the positions to which the floating features are guided are ones that show phonetic and/or psycholinguistic privilege, namely, stressed or word-initial syllables. Because the floating features become expressed in the licensing position, an identity constraint for this position is dominated in the hierarchy. Because the licensing position and the morpheme that introduces the floating feature are generally disjoint, alternations are seen in affixation. Direct licensing can be attributed to the work of a crisp edge constraint (in MSG, IDENT can also perform part of this labor). This prevents the floating feature from showing harmony across vowels of the morpheme with which it is affiliated and a vowel in licensing position. It is interesting, nevertheless, that both systems have evolved from patterns that formerly manifested vowel harmony or are hypothesized to have done so, tracing back originally to indirect licensing. In an indirect licensing system where the licensing position is the target for harmony, the restricted feature(s) are realized both in the morpheme in which they originate and the prominent site that serves to enhance them, thereby rendering their morphological association more transparent. If the system evolves into a direct licensing pattern where the feature(s) in question are no longer realized within segments of their sponsoring morpheme, their morphological affiliation is no longer overt. We could thus expect such patterns to show vulnerability to becoming moribund or frozen over time. Some instances of lexicalization of umlaut in MSG could be compatible with this course of development.

7.5 Direct licensing phenomena in review

To cap the preceding sections on direct licensing, this section summarizes the patterns and ranking structures.

Direct licensing patterns are characterized by the restriction of some material to a prominent position only. Many vowel patterns that show only direct licensing are faithful to the vowel in the licensing position and alter, reduce, or eliminate a vowel in a non-licensing position. In some cases a vowel in non-licensing position is statically impoverished for a contrast that is manifested by vowels in the licensing position. The table in (44) provides an overview of patterns of this kind that were examined in this chapter. In systems that alter or

Direct licensing phenomena in review 231

lack a contrast in non-licensing position, one or more IDENT(F) constraints are dominated in the constraint hierarchy. Where IDENT-IO(F) is indicated as the dominated constraint in (44), [F] refers to the same feature(s) as the feature(s) restricted by the licensing constraint. In systems where a vowel in non-licensing position undergoes deletion, MAX(segment) is the dominated faithfulness constraint. (As in previous chapters, the conventions used in constraints to characterize restrictions on features subject to licensing are used here.)

(44)　Direct licensing: patterns that show effacement or deficiency for a vowel in non-licensing position

	Pattern specifics	Faithfulness constraint(s) dominated	Language
i.	Licensing position = ó [F] = [−high]/[−low] The vowel in the stressed syllable is faithful.	IDENT-IO(low) IDENT-IO(round) IDENT-IO(back)	Belarusian
ii.	Licensing position = ó [F] = All vowel features/$\sigma_{post\text{-}tonic}$ The vowel in the stressed syllable is faithful.	IDENT-IO(F)	Dialect of Nova Siri
iii.	Licensing position = ó [F] = All vowel features/$\sigma_{post\text{-}tonic}$ The vowels in the stressed and final syllables are faithful.	IDENT-IO(F)	Dialect of Veroli
iv.	Licensing position = $\sigma_{Initial}$ [F] = [+round]/[−high] The vowel in the word-initial syllable is faithful.	IDENT-IO(F)	Ola Lamut
v.	Licensing position = ó [F] = [+high]/V_h (in inflectional suffixes) The vowel in the stressed syllable is faithful.	IDENT-IO(F)	Western Asturian dialects
vi.	Licensing position = ó [F] = [+high] The vowel in the stressed syllable is faithful.	MAX-IO(segment)	Northern dialects of Modern Greek

Other direct licensing patterns manifest a change or alternation in the licensing position. In general, where the identity of a vowel in licensing position is altered, a positional faithfulness constraint is dominated. Systems of this kind are summarized in (45). Constraints essential to preserving material that originates external to the licensing position and migrates to the licensing syllable are listed in the third labeled column from the left. Migration can arise when infixation shifts a vowel into the licensing position. When a diphthong results, as in old Piedmontese dialects, faithfulness constraints such as IDENT(F) and MAX(seg) are enforced at the cost of MORPHOLOGICAL-O-CONTIGUITY, which has a locus of violation in the licensing position. When coalescence occurs, as seen in dialects of Liguria, UNIFORMITY and identity constraints in the stressed position are also violated. In this case, preservation of the infixed vowel is driven by MAX(seg). A local conjunction that prevents derived non-high vowels in an unstressed syllable blocks the suffix vowel from undergoing lowering to bypass infixation. Association of a floating feature to the licensing position also incurs an identity violation, as seen in MSG and Esimbi. Here, preservation is accomplished by a faithfulness constraint for floating features.

(45) Direct licensing: patterns with an unfaithful vowel in licensing position

	Pattern specifics	Faithfulness constraint(s) dominated	Preservation of external material	Language
i.	Licensing position = ó [F] = All vowel features/[+high] (in inflectional suffixes) Infixation to form a diphthong: preserves vowels that originate in licensing position and word-final syllable.	MORPHOLOGICAL-O-CONTIG	MAX-IO(seg) IDENT-IO(high)	Old Piedmontese dialects
ii.	Licensing position = ΰ [F] = All vowel features/[+high] (in inflectional suffixes) Infixation to form a diphthong or coalesced vowel: preserves elements of vowels that originate in licensing position and word-final syllable.	MORPHOLOGICAL-O-CONTIG UNIFORMITY-IO IDENT-IO-ó(HEIGHT)	MAX-IO(seg) *ŏ/a,e•o &$_l$ IDENT-IO(high)	Dialects of Liguria

	Pattern specifics	Faithfulness constraint(s) dominated	Preservation of external material	Language
iii.	Licensing position = σ́ [F] = [−back] (in specific suffixes) Faithfulness is enforced for floating features.	IDENT-IO-σ́(F) IDENT-IO(F)	MAX-IO(FLOAT)	Modern Standard German
iv.	Licensing position = σ$_{Initial}$ [F] = [HEIGHT]/[−high] Faithfulness is enforced for floating root features.	IDENT-IO-σ$_{Initial}$(F) IDENT-IO(F)	MAX-IO-ROOT (FLOAT)	Esimbi

The overview of patterns in (44–45) reveals that prominence-based licensing that results in a direct licensing configuration can drive a diverse range of repairs, incurring violations of one or more of IDENT(F) (positional or non-positional), MAX(seg), MORPH-O-CONTIG, and UNIFORMITY. These produce a range of processes: reduction, static lack of contrast, deletion, infixation, coalescence, and association of floating features. The features that are subject to licensing in the patterns studied in this chapter are also diverse, including height features, [back], [round], or all vowel features together. Patterns that manifest indirect and identity licensing show a more limited range of types of phonological process (e.g. active assimilation in or from the licensing position, passive licensing), because those systems involve licensing outcomes where vowels in licensing position and non-licensing position show feature agreement.

As mentioned in §4.5, prominence-based licensing patterns that compelled violation of DEP(seg) could be imagined: for instance, where a vowel was inserted in a prominent position in order to serve as a licensor, forming a diphthong with the original vowel in that position. A scenario roughly along those lines – but that involved vowel fission rather than epenthesis – was proposed for the dialect of Francavilla Fontana (§6.3). A pattern could be expected in which a floating feature that was subject to licensing docked to an epenthetic vowel in a prominent position. This would allow the floating feature to be preserved, the licensing constraint to be satisfied, and the original vowel in the licensing position to remain faithful. Whether systems with these characteristics exist remains a question for further study.

7.6 Alternatives

This section discusses some alternative approaches to certain patterns that are discussed in this chapter.

PROCESS-BASED APPROACHES. Given that the vowel patterns considered in this chapter display a wide range of phonological processes, it is relevant to consider the alternative of a process-oriented framework where particular operations, such as vowel deletion or vowel reduction, manipulate phonological forms without the outcome being guided by reference to the well-formedness of the result. This would be true of a rule-based approach to the phenomena in question that did not also make use of output-centered constraints.

A problem that faces this alternative is that the factor that unites the vowel patterns examined in this work is not the processes or operations involved. Indeed, the processes can be quite different from pattern to pattern: they include vowel deletion, vowel quality reduction, vowel harmony, infixation sometimes combined with coalescence, and association of floating features. An account that is organized around phonological processes would thus treat the phenomena under study as disparate and unconnected. Furthermore, vowel patterns that are presented as static distributions in the language, such as static lack of contrast or static sequential dependencies (which fall under what I have labeled 'passive licensing') would be excluded from coverage by a process-oriented account, as they do not display an active process.

In contrast to the disconnected picture that emerges under a process-centered account, the generalized licensing constraint approach spotlights the common thread that links these phenomena, namely, they avert distinctive vowel qualities that are expressed only in non-prominent syllables. This explanation becomes available only when the well-formedness of output forms is considered as a driving force behind these patterns. It is independent from any process that leads to the output form, and thereby encompasses both static distributions as well as phenomena that show alternations. Prominence-based licensing vowel patterns thus provide powerful support for output-centered constraints, such as those employed in OT.

SONORITY MAXIMIZATION. An analysis of Belarusian proposed by de Lacy (2006: 321) attributes the lowering of mid vowels in unstressed syllables to a constraint within a family that serves to maximize the sonority of syllable nuclei. The particular constraint proposed to be active in Belarusian is $*\Delta_\sigma \leq \{e,o\}$, which is violated by any syllable with a nucleus whose sonority is less than or equal to that of mid vowels. This constraint dominates IDENT-IO(low) to produce lowering of mid vowels. High vowels are prevented from lowering by ranking

IDENT-IO(high) over *Δ$_σ$ ≤ {e,o} and stressed syllables are protected by a positional faithfulness constraint. The full ranking is IDENT-ǿ(low), IDENT(high) >> *Δ$_σ$ ≤ {e,o} >> IDENT(low).

The chief drawback of the sonority maximization approach to these data is that it does not encompass the breadth of vowel patterns that prominence-based licensing does. For example, it is not capable of driving the abundant systems of vowel assimilation described in chapters 5 and 6. In future work it would be valuable to explore whether licensing constraints could subsume other patterns to which *Δ$_σ$ ≤ X constraints have been applied. In the event that independent motivation for these constraints was confirmed, then the Belarusian pattern would remain consistent with a licensing analysis, but it would be ambiguous between this approach and an alternative in terms of sonority maximization.

POSITIONAL FAITHFULNESS. An alternative analysis of patterns that show positional neutralization or static lack of contrast in weak position uses positional faithfulness constraints and context-free markedness constraints (Beckman 1999). For example, the static absence of non-high round vowels in non-initial syllables of Ola Lamut has been analyzed using a constraint hierarchy structured as IDENT-IO-σ$_{Initial}$(round) >> *[−high, +round] >> IDENT-IO(round) (no shared features) (Walker 2001b: 868). In this ranking, a constraint that penalizes non-high round vowels dominates an identity constraint for [round], preventing non-high round vowels from occurring in general in the language. However, an identity constraint for [round] in the initial syllable dominates the markedness constraint to permit non-high round vowels when they occur in word-initial context. An initial syllable identity constraint for [high] would also need to dominate *[−high, +round] to prevent non-high round vowels from raising.

Cases such as this present a point of overlap in the potential coverage of prominence-based licensing constraints and positional faithfulness constraints. However, positional faithfulness cannot be a general solution for the vowel patterns under study in this work. Problems for a comprehensive approach to prominence-based licensing phenomena that uses positional faithfulness but lacks positional markedness constraints were discussed in §5.5. For some discussion of the future outlook for positional faithfulness constraints in the theory, see §9.2.3.

7.7 Conclusion

In this chapter, I have investigated patterns that show the direct licensing configuration only, where a restricted element is realized wholly in a prominent position. Each of the patterns studied in this chapter displays characteristics that fall in line with prominence-based licensing. The positions that serve as the locus for licensing in case studies in this chapter are stressed syllables and initial syllables. In addition, vowel patterns where the root serves as the position for direct licensing were noted for Modern German and Chumash in §7.2.2. These positions are expected to have the capacity to serve as licensors, on the basis of indicators of phonetic strength and psycholinguistic privilege discussed in chapter 2. The case of Veroli, where post-tonic vowel reduction occurs only in the penultimate syllable of proparoxytones, shows evidence of strength not just in the stressed syllable but also the final syllable. Weakness in post-tonic syllables is a characteristic of many Romance languages. In Veroli, the final syllable displays some strength (in the form of positional faithfulness) despite its post-tonic status, compatible with observations about the mixed strength/weakness of this position.

The material that is subject to licensing in patterns examined in this chapter is compatible with what is predicted on functional grounds. In some cases, it is restricted to content that usually serves as marked across languages, such as [+round] in a non-high vowel (in Ola Lamut). In others, the material is restricted to properties with the capacity to serve as marked, although with variability across languages; for example, [+high] (e.g. in northern dialects of Modern Greek) or [−high, −low] (in Belarusian). Yet other patterns restrict all values, as, for instance, in extreme cases where all vowel features are subject to licensing (e.g. in the dialect of Nova Siri). As expected, systems are not seen where a property that is clearly less marked is the only one that is subject to a licensing restriction.

This chapter has shown that direct licensing structures involving vowels can arise through the activity of several distinct processes. Direct licensing can also be displayed in phonological patterns that display a static lack of contrast in non-prominent positions. Since feature chains do not span more than one syllable in these patterns, a greater range of interactions between licensing and faithfulness constraints is made possible. Many of the patterns show effacement of unlicensed elements (e.g. neutralization, deletion) or a static absence of such material. These are compatible with the enforcement of faithfulness in the licensing position, which is consistent with its strength. However, some patterns were identified where vowel properties that originate outside the licensing position are preserved, either via infixation to the licensing position or via association of a floating feature. In the cases studied here, the preservation of this material, at the cost of some form of faithfulness in the licensing position, comes about through the activity of other faithfulness constraints, sometimes in conjunction with markedness. For the most part, these faithfulness constraints are not position sensitive (although root faithfulness is active in Esimbi). No position-sensitive constraints were called upon that overtly single out material in weak positions for preservation.

The diverse solutions that are witnessed in response to prominence-based licensing constraints for vowel properties bear out a fundamental prediction of OT in a striking way, namely, that linguistic phenomena will be characterized by heterogeneity of process, but homogeneity of outcome (McCarthy 2002; Prince and Smolensky 2004). The heterogeneity of process is well evidenced across the case studies presented in this chapter and in chapters 5 and 6. The homogeneity of outcome is evidenced in the shared result by which the vowel patterns prevent (certain) vowel qualities that are contained solely within a non-prominent position. A principal insight that emerges out of the studies that comprise these chapters is that the locus of explanation for these systems resides in the endpoint of the process or distribution, not the particular course by which that endpoint is attained.

Finally, it is important to note that not every vowel pattern that involves a general process named in this chapter or in chapters 5 and 6 is necessarily driven by prominence-based licensing constraints. A consequence of the output-centered perspective of OT is the need to diagnose the imperative for a process in the context of the particular linguistic system in which it occurs. For example, some patterns of vowel deletion have been shown to have a basis in improving the metrical structure of a language (e.g. Kager 1997). Also, some patterns of unstressed vowel neutralization have a source in prominence reduction of weak syllables (Crosswhite 2001; de Lacy 2006), as discussed in analyses of C'Lela (§5.2.2), central Veneto (§5.3), and Francavilla Fontana (§6.3). Likewise, vowel harmony patterns may differ in whether they are the product of prominence-based licensing or constraints on maximal licensing, as will be discussed in chapter 8, or perhaps other grammatical pressures. An explanatory categorization of vowel patterns is therefore not supplied by the process by which they are executed but rather by the result-centered imperative (i.e. constraint) that drives them. Different imperatives make different sets of predictions about the properties of a system. An implication is that effective study and theoretical analysis of vowel patterns requires careful diagnostic attention, an issue taken up again in the next chapter.

8 *Maximal licensing*

8.1 Introduction

This chapter turns to vowel patterns beyond those driven by prominence-based licensing. Under focus are unbounded harmony systems that involve a trigger that is weak or presents marked structure in some respect. Unlike harmony driven by prominence-based licensing, these patterns do not single out a prominent position as their final target. Instead, they are unbounded, producing assimilation as far as can be achieved while respecting other constraints that may prevent certain vowels from participating. They therefore serve to reduce perceptual difficulty for a vowel property by causing it to be realized in as many syllables as possible.

The proposal pursued in this chapter is that the unbounded systems under study are driven by maximal licensing constraints (building on Kaun 1995, 2004; Walker 2005; Jiménez and Lloret 2007). These constraints assign violations to every vowel (or segment) to which a chain for a given feature in a representation is not associated. They consequently drive harmony that propagates to the maximal extent.

Some differences between vowel harmony driven by prominence-based licensing versus maximal licensing are illustrated in (1). For the prominence-based cases, the stressed syllable serves as the strong licensing position for a feature specification [αF]. The illustrations for prominence-based licensing in (1a) depict some possible scenarios involving weak post-tonic syllables. Either harmony operates from a post-tonic syllable to the stressed syllable or the stressed syllable triggers harmony in post-tonic syllables, as shown in (1ai). However, prominence-based licensing does not predict harmony from a weak syllable that extends past the stressed licensing position to a pretonic syllable, as in (1aii). See the discussion of Jaqaru in §5.3 for an example of harmony that does not persist beyond the stressed syllable. Prominence-based licensing also does not predict harmony if assimilation does not succeed in reaching the licensing position, as in (1aiii). See the discussion of central Veneto in §5.3 for an example of this kind.

The scenarios considered for maximal licensing in (1b) involve either a weak post-tonic syllable or a weak vowel property [αF]. Maximal licensing has the capacity to operate in an unbounded fashion, extending as far as possible within a word, as in (1bi). However, if the extent of harmony is limited by the force of other constraints, it can be partial, proceeding up to the point where it is blocked, as shown in (1bii). In the figure on the left in this cell, harmony is blocked by the stressed syllable (e.g. because of a stressed syllable faithfulness constraint). In the figure on the right in (1bii), harmony is blocked by the pretonic syllable (e.g. because the particular vowel in this syllable is blocked from undergoing harmony by a markedness constraint). In some patterns, a given weak property only occurs contrastively in a strong position. In that case, unbounded harmony may be triggered by a vowel with that property in the strong position, as in (1biii).

(1) Some properties of prominence-based licensing versus maximal licensing

a. Harmony driven by prominence-based licensing (for weak post-tonic syllable)	b. Harmony driven by maximal licensing (for weak post-tonic syllable or weak [αF])

i. Terminates at strong position or originates from a strong position
 	
σ σ́ σ σ   σ σ́ σ σ
    ↘| |↙
   [αF]   [αF]
	i. Operates in an unbounded fashion
	
	σ σ́ σ σ
	   ↘↘↘|
	       [αF]

ii. Does not extend past strong position
 	
*σ σ́ σ σ
    ↘↘|
       [αF]
	ii. Can be partial, without reaching a specific uniform endpoint
	
	σ σ́ σ σ σ σ́ σ σ
	     ↘| ↘↘|
	    [αF] [αF]

iii. Does not occur if does not reach strong position
 	
*σ σ́ σ σ
     ↘|
    [αF]
	iii. Can originate from a strong position that is the locus of contrast for a weak quality
	
	σ σ́ σ σ
	   ↘|↙
	   [αF]

As with prominence-based licensing, harmony driven by maximal licensing can involve indirect licensing and identity licensing structures. Each of the structures illustrated in (1b) displays indirect licensing, where a single specification for [αF] comes to be present in licensing syllables by extending its duration. When a vowel is prevented from submitting to harmony because of a higher-ranked markedness or faithfulness constraint, the possibility of blocking or transparency arises.

*DUPLICATE(F) can discriminate between these choices. When *DUPLICATE(F) dominates a maximal licensing constraint, a vowel that cannot undergo harmony will block it, whereas if the maximal licensing constraint dominates *DUPLICATE(F), identity licensing may be available and transparency of a vowel that cannot undergo harmony could result. These two situations are outlined in (2). Consider a harmony driven by maximal licensing for [αF] and that a markedness constraint prevents a particular vowel from becoming [αF]. In (2) that vowel happens to be in the peninitial syllable. If *DUPLICATE(F) dominates the licensing constraint, then harmony will proceed up to the syllable adjacent to the peninitial syllable, but it will not affect the peninitial syllable or vowels beyond it, as in (2a). On the other hand, if the licensing constraint dominates *DUPLICATE(F), then harmony could proceed to the initial syllable via feature duplication in order to better satisfy the maximal licensing constraint, as in (2b).

(2)   Blocking and transparency effects in maximal licensing

a. Blocking: *DUPL(F) >> LICENSE(αF)   b. Transparency: LICENSE(αF) >> *DUPL(F)

$$\begin{array}{cccc} \sigma & \sigma & \sigma & \sigma \\ & | & \searrow & \downarrow \\ & [-\alpha F] & & [\alpha F] \end{array} \qquad \begin{array}{cccc} \sigma & \sigma & \sigma & \sigma \\ \nearrow & | & \searrow & \downarrow \\ [\alpha F]_i & [-\alpha F] & & [\alpha F]_i \end{array}$$

Four vowel harmony patterns driven by maximal licensing are examined in this chapter. First, two patterns where the trigger for harmony resides in a strong position are considered, one in Baiyinna Orochen, and the other in varieties spoken in the Vinalopó Mitjà region. Then a case study of the dialect of Servigliano is presented. Servigliano displays four vowel patterns that manifest sensitivity to relative weakness and/or positional prominence. It shows three vowel assimilation patterns, two of which it is proposed are driven by maximal licensing constraints. It also shows a reduction pattern in unstressed vowels. Issues explored in this case study include strength and weakness of triggers and targets, transparency effects, precedence sensitivity in maximal licensing, and interactions with prosodic structure.

8.2   Maximal licensing harmony from a strong position

In this section, I investigate harmony from a vowel in a prominent syllable driven by maximal licensing. Two cases are studied. In Baiyinna Orochen, unbounded harmony for [+round] is triggered by a root-initial syllable that contains a short non-high round vowel. The triggers for this harmony are asymmetrically weak, both with respect to quantity (short vowels) and quality (non-high round). In Valencian varieties spoken in the region of Vinalopó Mitjà,

Maximal licensing harmony from a strong position   241

unbounded harmony operates for all features of a stressed [−ATR] mid vowel. A non-low vowel that is [−ATR] has been characterized as marked. Although the harmony triggers are in a strong position in Baiyinna Orochen and Vinalopó Mitjà, this is also the only position in which the vowel qualities that characterize the trigger of harmony distinctively occur in these languages.

BAIYINNA OROCHEN. Baiyinna Orochen, a Tungusic language, shows a round harmony among non-high vowels that is described by Li (1996) and discussed by Kaun (2004). The language also shows a tongue root harmony that will be evident in the data but is not the subject of analysis. The language contrasts the following vowels /i ɪ ə a ɔ o ʊ u/, each of which may be distinctively long or short. It also exhibits the diphthongs /ie ɪɛ/. Short /o ɔ/ behave differently from long /oː ɔː/ as triggers for round harmony, so I discuss them in turn.

Short [o] and [ɔ] occur freely in the initial syllable of the root. Examples where they appear just in the initial syllable of a root are in (3a). These vowels appear in a non-initial syllable only when they immediately follow another syllable that contains a non-high round vowel. In addition, sequences in which a non-high unround vowel [ə əː a aː] occurs in a syllable immediately following a syllable with [o ɔ] are systematically absent: a non-high vowel in a syllable following [o ɔ] is round. Examples of this distribution in roots with short vowels are given in (3b).

(3)   a. mo̱liktə   'a kind of wild fruit'
        ɔ̱xɪxan   'flame'
   b. tʃo̱lpon   'morning star'
        mo̱ɣon   'silver'
        o̱ɲtot   'strange'
        sɔ̱bgɔ   'fish skin'
        ɔ̱rɔn   'reindeer'
        ɔ̱rɔktɔ   'hay'

Non-high round vowels condition round harmony in a non-high suffix vowel, as illustrated in (4a). Unround realizations of vowels in the same suffixes after roots whose last syllable does not contain a non-high round vowel are shown in (4b). These data, together with those in (3), are indicative of an active round harmony that traces back to a round vowel in the initial syllable.

(4)   Indef. acc.   Immed. imp. mood, 2 pers.
   a. somsok-jo̱   'pasture'   olbos-ko̱l   'to swim'
      ɔlɔ-jɔ̱   'fish'   bɔdɔ-xɔ̱l   'to think'
   b. urə-jə̱   'mountain'   iː-xə̱l   'to enter'
      bɪra-ja̱   'river'   taŋ-ka̱l   'to count'

Like their short counterparts, [oː] and [ɔː] are not restricted in the initial root syllable, but they occur in a non-initial syllable only following another syllable that contains a non-high round vowel. Examples of roots in which [oː ɔː] occur only in the initial syllable are provided in (5a), and roots where they occur following a syllable with a non-high round vowel are given in (5b).

(5)   a. boːsu   'cloth'
         toːri-   'to lose one's way'
         ɔːmɪ   'large intestines'
         nɔːnɪn   'he, she'
     b. sokkoː   'muddy (water)'
         oloːk   'lie'
         gɔlɔː   'log'
         ɔmɔːŋ   'fatty meat (of deer)'

The long vowels [oː ɔː] differ from their short counterparts in that they do not trigger round harmony, as illustrated with the roots in (6a) and the suffixed forms in (6b).

(6)   a. oːdən   'velvet'
         koːməxə   'windpipe'
         kɔːɲakta   'hand-bell'
         tɔːlga   'pole used for supporting the coffin'
     b. boːl-jə   'slave (indef. acc.)'
         gɔːl-ja   'policy (indef. acc.)'
         kɔː-wkaːn-   'sharpen with a knife (caus.)'
     cf. sɔŋɔ-wkɔːn-   'weep (caus.)'

Despite not triggering round harmony, [oː ɔː] can be the product of round harmony and propagate it onward. The pair in (7a) shows that a long non-high vowel can be the target of round harmony in a suffix. In (7b) roots with [oː] or [ɔː] in the final syllable trigger round harmony in a suffix. In (7c), round harmony produces [oː] or [ɔː] in a suffix and continues to a following suffix. The examples in (7d) show unround alternants of the suffixes in (7c), when conditions for round harmony are not met. The root forms in (5b) also support the participation of [oː ɔː] in round harmony. The examples in (6) showed that long non-high round vowels do not trigger round harmony; therefore the harmony in (7b–c) must trace back to the short round vowel in the initial syllable.

(7)   a. bɔsɔ-mkɔːn   'catch up (caus.)'
         amʊ-mkaːn   'defecate (caus.)'
     b. sokkoː-mɲo   'muddy (water) (contem.)'
         ɔmɔːŋ-mɔ   'fatty meat (of deer or roe deer) (def. acc.)'
     c. ɲoɲo(xo)-xoːn-mo   'bear (dim., def. acc.)'
         oloː-wkoːn-no-   'cook (caus., pres.)'

		dʒɔlɔ-xɔːn-mɔ̠	'stone (dim., def. acc.)'
		bɔdɔ-wkɔːn-nɔ̠-	'think (caus., pres.)'
	d.	luxi-xəːn-mə̠	'arrow (dim., def. acc.)'
		buː-wkəːn-nə̠-	'give (caus., pres.)'
		bɪra-xaːn-ma̠	'river (dim., def. acc.)'
		waː-wkaːn-na̠-	'kill (caus., pres.)'

Unlike their non-high counterparts, high round vowels occur freely in non-initial syllables (8a), and they do not trigger round harmony (8b). High vowels, whether round or unround, block round harmony (8c).

(8)	a.	imu̠ksə-ru̠k	'oil container'
		kiluːr	'large piece of ice'
		pəntuː	'pilose antler'
		ʃɪlʊ̠kta	'intestines'
		amʊ̠(n)-ru̠k	'toilet'
		akkʊː	'filled, solid'
	b.	ɲurɪktə̠	'hair'
		uʃiː	'rope'
		suxə̠	'axe'
		urəː	'earthworm'
		dʒuːxi̠n	'otter'
		bəju(n)-ksə̠	'elk hide' cf. ɲoɲoxo-kso̠ 'bear hide'
		gʊgdɪ	'bitter'
		ʊxɪːn	'spark'
		ʊnta̠	'leather shoe'
		gʊraːn	'male roe deer'
		tʃʊːxa̠	'grass'
		ʊːlɪn	'cheek'
	c.	bolboxi-wə̠	'wild duck (def. acc.)'
		bomboŋkie-wə̠	'Shaman's hat (def. acc.)'
		owon-dulə̠ː	'pancake (destin.)'
		tʃɔlɪk-pa̠	'cloud-shaped design (def. acc.)'
		ɔmɔlɪɛ-xa̠l[1]	'grandson (pl)'
		ɔrɔn-dʊla̠ː	'reindeer (destin.)'

To summarize, in Baiyinna Orochen rounding contrasts in non-high vowels are restricted to the root-initial syllable.[2] A short non-high round vowel in the initial syllable triggers round harmony in non-high vowels, both long and short. A long non-high round vowel in the initial syllable does not trigger round harmony. High vowels block harmony, and high round vowels do not trigger round harmony.

In Baiyinna Orochen, rounding occurs in non-initial non-high vowels only through assimilation tracing back to a short non-high round vowel in the initial syllable. A prominence-based licensing constraint is not suitable for this

244 *Maximal licensing*

pattern. Consider a licensing constraint penalizing [+round] in non-high vowels when not licensed by the initial syllable. This would produce a passive licensing pattern like that seen in Classical Mongolian (§5.2.2), where, rather than showing consistent rounding assimilation, [ə əː a aː] and their round counterparts would both be permitted in syllables following [o] and [ɔ]. Round harmony from the initial syllable could be driven by a licensing constraint penalizing both values for [round] in non-high vowels when not licensed in initial position. However, this constraint does not predict the failure of long [oː ɔː] to trigger harmony, because there is no reason to expect them not to serve as the host for [+round] shared with a non-initial syllable. Indeed, because of their longer duration, [oː] and [ɔː] could be expected to be preferred licensors for [+round] in the initial syllable.

(9) Prominence-based licensing by initial syllable does not predict only short vowel triggers
 LICENSE([rd]/[–hi], $\sigma_{Initial}$), IDENT-IO-$\sigma_{Initial}$(rd) >> IDENT-IO(rd), CRISP EDGE([rd], σ)

Input	Output	LICENSE ([rd]/[–hi], $\sigma_{Initial}$)	IDENT $\sigma_{Initial}$(rd)	IDENT (round)	CRISPEDGE ([rd], σ)
i. /olɔːk/	☞ a. oloːk			*	*
	b. olɔːk	*!			
	c. əlɔːk		*!	*	*
ii. /boːl-jə/	×☞ a. boːljo			*	*
	b. boːljə	*!			
	c. bəːljə		*!	*	*

The problem is illustrated in (9). The top stratum of this constraint hierarchy has a licensing constraint for both values of [round] in a non-high vowel, together with IDENT-IO-$\sigma_{Initial}$(round), to achieve control of harmony by the initial syllable. The licensing constraint dominates non-positional IDENT-IO(round) and CRISPEDGE([round], σ) to produce indirect licensing. The evaluation in (9i) shows how this ranking is successful for harmony triggered by a short vowel. A hypothetical input is considered where a short non-high round vowel is followed by a long non-high unround vowel in a root. The faithful output in (b) is ruled out by the licensing constraint, and a candidate with harmony from the non-initial vowel to the vowel in the initial syllable, in (c), is ruled out by the initial syllable faithfulness constraint. The winner, in (a), satisfies the licensing constraint through round harmony from the initial syllable to the non-initial vowel. This violates the dominated constraints, IDENT(round) and CRISPEDGE([round], σ). Although the result in (9i) is the expected one for Baiyinna Orochen, a difficulty arises when the initial syllable contains a long non-high round vowel, as in (9ii). The output predicted by the hierarchy is the one in (9iia), with progressive round harmony. However, this is not the attested form in the language, as indicated by 'x☞' in the tableau. The attested form is the candidate in (9iib), without harmony. For this candidate to be selected by the constraints shown, either IDENT-IO(round) or the crisp edge constraint must dominate the licensing constraint. That solution is not viable, however, because the revised ranking would incorrectly prevent round harmony in (9i).

The problem could not be solved by restricting the first argument of the licensing constraint to round non-high vowels that are short, because then long non-high vowels would not be expected to undergo round harmony, wrongly predicting that [olə:k] would be well formed in the language. The correct result could be obtained if the licensor were restricted to an initial syllable that contains a short vowel; however, this runs counter to the claim that the π argument in a prominence-based licensing constraint is a prominent position, since a short vowel is weaker in articulation and exposure of perceptual cues than its long counterpart.

It is noteworthy that the triggers for round harmony in Baiyinna Orochen show asymmetric weakness, an observation made by Kaun (2004). A short non-high round vowel is weak in comparison to its long counterpart, as just mentioned, and it is weak in comparison to its high counterpart, because rounding in a non-high vowel has been argued to be perceptually weaker than in a high vowel. Versions of constraints that require a property of a weak vowel to be maximally realized throughout the word have been proposed by Kaun (1995, 2004) (EXTEND[F]if[αG], ALIGN[F]/[αG]) and Walker (2005) (SPREAD[F]ifX). Jiménez and Lloret (2007) have suggested that maximal extension patterns for weak triggers involve the activity of licensing more broadly interpreted than positional licensing effects. With inspiration from that work, I propose that round harmony in Baiyinna Orochen is caused by a maximal licensing constraint. When a particular property is present in a word, this constraint assigns a penalty to each vowel in the word in which that property is not realized. This differs from prominence-based licensing, which penalizes a feature chain that does not find expression in a specific position. The general schema for a maximal licensing constraint pertaining to features is given in (10). In practice, I will refer to maximal licensing constraints with the label LICENSE([F], $\forall \upsilon$).

(10) *Maximal Licensing constraint schema*: LICENSE([F], $\forall \upsilon$)
$*\upsilon/\neg\text{LICENSE}([F], \upsilon) \equiv_{\text{def}}$
Let any occurrence of [F], a given feature, in a chain $C_j([F])$ be $[F]_j$, and any occurrence of υ, a given type of phonological unit (e.g. segment, vowel), be u. Then for every pair $<C_j([F]), u>$ such that $\exists [F]_j [P([F]_j)] \wedge \neg\text{Coincide}(C_j([F]), u)$, assign a violation to u.

As in the schema for prominence-based licensing constraints, $P([F]_j)$ serves as a place holder for restrictions on the value or context for [F]. When no such restriction is visible, $P([F]_j)$ will be ID, i.e. $[[F]_j = [F]_j]$, so that it has no visible effect on the evaluation of the constraint. I assume that the same kinds of restrictions on F for prominence-based licensing constraints are available for maximal licensing constraints. In addition to ID, these are (i) $[F]_j = [\alpha F]$, (ii) [F]/[βG], and (iii) [F]/Weak (§3.4.1). For the round harmony of Baiyinna Orochen, [F] will be restricted to [+round] in a short non-high vowel: [+round]/ V_μ[−high]. For every chain for a given feature in a representation for which P is true, violations of the maximal licensing constraint are assigned to every occurrence of phonological unit υ with which the chain for the feature does not coincide. (On the Coincide relation, see §3.4.1.) The phonological unit in question could perhaps be uniformly defined as a segment; however, to simplify assessment, I will allow the possibility that it could be defined as a vowel, since we are considering patterns of vowel harmony. Apart from convenience, there may be a substantive basis for this assumption. Because vowels form the nucleus of a syllable – the component with highest sonority – it is conceivable that vowels could be singled out as licensors.

The formulation in (10) does not place an upper limit on the prosodic or morphological domain in which a maximal licensing constraint is assessed. In this chapter I will be concerned with phenomena of licensing that occur within a phonological word, which in some cases can include clitics. Restricting maximal licensing phenomena to smaller prosodic domains can be obtained using crisp edge constraints, as we will see in §8.3. Whether there is a maximal domain across languages for such phenomena – for example, the phonological word – which should be stipulated in the definition of maximal licensing constraints is a question that I will leave open. The constraint statement could easily be augmented in this way.

Other patterns considered later in this chapter will motivate extending the maximal licensing constraint schema so that it is sensitive to precedence, that is, whether the vowels that fail to realize a feature chain come before or after segments to which that chain is associated. This will be introduced in the analysis of the Servigliano dialect in §8.3.

Maximal licensing phenomena could also be obtained using the ALIGN, EXTEND, or SPREAD constraints mentioned above. However, McCarthy (2003) has objected to constraints like ALIGN because of their gradient assessment, which, he argues, makes problematic typological predictions. The maximal licensing constraint is formulated so as to make evident that the locus of violation for this constraint is ʊ, in conformity with the categorical markedness constraint schema that McCarthy advocates.[3] In addition, the proposed formalism connects weak trigger effects that involve prominence-based licensing or maximal licensing by positing that both are driven by avoidance of certain non-coincident structures, that is, elements that do not satisfy a particular Coincide relation.

AGREE(F) is another constraint that has been used to drive vowel harmony (Baković 2000). AGREE(F) requires that adjacent elements have the same value for the feature [F]. Because this constraint is local, that is, it imposes a restriction on adjacent elements, it could not obtain the round harmony of Baiyinna Orochen. Consider a sequence of syllables where a short non-high vowel is preceded by a long non-high round vowel, e.g. [… oːCə …]. Whether harmony occurs could depend on a syllable that is not adjacent to the unrounded target vowel, namely, a short non-high round vowel in a prior syllable. Recall that if the sequence in question occurred in the first two syllables of the word, round harmony would not take place (see [6a]).[4]

I thus proceed to a treatment of round harmony in Baiyinna Orochen as driven by a maximal licensing constraint. The top stratum of the constraint hierarchy will contain an initial syllable faithfulness constraint, IDENT-IO-σ_{Initial}(round).[5] The active licensing constraint is LICENSE([+round]/ V_μ[−high], $\forall V$), which penalizes vowels that do not coincide with a chain for [+round], when it occurs in combination with [−high] in a short vowel (V_μ). A non-high round vowel will be retained in the initial syllable even if there are vowels in the word that do not coincide with the chain for its round feature. Therefore, IDENT-IO-σ_{Initial}(round) dominates the licensing constraint. Non-high round vowels can appear in non-initial syllables as the product of licensing-driven harmony, and they may occur in initial syllables. This signals that *[+round, −high] is dominated by the licensing constraint and initial syllable faithfulness. Non-high round vowels are absent otherwise, which is captured by *[+round, −high][6] >> IDENT-IO(round). Because licensing can cause round harmony, the licensing constraint will dominate CRISPEDGE([round], σ).

The evaluations in (11i–ii) illustrate the assessment of the same forms as in (9), where the derivation for the second input proved problematic for prominence-based licensing. The crisp edge constraint is included in the same stratum as *[+round, −high] in the tableau, but there is no evidence from these forms that it must dominate IDENT-IO(round). The evaluation in (11i) illustrates a case where round harmony issues from a short non-high round vowel in the initial syllable. This outcome, in (a), satisfies the licensing constraint, but it earns violations of *[+round, −high], the crisp edge constraint, and IDENT(round). Candidate (b) is faithful, but it incurs a fatal violation of the licensing constraint. The alternative in (c), where the vowel in the initial syllable becomes [−round], violates the initial syllable faithfulness constraint in the top stratum. For symmetry with the tableau in (9), I assume that this candidate shares [−round] across syllables, but whether [−round] is shared or not will not alter the outcome of the selection.

In (11ii), the initial syllable contains a long non-high round vowel. In this case, the faithful candidate in (a), without harmony, obeys the licensing constraint, because there is no chain for [+round] that is associated with a short non-high vowel. This candidate is favored over one with progressive round harmony, in (b), which (a) harmonically bounds with this constraint set. As in (11i), altering rounding in the initial syllable, in (c), is ruled out by the positional faithfulness constraint. The maximal licensing constraint thus obtains the generalization that short non-high round vowels trigger round harmony but their long counterparts do not. That a long non-high vowel can propagate harmony triggered by a short vowel is verified by the evaluation in (11iii). The licensing constraint drives maximal harmony from the initial short non-high round vowel.

(11)   Only short vowels trigger round harmony
       ID-σ$_{Initial}$(rd) >> LICENSE([+rd]/V$_\mu$[−hi], ∀V) >> *[+rd, −hi], CRISPEDGE([rd], σ) >> ID(rd)

Input	Output	IDENT σ$_{Initial}$(rd)	LICENSE([+rd]/ V$_\mu$[−hi], ∀V)	*[+rd, −hi]	CRISPEDGE ([rd], σ)	IDENT (rd)
i. /oləːk/	☞ a. oloːk			**	*	*
	b. oləːk		*!	*		
	c. ələːk	*!			*	*
ii. /boːl-jə/	☞ a. boːljə			*		
	b. boːljo			**(!)	*(!)	*
	c. bəːljə	*!			*	*
iii. /ɔmaːŋ-ma/	☞ a. ɔmɔːŋmɔ			***	*	**
	b. ɔmɔːŋma		*!	**	*	*
	c. ɔmaːŋma		*!*	*		

Maximal licensing harmony from a strong position 249

The feature specification [+round] can only assimilate among non-high vowels. This is obtained by GESTURALUNIFORMITY([+round], [high]), which penalizes a sequence of adjacent vowels that differ in height and are associated to the same specification of [+round] (§5.2.2). Since GESTURALUNIFORMITY can cause blocking effects in round harmony, it dominates the licensing constraint. The tableaux in (12–14) illustrate cases where round harmony is partial in the word or does not occur. For reasons of space, the crisp edge constraint is not shown; it does not affect the decision in the evaluations shown. In (12), a hypothetical input is considered with a high round vowel in the initial syllable and a non-high round vowel in the second syllable. In candidate (c), each vowel has a separate specification for [+round], belonging to separate chains. This incurs a violation of the licensing constraint. In candidate (b), [+round] is shared across the vowels. This satisfies the licensing constraint, but it violates GESTURALUNIFORMITY. The selected form in (a) eliminates [+round] in the non-high vowel, which satisfies the licensing constraint but earns a violation of IDENT-IO(round). This shows that a high round vowel cannot serve to rescue [+round] in a non-high vowel in a following syllable, nor is round harmony expected in this context.

(12)   High vowels do not share [+round] with a non-high vowel
       GESTURALUNIFORMITY([+round], [high]) >> LICENSE([+round]/V_μ[–high], $\forall V$) >> IDENT(round)

/ʊntɔ/	GESTUNI ([+rd], [hi])	IDENT σ_{Init}(round)	LIC([+round]/ V_μ[–high], $\forall V$)	*[+round, –high]	IDENT (round)
☞ a. ʊnta					*
b. ʊntɔ \ / [+rd]	*!			*	
c. ʊntɔ | | [+rd]$_i$ [+rd]$_j$			*!	*	

The tableau in (13) illustrates a case where a high vowel blocks harmony. Because round harmony cannot skip a high vowel, *DUPLICATE(F) must belong to the set of constraints that dominate the licensing constraint. *DUPLICATE(F) rules out candidate (d), where [+round] is duplicated in the final non-high vowel, skipping the high vowel. In candidate (c), round harmony from [ɔ] in the initial syllable conducts fully in the word. This outcome is ruled out by the gestural uniformity constraint, because [+round] is shared across high and non-high vowels. One violation is assigned for the [...ɔCCʊ...] sequence and one for the [...ʊCɔː ...] sequence. Candidate (e) eliminates [+round] in the vowel of the initial syllable. This satisfies the licensing constraint but is ruled out by initial syllable faithfulness. The selected output, in (a), shows partial round harmony. Two violations of the licensing constraint are tallied: one for the high vowel and one for the final non-high vowel, each of which does not coincide with the chain for [+round] that is associated with non-high vowels in the first two syllables. Candidate (b) does not spread [+round] at all from the [ɔ] in the initial syllable. This incurs one more violation of licensing than (a), because [a] in the second syllable is a third locus of violation of the maximal licensing constraint. I assume that IDENT-IO(high) (not shown) is in the top stratum to prevent any changes in the height of vowels that would facilitate the satisfaction of licensing.

(13) High vowels block round harmony
      *DUPLICATE(F), GESTUNI([+round], [high]) >> LICENSE([+round]/V$_\mu$ [–high], ∀V]

/ɔran-dʊla:/	*DUPL(F)	GESTUNI ([+rd], [hi])	IDENT σ$_{Init}$(rd)	LIC([+rd]/ V$_\mu$[–hi], ∀V)	*[+rd, –hi]	IDENT (rd)
☞ a. ɔrondʊla: \/ | [+rd] [+rd]				**	**	*
b. ɔrandʊla: | | [+rd]$_i$ [+rd]$_j$				***!	*	
c. ɔrondʊlɔ: ⌣ [+rd]		*!*			***	**
d. ɔrondʊlɔ: \/ | [+rd]$_i$ [+rd]$_i$	*!			*	***	**
e. arandʊla:			*!			*

Tableau (14) demonstrates how the ranking obtains an unrestricted distribution for rounding in high vowels. The input contains a high round vowel in a syllable following an unround vowel. This form will map faithfully to the output, satisfying all constraints under consideration. An alternative that eliminates rounding in the high vowel is suboptimal because it incurs a violation of IDENT(round). If there were a constraint against the feature combination [+round, +high], it must be dominated by IDENT(round).

(14) The distribution of high round vowels is not restricted

/ʃɪlʊkta/	*DUPL(F)	GESTUNI (+rd, hi)	IDENT σ$_{Initial}$(rd)	LIC([+rd]/ V$_\mu$[–hi], ∀V)	*[+rd, –hi]	IDENT (rd)
☞ a. ʃɪlʊkta						
b. ʃɪlɪkta						*!

A summary of some basic rankings for the analysis of Baiyinna Orochen is given in (15).

(15) Some main constraint interactions in Baiyinna Orochen
   a. IDENT-IO-σ_Initial(round), LICENSE([+round]/V_μ[−high], ∀V) >> *[+round, −high], CRISPEDGE([round], σ) >> IDENT-IO(round)
   Licensing-driven maximal harmony for [+round] issues from short non-high round vowels in the initial syllable; apart from round harmony contexts, non-high round vowels do not occur in non-initial syllables.
   b. IDENT-IO-σ_Initial(round) >> LICENSE([+round]/V_μ[−high], ∀V)
   A short non-high round vowel will be retained in the initial syllable, even if licensing-driven harmony fails to propagate to every vowel in the word.
   c. GESTURALUNIFORMITY([+round], [high]) >> LICENSE([+round]/V_μ[−high], ∀V)
   Harmony for [+round] does not operate across vowels that differ in height.
   d. *DUPLICATE(F) >> LICENSE([+round]/V_μ[−high], ∀V)
   Identity licensing structures do not occur, with the result that high vowels block licensing-driven round harmony.

To conclude, Baiyinna Orochen presents a case of round harmony that is not driven by prominence-based positional licensing. The approach pursued here employs a maximal licensing constraint, which drives round harmony from a vowel that presents perceptual difficulty to all other vowels. In contrast to a harmony pattern driven by prominence-based licensing where the initial syllable licenses [+round], the maximal licensing pattern reflects that short vowels in the initial syllable trigger round harmony but not long ones. A position-sensitive effect is nevertheless seen in the lack of restriction on rounding in vowels in the initial syllable, obtained with a positional faithfulness constraint.

VINALOPÓ MITJÀ. Jiménez (1998) provides a valuable study of vowel patterns in Valencian Catalan that intersects with issues under consideration here. Valencian varieties distinguish seven vowels /i e ɛ a ɔ o u/ (some dialects also present /ə/). In Valencian Catalan dialects, /ɛ ɔ/ generally occur in stressed syllables only. In an unstressed syllable, underlying /ɛ ɔ/ become [e o], respectively. However, in some varieties of Valencian Catalan [ɛ ɔ] can occur as contextually conditioned allophones of /a/ in an unstressed syllable, such as through harmony. In varieties spoken in localities of the Vinalopó Mitjà region, stressed [ɛ ɔ] cause unstressed /a/ in preceding and following syllables to raise to [ɛ] or [ɔ], respectively, as illustrated in (16). The hypothesized underlying forms follow Jiménez, who performed a comparative study of dialects in the region. Although Jiménez does not include examples where harmony does not occur, his description indicates that the triggers for this process are specifically stressed /ɛ ɔ/.

(16) afecta   /afɛkta/   ɛfɛ́ktɛ   'it affects'   cf. València: afɛ́kta
      Ayela   /ajɛla/   ɛjɛ́lɛ   'a town'
      tovallola /tovaʎɔla/   tovɔʎɔ́lɔ   'towel'
      carxot   /kartʃɔt/   kɔrtʃɔ́t   'slap'

Jiménez hypothesizes that the goal of this harmony is to improve perceptibility of the marked vowels [ɛ ɔ]. In agreement with his perspective, I analyze the harmony as driven by a maximal licensing constraint for all features in these vowels, with restriction of harmony to the [−ATR] vowels through the interaction of certain constraints, discussed below. Motivation from various phonological patterns for a constraint that prohibits the feature combination [−ATR, −low] is discussed by Archangeli and Pulleyblank (1994). They argue that this constraint (a grounded condition in their theoretical terms) has a physiological basis in sympathetic movements of parts of the tongue.

There is reason to suppose the harmony of Vinalopó Mitjà is caused by maximal licensing rather than prominence-based licensing. If it were caused by the latter, it would require a constraint that penalizes feature chains associated with [a] that are expressed only in an unstressed syllable. This runs counter to expectations: with the exception of word-final position, a low vowel in an unstressed syllable does not present increased perceptual difficulty relative to other vowel qualities, particularly in inventories with a single low vowel (see §2.6). A prominence-based licensing constraint that takes properties of [a] in all unstressed syllables as its first argument is therefore problematic. On the other hand, there is support for the claim that [ɛ] and [ɔ] can serve as marked. This is addressed by a maximal licensing constraint, which can drive a pattern that expands the opportunities for perception of the features in these segments.

Before proceeding further with the maximal licensing approach, let us first consider whether harmony that targets unstressed /a/ could be a case of unstressed vowel reduction, driven by a constraint that serves to minimize the prominence of non-head syllables, such as unstressed syllables (e.g. Crosswhite 2001, 2004; de Lacy 2002, 2006, 2007a). There is reason to doubt that this is the source for the vowel harmony in Vinalopó Mitjà. An initial reason to give us pause is that assimilation in height to a neighboring syllable is not the usual way in which reduction-driven raising of vowels is achieved. More persuasively, the acquisition of color features from the stressed vowel would not be motivated by reduction-driven raising. If prominence of the unstressed syllable alone were at stake, /a/ could be expected to systematically raise to just one of [ə], [ɛ] or [ɔ]. Indeed, Jiménez (1998: 140f.) finds evidence of such fixed quality reduction of final unstressed /a/ in some related varieties (see §7.2.2), and he argues that it is distinct from harmony that affects /a/. Conversely, the extension of vowel features from /ɛ/ and /ɔ/ is expected if a maximal licensing constraint for the features in these vowels is in force.

The licensing constraint that I propose is active in Vinalopó Mitjà is LICENSE([V-FEATURE]/[−ATR, −low], ∀V), which enforces maximal licensing for vowel features in a [−ATR] non-low vowel. This constraint will dominate *[−ATR, −low] and IDENT constraints for [low], [round], and [back] to produce raising of /a/ to [ɛ] and [ɔ]. It will also dominate crisp edge constraints for vowel features, because it results in harmony. The licensing constraint will itself be dominated by IDENT constraints for the features [low] and [ATR] in the stressed syllable to preserve [ɛ] and [ɔ] in this context even if licensing is not satisfied.

An illustration of how this ranking obtains harmony of unstressed /a/ to [ɛ] is given in (17). The input contains a form in which /ɛ/ occurs in the syllable that is assigned stress. The vowel /a/ occurs in the preceding and following syllables. Candidates (d) and (e) satisfy the licensing constraint by altering height features in the stressed syllable, but this is ruled out by faithfulness for height in this position. Candidates (b) and (c) violate the maximal licensing constraint. In (c), both unstressed vowels form the locus of violation, and in (b), just the final unstressed vowel does. (For simplicity, just one mark is shown for each vowel that fails to license the features of [ɛ].) Candidate (a), which satisfies licensing by harmony from the stressed syllable to both unstressed vowels, is selected. This form incurs two violations for each of IDENT(low) and IDENT(back) and three violations of *[−ATR, −low]. The ranking of the licensing constraint over IDENT(round) is not essential for this particular form, but it will be necessary for harmony that produces mapping of unstressed /a/ → [ɔ], as shown in (18).

(17) Maximal harmony from a stressed [−ATR] mid vowel
      ID-IO-ó(ATR), ID-IO-ó(low) >> LICENSE([V-FEATURE]/[−ATR, −low], ∀V)
      >> ID(low), ID(round), ID(back), *[−ATR, −low]

/afɛkta/	ID-ó(ATR) ID-ó(low)	LICENSE([V-F]/ [−ATR,−lo], ∀V)	IDENT (low)	IDENT (round)	IDENT (back)	*[−ATR, −low]
☞ a. ɛfɛ́ktɛ			**		**	***
b. ɛfɛ́kta		*!	*		*	**
c. afɛ́kta		*!*				*
d. afákta	*!(low)		*		*	
e. afékta	*!(ATR)					

Harmony propagates only among [−ATR] vowels. Following Jiménez, I attribute this to a gestural uniformity constraint. The constraint, which I assume is GESTURALUNIFORMITY([V-FEATURE], [ATR]), assigns a penalty to any sequence of adjacent vowels that are linked to the same vowel feature and differ in [ATR] specification. The gestural uniformity constraint dominates the licensing constraint, because it can prevent its satisfaction, as seen in (18) with the evaluation of a hypothetical form. The input contains /ɔ/ in the syllable that is assigned stress. The initial syllable contains /i/, which does not harmonize with stressed [ɔ]. In (b), the high vowel shows harmony for color features with [ɔ], violating the gestural uniformity constraint. This better satisfies the licensing constraint than the selected form in (a), in which the high vowel shows no harmony with the stressed vowel. Candidate (c) is the faithful form, but it loses to (a), because it incurs more violations of the licensing constraint. To minimize clutter in this tableau, I have assigned a mark for violations of the licensing constraint only for color features. If violations for height features were also shown, it would still be the case that (c) would have more violations of the licensing constraint than (a), which would have more violations than (b).

(18) Harmony propagates only among [−ATR] vowels
      GESTURALUNIFORMITY([V-FEAT], [ATR]) >> LICENSE([V-FEAT]/
      [−ATR, −low], ∀V)

/tivɔla/	GESTUNI ([V-F], [ATR])	ID-ó(ATR) ID-ó(low)	LICENSE ([V-F]/ [−ATR, −lo], ∀V)	ID (low)	ID (rd)	ID (bk)	*[−ATR, −low]
☞ a. tivɔ́lɔ			*	*	*		**
b. tuvɔ́lɔ	*!			*	**		**
c. tivɔ́la			**!				*

Another possible candidate is [tɔvɔ́lɔ], where /i/ becomes [ɔ] in order to satisfy licensing. This can be ruled out by the local conjunction *ŏ/a,ɛ•ɔ &$_l$ IDENT-IO(ATR), which will penalize a [−ATR] unstressed vowel that also violates IDENT(ATR); it will prevent a mapping from /i e o u/ to unstressed [ɛ a ɔ]. The local conjunction belongs to the top stratum of the constraint hierarchy.

An interesting aspect of the Vinalopó Mitjà system is that unstressed [ɛ] and [ɔ] can be derived through vowel harmony but underlying /ɛ ɔ/ apparently raise to [e o] in an unstressed syllable. Although Jiménez does not provide examples to show raising of /ɛ ɔ/ in Vinalopó Mitjà, he reports that this pattern is true of Valencian Catalan varieties, as in all other Catalan dialects (1998: 143). This could be obtained by ranking *[−ATR, −low] over IDENT-IO(ATR).[7] As a result, if an input contained /ɛ/ or /ɔ/ in a syllable that was not assigned stress, the vowel in question would be expected to map to [e] or [o], respectively.

While an analysis of raising of /ɛ ɔ/ to [e o] is straightforward in itself, in Vinalopó Mitjà there is the potential for an interaction between raising of unstressed /ɛ ɔ/ and the derivation of these vowels in harmony. Specifically, when the stressed syllable contains [ɛ] or [ɔ], we may wonder if unstressed /ɛ ɔ/ in a neighboring syllable will undergo raising to [e o] when these vowels could instead remain faithful and serve to satisfy the licensing constraint via harmony with the stressed syllable. The data that were available to me do not bear on what transpires in this circumstance. If unstressed /ɛ ɔ/ were found to undergo raising to [e o] when they could have been the target of harmony from stressed [ɛ ɔ], the pattern could perhaps be treated as a kind of derivational opacity (or its equivalent) in which unstressed vowel raising occurs prior to harmony from the stressed syllable. Further investigation on this question would be useful to obtain a more complete picture of vowel processes in this language.

SUMMARY. In closing §8.2, we have seen examples of harmony driven by maximal licensing that involves the feature [+round] in Baiyinna Orochen and all vowel features in varieties spoken in Vinalopó Mitjà. Each of these harmonies is hypothesized to be motivated by licensing constraints that produce maximal extension of features in specific marked vowels to other vowels in the word. These patterns serve to increase the exposure for the features in question, improving their perceptibility. The control of harmony by vowels in strong positions in these patterns was the effect of positional faithfulness constraints that served to restrict contrastive occurrences of the marked vowels to a specific strong position. Jiménez and Lloret (2007) have proposed a similar analysis for [−ATR] harmony in Eastern Andalusian that is maximal in the word, as attested in forms where harmony from the final syllable persists to pretonic syllables (see §6.4). In the next section, I propose that maximal licensing is active in two vowel harmonies in the dialect of Servigliano, as part of a case study of vowel patterns in that language. Different from the cases just considered, in these Servigliano patterns, harmony can be triggered by vowels in positions that show comparative weakness and that are not the privileged locus of contrast for the features that characterize harmony triggers.

8.3 Case study: Servigliano

This section presents a case study of vowel patterns in the Romance dialect of Servigliano (Marche). The language presents three vowel harmony patterns as well as vowel reduction in unstressed syllables. Each of the harmonies fits within the context of either maximal licensing or prominence-based licensing. The data and description of the phonological patterns is due to Camilli (1929) with subsequent interpretation and analysis by Kaze (1989), Maiden (1995) and Nibert (1998), the latter being especially detailed.[8]

For the present study, all words of Servigliano contained in the grammatical description and glossary of words in the article by Camilli were entered into an electronic database.[9] The resulting database contained a total of 3,240 words or short phrases. Items in the database were coded for properties under investigation, which allowed searches and counts for forms that display certain patterns.

Since the Servigliano system will be explored in some depth here, I begin with an overview of its inventory of segments. The vowel inventory is given in (19). Seven vowels occur in stressed syllables. In unstressed syllables, the inventory is reduced to five vowels – unstressed [ɛ] and [ɔ] do not occur. In agreement with Nibert, I will characterize [e o] as [+ATR] and [ɛ ɔ] as [−ATR] in Servigliano.

(19)   Vowel inventory
      a. Stressed   b. Unstressed
        i   u   i   u
        e   o   e   o
        ɛ   ɔ   a
          a

The consonant inventory is provided in (20). A noteworthy feature of the consonant system is its rich set of geminates, although these will not figure in the vowel patterns under study.

(20)   Consonant inventory

	Bilabial	Labiodental	Apico-dental/ Alveolar	Palatal	Velar
Stop	p b pp bb	f v ff vv	t d tt dd	c ɟ cc ɟɟ	k g kk gg
Fricative			s ss	ʃ ʒ ʃʃ ʒʒ	
Affricate			ts dz tts ddz	tʃ dʒ ttʃ ddʒ	

	Bilabial	Labiodental	Apico-dental/ Alveolar	Palatal	Velar
Nasal	m mm		n nn	ɲɲ	ŋ ŋŋ
Flap			ɾ		
Trill			r		
Lateral Approximant			l ll		
Glide				j jj	w

The first vowel pattern of Servigliano that I consider is metaphony. In this pattern, post-tonic high vowels [i] and [u] cause raising of a stressed mid vowel: /e o/ become [i u], as in (21a), and /ɛ ɔ/ become [e o], as in (21b).

(21)   a. /e/
           kréd-o   kríd-i   'I/you believe'
           métt-o   mítt-i   'I/you put'
           kwést-o   kwíst-u   'this (neut/m sg)'
           pés-a   pís-u   'heavy (f sg/m sg)'
        /o/
           fjóɾ-e   fjúɾ-i   'flower (m sg/m pl)'
           pótʃ-e   pútʃ-i   'flea (m sg/m pl)'
           scifós-a   scifús-u   'picky eater (f sg/m sg)'
           lóŋg-a   lúŋg-u   'long (f sg/m sg)'
    b. /ɛ/
           pɛ́tten-e   péttin-i   'comb (m sg/m pl)'
           tʃilɛ́stɾ-a   tʃiléstɾ-u   'heavenly/pale blue (f sg/m sg)'
           sgwɛ́ts-a   sgwéts-u   'suspicious (f sg/m sg)'
           ʃʃuɛ́ɾt-a   ʃʃuéɾt-u   'strange (f sg/m sg)'[10]
        /ɔ/
           mɔ́ɾ-e   móɾ-i   'he dies/you die'
           sprɔ́t-a   sprót-u   'pedantic (f sg/m sg)'
           biɾikɔ́kan-a biɾikókun-u 'apricot (tree) (f sg/m sg)'
           mɔ́ʃ-a   móʃ-u   'dejected (f sg/m sg)'

As seen in (22), stressed /i a u/ do not assimilate in height with the following vowel.

(22)   /i/
         amík-a   amík-u   'friend (f sg/m sg)'
         dítʃ-e   dítʃ-i   'he says/you say'

/u/
mút-a	mút-i	'mute (f sg/m pl)'
múɾ-e	múɾ-u	No gloss (m pl/m sg)

/a/
pátɾ-e	pátɾ-i	'father (m sg/m pl)'
ɾáp-a	ɾáp-i	No gloss (f sg/f pl)
pánn-u	páɲɲ-i	No gloss (m sg/m pl)

Exceptions to metaphony exist (Camilli 1929: 224; Nibert 1998: 81). These include the adverbs [ékko] 'here,' [ésso] 'there,' and [éjjo] 'there' when they occur with an enclitic that contains a high vowel, e.g. [ékki=li] (this form shows a post-tonic vowel assimilation, discussed below). Occurrences of the vowel [o] historically derived from [au] also form a set of exceptions, e.g. [kós-a]/[kós-u] 'thing,' [trópp-a]/[trópp-u] 'too much.' A limited number of other exceptions were found in the glossary. The bulk of these contain stressed [ɛ] or [ɔ] with a post-tonic high vowel (17 words), e.g. [séllur-u] 'celery,' [morɔ́ʃ-u] 'ogre.' Nevertheless, on the whole metaphony is a widespread characteristic of Servigliano and is responsible for productive alternations, as seen in (21).

The metaphony system of Servigliano exhibits hallmarks of a phenomenon driven by prominence-based licensing. Properties of a weak (unstressed) vowel come to be expressed in a prominent syllable; this system shows indirect licensing by the stressed syllable for [+high] and [+ATR] when they belong to a post-tonic high vowel. Only indirect licensing occurs. As I will discuss later, there is complete harmony among post-tonic vowels, which removes possible contexts for identity licensing in metaphony. The metaphony pattern can be analyzed using a prominence-based licensing constraint for the class of height features belonging to a high post-tonic vowel: LICENSE([HEIGHT]/$\sigma_{post-tonic}$[+high], ó) (see §3.4.2 on HEIGHT). Two licensing constraints, one for [high] and one for [ATR] would also be possible, but the generalization of the constraint to the class of height features captures the common factor of the features involved in the assimilation. The licensing constraint will dominate CRISPEDGE([HEIGHT], σ), IDENT-IO(high), and IDENT-IO(ATR). Because the raised vowel occurs in the stressed syllable, position-sensitive IDENT-IO-ó(high) and IDENT-IO-ó(ATR) will also be dominated by the licensing constraint. IDENT-IO-ó(low) will outrank the licensing constraint to prevent /a/ from undergoing metaphonic raising. Although the data thus far would also be compatible with positing that it is non-positional IDENT-IO(low) that dominates the licensing constraint, we will see later that IDENT-IO(low) is lower ranked.

The core of the analysis is illustrated in (23). The input in (i) contains a final high vowel and a mid [+ATR] vowel in the syllable that receives stress. The winner in (23ia) obeys the licensing constraint by sharing specifications for all height features ([high], [ATR], [low]) across the final and stressed syllable. This incurs three violations of the crisp edge constraint. The loser, in (23ib), is faithful to its input height feature specifications, but it violates licensing for [+high]. This candidate is assumed to have satisfied licensing for [+ATR] and [−low] by shared specifications across [o] and [i]. The evaluation in (ii) shows an instance where licensing is wholly prevented, because the syllable that receives stress contains a low vowel in the input. High-ranked IDENT-ó(low) prevents the stressed vowel from raising to a high vowel, as in (23iib). It would likewise prevent any raising scenario, such as to [e] or [ɛ] or their back counterparts. The faithful candidate in (23iia) therefore wins at the cost of licensing for all height features in the final high vowel.

(23) Metaphony raises mid stressed vowels but not low vowels
 IDENT-ó(low) >> LICENSE([HEIGHT]/σ$_{post-tonic}$[+high], ó) >>
 CRISPEDGE([HEIGHT], σ), IDENT-ó(high), IDENT-ó(ATR)

Input	Output	ID-ó (low)	LIC([HEIGHT]/ σ$_{post-tonic}$[+high], ó)	CRISPEDGE ([HEIGHT], σ)	ID-ó (high)	ID-ó (ATR)
i. /fjor-i/	☞ a. fjúri			***	*	
	b. fjóri		*!	**		
ii. /patr-i/	☞ a. pátri		***			
	b. pítri	*!		***	*	*

The assimilation in (23ia) is controlled by the vowel in the final syllable. I attribute this to a constraint that enforces faithfulness for vowel height features in final position: IDENT-IO-σ$_{Final}$(high). This constraint must dominate identity constraints for [high] and [ATR] in the stressed syllable. Consider the alternative failed candidates in (24). The evaluation in (i) compares two candidates that each satisfy licensing by assimilation: (24ia) by harmony from the final vowel and (24ib) by harmony from the stressed vowel. Candidate (a) wins because it respects word-final faithfulness, even though this is at the cost of faithfulness in the stressed licensing position. The candidates in (24i) do not provide evidence for ranking IDENT-IO-σ$_{Final}$(high) over IDENT-ó(ATR). That ranking will be necessary to select /mɔʃ-u/ → [móʃu] (violating IDENT-ó[ATR]) over /mɔʃ-u/ → *[mɔ́ʃo] (violating IDENT-IO-σ$_{Final}$[high]). The evaluation in (24ii) shows another effect of the word-final faithfulness constraint in the system.

When licensing fails, it will prevent lowering of the final high vowel in (24iib), instead favoring a faithful realization. This indicates that IDENT-IO-σ_Final(high) dominates the licensing constraint.

(24) The final syllable remains faithful and controls metaphony
 ID-σ_Final(high) >> LICENSE([HEIGHT]/σ_post-tonic[+high], ó) >> ID-ó(high), ID-ó(ATR)

Input	Output	IDENT-σ_Final(high)	LIC([HEIGHT]/σ_post-tonic[+high], ó)	IDENT-ó (high)	IDENT-ó (ATR)
i. /fjoɾ-i/	☞ a. fjúɾi			*	
	b. fjóɾe	*!			
ii. /patɾ-i/	☞ a. pátɾi		***		
	b. pátɾe	*!			

I discuss faithfulness in final position further when I turn to the harmony that operates among post-tonic vowels, which is also controlled by a final vowel.

Another property of Servigliano's metaphony is that it shows stepwise vowel raising. That is, mid [−ATR] /ɛ ɔ/ become mid [+ATR] [e o], and mid [+ATR] [e o] become high [+ATR] [i u]. In each case, raising alters only one height feature specification. After Kirchner (1996), I analyze this with the local conjunction of faithfulness constraints given in (25) (see also Moreton and Smolensky 2002; Miglio 2005; Walker 2005; cf. Cole 1998).

(25) IDENT-IO-ó(high) &_l IDENT-IO-ó(ATR)
 If a segment in a stressed syllable violates IDENT-IO(high), then it obeys IDENT-IO(ATR), and vice versa.

Local conjunction theory was introduced in §4.3. The minimal domain evaluable by two IDENT(F) constraints is the segment. The local conjunction in (25) is violated by a segment in a stressed syllable that incurs violations of both IDENT(high) and IDENT(ATR). It will dominate the licensing constraint with the effect of preventing metaphony from raising /ɛ ɔ/ to [i u], but it permits them to become [e o]. The restriction to the stressed syllable is necessary because, as we will see, certain vowel processes in unstressed syllables have the capacity to change a vowel's [ATR] and [high] specifications simultaneously.

The ranking is illustrated in (26). The syllable that receives stress contains mid [−ATR] /ɛ/ in the input. Candidate (c) perfectly satisfies licensing by raising the vowel to [i], but it is ruled out by the local conjunction. The faithful candidate in (b) violates the licensing constraint twice for unlicensed [+high] and [+ATR]. The winner in (a) improves on satisfaction of the licensing constraint by raising to [e], which alters only the [ATR] specification in the stressed vowel.

(26)   Stepwise raising of mid [−ATR] vowels
       IDENT-ó(high) &$_l$ IDENT-ó(ATR) >> LICENSE([HEIGHT]/σ$_{\text{post-tonic}}$[+high], ó)

/sgwɛts-u/	ID-ó(high) &$_l$ ID-ó(ATR)	LIC([HEIGHT]/ σ$_{\text{post-tonic}}$[+high], ó)	IDENT-ó (high)	IDENT-ó (ATR)
☞ a. sgwétsu		*		*
b. sgwɛ́tsu		**!		
c. sgwítsu	*!		*	*

A summary of the rankings established for metaphony in Servigliano is provided in (27).

(27)   Ranking lattice for metaphony
       IDENT-IO-ó(high) &$_l$ IDENT-IO-ó(ATR)
       IDENT-IO-σ$_{\text{Final}}$(high)
       IDENT-IO-ó(low)
         |
       LICENSE([HEIGHT]/σ$_{\text{post-tonic}}$[+high], ó)
         |
       IDENT-IO-ó(high)
       IDENT-IO-ó(ATR)
       IDENT-IO(high)
       IDENT-IO(ATR)
       CRISPEDGE([HEIGHT], σ)

To review, the metaphony system of Servigliano represents a vowel pattern that shows positional asymmetries where the stressed syllable functions as prominent and post-tonic syllables function as weak, consistent with expectations about the relative strength of these positions. This pattern causes height features in high vowels of post-tonic syllables also to be realized in the stressed syllable, in an indirect licensing configuration. As a result, these features receive enhanced exposure through their overlap with a prominent vowel.

Next I consider vowel reduction in unstressed syllables. As mentioned in the introduction to the vowel inventory, [−ATR] mid vowels [ɛ] and [ɔ] are absent in unstressed syllables of Servigliano. In unstressed syllables these vowels become [+ATR] [e] and [o], as illustrated in (28).

(28)   /ɛ/
       vɛ́ŋgo   'I come'   venéte   'you (pl) come'
       llɛ́tto   'I call (animals)'   llettá   'to call (animals)'

spéllo   'I fleece'   spellá   'to fleece'
/ɔ/
pɔ́ttso   'I am able to'   potéte   'you (pl) are able to'
vɔ́jjo   'I want'   volé   'to want'
skɔ́rdo   'I listen'   skordá   'to listen'

This pattern of mid vowel reduction is attested in many Romance varieties spoken in Italy, including Standard Italian (e.g. Crosswhite 2001, 2004; Flemming 2004, 2005; Barnes 2006; Kingston 2007; Krämer 2009). Following analyses by Crosswhite (2004) and Walker (2005) for other Romance varieties of Italy, I analyze this phenomenon as an effect of constraints that minimize the sonority of unstressed syllables. Examples of this type of constraint discussed earlier include cases in central Veneto (§5.3), Francavilla Fontana (§6.3), dialects of Liguria (§7.3), and Vinalopó Mitjà (§8.2). The constraint that prohibits unstressed vowels with sonority greater than or equal to [ɛ ɔ] is *ŏ/a,ɛ•ɔ. The ranking that promotes raising of unstressed /ɛ/ and /ɔ/ is *ŏ/a,ɛ•ɔ >> IDENT-IO(ATR). In addition, IDENT-IO(high) will dominate IDENT-IO(ATR) to prevent the mappings /ɛ/ → [ɪ] and /ɔ/ → [ʊ].[11]

The tableau in (29) illustrates the effect of this ranking in a word with an underlying /ɔ/ in a syllable that is not assigned stress. The selected candidate in (a) raises the [−ATR] mid vowel to [o], violating IDENT(ATR). The faithful candidate in (b) is eliminated on the basis of its violation of the prominence reduction constraint. Candidate (c), which raises /ɔ/ to [ʊ], is ruled out by IDENT(high).

(29)   Unstressed mid [−ATR] vowels reduce to mid [+ATR]
        IDENT-IO(high), *ŏ/a,ɛ•ɔ >> IDENT-IO(ATR)

/pɔt-ete/	IDENT-IO(high)	*ŏ/a,ɛ•ɔ	IDENT-IO(ATR)
☞ a. potéte			*
b. pɔtéte		*!	
c. pʊtéte	*!		

Because /ɛ/ and /ɔ/ also do not occur in a final unstressed syllable, IDENT(high) and *ŏ/a,ɛ•ɔ will additionally dominate the positional faithfulness constraint: IDENT-IO-σ_{Final}(ATR).

Mid [+ATR] vowels /e/ and /o/ do not undergo reduction-based raising in an unstressed syllable (although they can undergo harmony, as we will see below). This motivates the ranking IDENT-IO(high) >> *ŏ/a,ɛ•ɔ,e•o. This ranking will also prevent /ɛ/ and /ɔ/ from raising to [i] and [u]. The tableau in (30) demonstrates. In candidates (c-e), one or more unstressed mid vowels raise to high. Although this improves satisfaction of *ŏ/a,ɛ•ɔ,e•o, it incurs a fatal violation of IDENT(high). Candidate (a), with reduction of /ɔ/ to [o], is more harmonic than the faithful candidate in (b), because it obeys *ŏ/a,ɛ•ɔ.

(30)   Unstressed underlying [+ATR] mid vowels do not undergo reduction-based raising
       IDENT-IO(high) >> *ŏ/a,ɛ•ɔ,e•o

/pɔt-ete/	IDENT-IO(high)	*ŏ/a,ɛ•ɔ,e•o	*ŏ/a,ɛ•ɔ
☞ a. potéte		**	
b. pɔtéte		**	*!
c. potéti	*!	*	
d. putéte	*!	*	
e. putéti	*!*		

The lack of reduction-induced raising of the more sonorous vowel /a/ is achieved by the ranking: IDENT-IO(low) >> *ŏ/a, *ŏ/a,ɛ•ɔ, as illustrated in (31).

(31)   Unstressed low vowels do not undergo reduction-based raising
       IDENT-IO(low) >> *ŏ/a, *ŏ/a,ɛ•ɔ

/sprɔt-a/	IDENT-IO(low)	*ŏ/a	*ŏ/a,ɛ•ɔ
☞ a. sprɔ́t-a		*	*
b. sprɔ́t-ɛ	*!		*
c. sprɔ́t-e	*!		

The combined ranking for unstressed [−ATR] mid vowel reduction in Servigliano is summarized in (32).

(32)   Ranking lattice for unstressed [-ATR] mid vowel reduction

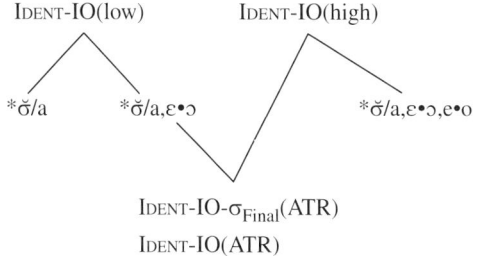

IDENT-IO-σ_Final(ATR)
IDENT-IO(ATR)

This reduction pattern is analyzed as driven by prominence-reduction constraints, because of a tendency seen in dialects of Italy for sonority minimization in unstressed syllables. Alternatively, a licensing constraint that penalizes [−ATR] in unstressed mid vowels could be invoked to drive reduction, assuming that only direct licensing were permitted. However, a licensing approach would not have any built-in predictions about whether unstressed mid [−ATR] vowels would be resolved by raising or lowering, whereas the prominence-reduction approach predicts raising.

I consider next vowel copy harmony in Servigliano. Vowels in post-tonic syllables assimilate for all of their features. The vowel that controls assimilation is a final stem or clitic vowel. The examples in (33) show vowel copy harmony among post-tonic vowels that is controlled by the final stem vowel. Certain examples in (33a–b) demonstrate that post-tonic vowel copy harmony can feed metaphony. The examples in (33c) show that copy harmony cannot skip the stressed syllable or otherwise persist to pretonic vowels.

(33) a. prédok-o   'I preach'
          prédak-a   's/he preaches'
          prédik-i   'you preach'   (/ɛ/ → [é] by metaphony)
      b. pérsak-a   'peach tree'
          pérsek-e   'peaches' (generic)
          pérsuk-u   'peach'   (/ɛ/ → [é] by metaphony)
          pérsik-i   'peaches'
      c. doménnak-a   'Sunday'
          doménnek-e   'Sundays'
      d. stómmuk-u   'stomach'[12]
          stómmik-i   'stomachs'
      e. álam-a   'soul'
          álem-e   'souls'

The examples in (34) demonstrate post-tonic vowel copy harmony that is controlled by a final clitic. In these data "-" occurs at the site of attachment for an affix and '=' for a clitic. As in (33), some of the examples in (34a) show that copy harmony can feed metaphony.

(34) a. métt-a=tʃa=la   'put it (f sg) there'   cf. métte 's/he puts', tʃe 'there'
          métt-e=tʃe=le   'put it (f pl) there'
          métt-o=tʃo=lo   'put it (neut) there'
          mítt-u=tʃu=lu   'put it (m sg) there'   (/e/ → [í] by metaphony)
          mítt-i=tʃi=li   'put it (m pl) there'   (/e/ → [í] by metaphony)
      b. párd-u=tu   'your father'   cf. pátre   'father'
      c. mátr-a=ta   'your mother'   cf. mátre 'mother'

Camilli (1929: 225) notes two exceptions to post-tonic vowel copy harmony: [ákor-e] 'country maple tree (pl)' and [fíkor-e] 'September fig tree (pl)'. The database also revealed two apparent exceptions in the glossary: [píola] 'jew's harp' and [láuro] 'laurel'. Possibly the latter example contains a diphthong, in which case it would not be an exception.

Vowel copy harmony also operates among vowels in proclitics. The vowel in the last proclitic controls harmony, as seen in (35).

(35) to=lo=dík-o   'I tell it (neut) to you (sg)'   cf. te 'to you'
      tʃi=li=métt-o   'I put it (m pl) there'   cf. tʃe 'there'
      ttu=lu=ʃíɲɲ-a   'he marks it (m sg) down for you (sg)'[13] cf. te 'for you'

Vowel copy harmony optionally affects the prepositions [pe] 'for, by, through' and [de] 'from' when they occur before a definite article ([lu], [la], [lo], [li], [le]). Examples are provided in (36a). The same pattern occurs when [ke] 'that (rel. pron.)' or [no] 'no' occurs preceding these same clitics functioning as direct object pronouns, as in (36b).

(36) a. pe lo=kállo   ~ po lo=kállo   'through the corn (collective)'
         de lu=pórku   ~ du lu=pórku   'from the pig'
      b. ke la=píjja   ~ ka la=píjja   'that takes it (f sg)'
         no lu=fá   ~ nu lu=fá   'he doesn't do/make it (m sg)'

Camilli (1929: 224) describes copy harmony as occurring frequently in these sequences, in contrast to the obligatory operation of harmony in the sequences in (35). Nibert (1998: 76, n. 8) suggests that the optionality of harmony in the forms in (36) could be indicative of optionality in the interpretation of the first item in prosodic phrasal structure. When harmony occurs, the first element is interpreted as a proclitic dependent on the following noun or verb, and when harmony does not occur, it is interpreted as an independent element. I will assume that this is the case. This means that in the examples where harmony occurs, it would be appropriate for the first element to be followed by an '=', e.g. [po=lo=kállo].

Pretonic stem vowels do not show vowel copy harmony with each other, as illustrated by the examples in (37a). They also do not show harmony with proclitics, as seen in (37b).

(37) a. ɲɲenoccó   'kneeling'
         kompaɲɲía   'procession'
         kurintí   'stable aisle'
         mannikéttu   'cuff'
      b. jje=ttunnímo   'we cut it/them'
         tʃe=fatʃímo   'we make ourselves'
         lu=rastéllu   No gloss
         li=krutʃíʃʃi   No gloss
         lo=maɲɲá   No gloss

266 *Maximal licensing*

Some data involving proclitics point to a possible interaction between copy harmony and secondary stress, although the generalizations are hard to pin down. Proclitics that bear a secondary stress apparently show the capacity to resist and block copy harmony, as seen in (38a). However, for sequences of three or more proclitics, another less frequent pattern of secondary stress occurs where the second proclitic preceding the stem receives secondary stress. In this case, the stressed proclitic does not block vowel copy harmony, as shown in (38b) for sequences of three proclitics. Under this alternate stress pattern, in a series of four proclitics, the stressed proclitic second from the stem does not block harmony, but the first proclitic does, as in (38c).

(38) a. mè=ssa=la=píjj-a   'he takes it (f sg) from me'   cf. se = reflexive pronoun
     tè=ttʃo=lo=dák-o   'I give it (neut) to you (sg)'   cf. tʃe = reiterative pronoun
     me=ttè=ssa=la=píjj-a 'he takes it (f sg) from me…?'[14]
  b. ma=ssà=la=píjj-a   'he takes it (f sg) from me'
     to=ttʃò=lo=dák-o   'I give it (neut) to you (sg)'
  c. mè=tta=ssà=la=píjj-a 'he takes it (f sg) from me…?'

These data do not establish a clear relationship between secondary stress and blocking (Maiden 1991b: 234 n. 2; cf. Nibert 1998). Given the absence of fuller information about secondary stress in Servigliano and the nature of its variation, I will not analyze the variations in blocking versus participation in copy harmony in (38), but further investigation of these aspects of Servigliano would be valuable. Comparative evidence also gives reason for caution. The very existence of secondary stress within Standard Italian, a sister language, has been the subject of debate; see Krämer (2009: 194f.) for an overview of the issues. As to the resistance of the first proclitic of four to vowel copy harmony, Maiden suggests that the concatenation of three or more proclitic pronouns would be rare and could be perceived as not very natural. Drawing on the standard language (by which I infer him to mean Italian), he suggests that when speakers are induced to produce a clitic sequence of three or more pronouns, the first could be pronounced strongly and function as external to the prosodic constituent that contains the following proclitics and stem.

To summarize, the descriptive characteristics of vowel copy harmony in Servigliano are as follows. A regressive vowel copy harmony operates among post-tonic syllables, including enclitics, and among proclitics. Pretonic vowels do not participate, nor does the vowel that is assigned primary stress. The relationship between secondary stress in proclitics and blocking is unclear and complicated by variation in the system.

Before addressing what drives vowel copy harmony, I consider the domain in which it operates. This necessitates considering the prosodic phrase structure of complexes that contain clitics in Servigliano. The levels of the prosodic hierarchy that I assume are shown in (39) (Selkirk 1978, 1995). I refer to the word level constituent as the phonological word, although some researchers refer to it as the prosodic word. In agreement with Selkirk (1995) among others, I do not postulate a clitic group constituent (cf. Nespor and Vogel 1986; Hayes 1989).

(39)   Prosodic hierarchy
        Utt   Utterance
        IP   Intonational phrase
        PPh   Phonological phrase
        PWd   Phonological word
        Ft   Foot
        σ   Syllable

Following Loporcaro (2000), I posit that clitics in Servigliano attach via adjunction at the PWd level. Loporcaro makes this claim generally for all Romance clitics. I concentrate here simply on evidence for this structure in Servigliano.[15] The representation for attachment of an enclitic is shown in (40). Proclitics will attach via a mirror image representation. In the terminology of Selkirk (1995: 441), clitics in Servigliano are thus 'affixal clitics'; they are dominated by a PWd node and are sister to a PWd.

(40)   Clitic adjunction to PWd

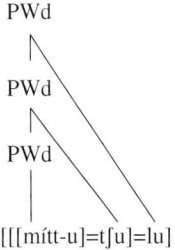

Stress is often used as a prime diagnostic for prosodic structure involving clitics (e.g. Peperkamp 1996, 1997); however, Loporcaro points out that other phonological phenomena, such as vowel harmony, may be revealing about the level of attachment for a clitic. Let us first consider the interaction between clitics and the assignment of stress in Servigliano. Primary word stress falls on one of the last three syllables of the word not including enclitics. Examples of stress on the final syllable, the penult, and the antepenult are given in (41a). The examples in (41b) show that the addition of enclitics does not affect the assignment of primary stress within the stem.

(41)   a. kontʃá   'to sift, weigh'
            fítsa   'string'
            béllara   'weasel'
       b. mítt-i   'you (sg) put'
            mítt-i=li   'put it (m pl)'
            mítt-i=tʃi=li 'put it (m pl) there'

The lack of stress shift under cliticization in Servigliano indicates that clitics are not incorporated directly within the PWd of the host (i.e. without adjunction), a structure that has been posited for certain cases of clitic attachment in other languages (e.g. Selkirk 1995; Peperkamp 1996, 1997). Loporcaro distinguishes Romance varieties like Servigliano, in which the attachment of enclitics never alters the assignment of primary stress, from ones where enclitics can cause a stress shift (e.g. in the Neopolitan and Stabiese dialects), by positing that the former do not allow stress to be reassigned post-lexically, but the latter do. I reinterpret this conceptualization using reference to maximal and minimal projections for a category, as defined in (42) after Itô and Mester (2009a, b).

(42)   Maximal and minimal projections of category κ
       a. $\kappa_{max(imal)} =_{def} \kappa$ not dominated by κ
       b. $\kappa_{min(imal)} =_{def} \kappa$ not dominating κ

In the structure in (40), [mítt-u] is PWd_{min} and [[[mítt-u]=tʃu]=lu] is PWd_{max}. In languages where clitics attach via adjunction to PWd, those where clitics can show a stress shift allow the possibility that stress be assigned within PWd_{max}, whereas in languages like Servigliano, in which clitics do not cause a stress shift, primary stress is only assigned within PWd_{min}. This can be accomplished by making either PWd_{max} or PWd_{min} the category projection that is referred to by constraints that assign stress. A similar assumption is made by Krämer (2009) for the case of Italian, where clitics do not cause stress shift. Krämer proposes that the majority of constraints relevant for stress assignment refer to PWd_{min} in the Italian system. Camilli shows that proclitics can be assigned a secondary stress (see [38]). I thus assume that secondary stress can be assigned within PWd_{max} in Servigliano, although, as I already mentioned, further investigation of secondary stress is needed.

Vowel copy harmony in Servigliano can operate across enclitics and stem vowels in post-tonic syllables. Copy harmony thus operates within PWd_{max}. The vowel that controls harmony in post-tonic syllables is in the final syllable of PWd$_{max}$. For clarity, I will henceforth notate faithfulness constraints for the final syllable in Servigliano as σ$_{FinalPWdMax}$. The lack of harmony between pretonic vowels and proclitics will require some further consideration, and is taken up below. The operation of harmony across enclitics and post-tonic stem vowels bears on the viability of another conceivable structure of clitic attachment, namely incorporation into the phonological phrase without being organized into a PWd, e.g. [[mítt–i]$_{PWd}$=li]$_{PPh}$, a structure that Peperkamp posits for Standard Italian. If this were the structure for Servigliano, then it would be necessary to make the phonological phrase the domain for vowel copy harmony. However, copy harmony never operates across word boundaries except between clitics and their host. If the PPh incorporation structure were assumed, copy harmony could be expected to occur in more contexts than where it is attested.

Having established the domain of copy harmony, I turn to the vowels that participate in the assimilation. Copy harmony in Servigliano is limited to weak vowels only. Stressed vowels are not affected (but note [38]), nor are pretonic vowels. There is reason to suppose that unstressed proclitic vowels and post-tonic vowels show weakness compared to other vowels in the language. First, there is no stress-based prominence reported for these vowels. Second, the majority of these vowels belong to dependent morphemes, either suffixes or clitics. Further, numerous other Romance varieties show more extreme vowel reduction or assimilation in post-tonic vowels than in pretonic stem vowels. Examples include the southern Lucanian dialect of Nova Siri (see §7.2.1), dialects of central Italy, the Lazio dialect of Sant' Oreste, the Montefalcone dialect (the foregoing discussed by Maiden 1995), the Francavilla Fontana dialect (Calabrese 1985; Sluyters 1988), and Brazilian Portuguese (Major 1992; Crosswhite 2001, 2004).

Based on the asymmetries witnessed in pretonic versus post-tonic syllables in Romance varieties, and the positional asymmetries displayed by vowel copy harmony in Servigliano, I propose the prominence scale in (43), applicable to Servigliano and certain other varieties (cf. Canalis 2007b and see §5.2.1).

(43)   Prominence scale (Servigliano)
        V/Strong (ó) > V/Weak (Pretonic stem) > V/Extra-Weak (Post-tonic, Unstressed clitic)

This scale posits that stressed vowels are more prominent than pretonic stem vowels, which in turn are more prominent than post-tonic vowels and vowels in unstressed clitics.[16] The vowels that are extra weak are the ones that participate in vowel copy harmony in Servigliano.

The scale in (43) is not intended to claim that all pretonic vowels or all post-tonic vowels necessarily show uniform equality in strength. Some studies have found evidence of a stronger position within these sequences in particular languages. Within post-tonic syllables, a final syllable exhibits greater phonetic and/or phonological strength than a non-final syllable in language varieties such as the dialects of Cortona and Umbertide (Canalis 2009), and southern Lazio dialects (Maiden 1995; Canalis 2009, and see §7.2.1). The immediate pretonic syllable is generally found to be stronger than pretonic syllables that come earlier in the word in Brazilian and European Portuguese (Chitoran and Hualde 2007), Catalan (Recasens 1991),[17] Romanian (Hualde and Chitoran 2003; Chitoran and Hualde 2007), and Spanish (Hualde and Chitoran 2003; Hualde 2004; Chitoran and Hualde 2007).[18] Related findings have been reported for pretonic syllables in Slavic languages (Bethin 1998, 2006; Crosswhite 2001, 2004; Padgett and Tabain 2005; Barnes 2006). These differences among post-tonic vowels on the one hand and pretonic vowels on the other could be reflected in phonological patterns such that the more prominent vowels within these sequences show less extreme reduction or they control assimilation, which could be captured by positional faithfulness constraints for the stronger vowels. Servigliano presents a case where the final post-tonic vowel in the maximal PWd controls harmony via faithfulness to this position.

I propose that the weakness of the 'extra-weak' vowels in Servigliano gives rise to a maximal licensing constraint for these vowels. This constraint drives vowel copy harmony, which expands the chances for perception of the quality of these vowels. The pattern does not fit under prominence-based licensing, because a prominent position is not consistently present to fulfill the role of licensor. I assume that copy harmony among post-tonic syllables and proclitics is a manifestation of the same process, and is driven by the same constraint. Although the final syllable could be considered prominent among the post-tonic syllables, the proclitic closest to the stem does not fall in a position that is expected to function as prominent. In addition, harmony among post-tonic syllables terminates at the main stressed syllable. Given the ubiquitous licensing role for the stressed syllable in Servigliano and related dialects, we could have expected copy harmony to necessarily *reach* the stressed syllable if this system were driven by prominence-based licensing. These considerations motivate a maximal licensing approach.

Vowel copy harmony only operates among vowels starting from the rightmost syllable of a sequence of extra-weak syllables. To capture this property of the harmony, I posit a precedence-sensitive version of the maximal licensing constraint, formulated in (44), for regressive maximal licensing phenomena involving vowels. This schema is formulated along the same lines as that of the non-precedence-sensitive maximal licensing constraint schema in (10) except that only vowels that precede a segment to which a chain for [F] is associated are eligible to be assigned a violation. (On P([F]$_j$), see discussion surrounding [10].) Provided that [F] is present in a form and any restrictions on it are fulfilled, this constraint will assign a violation to every vowel that is not a member of a chain for [F] and precedes a vowel that is.

(44)   *Precedence-sensitive Maximal Licensing constraint*: LICENSE([F], $\forall V_{Left}$)
       *V/¬LICENSE([F], V$_{Left}$) ≡ $_{def}$
       Let any occurrence of [F], a given feature, in a chain C$_j$([F]) be [F]$_j$, any occurrence of a vowel be v, and v > C([F]) mean that v precedes a segment to which C([F]) is associated.
       Then for every pair <C$_j$([F]), v> such that $\exists$ [F]$_j$ [P([F]$_j$)] $\wedge$ [v > C$_j$([F])] $\wedge$ [¬Coincide(C$_j$([F]), v)], assign a violation to v.

More generally, precedence-sensitive maximal licensing constraints will take the form LICENSE([F], $\forall \upsilon_D$), where D is drawn from the set {Left, Right} according to whether the restriction holds of preceding elements (left) or following elements (right). If we were to assume that all maximal licensing constraints are precedence sensitive, then bidirectional patterns of harmony driven by maximal licensing constraints could involve the activity of both left and right versions of the harmony-driving constraint. The specific constraint for Servigliano vowel copy harmony is LICENSE([V-FEATURE]/σ$_{xweak}$, $\forall V_{Left}$), which is violated when vowel features belonging to extra-weak syllables are not licensed by affiliation with preceding vowels. As we will see, this precedence-sensitive formulation will be important when considering the operation of harmony at the juncture of the stem and proclitics; specifically, it will prevent the vowel in the stem-initial syllable from controlling harmony in proclitics.

A crisp edge constraint for the minimal PWd could not be used to prevent vowel copy harmony from a stem syllable to proclitics, because copy harmony can span the minimal PWd boundary in post-tonic syllables. Although this problem could perhaps be addressed by altering the formulation of crisp edge constraints so that they may penalize a non-crisp boundary at a particular edge (left or right) of a constituent, there is independent motivation for directional harmonies that supports instead extending the harmony-driving constraint to include reference to the precedence of elements, as in (44). A precedence-sensitive version of the maximal licensing constraint will be necessitated for an unstressed vowel raising harmony in Servigliano, discussed below. See Rose and Walker (in press) for an overview on directionality in other harmony systems.

I turn now to the constraint rankings needed for the vowel copy harmony, focusing first on forms where the harmony operates among post-tonic syllables. Since copy harmony can cause any vowel feature to be altered in a target vowel, and it produces representations in which a feature chain spans more than one syllable, LICENSE([V-FEATURE]/σ$_{xweak}$, ∀V$_{Left}$) must dominate IDENT-IO(V-FEATURE) and CRISPEDGE([V-FEATURE], σ). This harmony can also generate unstressed non-high vowels, indicating that the maximal licensing constraint dominates not only *ŏ/a,ɛ•ɔ,e•o, *ŏ/a,ɛ•ɔ, and *ŏ/a, but also the local conjunction *ŏ/a,ɛ•ɔ,e•o &$_l$ IDENT-IO(high). The latter penalizes non-high vowels that incur a violation of IDENT(high). I consider the local conjunction here, because it plays a role in the unstressed vowel-raising harmony discussed later. Since a primary stressed syllable halts copy harmony, IDENT-IO-ó(V-FEATURE) must outrank the licensing constraint. Control of the harmony in post-tonic syllables by the final vowel will be achieved by IDENT-IO-σ$_{FinalPWdMax}$ for [high], [low], and [COLOR], that is, for all vowel features except [ATR], which is ranked lower in the hierarchy because of unstressed vowel reduction. I place these identity constraints for the final syllable in the top stratum. They will dominate the constraints that penalize unstressed non-high vowels. Finally, it was mentioned before that copy harmony operates within PWd$_{max}$. This domain is obtained by ranking CRISPEDGE([V-FEATURE], PWd$_{max}$) over the licensing constraint, to prevent vowel assimilation across a maximal PWd in longer utterances.

The tableau in (45) demonstrates the main workings of the hierarchy. For simplicity, a single violation per vowel is shown for violation of the licensing constraint and the identity constraints for vowel features, even where more than one feature is concerned. Any additional violations incurred by the candidates considered would not affect the outcome. The input in (45) has /a/ in the final syllable, preceded by two post-tonic syllables with vowels of different qualities. In candidate (c) copy harmony in post-tonic syllables is controlled by the vowel in the penultimate syllable and in (d) it is controlled by the vowel in the antepenult. Each of these candidates incurs fatal violations of identity constraints for the final syllable. Candidate (a) is the winner, with copy harmony from /a/ to the preceding post-tonic vowels, violating the local conjunction for the mapping of /i/ → [a] and IDENT(V-FEATURE). Observe that (d), with raising of post-tonic vowels fares better with respect to the local conjunction than the winner in (a), which shows lowering of post-tonic vowels by assimilation to final /a/. This supports the ranking of IDENT constraints for the final syllable over the local conjunction. Candidate (e) shows copy harmony controlled by final /a/ that persists to stressed /e/. Even though this candidate perfectly satisfies the licensing constraint, it is ruled out by the stressed syllable faithfulness constraint. In contrast, the selected form incurs one violation of the licensing constraint, because post-tonic vowel features are not licensed by the stressed syllable, but it satisfies faithfulness for the stressed syllable. The faithful candidate in (b) is eliminated because it incurs six violations of the licensing constraint: three for [a] (one each for the three unassimilated vowels that precede [a]), two for post-tonic [e], and one for [i]. Note that candidates (b) and (d) would be expected to show metaphonic raising of stressed /e/ → [i] because of the following high vowel, but I do not show that in these candidates because the metaphony-driving constraint is not included here. I address the interaction of these harmonies below.

(45)   Vowel copy harmony in post-tonic syllables
       IDENT-IO-$\sigma_{FinalPWdMax}$(high)/(low)/(COLOR),   IDENT-IO-ó(V-FEATURE) >>
       LICENSE([V-FEATURE]/σ_{xweak}, $\forall V_{Left}$) >> IDENT-IO(V-FEATURE), *ŏ/a,ɛ•ɔ,e•o
       &$_l$ IDENT-IO(high)

/mett-i=tʃe=la/	IDENT$\sigma_{FinPWdMax}$ (high)/(low)/ (COLOR)	IDENT-ó (V-FEAT)	LICENSE ([V-FEAT]/ σ_{xwk}, $\forall V_{Left}$)	IDENT (V-FEAT)	*ŏ/a,ɛ•ɔ,e•o &$_l$ IDENT(hi)
☞ a. métt-a=tʃa=la			*	**	*
b. métt-i=tʃe=la			**!*, **, *		
c. métt-e=tʃe=le	*(!)(low) *(!)(COLOR)			**	*
d. métt-i=tʃi=li	*(!)(high) *(!)(low) *(!)(COLOR)		*	**	
e. mátt-a=tʃa=la		*!		***	*

Examples in (33–34) showed that vowel copy harmony can feed metaphony. The analysis of metaphony established that the constraint that drives metaphony, LICENSE([HEIGHT]/$\sigma_{post-tonic}$[+high], ó), is dominated by the constraint that enforces identity for [high] in the final syllable, and it dominates constraints that enforce identity for [high] and [ATR] in the stressed syllable. These faithfulness constraints for the final syllable and the stressed syllable dominate the maximal licensing constraint that drives post-tonic vowel harmony. The combined ranking, showing IDENT constraints for the features concerned in metaphony is shown in (46). This tableau does not include the local conjunction, *ŏ/a,ɛ•ɔ,e•o &$_l$ IDENT-IO(high), because it is ranked sufficiently low in the hierarchy so as not to affect the selection with the candidates under consideration. The input in (46) has a high vowel in the final enclitic and a mid

[+ATR] vowel in the syllable that is assigned stress. Candidates (d) and (e) show post-tonic copy harmony from a non-final vowel, which violates the top-ranked identity constraints for [high] and color features in the final syllable. Candidate (c) is fully faithful, and (b) shows post-tonic copy harmony controlled by the final vowel. Each of these candidates has post-tonic high vowels but does not show raising in the stressed syllable, violating the licensing constraint that drives metaphony. Candidate (a) shows post-tonic copy harmony controlled by the final vowel and it displays metaphony. This satisfies the two highest-ranked constraints, causing it to win over the competitors. The rankings that have been worked out for metaphony and post-tonic copy harmony thus integrate to predict correctly that the latter feeds the former.

(46)   Vowel copy harmony feeds metaphony

/mett-i=tʃe=lu/	IDENTσ$_{\text{FinPWdMax}}$ (high)/(low)/ (COLOR)	*Metaphony* LICENSE ([HEIGHT]/ σ$_{\text{post-tonic}}$ [+high], ó)	IDENTó (high)/ (ATR)	*Vowel copy* LICENSE ([V-FEAT]/ σ$_{\text{xweak}}$, ∀V$_{\text{Left}}$)	IDENT (V-FEAT)
☞ a. mítt-u=tʃu=lu			*(high)	*	***
b. métt-u=tʃu=lu		*!		*	**
c. métt-i=tʃe=lu		*!*		***, **, *	
d. métt-e=tʃe=le	*(!)(high) *(!)(COLOR)				**
e. métt-i=tʃi=li	*!(COLOR)	*		*	**

We have established that the failure of the stressed syllable to undergo copy harmony is obtained by stressed syllable faithfulness constraints. This syllable blocks copy harmony rather than behaving as transparent and permitting copy harmony in pretonic syllables, as in [doménnaka], *[daménnaka] 'Sunday.' Although this might seem to suggest that *DUPLICATE(F) prevents harmony across a stressed syllable that does not harmonize with post-tonic vowels, the issue is more general than that. Even if the vowel in the stressed syllable happens to have the same quality as the post-tonic vowels, harmony does not persist to pretonic vowels [doménneke], *[deménneke] 'Sundays.' However, we will see later that the stressed syllable can trigger harmony for [+high] in pretonic syllables, and this also occurs when a high stressed vowel is the product of metaphony from a post-tonic syllable.

It thus appears that the stressed syllable serves as a barrier to assimilation specifically for [low], [–high], and [COLOR]. I suggest that this is the work of crisp edge constraints for a foot. I postulate that the core stress foot is binary, which would exclude the final syllable in a word like [doménneke]. For some Romance varieties, Flemming (1993) suggests that post-tonic syllables that are not part of the main stress foot are adjoined to the final foot. I hypothesize this structure exists in Servigliano. Given Itô and Mester's definition of maximal and minimal category projections, the core stress foot would be identified as Ft_{min} and the foot plus all adjoined post-tonic syllables would be Ft_{max}. This latter projection is the one to which the crisp edge constraint makes reference for barrier effects by the stressed syllable. It could not be Ft_{min}, because vowel copy harmony can operate across a Ft_{min} boundary. CRISPEDGE([low], Ft_{max}), CRISPEDGE([–high], Ft_{max}) and CRISPEDGE([COLOR], Ft_{max}) will dominate LICENSE([V-FEATURE]/σ_{xweak}, $\forall V_{Left}$). This is illustrated in (47). The hypothetical input for [doménneke] here has /e/ in the penultimate syllable. In the candidate outputs, the boundaries of Ft_{max} are shown. Candidate (b) fully satisfies the licensing constraint, but it violates the crisp edge constraints, because [–round], [–back], [–high], and [–low] span the Ft_{max} boundary. Candidate (a) is selected, because even though it violates the licensing constraint, it satisfies the higher ranked crisp edge constraints. Following earlier practice, a single violation is tallied for unlicensed vowel features for simplicity.

(47)   Vowel copy harmony does not persist to pretonic vowels
         CRISPEDGE([COLOR/low/–high], Ft_{max}) >> LICENSE([V-FEATURE]/σ_{xweak}, $\forall V_{Left}$)

/domennek-e/	CRISPEDGE ([COLOR]/[–high]/[low], Ft_{max})	LICENSE([V-F]/ σ_{xweak}, $\forall V_{Left}$)
☞ a. do(ménneke)$_{max}$		*
b. de(ménneke)$_{max}$	*(!)*(COLOR) *(!)(–high) *(!)(low)	

The crisp edge constraints shown in (47) will also serve to prevent copy harmony across a transparent stressed syllable in words where the stressed syllable does not happen to show the same quality as the post-tonic vowels. This will be important once we consider unstressed vowel-raising harmony, which shows that *DUPLICATE(F) is lower ranked in the constraint hierarchy, and thus is not the cause of blocking by the stressed syllable in vowel copy harmony.

I consider next vowel copy harmony involving proclitics. In this context, positional faithfulness for the final syllable will not come into play. This raises the question of what determines control of harmony by the proclitic that is closest to the stem. I propose to capture this using an identity relation between the base of cliticization and the cliticized form, building on a similar relation proposed by Krämer (2009: 201) for Italian. I formulate this relation as an extension of base-affixed form transderivational identity (IDENT-BA(F)) (Benua 1995), a version of which is used by Baković (2000) to obtain cyclic effects in vowel harmony systems. I extend 'affixed forms' to include constituents formed by attachment of affixal clitics. Thus, in a structure such as [to=[lo=[dík-o]]], IDENT-BA(F) will enforce identity for (F) for segments in [lo=dík-o] to their correspondents in [dík-o], and likewise for segments in [to=lo=dík-o] to their correspondents in [lo=dík-o]. Because new material added at each cycle of cliticization will not have corresponding segments in the base, it will not be subject to IDENT-BA(F), and therefore can undergo alteration for [F] in phonological processes from which the segments of the base may be protected.[19] The definition of IDENT-BA(F) is given in (48), after Kager (1999).

(48)   IDENT-BA(F)
Let α be a segment in the base and β be a correspondent of α in the affixed form. If α is [γF], then β is [γF].

Copy harmony can produce complete assimilation, necessitating the constraint IDENT-BA(V-FEATURE). Like IDENT-IO constraints for the final syllable, IDENT-BA(V-FEATURE) dominates constraints that penalize unstressed non-high vowels, including the local conjunction. Because copy harmony in post-tonic syllables is controlled by the final syllable rather than the innermost suffix or enclitic, IDENT-IO–$\sigma_{FinalPWdMax}$ constraints for [high], [low], and [COLOR] will dominate IDENT-BA(V-FEATURE) to neutralize its effect in post-tonic sequences.

The operation of vowel copy harmony in proclitics is illustrated in (49). The input is a form with two proclitics. All candidates will earn three violations of the maximal licensing constraint for the final unstressed [a], from which harmony is blocked by the stressed syllable. These violations are not shown in the tableau as they will not factor into the outcome here. Candidate (d), which shows progressive assimilation from the first proclitic to the second is eliminated because it violates IDENT-BA. This violation is incurred because the base for attachment of the outermost proclitic is [lu=ʃiɲɲ-a], and the proclitic vowel /u/ maps to [e] in (d). Candidate (c) with regressive copy harmony from the first syllable of the stem likewise violates IDENT-BA(V-FEATURE).

The faithful candidate in (b) is ruled out on the basis of its violation of the licensing constraint. Candidate (a) is selected, which violates only IDENT-IO(V-FEATURE). This particular vowel sequence in the proclitics does not necessitate ranking IDENT-BA(V-FEATURE) over constraints that prohibit unstressed non-high vowels. That would be supported by a hypothetical proclitic sequence /Ci=Ce=.../ mapping to [Ce=Ce=...], which respects IDENT-BA and lowers a high clitic vowel by regressive assimilation, rather than to *[Ci=Ci=...], which violates IDENT-BA and shows raising by progressive assimilation.

(49)   Vowel copy harmony in proclitics
       IDENT-BA(V-FEATURE), LICENSE([V-FEATURE]/σ_{xweak}, $\forall V_{Left}$) >> IDENT-IO
       (V-FEATURE), *ŏ/a,ɛ•ɔ,e•o &$_l$ IDENT-IO(high)

/te=lu=ʃiɲɲ-a/	IDENT-BA (V-FEATURE)	LICENSE ([V-FEATURE]/ σ_{xweak}, $\forall V_{Left}$)	IDENT-IO (V-FEATURE)	*ŏ/a,ɛ•ɔ,e•o &$_l$ IDENT-IO(high)
☞ a. ttu=lu=ʃíɲɲ-a			*	
b. tte=lu=ʃíɲɲ-a		*!		
c. tti=li=ʃíɲɲ-a	*!		**	
d. tte=le=ʃíɲɲ-a	*!		*	*

There are two observations to be made about what precedence sensitivity in the licensing constraint does and does not capture in this system. First, the control of copy harmony by the vowel in the final syllable within a sequence of extra weak syllables does not follow from the precedence sensitivity. Both candidate (49a), with regressive harmony, and (49d), with progressive harmony, satisfy the licensing constraint. Although (49d) violates the local conjunction (*ŏ/a,ɛ•ɔ,e•o &$_l$ IDENT-IO(high)), this is incidental to the vowels in this particular form and will not guarantee control by the proclitic that is closest to the stem. Control by the innermost proclitic is instead assured by IDENT-BA. Likewise, control of copy harmony by the final vowel in post-tonic syllables is achieved by faithfulness to the final syllable, not precedence sensitivity in the licensing constraint.

The second observation is that the precedence sensitivity in the licensing constraint is important to prevent harmony from the initial stem syllable to the closest proclitic. Consider a form with a single proclitic, shown in (50). Focusing on licensing violations for features of the proclitic only, the precedence-sensitive licensing constraint penalizes only non-harmonizing vowels that precede the proclitic vowel, so both candidate (a), with no copy harmony, and (b), with copy harmony from the stem to the proclitic, satisfy the licensing constraint. Candidate (b) loses, because it incurs an unnecessary violation of IDENT-IO(V-FEATURE) and the local conjunction. If, on the other hand, a version of the licensing constraint were assumed that was not precedence sensitive, as in (51), then (a) would earn two violations of the licensing constraint with respect to the proclitic vowel for the two syllables that do not actively harmonize with it. Candidate (b) would be erroneously selected, as called out by 'x☞', because the harmony from the initial stem vowel would cause it to incur only a single violation of the licensing constraint with respect to the proclitic. Complete harmony across all syllables in this form would not be expected because it has been established that identity constraints for the stressed syllable and the final syllable dominate the maximal licensing constraint. The problem for a non-precedence-sensitive version of the licensing constraint could not be solved by appealing to IDENT-BA to block harmony from the stem, because the proclitic vowel /u/ does not have a correspondent in the base for cliticization, which is [pórk-u].

(50)   The role of precedence sensitivity in the licensing constraint

/lu=pork-u/	IDENT-BA (V-FEATURE)	LICENSE ([V-FEATURE]/ σ_{xweak}, $\forall V_{Left}$)	IDENT-IO (V-FEATURE)	*ŏ/a,ɛ•ɔ,e•o &$_l$ IDENT-IO(high)
☞ a. lu=pórk-u				
b. lo=pórk-u			*(!)	*(!)

(51)   Problem for a licensing constraint that is not precedence sensitive

/lu=pork-u/	IDENT-BA (V-FEATURE)	LICENSE ([V-FEATURE]/ σ_{xweak}, $\forall V$)	IDENT-IO (V-FEATURE)	*ŏ/a,ɛ•ɔ,e•o &$_l$ IDENT-IO(high)
a. lu=pórk-u		**!		
x☞ b. lo=pórk-u		*	*	*

A summary of the rankings established for vowel copy harmony in Servigliano is given in (52).

(52)   Ranking lattice for vowel copy harmony

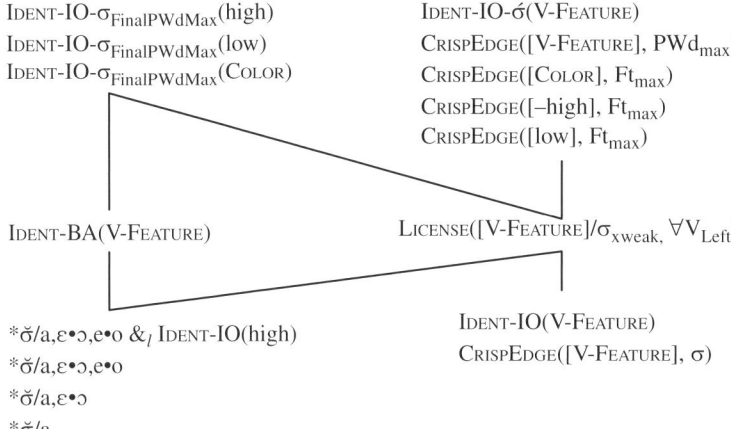

To recap some main themes, vowel copy harmony in Servigliano is a pattern that presents positional asymmetries. Harmony operates among what could plausibly be considered extra-weak vowels in the language, namely, those that occur in post-tonic syllables and unstressed clitics. Harmony is blocked by stressed syllables (although the facts surrounding secondary stressed syllables are not firmly understood). In this respect, copy harmony shows an important difference from metaphony, where assimilation necessarily propagates to the stressed syllable. Furthermore, in its operation among proclitics, copy harmony does not conform with a system where features come to be expressed in a prominent position. The pattern is thus consistent with a drive for maximal licensing instead of prominence-based licensing. As a maximal licensing system, copy harmony serves to increase the exposure of vowel features in extra-weak syllables in an unbounded fashion. The primary stressed syllable does not visibly participate in the harmony, in conformity with the strength of this position. As for control of copy harmony, the vowel in the final syllable governs harmony among post-tonic syllables through faithfulness to this position, which falls in line with expectations about this position's potential to show aspects of strength, despite its status as a weak post-tonic syllable. In the case of proclitics, it is not positional strength that decides control for harmony but rather the enforcement of an identity relation between a cliticized form and its base. Prosodic constituents and precedence sensitivity in the licensing constraint figure in determining the domains for harmony.

The last vowel pattern in Servigliano that I examine is an unstressed vowel raising harmony. Servigliano presents two vowel-raising harmonies. One is the

280 *Maximal licensing*

metaphony described above, where post-tonic [i u] cause stressed /e o/ to raise to [i u] and stressed /ɛ ɔ/ to raise to [e o], respectively. In the second raising harmony, [i u] cause preceding unstressed [e o] in the stem to raise to [i u], respectively. I discuss reasons to analyze unstressed raising harmony and metaphony as separate phenomena after presenting the data. Because of the other vowel harmonies that are active in Servigliano, unstressed raising harmony is witnessed only in pretonic vowels. I consider first data where the stressed vowel is the trigger, starting with the examples in (53).

(53)   leg-éte   lig-ímo   'you (pl)/we tie'
       sténn-ete   stinn-í   'you (pl) spread/to spread'
       verd-ó   virdú   'very green (m sg/pl)'
       nfork-éte   nfurk-ímo   'you (pl)/we mount'
       fol-émo   ful-ísti   'we/you (sg) were (perf.)'
       kost-é   kust-ú   demonstrative pronouns
       kommonek-á   kummunik-íno   'to communicate/? communicate'[20]
       bollétt-a   bullitt-í   No gloss
       ɲɲenocc-ó   ɲɲinucc-ú   'kneeling'/No gloss

Stressed vowels that are high as the result of metaphony also trigger raising, as shown in (54).

(54)   stommekós-a   stummikús-u   'nauseating (f sg/m sg)'
       battetó-re   battitú-ri   'beater (hunt) (m sg/pl)'
       kos-étt-a   kus-ítt-u   No gloss
       dolór-e   dulúr-i   'sorrow (m sg/pl)'

Observe that the forms in (54) will obey the crisp edge constraints for Ft_{max} postulated for vowel copy harmony, because they were for [COLOR], [−high] and [low]. The feature that spans the Ft_{max} boundary in these forms is [+high].

Triplets of related forms given in (55) show that mid [−ATR] vowels that normally undergo raising to mid [+ATR] in an unstressed syllable can raise to [+high] in unstressed raising harmony.

(55)   a. véŋg-o   'I come'
          ven-éte   'you (pl) come'
          vin-í   'to come'
       b. téŋg-a   'to hold'
          ten-éte   'you (pl) hold'
          tin-ímo   'we hold'
       c. vɔ́jj-o   'I want'
          vol-éte   'you (pl) want'
          vul-ímo   'we want'
       d. bbesɔ́ɲɲ-a   'need (f sg)'
          bbesoɲɲ-á   'to need'
          bbisuɲɲ-ímo   'we need'

The examples in (56) show that unstressed raising harmony does not persist to proclitics.

(56)   j̲j̲e̲=dítʃe   'he says to him/her/them'
       j̲j̲e̲=ttu̲nnímo   'we cut it/them'
       le̲=fíkore   'the September fig tree (pl)'
       le̲=múre   No gloss

Pretonic /a/ does not undergo raising in this harmony, as the data in (57) demonstrate. Observe that in examples in (57c), a pretonic mid unstressed vowel undergoes raising, which indicates that these forms are not lexical exceptions to the process.

(57)   a. fakkí   'laborer'
           tarína   'soup tureen'
           sapútu   'dandy'
           aŋgunía   'agony'
       b. sap-éte   sap-ímo   'you (pl)/we know'
           fatʃ-énno   fatʃ-ímo   'doing/we do'
       c. bjaŋkɔ́   bjaŋkulí   'type of ox'
           battetóre   battitúri   'beater (hunt) (m sg/pl)'

The data in (58) support the conclusion that the height assimilation involving unstressed pretonic vowels is indeed a raising harmony. Unstressed high vowels that occur preceding a stressed non-high vowel do not undergo lowering.

(58)   /i/
       ditʃéte   'you (pl) say'
       ɲɲikósa   indefinite particle
       tʃiléstra   'heavenly/pale blue (f sg)'
       kriʃʃikɔ́re   'suckling baby's cry'
       gajjináttʃu   'turkey (m sg)'
       /u/
       budéllu   No gloss
       bruɲɲólu   'type of tree (blackthorn)'
       nutʃélla   'hazel nut/hazel tree'
       kuttʃɔ́la   'snail'
       cidunátru   indefinite particle

The data pertaining to unstressed vowel-raising harmony considered so far show that stressed high vowels can trigger the raising. A search was performed on the Servigliano database for forms with a high vowel in the stressed syllable and one or more pretonic non-low vowels. There were 316 words of this kind that were consistent with a distribution in which stressed high vowels trigger height assimilation in preceding mid vowels. Not all of these showed alternations; for some there was evidence of active raising, in others the pretonic vowel(s) were underlyingly high, and in other cases there was insufficient information to determine the underlying height of the pretonic vowels. The database contained two exceptions to raising triggered by a stressed high vowel [eʃʃí] 'yes (emph.),' [nnentsú] 'over there?' These counts do not include forms where unstressed /a/ intervenes between the stressed vowel and a pretonic non-low vowel, which I consider later.

Although a prior analysis has characterized the unstressed vowel-raising harmony as triggered by stressed vowels (Nibert 1998), the question of whether pretonic high vowels can trigger raising in pretonic mid vowels merits investigation. Camilli describes pretonic mid vowels as undergoing raising if the following vowel is high – he does not indicate a condition that the following high vowel must be stressed (1929: 224). The examination by Maiden (1995: 119) of the historical development of several Servigliano forms with pretonic high vowels points to the conclusion that regressive raising harmony in unstressed non-low vowels can be triggered by unstressed high vowels (59a), as well as stressed high vowels (59b).

(59) a. viritá   < *veritáte   'truth'
        bbiʃʃiká   < *vessikáre   'to remove the bladder'
        dilibberá   < *deliberáre   'to set free'
        suspirá   < *sospiráre   'to sigh'
        kuntsumá   < *konsumáre   'to consume'
        furmikétta   < *formikétta   'ant'
     b. putímo   < *potímo   'we can'
        fjurillítti   < *fjorellítti   'little flowers'

The following pair also suggests that unstressed high vowels can trigger raising harmony: [meterélla], [mitirélla]. Camilli lists both as forms for a word meaning 'endive' (1929: 259). It is interesting that the second form, in which both pretonic vowels are high, is consistent with a distribution expected for unstressed raising harmony if it could be triggered by an unstressed high vowel. That is, if one of the pretonic vowels is high, both become so. This form does not bear on directionality in the harmony, however.

To investigate this pattern further, the database was examined for words containing a stressed non-high vowel and two or more pretonic non-low vowels, at least one of which was high. There were eighty-three such words that were consistent with a distribution where unstressed high vowels trigger unstressed raising harmony. For the most part, alternations do not occur in this context. Some examples are given in (60) (see also [59a]).

(60)   riʃibbála   'strep throat'
       ʃʃinikɔ́ka   'whimpering'
       stimmulá   'to goad, prod'

cid̪unátru	indefinite particle
bujjirélla	'spring'
bbut̪iná	'to wrap'
kuk̪umétta	'rummy (card game)'
funnurujjá	'dregs'

There were fifteen words in which a mid pretonic vowel preceded or followed a high pretonic vowel. I consider those forms more closely in what follows.

Seven examples were found in the database that did not conform to the distribution of unstressed raising harmony in the regressive direction triggered by an unstressed high vowel. In four of these, the vowel that did not undergo harmony was [e] preceded by [r], as shown in (61b). The remaining three forms are given in (61a).[21]

(61) a. boŋkristiá   No gloss
         montefurtí   No gloss
         occuvɔ́   'type of bird (long-tailed tit)'
      b. refiná   'to stop'
         remmuccá   'to support'
         rentrufásse   'to find (about wood in water)'
         reppujjásse   'to lodge'

I speculate that the first two words in (61a) might be compounds, with raising harmony failing to operate across the stem boundary. Perhaps the third word in (61a) has the status of a learned form, causing it to not show harmony, but this requires further investigation. Thus, even though they may be exceptions, the forms in (61a) do not seem to cast significant doubt on the existence of regressive raising harmony triggered by an unstressed high vowel.

The forms in (61b) show a common context where harmony does not occur, namely, in [re] sequences. However, it is not the case that unstressed [ri] sequences never occur in Servigliano, e.g. [rivústu] 'robust.' An instance where /e/ following [r] actively undergoes unstressed vowel raising is evidenced by the pair: [réʃʃo]/[riʃʃí] 'I come out/to come out.' This state of affairs is reminiscent of a phenomenon reported for a height harmony in the Pasiego Romance dialect of the Cantabrian Montaña. A non-low vowel preceding a stressed high vowel in Pasiego is usually high. However, Penny (1969: 154f.) observes that a front vowel adjacent to [r] may resist harmony, e.g. [rendír] ~ [rindír] 'to give in,' [rebUltÚsU] ~ [ribUltÚsU] 'disobedient' (in Pasiego, [U] represents a high back round vowel that is centralized and more open than [u]). It is also interesting that Flemming (1993) has argued that the height harmony in Pasiego can be triggered by both stressed and unstressed high vowels. In the database for Servigliano, there were thirty-six words with the sequence [re] in an unstressed syllable versus just eleven words with the sequence [ri] in an unstressed syllable – counting all words, not just ones with contexts for unstressed raising harmony. I will assume that a phonotactic constraint is active in Servigliano that disfavors [ri] sequences in an unstressed syllable. I assume that the constraint is lexically indexed in Servigliano with the result that [e] preceded by [r] does not undergo harmony in certain words. My conclusion is that the Servigliano data are compatible with the descriptive generalization that an unstressed high vowel can trigger regressive unstressed raising harmony.

Let us now consider data bearing on whether an unstressed high vowel can trigger progressive unstressed raising harmony. There were eight words in the database in which a high pretonic vowel was followed by a mid pretonic vowel, listed in (62).

(62)   birokókwala   No gloss
       finestrélla   'buttonhole'
       kuppolétta   'head of a spindle'
       mukkolétta   'buckle'
       sbriskolá   'to hit'
       tʃitʃeró   'plump'
       tʃitʃeróttu   'plump'[22]
       ttʃimentá   'to insult'

The absence of harmony in the words in (62) does not appear readily attributable to a particular phonological context, morphological structure, or learned vocabulary. Even in the event that one or two of these forms could be explained in this way, this set of data seems to point to the conclusion that progressive unstressed vowel harmony is not enforced in Servigliano. This conclusion is consistent with Camilli's description, which characterized pretonic vowel assimilations as dependent on a following vowel. I will thus assume that unstressed raising harmony is regressive and triggered by a high vowel, whether stressed or unstressed.[23]

The next issue to consider is the status of intervening unstressed /a/. This vowel has been characterized as transparent to the raising of unstressed vowels (Kaze 1989; Nibert 1998), because of the alternations shown in (63a). There were eight additional forms in the database that were consistent with the analysis of /a/ as transparent (not shown here). However, since those additional forms did not show alternations, it is also possible that the vowel in the syllable preceding /a/ in those forms is underlyingly high and not the product of raising harmony. On the other hand, there were thirty-one forms in the database where unstressed /a/ blocked regressive unstressed raising harmony. Some examples are given in (63b).

(63)   a. bokalétt-a   bukalítt-u   No gloss
           bokkal-ó   bukkal-ú   'foolish (m sg/m pl)'

b. setattʃíttu   'tomato strainer'
   menattʃútu   'violent, hot-tempered'
   merkantsía   No gloss
   skrokkafúse   'a type of fritter'
   skottʃamúsu   'bit for a reluctant horse'
   golantrína   'lady bug'
   tresomarí   'rosemary'

The examples in (63a) show that it is possible for /a/ to be transparent to unstressed vowel-raising harmony. However, the abundance of forms in which /a/ blocks the harmony indicate that a significant number of lexical exceptions exist. I will treat both scenarios in the analysis.

To summarize the conclusions at this point, the pattern of unstressed vowel-raising harmony in Servigliano is such that a high vowel – stressed or unstressed – causes a preceding unstressed mid vowel in the stem to raise to high. In a number of forms /a/ blocks this harmony, although /a/ is transparent to the assimilation in some words.

Given that both metaphony and unstressed vowel-raising harmony cause [e] and [o] to raise to [i] and [u], the question arises whether the harmonies are distinct in this dialect or instances of a single harmony process. Typological evidence provides a main reason to suppose that metaphony and unstressed vowel raising are distinct phenomena (Maiden 1995; Nibert 1998). Many of the minor Romance languages show metaphony only (i.e. raising that affects the stressed vowel but not pretonic vowels), and the stepwise raising seen in the metaphony of Servigliano is not unusual in Romance metaphonies (Maiden 1991a). The domains for the raising phenomena are also a factor. Raising in the stressed syllable (metaphony) can be caused by a feature that spans a boundary between stem and clitic, whereas raising of vowels preceding the stressed syllable (unstressed vowel raising) may not give rise to representations that span this boundary, a difference that suggests these patterns are not unitary.[24] For these reasons, I will assume that metaphony and unstressed raising harmony in Servigliano are distinct and driven by separate constraints.[25]

Unstressed vowel raising harmony increases the extent of realization for [+high] in a word. I propose that it is driven by a maximal licensing constraint that penalizes vowels that do not harmonize for [+high] with a following high vowel: LICENSE([+high], $\forall V_{Left}$). We have seen that [+high] has a capacity to serve as marked, which is consistent with its being singled out for expansion in this pattern. The harmony is not suitable for treatment in terms of prominence-based licensing, because it does not regularly produce outcomes where [+high] belongs to a prominent position. Although unstressed raising harmony can issue from the stressed syllable, in some forms it operates among pretonic syllables only.

Because the licensing constraint drives raising harmony, it dominates IDENT-IO(high) and CRISPEDGE([high], σ). I attribute control of the harmony by a high unstressed trigger to the local conjunction that penalizes vowels that have lowered from high to non-high: *ŏ/a,ɛ•ɔ,e•o &$_l$ IDENT-IO(high). This constraint will prevent vacuous satisfaction of the licensing constraint that drives unstressed raising harmony by lowering an unstressed high vowel that is a potential trigger. Control by a stressed high vowel can be obtained with an identity constraint for [high] in the stressed syllable. The local conjunction and IDENT-IO-ó(high) will dominate the licensing constraint.

The ranking is illustrated in (64). The evaluation in (64i) operates on an input with a high vowel in the syllable that is assigned stress with preceding mid and low vowels. None of the candidates considered raises pretonic /a/. This will be enforced by IDENT-IO(low), as will be discussed below. Candidate (64ib) is faithful for [high], and it satisfies the crisp edge constraint, but it incurs two violations of the maximal licensing constraint (the expected reduction of unstressed /ɔ/ to [o] is shown here). Candidate (64ic) satisfies the maximal licensing constraint by lowering the stressed vowel to mid, but this outcome is ruled out by IDENT-ó(high). In candidate (a), the mid pretonic vowel shows raising harmony. This candidate is selected, because it satisfies the two top-tier constraints and it fares better with respect to the licensing constraint than (b), at the cost of IDENT(high) and the crisp edge constraint. The evaluation in (64ii) is for the derivation of [kaliʃá] 'to slide.' Again, pretonic /a/ will not raise. The optimal output in (64iia) retains the pretonic high vowel, even though this causes the form to incur a violation of the licensing constraint. The alternative in (b), which satisfies the licensing constraint by lowering the pretonic high vowel, is eliminated because it violates the higher-ranked local conjunction.

(64) Unstressed vowel-raising harmony
IDENT-IO-ó(high), *ŏ/a,ɛ•ɔ,e•o &$_l$ IDENT-IO(high) >> LICENSE([+high], ∀V$_{Left}$) >> IDENT-IO(high), CRISPEDGE([high], σ)

Input	Output	IDENT-ó(high)	*ŏ/ a,ɛ•ɔ,e•o &$_l$ ID(high)	LICENSE ([+hi], ∀V$_{LL}$)	IDENT (high)	CRISPEDGE ([high], σ)
i. /bjaŋkɔli/	☞ a. bjaŋkulí			*	*	*
	b. bjaŋkolí			**!		
	c. bjaŋkolé	*!			*	
ii. /kaliʃa/	☞ a. kaliʃá			*		
	b. kaleʃá		*!		*	

It was previously determined that *ŏ/a,ɛ•ɔ,e•o &$_l$ IDENT-IO(high) is dominated by the constraint that drives vowel copy harmony, which in turn is dominated by the constraint that drives metaphony. That implies that the portion of the constraint hierarchy that implements the processes of copy harmony and metaphony will be higher ranked than the maximal licensing constraint that drives unstressed vowel raising. We therefore expect that the distributions associated with vowel copy harmony and metaphony could not be sacrificed in order to improve performance with respect to unstressed raising harmony, as is consistent with the data. Indeed, metaphony feeds unstressed vowel raising, as seen in (54).[26] This traces back to control by the word-final syllable: a faithfulness constraint for [high] is in the top stratum of the constraint hierarchy.

The tableau in (65) shows the application of the hierarchy for unstressed raising harmony to a form in which a pretonic high vowel is flanked by unstressed vowels that are mid in the input. This tableau considers a hypothetical input for [dilibberá], which reflects the historical development of this form. The faithful candidate in (c) is ruled out by its violation of the licensing constraint. Candidates (a) and (b) both show raising harmony, (a) displays regressive harmony only and (b) displays raising harmony in both directions. Candidate (a) is favored over (b), because it incurs the minimal IDENT(high) violations needed to satisfy the licensing constraint. Observe that if the licensing constraint that drives unstressed raising harmony were not precedence sensitive, then (b) would incorrectly be favored over (a). Candidate (d) achieves satisfaction of the licensing constraint by lowering the pretonic high vowel to mid, but it is ruled out by the local conjunction.

(65)   Regressive directionality in unstressed raising harmony

/delibber-a/	*ŏ/ a,ɛ•ɔ,e•o &$_l$ ID(high)	LICENSE ([+high], ∀V$_{Left}$)	IDENT (high)	CRISPEDGE ([HEIGHT], σ)
☞ a. dilibberá			*	*
b. dilibbirá			**!	*
c. delibberá		*!		
d. delebberá	*!		*	

It was noted earlier that in some particular languages, Romance and otherwise, the immediate pretonic syllable shows greater strength than other pretonic syllables. It might seem that a positional faithfulness constraint for [high] in the immediate pretonic syllable could be applicable to directionality effects in the system of unstressed vowel raising. For instance, we could speculate that a constraint IDENT-IO(high)$_{immed.pretonic}$ could block harmony to the immediate pretonic vowel in (65a) and thereby obviate the need for precedence sensitivity in the licensing constraint. That would require IDENT-IO(high)$_{\text{immed.pretonic}}$ to dominate the licensing constraint. However, the reverse ranking would be required for unstressed vowel raising triggered by a stressed high vowel, which can cause raising of a mid vowel in an immediate pretonic syllable. That approach would thus lead to a ranking paradox. The output in (65a) also bears on the analysis of trigger control. We could consider invoking IDENT-IO(high)$_{\text{immed.pretonic}}$ to obtain control of unstressed raising harmony that is triggered by a high vowel in an immediate pretonic syllable, as in [viritá] 'truth', and it could block lowering of the immediate pretonic high vowel in (64ii), where raising harmony is blocked by a preceding low vowel. However, this strategy would erroneously predict that pretonic syllables other than the immediate pretonic one would not control raising harmony, with the result that (65d) would be expected to win over (65a). Faithfulness for the immediate pretonic syllable thus does not figure in the analysis of Servigliano unstressed vowel-raising harmony.

The next property of the system that I analyze is that unstressed raising harmony does not persist to proclitics. The domain of the harmony can be obtained by ranking CRISPEDGE([high], PWd$_{\text{min}}$) over LICENSE([+high], $\forall V_{\text{Left}}$). This agrees in the main with Vogel (1997: 59f.), who analyzes the harmony as applying within PWd. The PWd constituent that she assumes corresponds to PWd$_{\text{min}}$ here. The ranking is demonstrated in (66) with an input that contains a proclitic with a mid vowel. In candidate (c), the stressed high vowel causes raising of the pretonic mid vowel in the stem and the proclitic vowel. This satisfies the licensing constraint, but it violates the crisp edge constraint, because a chain for [+high] spans the PWd$_{\text{min}}$ boundary. Candidate (a), with raising harmony in the immediate pretonic vowel, is selected over candidate (b), with no raising harmony, because (a) better satisfies the licensing constraint.

(66)   Unstressed vowel raising does not affect proclitics
        CRISPEDGE([high], PWd$_{\text{min}}$) >> LICENSE([+high], $\forall V_{\text{Left}}$)

/jje=ttonn-imo/	CRISPEDGE([hi], PWd$_{\text{min}}$)	LICENSE([+hi], $\forall V_{\text{Left}}$)	IDENT(high)
☞ a. jje=ttunnímo		*	*
b. jje=ttonnímo		**!	
c. jji=ttunnímo	*!		**

Lastly, I consider the behavior of /a/. Unstressed raising harmony does not cause /a/ to raise, which is captured by ranking IDENT-IO(low) over the licensing constraint. It was established that /a/ blocks the harmony in some words and is transparent to the harmony in others. I assume that transparency in unstressed raising harmony involves a duplication of [+high] across the transparent segment, producing identity licensing by the preceding non-low vowel. I propose to obtain the possibilities of blocking and transparent /a/ using lexical indexation of *DUPLICATE(F) for the stems that show blocking by /a/. Lexically indexed *DUPLICATE(F)$_L$ will dominate the licensing constraint, because it can prevent fuller satisfaction of the licensing constraint. The licensing constraint will in turn dominate non-indexed *DUPLICATE(F) so that /a/ will be transparent in stems that are not indexed to *DUPLICATE(F)$_L$.

The occurrence of transparency and blocking is illustrated in (67) with two inputs that have an /a/ intervening between a potential trigger and target. The input in (67i) is not indexed to *DUPLICATE(F)$_L$. This allows satisfaction of the licensing constraint to drive a duplicated feature structure, as in (67ia), where /a/ is transparent to the raising harmony and licensing by the first vowel is achieved by identity licensing. This candidate incurs one violation of the licensing constraint, because /a/ does not undergo harmony. Candidate (67ib) fares more poorly on the licensing constraint, because two vowels that precede the high vowel do not undergo harmony. Candidate (67ic) shows an indirect licensing structure with harmony that also affects /a/, but that violates the higher-ranked IDENT(low) constraint. The input in (67ii) is indexed to *DUPLICATE(F)$_L$. The candidate in (67iib) with a duplicated feature therefore violates this constraint, despite its earning one fewer violation of licensing than the selected form in (67iia), where /a/ blocks harmony. *DUPLICATE(F)$_L$ thus serves to prevent identity licensing structures in words that are indexed to this constraint. Another candidate that raised the intervening /a/ would be ruled out by IDENT(low), like (67ic).

(67)   Transparency and blocking effects with /a/
       IDENT-IO(low), *DUPLICATE(F)$_L$ >> LICENSE([+high], $\forall V_{Left}$) >> *DUPLICATE(F)

Input	Output	IDENT (low)	*DUPL(F)$_L$	LICENSE ([+high],$\forall V_{Left}$)	*DUPL(F)
i. /bokkal-u/	☞ a. bukkalú [+hi]$_i$ [+hi]$_i$			*	*
	b. bokkalú [+hi]			**!	
	c. bukkilú [+hi]	*!			
ii. /golantrin$_L$-a/	☞ a. golantrína [+hi]			**	
	b. gulantrína [+hi]$_i$ [+hi]$_i$		*!	*	*

It is noteworthy that blocking of harmony by /a/ is obtained using a lexically indexed markedness constraint. Recall that lexically indexed faithfulness constraints are often behind morpheme-specific blocking and various lexically indexed markedness constraints can produce morpheme-specific triggering (see Pater 2009a and discussion in §3.6, §5.3 and chapter 6). Lexically indexed *DUPLICATE(F) renders /a/ opaque to harmony within specific morphemes by preventing the occurrence of a particular structure, namely, a duplicated feature. More generally, a lexically indexed markedness constraint could potentially cause blocking for an assimilation when the structure that would have resulted from the assimilation is marked.

A summary of the rankings established for unstressed vowel-raising harmony in Servigliano is provided in (68).

(68) Ranking lattice for unstressed vowel-raising harmony

IDENT-IO-ó(high)
*ŏ/a,ɛ•ɔ,e•o &$_l$ IDENT-IO(high)
IDENT-IO(low)
CRISPEDGE([high], PWd$_{min}$)
*DUPLICATE(F)$_L$
|
LICENSE([+high], ∀V$_{Left}$)
|
CRISPEDGE([high], σ)
IDENT-IO(high)
*DUPLICATE(F)

To review, unstressed raising harmony is the second vowel pattern in Servigliano that is driven by maximal licensing. This harmony expands the scope of realization for [+high] specifications to as many preceding vowels as is possible within the limits of other constraints. Triggers can occur in a strong position (stressed) or a weak one (unstressed). Control by a stressed vowel is handled by faithfulness for this position, whereas trigger control in the case of unstressed vowels is attributed to prominence reduction, using a local conjunction that prevents high unstressed vowels from lowering. In forms where unstressed vowels are the trigger for raising, harmony operates among unstressed syllables only. This diagnoses the pattern as driven by maximal licensing rather than organized around a prominent licensing position.

Rankings that were worked out for each of the four vowel patterns in Servigliano are combined in (69). For ease of interpretation, the constraints that drive each of the processes are called out at the left.

(69)   Ranking lattice for vowel patterns in Servigliano

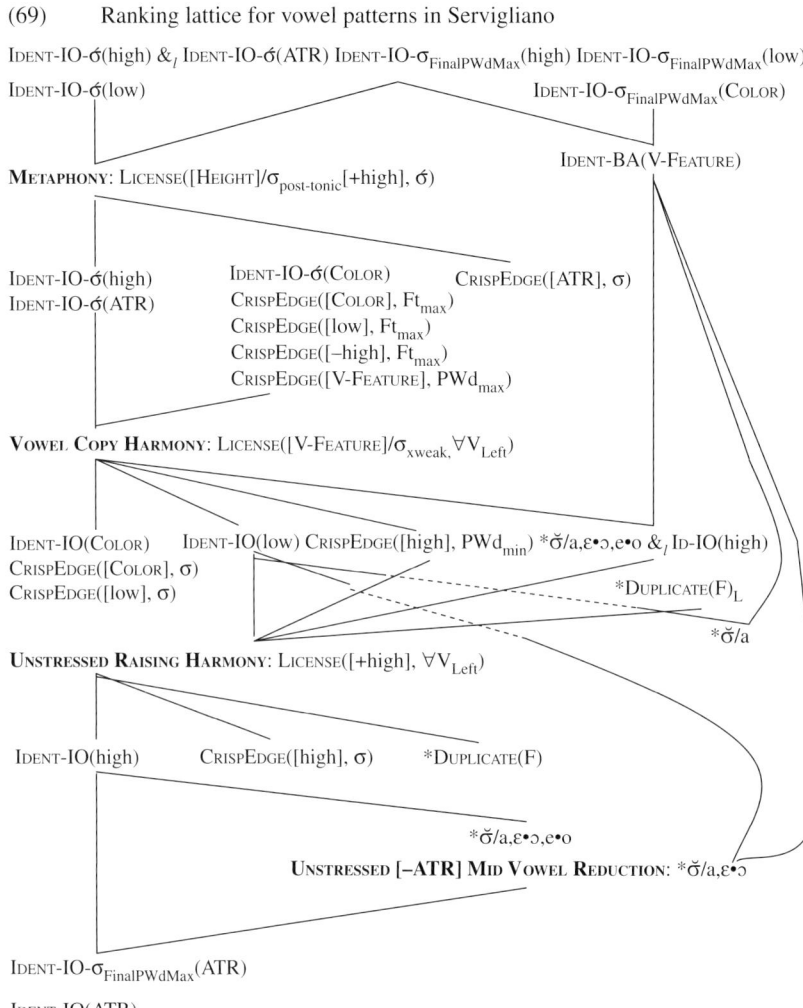

The combined ranking lattice shows that the constraint hierarchies that were determined for the individual patterns are compatible in combination with each other. The harmony and reduction processes do not generally conflict with one another. Their hierarchical ordering results primarily from intercalated faithfulness constraints. At the top of the hierarchy are identity constraints for the final syllable for all vowel features except [ATR]. Also in this tier are the local conjunction of faithfulness that produces stepwise raising in stressed syllables in metaphony and the faithfulness constraint for [low] in the stressed syllable, which prevents stressed /a/ from undergoing harmony. These dominate the prominence-based licensing constraint that drives metaphony, which itself outranks faithfulness constraints for [high] and [ATR] in the stressed syllable. Stressed syllable identity constraints dominate the maximal licensing constraint that causes vowel copy harmony, because the stressed syllable is not affected by this harmony. The stressed syllable forms a left boundary for this harmony among post-tonic vowels. The constraint that promotes vowel copy harmony dominates all non-positional identity constraints for vowel features as well as the local conjunction that prohibits lowering of a high vowel in an unstressed syllable. That conjunction and IDENT-IO(low) outrank the maximal licensing constraint that drives unstressed vowel raising, which in turn dominates IDENT-IO(high), because it causes mid vowels to raise to high. IDENT-IO(low) also dominates the prominence reduction constraint that drives unstressed mid vowels to reduce to [+ATR]. The partially dashed lines have the same status as all other ranking lines: dashed portions simply make them easier to follow where they cross others in the figure. Finally, IDENT-IO(high) and the prominence reduction constraint outrank IDENT-IO(ATR) and faithfulness for [ATR] in the final syllable.

Quite generally, within the combined constraint hierarchy, where harmony-driving constraints are not fully satisfied in a given form, the limits on their satisfaction are achieved by their interaction with other constraints. Because the harmonies do not interact opaquely with one another, no serial ordering of the processes is required. Thus, despite the complexity of the vowel patterns taken together, a sequential derivation using intermediate forms is not called for.

Observe that the constraint that prevents identity licensing, *DUPLICATE(F) (not lexically indexed) is dominated by all of the harmony-driving constraints. Yet transparent vowels are witnessed only in unstressed vowel-raising harmony. In the case of metaphony, the circumstances that could motivate transparency do not arise, because the features that are licensed by the stressed syllable in metaphony are present in the entire sequence of post-tonic vowels. In vowel copy harmony among post-tonic syllables, a potential circumstance for transparency arises with the stressed syllable, which does not undergo copy harmony and blocks it from proceeding to pretonic syllables. This blocking behavior was captured with crisp edge constraints that cause the stressed syllable to be a barrier for harmony of [low], [−high] and color features. These constraints explain why the stressed syllable blocks harmony even when it displays the same features as the post-tonic vowels. Therefore, even though *DUPLICATE(F) is situated relatively low in the constraint hierarchy, the transparency effects that are predicted in Servigliano are quite limited.

Taken together, the vowel patterns in Servigliano constitute a striking example of how various phenomena sensitive to positional prominence and/or reduction of perceptual difficulty can produce effects that are extensive and interactive within a language. Harmony that revolves around a prominent position is witnessed in the metaphony pattern. This pattern shows the marks of prominence-based licensing in ways that are by now familiar. Vowel copy harmony and unstressed vowel-raising harmony enlarge the picture to encompass maximal licensing. In these patterns, a restricted feature's expression in the word is expanded through the action of a constraint that drives it to be realized in every vowel rather than in a specific prominent position. Copy harmony operates among extra-weak vowels in the language (post-tonic vowels and unstressed clitics). Vowels in these contexts could be expected to suffer a perceptual disadvantage, which is consistent with their triggering licensing-driven harmony. Unstressed raising harmony is triggered by vowels that are [+high], a value that can serve as marked. The combined effect is such that every syllable in the maximal phonological word is a potential participant in one harmony pattern or another (subject to restrictions on vowel quality), and the harmonies show the potential for interaction such that copy harmony can feed metaphony and metaphony can feed unstressed raising harmony. Other position-sensitive effects in the system are witnessed, including faithfulness to strong positions, which can determine trigger control and resistance to harmony, and prominence reduction effects in non-prominent (unstressed) syllables. As this case study has shown, the relevant phenomena are compatible with what could be expected on the basis of positional prominence and strength asymmetries and vowel markedness.

8.4 Conclusion

In this chapter I have explored extending the concept of licensing from the prominence-based licensing systems studied earlier in this book to maximal licensing systems, which drive unbounded harmony from a weak trigger. Rather than being organized around expressing a feature in a prominent position, these patterns increase opportunities for the perception of the harmonizing property by realizing it in as many vowels as possible.

The table in (70) provides a summary of descriptive characteristics of the maximal licensing harmony systems that were examined in this chapter. In discussion that follows, I review various distinguishing properties of these systems.

(70)   Maximal licensing: patterns studied in this chapter

	Harmonizing features	Triggers	Targets	Blocking effects	Transparent vowels	Directionality	Language
i.	[+round]	Short round non-high vowels (in σ$_{initial}$). [+round, −high] vowels are contrastive in initial σ only.	Non-high vowels	High vowels	None	Progressive; follows from initial σ trigger.	Baiyinna Orochen
ii.	All vowel features	Non-low [−ATR] vowels (in σ́). When not participants in harmony, [−low, −ATR] vowels are neutralized in σ̆.	[−ATR] vowels	No data	No data	Bidirectional	Vinalopó Mitjà
iii.	All vowel features	Vowels in extra-weak σs: post-tonic, unstressed clitic.	Vowels in extra-weak σ	σ́, Ft$_{max}$ boundary	None	Regressive	Servigliano
iv.	[+high]	High vowels	Non-low vowels	PWd$_{min}$ boundary, /a/ in some words	/a/ in some words	Regressive	Servigliano

Maximal licensing systems for [+round], [+high], and all vowel features are included here. Jiménez and Lloret (2007) discuss a case involving [−ATR] in Eastern Andalusian. Other unbounded weak trigger harmonies involving [+round] are studied by Kaun (1995, 2004) and another system involving [+high] is discussed by Walker (2005).

Conclusion   295

Various characteristics of harmony that is driven by maximal licensing rather than prominence-based licensing were described in the introduction to this chapter. A primary characteristic is that harmony is in principle unbounded. That is true of each of these systems. Nevertheless, some maximal licensing harmonies operate only within particular domains. These effects were obtained using crisp edge constraints in Servigliano. For vowel copy harmony, crisp edge constraints for Ft_{max} prevent harmony from persisting from post-tonic syllables to pretonic ones, and for unstressed vowel-raising harmony, CRISPEDGE([high], PWd_{min}) prevents harmony from affecting proclitics.

Another characteristic of maximal licensing is its potential to show partial harmony without reaching a specific endpoint. This characteristic was found in all of the harmonies examined. In Baiyinna Orochen, high vowels block harmony. In Vinalopó Mitjà, only [−ATR] vowels undergo harmony. There were not data, however, to indicate whether [+ATR] vowels function as blockers or are transparent. In Servigliano vowel copy harmony, only vowels in other extra-weak syllables undergo harmony. Stressed syllable faithfulness and the boundary of Ft_{max} served as a barrier to harmony from post-tonic syllables to syllables that come earlier in the word. In the unstressed raising harmony of Servigliano, pretonic /a/ blocks harmony in some words. Despite these circumstances where harmony could not be complete in the form, those vowels that were not prevented from undergoing harmony showed assimilation.

When a form contains a vowel that cannot undergo a harmony driven by a maximal licensing constraint, it is possible for it to block or be transparent. The contrast is seen in blocking by high vowels in Baiyinna Orochen versus transparency of low vowels in some words in unstressed raising harmony in Servigliano. This difference is obtained through different ranking of *DUPLICATE(F) with respect to the licensing constraint that causes harmony. When *DUPLICATE(F) is dominated by the licensing constraint, as in Servigliano, identity licensing becomes available. Under the opposite ranking, harmony can only generate indirect licensing structures, with the result that non-participating vowels block harmony.

A further characteristic of maximal licensing is that harmony may consistently originate from a strong position when it is the locus of contrast for the marked properties that give rise to the licensing phenomenon. This was observed in Baiyinna Orochen, in which short non-high round vowels occur contrastively only in the initial syllable. In Vinalopó Mitjà, non-low [−ATR] vowels are unrestricted in stressed syllables, but they are subject to reduction-based neutralization in unstressed syllables when they are not participants in harmony. However, not all maximal licensing harmonies issue strictly from contrasts within a strong position. In the unstressed raising harmony of Servigliano, both stressed and unstressed high vowels trigger assimilation, and the vowel copy harmony of Servigliano is triggered by vowels in extra-weak syllables. The source of trigger control in each of these cases was addressed in the context of their analysis above. The common factor across these patterns is that all of the maximal licensing harmonies involve triggers that are weak or marked in some respect.

In closing, it is important to recognize that not all unbounded vowel harmony that issues from a strong position involves vowel properties that present some form of relative perceptual difficulty or markedness. For example, in Old Norwegian, height harmony is initiated by stressed long low vowels (Hagland 1978; Majors 1998). Clearly, the triggers for height harmony in Old Norwegian do not face an asymmetric perceptual threat. A case like Old Norwegian differs from harmony driven by maximal licensing in that it is hypothesized to originate in the strong coarticulatory influence of the stressed syllable (Majors 1998, see also Ringen and Heinämäki 1999). There thus can be more than one source for vowel harmony from a stressed syllable. The aspects of asymmetric weakness or markedness of the vowels that trigger harmony in Baiyinna Orochen and Vinalopó Mitjà motivate their treatment in terms of maximal licensing. Investigation of the different typological properties of unbounded harmonies with different sources would be a valuable aim for future study.

9   *Conclusion and final issues*

9.1   Licensing and vowel patterns

This chapter reviews what has been accomplished in this book and looks ahead to issues that remain to be resolved. This first section consolidates the leading results of the research in this work. In the next section, I identify topics that need attention in the future in order to make further progress.

As discussed in chapter 1, this work revolves largely around two themes: (1) how word position affects the way in which vowels function in sound patterns, and (2) how aspects of the perception and production of speech affect vowel patterns. Bearing on these issues, a fundamental insight this work brings to the understanding of vowel phenomena is that diverse systems in numerous languages serve to prevent the expression of distinctive phonological content solely in a weak position. Further, these patterns are hypothesized to have functional underpinnings such that they serve in large part to reduce perceptual difficulty in language.

The formal approach advanced in this work posits licensing constraints as the imperative that is the common factor for the vowel phenomena under study. These licensing constraints are cast as markedness constraints. Effects that involve licensing by a prominent position are united under the umbrella of a generalized prominence-based licensing constraint schema. This schema is such that prominence-based licensing constraints can be satisfied by multiple configurations for the restricted element: identity licensing, indirect licensing, direct licensing, and absence of the element, with the solution being determined by the interaction with other constraints in the grammar of language. Importantly, the licensing imperative is formulated so as to be applicable at the level of output forms of the grammar, which yields the observed multiplicity of processes and distributions that display a common lack of distinctive elements contained wholly within a weak position. This property of the formal system is predicted by OT, and it can be counted as a genuine success of the framework.

A further proposal developed in this work is that another category of licensing phenomena exists, which involves maximal licensing. Unlike prominence-based licensing, where licensing for an element is achieved by membership in a specific prominent position, maximal licensing is achieved by membership of an element in every vowel of an output (or perhaps in every segment). The maximal licensing constraint is evaluated so that a penalty is assigned to every vowel to which some restricted element in the word is not associated, which can produce harmony that proceeds as far as possible within a form. In patterns that show licensing-driven vowel harmony, prominence-based licensing will promote assimilation that is bounded by the prominent licensing position, whereas maximal licensing will promote unbounded assimilation. Despite this difference, maximal licensing phenomena are prone to restrict elements that show comparative perceptual difficulty, like prominence-based licensing patterns. Prominence-based licensing and maximal licensing constraints are thus grammatical imperatives that each serve to penalize marked elements that occur with insufficient expression, but what constitutes sufficient expression differs: in one case it is expression in a prominent position, and in the other it is expression in every position.

The proposed functional grounding for licensing patterns gives rise to various predictions, introduced in chapter 2. It is expected that licensing phenomena could penalize all vowel qualities (or values of a feature) when not licensed, or they could single out particular properties or positions. A joint prediction of prominence-based and maximal licensing phenomena is that vowels that are asymmetrically strong will not be singled out for a licensing restriction. Asymmetric strength could be in the form of perceptual cues. This predicts, for example, that low vowels that lack a backness/rounding contrast (in non-final position) will not be isolated as the subject of a licensing pattern. Likewise, vowels in a singularly strong position are not expected to be singled out for licensing-based restrictions.[1]

What positional effects are expected then? Prominence-based licensing constraints introduce positional effects by virtue of identifying a prominent position that serves as a licensor. In constraints for prominence-based licensing and maximal licensing, positional effects can also arise from the characterization of the structure that is subject to licensing, which can be restricted to elements that occur in a weak position. Positional asymmetries that are predicted by licensing constraints are therefore that elements in weak positions could be singled out for a licensing-driven restriction, and that a prominent position could be singled out as a licensor.

It falls to the interaction of other constraints to determine whether material in the licensing position or the non-licensing position will be preserved. In the analyses proposed in this work, a constraint type that plays a primary role in this regard is positional faithfulness, which enforces preservation of material in some position that is strong by virtue of prosodic or morphological factors. A vowel in a non-licensing position that occurs in a context for positional faithfulness can control licensing-driven assimilation, resulting in a weak trigger harmony. Beyond the specific function of trigger control, positional faithfulness serves more generally to obtain phenomena where strong positions display resistance to neutralization. This includes phenomena that are characterized as the blocking of a neutralizing process, such as vowel reduction, and position-sensitive contrast, such as the restriction of certain marked structures to some strong position. This last function overlaps to some extent with the labor of prominence-based licensing constraints, an issue that I take up in §9.2.3.

Three additional types of constraints were utilized for weak trigger control in particular patterns. These were non-positional faithfulness, position-sensitive markedness, and the local conjunction of these two types of constraints. A case of non-positional faithfulness was employed for the combination of features that characterize a high front vocoid to obtain trigger control by these segments in the umlaut of OHG. This was suggested to be grounded in the strong coarticulatory resistance of these vocoids. A position-sensitive markedness constraint was employed for trigger control in the dialect of Francavilla Fontana. A prominence reduction constraint that prohibits unstressed non-high vowels was invoked to capture control of metaphony by high vowels. The constraint in question is independently motivated for this dialect by the raising of unstressed mid vowels to high, and it serves to block unstressed vowel lowering. This same constraint was used in a local conjunction with a faithfulness constraint for [high] for control by unstressed high vowels in the metaphony of central Veneto. Central Veneto differs from Francavilla Fontana in blocking only non-high unstressed vowels that are derived, whereas Francavilla Fontana prevents unstressed mid vowels whether derived or not. The resulting picture, then, is one in which weak trigger control effects can come about from markedness constraints or faithfulness constraints or a conjunction of constraints, and these constraints could be position sensitive or not, depending on specifics of the pattern in question.

The approach taken in this work has sought to diagnose the source of trigger control, where possible, in the context of the overall system in which a given pattern occurs. In some cases this points towards a particular conclusion, although in others more than one strategy for obtaining trigger control is available and they appear equally motivated. In the latter situation, I have adopted positional faithfulness when it is an option. Overall, the prediction of a grounded approach is that weak trigger control for assimilation will occur only under circumstances where there is some basis in markedness, positional strength, or inherent strength (e.g. coarticulatory strength) to prevent the vowel in non-licensing position from capitulating to assimilation from the licensing position. This prediction and the others mentioned above in this section are borne out by the vowel patterns studied in this work and they look promising as generalizations that are likely to persist as further patterns are investigated.

9.2 Vowel patterns and prominence in the future

This section turns to issues related to licensing-driven vowel patterns that would benefit from further research and whose investigation could be important in refining our understanding of surrounding issues that are typological, evolutionary, and formal in nature.

9.2.1 Refining descriptive generalizations

This work has established a number of descriptive generalizations about licensing-based vowel patterns. As outlined in broad strokes in the previous section, many of these generalizations fall firmly in line with what is expected given the formal approach advanced here and the hypothesized functional grounding for these patterns. This section highlights some additional observations about the vowel patterns examined in this work and raises some questions about their status to guide future typological investigation.

Chapter 2 surveyed phonetic, psycholinguistic, and phonological evidence for positional licensing asymmetries and vowel markedness. Let us recall first the discussion surrounding strong and weak positions. Strong positions that were identified include initial positions, stressed positions, and morphological roots/stems. Weak positions were unstressed syllables and affixes (especially inflectional). Final positions were identified as showing evidence of mixed strength and weakness. On the basis of the evidence for their increased prominence, we could expect initial syllables, stressed syllables, and roots/stems to serve as the π argument in prominence-based licensing constraints. Evidence for each of these positions serving as prominent in a licensing constraint was identified among the languages studied in this book. With respect to vowel harmony that is driven by prominence-based licensing, we could further expect that each of these positions could serve as either the trigger or target of assimilation. As summarized in (1), this was found to be true for stressed syllables and roots/stems, but it was only partly verified for word-initial syllables.

(1) Attested function of prominent positions in vowel harmony driven by prominence-based licensing
  i. Stressed syllable
    a. Trigger of assimilation: exx. Buchan Scots (+high), Eastern Meadow Mari (+round).
    b. Target of assimilation: exx. central Veneto (+high), Old High German (−back), Eastern Andalusian (−ATR), Jaqaru (all vowel features).
  ii. Root/stem
    a. Trigger of assimilation: exx. Macuxi (color), Lango (ATR), Mazahua (all vowel features) (after Steriade 1995b).
    b. Target of assimilation: exx. Lango (ATR), Chamorro (−back) (after Kaplan 2008a).
  iii. Word-initial syllables
    a. Trigger of assimilation: ex. Eastern Meadow Mari (back).
    b. Target of assimilation: pattern not identified.

Patterns in which a word-initial syllable was a trigger for licensing-driven harmony were identified, but patterns in which this position was a target of harmony driven by prominence-based licensing were not discovered.[2] To be clear, however, this work did not undertake an exhaustive survey of vowel patterns that show prominence-based licensing. Rather, a broad selection of systems that exemplify a range of the patterns known to be attested were examined and analyzed. Therefore, while I would not say that I am confident that no patterns of type (1iiib) exist, they appear to at least be rare. This could be related to the fact that not many patterns of vowel harmony driven by prominence-based licensing were found in general where the initial syllable served as licensor. The lack of word-initial targets in harmony driven by prominence-based licensing could also be related to the finding of Smith (2005) that positional augmentation phenomena do not promote neutralization of segmental contrasts in word-initial positions except when they would serve to demarcate the left boundary of a word-initial syllable. Smith relates this to the importance of word-initial material in early-stage word recognition. Perhaps the rarity or absence of prominence-based harmony patterns that target the initial syllable could be due to the same cause. Determining whether patterns of type (1iiib) are a systematic typological gap remains for further investigation.

The survey of research on final syllables in §2.4 found that final syllables show evidence of both strength and weakness. Barnes (2006) noticed that final syllables rarely (perhaps never) serve as the only prominent syllable within the word domain. Interestingly, the vowel patterns studied in this work are largely consistent with Barnes' observation. No prominence-based licensing patterns were found in which a word-final syllable serves as the licensing position. Yet, consistent with the prediction of possible weakness, some licensing patterns singled out material in word-final syllables for restriction by a licensing effect (e.g. C'Lela, Eastern Meadow Mari, Ticinese). On the other hand, evidence was found for strength of word-final syllables in the form of trigger control by this position in some patterns of licensing-driven harmony (e.g. Jaqaru, Servigliano) and in the form of resistance to neutralization of structure that fails to coincide with a prominent position that serves as licensor (e.g. Veroli, Servigliano). These characteristics were captured in the formal system using a positional faithfulness constraint for the final syllable. The rarity of prominence-based licensing patterns where the final syllable serves as a licensor – perhaps being a systematic absence – suggests the possibility that the threshold of prominence for a position to serve as a licensor for prominence-based licensing is higher than that required for positional faithfulness effects. Alternatively, it could be the case that the basis for positional prominence is different for positional faithfulness versus prominence-based licensing. These questions remain open.

On the topic of markedness of specific vowel qualities, a review of previous research in §2.6 identified some consistent markedness asymmetries and others that seem to be variable across languages and phonological phenomena. An example of a feature combination whose relative markedness is cross-linguistically consistent is [+round, –high] > [+round, +high]. The feature [+round] in a non-high vowel was restricted by licensing constraints in Classical Mongolian (indirect licensing), Ola Lamut (direct licensing), and Baiyinna Orochen (maximal licensing; further restricted to short vowels). Moreover, no pattern singled out high round vowels or unround non-high vowels for a licensing restriction.

Turning to a case of variable markedness, evidence concerning the relative markedness of different vowel heights in an unstressed syllable does not point in a uniform direction, although some generalizations were distilled. In a weak position, especially one with impoverished duration, both high and mid vowels have aspects that could be expected to increase their perceptual difficulty. On the other hand, low vowels in an inventory with a single low vowel are not expected to present greater perceptual difficulty than higher vowels. Final position was noted to be an exception, because properties of this position could interfere with the perception of low vowels. As summarized in (2), each of the potentially marked qualities for vowel height was found to be restricted in a licensing pattern studied in this work.

(2) Licensing patterns that impose restrictions on vowels of particular heights
 i. [+high]
  Exx. Buchan Scots, central Veneto, Servigliano (harmony), C'Lela (passive licensing), Modern Greek (deletion), Western Asturian dialects (static lack of contrast).

ii. [−high, −low]
Exx. Belarusian, northern Mantuan (neutralization with alternations), note also Chumash (static lack of contrast for non-peripheral vowels and possibly harmony) (after Steriade 1995b), Esimbi (alternations induced by association of a floating feature, includes mid and low vowels).
iii. [+low] in final position
Exx. Ticinese (harmony), Valencian dialects (neutralization) (after Jiménez 1998).

Licensing phenomena that single out high vowels are numerous and span many different types of processes and distributions. Licensing phenomena that single out mid vowels seem to be fewer, at least of certain types. Cases involving neutralization were identified. The place of Chumash in the typology warrants further study. In Chumash, mid vowels and [ɨ], characterized by Steriade (1995b) as the set of non-peripheral vowels, are singled out in a pattern that shows a static lack of contrast in affixes. This language also shows a harmony from the root to affixes that can produce non-peripheral vowels in affixes, but whether that harmony is licensing-driven remains to be determined. The pattern of vowel height alternations in prefixes of Esimbi also deserves comment. In Esimbi, non-high vowel height is restricted by the licensing constraint. Non-high vowel features characterizing mid and low occur with front, central, and back vowels underlyingly.[3] In this case, mid vowels serve as marked, as well as low vowels, because they present backness/rounding (F2) contrasts, which tend to be less dispersed at lower heights. Turning to low vowels in inventories where these vowels lack an F2 contrast, two licensing patterns that single out /a/ in final position were identified, involving harmony and neutralization.

The patterns studied in this work thus seem to be consistent with the expectation that high and mid vowels could be variably marked for purposes of licensing, and low vowels in inventories with a single vowel at that height will not serve as marked for this purpose, except in final position. Nevertheless, it appears that licensing phenomena that single out high vowels are more numerous and perhaps more diverse. As mentioned in §5.5, this could be related to the finding of Mielke (2008) that high vowels are more active than mid vowels as a natural class in phonological phenomena in general. Also, genealogical relations could factor into an asymmetry in attestation, especially in view of the fact that among the languages studied in this work, Romance languages receive some emphasis. In future typological research, it would be valuable to probe further into licensing-driven patterns that involve mid or non-peripheral vowels. Such inquiry could lead to a better understanding of the nature of markedness of mid versus high vowels and whether there are any significant gaps in the typology that warrant characterization.

9.2.2 Paths of historical development

This section briefly considers the historical progression of some prominence-based licensing patterns that originate in harmony controlled by a vowel in a non-licensing position, which that may bring insight into their evolutionary cycle. The diachronic development of umlaut in German and the presentation of metaphony across Romance dialects are particularly relevant.

As discussed in §5.3, Iverson and Salmons (2003) have suggested that umlaut in Germanic has phonetic origins in vowel-to-vowel coarticulation. Phonetic processes tend to be gradient and show greater variance in their execution. Umlaut developed into a phonological process in Old High German, when it became a categorical generalization in the grammar. By Middle High German, the phonological phenomenon of umlaut started to show some morphological restrictions, and its potential for action-at-a-distance – across formerly blocking consonants – signaled a loss of phonetic conditioning (Iverson and Salmons 1996). In Modern Standard German, umlaut became highly morphologically specific and overt phonological conditioning was lost, resulting in the floating feature analysis of Lieber (1987), among others. In terms of licensing configurations, a progression is witnessed in the history of German from indirect licensing to identity licensing to direct licensing.

The diachronic development of licensing for floating height features in Esimbi could be reconstructed along similar lines with a progression from indirect licensing to direct licensing (see §7.4 and Stallcup 1980a, b). For Esimbi, however, an intermediate step of identity licensing has not been postulated.

The presentation of metaphony across Romance languages shows parallels. Depending on the dialect, metaphony in the present day may be (i) an incipient phonetic process, (ii) a productive phonological pattern, (iii) a productive phonological pattern restricted to certain morphological categories, (iv) a productive morphologically conditioned pattern, lacking an overt phonological trigger, and (v) a largely moribund morphologically specialized phenomenon, with exceptions (Maiden 1991a; Dyck 1995). Furthermore, within dialects, morphological conditioning develops later: Maiden argues that "The origins of metaphony show every sign of being purely phonetic, and wholly independent ... of the semantic or morphosyntactic categories with which metaphony may ultimately become associated" (p. 134). In addition, in dialects where the overt phonological conditioning for metaphony is missing due to neutralization of post-tonic vowels (usually to [ə]), the phonological conditioning is reconstructed as overtly present in a prior stage (Maiden p. 148). The various stages across Romance dialects in the present day suggest that metaphony tends to follow an evolutionary sequence along similar lines to German umlaut, with different pacing across dialects, and in some cases with a stage permitting identity licensing. Notice also that, like German, the sequence apparently originates from a gradient phonetic conditioning, developing later into an obligatory and productive phonological process with stages that involve morphological conditioning.

While not all phonological phenomena show this course of development, it suggests a kind of canonical evolutionary sequence for patterns of certain types. Possibly licensing-driven vowel assimilation patterns in which harmony is controlled by a vowel in a non-licensing position tend to be phonologically unstable, especially when non-local identity licensing is involved, and they are prone to evolve into direct licensing configurations. Perhaps there are other canonical evolutionary paths with licensing-based vowel patterns.[4] This opens fresh avenues to pursue in the cause and direction of sound change that involves licensing phenomena.

On a related topic, Walker (2005: 959f.) has suggested that metaphony across Romance dialects could be unified if it were driven by a constraint equivalent to LICENSE([HEIGHT]/$\sigma_{\text{post-tonic}}$[+high], σ), which penalizes height features in a post-tonic high vowel that are not licensed by the stressed syllable. This constraint has the capacity to drive licensing-driven assimilation for [+high], [+ATR], and [−low] from a high post-tonic vowel, all of which are attested in some pattern of Romance metaphony. Under this approach, patterns in which assimilation for only some of these features occurs are obtained by ranking IDENT constraints for the non-assimilating features above the licensing constraint. (Other constraints can also serve to inhibit some of these features from assimilating.) In the analyses of metaphony within this book, I have generally postulated licensing constraints for the entire class of height features only if there is evidence of assimilation for multiple features; however, the alternative with a licensing constraint for [HEIGHT] used across all dialects could be substituted.[5] If the latter constraint were used, the analysis would provide a more uniform treatment of the metaphony-driving constraint across related languages, allowing for a formal analysis of a common origin that is retained in the present day. Such an account could be supported synchronically if speakers of individual dialects where certain height features never assimilate in metaphony were to show evidence of a bias to metaphony involving those features under some conditions, such as in an experimental context. Alternatively, speakers might show evidence supporting metaphony-driven constraints that are specific just to the features that assimilate in their language. In that case, it would appear that the specifics of an original metaphony-driving constraint could have become differentiated across a number of dialects over time. Pursuit of these issues is left open for future research.

9.2.3 Refining outcomes and constraints

I turn now to areas relating to this research where the goodness-of-fit between the typology predicted by the constraint set and the attested patterns in language could be refined. I will not solve these issues here, but rather highlight relevant research that has made progress in addressing them and point to directions to pursue in the future.

I consider first some problems involving overgeneration by the constraint set, corresponding in the literature to what is known as the 'too-many-solutions' problem (e.g. Steriade 2009). One issue concerns the potential for licensing constraints to influence the location of a prominent position. Many different patterns that satisfy prominence-based licensing are exhibited in this work, including assimilation, neutralization, deletion, infixation, passive licensing, and others. At the same time, a licensing pattern appears to be unattested: a case where prominence shifts, i.e. stress shifting to a vowel with a perceptually weak quality (Walker 2005).[6] This connects to a wider generalization in phonological patterns, namely, that stress assignment is never conditioned by segmental features (de Lacy 2002, 2006, 2007a; Blumenfeld 2006),[7] although stress can influence the distribution of segmental features.

To illustrate the problem, consider a ranking in which a constraint that penalizes [+high] when not licensed by a stressed syllable (LICENSE([+high], σ)) and IDENT-IO(high) dominate the constraints responsible for penultimate stress assignment (e.g. TROCHEE, plus other constraints not shown here). The operation of the hierarchy over two different inputs is illustrated in (3). In (3i), assignment of stress to the penult is possible while also satisfying the licensing constraint and IDENT(high). However, in (3ii), the vowel in the penultimate syllable is non-high whereas the vowel in the final syllable is high. Here, the licensing constraint and IDENT are satisfied at the cost of TROCHEE, resulting in assignment of stress to the final syllable, a feature-driven stress shift that does not seem to be attested.[8]

(3) Unwanted prediction of a stress shift driven by a licensing constraint

Input	Output	LICENSE ([+high], σ)	IDENT (high)	TROCHEE
i. /bite/	☞ a. (bíte)			
	b. (bité)	*!		*
ii. /beti/	☞ a. (betí)			*
	b. (béti)	*!		
	c. (béte)		*!	

As I have pointed out previously (2005: 974), this problem is not specific to the analysis of prominence-based vowel patterns in OT; the fundamental question of why such phenomena appear to be unattested in language would likewise confront a rule-based approach to the patterns under study in this work.

In order to address this issue, Blumenfeld has proposed a novel type of constraint applicable to asymmetries of the type *A conditions B, but not vice versa* in the interaction between two components of phonological structure. The constraints in question, which Blumenfeld calls 'procedural markedness constraints' (2006: 85) are expressed as implications of the type 'If P has property x, then Q has property y.' Importantly, procedural markedness constraints not only state a relationship between two phonological categories, but they also enforce the direction of their interaction: the property named in the antecedent of the implication can influence the property named in the consequent but not vice versa. Procedural markedness constraints can thus prevent segmental features from affecting stress assignment if stress is the property named in the antecedent and a feature is named in the consequent.

I will not spell out all of the details of Blumenfeld's implementation of this approach here. For the present purposes it is sufficient to understand that Blumenfeld has made a proposal to address the problem, but it involves making certain changes to the architecture of some constraints and aspects of the evaluation mechanism that depart from those in classic OT. Further assessment of the implications of these changes for phonological theory is an important part of ongoing research on this problem. In addition, if this approach were pursued with respect to licensing phenomena, it would necessitate reformulating licensing constraints in Blumenfeld's procedural terms, the feasibility of which needs to be examined.

A second issue of overgeneration has to do with predictions of the constraint that drives unbounded harmony. Some problems with harmony-driving constraints like ALIGN(F), SPREAD(F), and EXTEND(F) have been discussed by Wilson (2003, 2006) and McCarthy (2004, 2009). They identify pathological predictions such as harmony-triggered deletion, metathesis, affix repositioning, and allomorph choice, as well as harmony-blocked epenthesis, all of which could come about under certain constraint rankings when harmony would otherwise be blocked from propagating fully in the word. Although their exemplification centers on examples of nasal harmony, the foregoing are largely applicable to unbounded vowel harmony with or without weak triggers, and maximal licensing constraints could likewise present these problems.

The problem of harmony-triggered vowel deletion is illustrated in (4). In the hypothetical ranking shown here, a maximal licensing constraint

LICENSE([+round]/[−high], ∀ V), and GESTURALUNIFORMITY([+round], [high]) dominate MAX-IO(seg), which in turn dominates IDENT(round). In words with a non-high round vowel, the maximal licensing constraint assigns a penalty to each vowel with which the [+round] feature in the non-high round vowel does not coincide. The gestural uniformity constraint prohibits a sequence of adjacent vowels that differ in height to which a [+round] specification is linked, effectively restricting round harmony to non-high vowels. The evaluation in (4i) shows that this ranking will promote harmony among non-high vowels: the form that exhibits round harmony, in (a), is selected over a disharmonic but faithful form, in (b), as well as a form that deletes a vowel that is [−round] in the input, in (c). This result is not problematic. However, the result for the input in (4ii) presents a so-called pathology. The input contains a non-high round vowel followed by a syllable with a high unround vowel. Here the gestural uniformity constraint blocks harmony between the vowels in (c), and the licensing constraint rules out a disharmonic form (b). The winner is (a), which satisfies the licensing constraint via deletion of the high vowel. This represents an unattested outcome of harmony-triggered deletion. Notice that we could rule out another candidate, [bɑt], using a faithfulness constraint for [round] in the initial syllable, so this alternative could not consistently serve as a way out. The same goes for a candidate [boto], which could be prevented by IDENT(high).

(4) Unwanted prediction of vowel deletion driven by a maximal licensing constraint

Input	Output	LICENSE ([+rd]/[−hi], ∀V)	GESTUNI ([+rd], [hi])	MAX (seg)	IDENT (round)
i. /bota/	☞ a. boto				*
	b. bota	*!			
	c. bot			*!	
ii. /botɯ/	☞ a. bot			*	
	b. botɯ	*!			
	c. botu		*!		*

The problems presented by the unbounded harmony-driving constraints in question have engendered different types of solutions. Wilson (2003, 2006) proposes to model the constraint as 'targeted,' an approach where the constraint specifies a marked configuration and a repair. Other applications of targeted constraints to harmony phenomena include Baković (2000), Baković and Wilson (2000), and Hansson (2001). Like Blumenfeld's procedural constraints, targeted constraints represent a departure from the traditional constraint architecture and aspects of the evaluation procedure.

McCarthy (2004) proposes to address the problems with a proposal that the representations over which harmony operates are headed 'feature spans.' In this approach, unbounded harmony is driven by a constraint that prohibits adjacent feature spans. When an intervening segment blocks harmony, it thereby avoids the prediction that the harmony-driving constraint would necessarily penalize disharmonic segments that occur beyond the blocking segment. Furthermore, because of the assumption that spans are headed and particulars of the way this is implemented in the constraint set, harmony-triggered deletion is not predicted. See O'Keefe (2007) for other work pursuing a span-based approach to harmony.

A proposal to address pathological predictions of constraints that drive unbounded harmony is developed in another vein by McCarthy (2009, in press). This approach is couched within Harmonic Serialism, a version of OT in which GEN is restricted to making a single change at a time, with the potential for a derivation involving multiple passes through GEN and EVAL. The harmony-driving constraint that McCarthy proposes in this account is SHARE(F), a constraint that penalizes pairs of adjacent elements that are not linked to the same token of [F]. The SHARE constraint departs from traditional versions of harmony-driving constraints in that it assigns a penalty even when [F] is wholly absent (McCarthy assumes that features are privative). For additional work on Harmonic Serialism, see McCarthy (2007b, 2008a, b), among others.

Clearly, multiple strategies have been leveled at the problem of pathological predictions that can be made by constraints that drive unbounded spreading, involving variously the representations involved, the constraints themselves, and the evaluative system within which they are situated. Because certain of these approaches involve significant departures from classic OT, their predictions for phonological theory are still being explored, and we can therefore anticipate that their relative merits will be better understood in the future. More specific to the issues under focus in this work, it is essential to explore the applicability of these different proposals to unbounded harmony that involves weak triggers, as maximal licensing constraints were postulated as an imperative for these patterns.

Let us turn our attention next to positional faithfulness constraints. As discussed in §7.6, there is some degree of overlap in the analysis of positional licensing phenomena as positional markedness (analyzed here with prominence-based licensing constraints) versus positional faithfulness. For example, both types of constraint have the capacity to capture the static absence of marked structure in weak positions, such as the absence of non-high round vowels in non-initial syllables of Ola Lamut. Some redundancies between these constraint families are also highlighted in recent work by Jesney (in press b). Despite these redundancies, however, the two constraint families each perform some unique labor in the typology of positional licensing phenomena. As discussed in §3.2, only positional markedness constraints predict attested phenomena where a specification [F] in a licensing position is altered in order to license a specification that originated elsewhere, for instance, in a position that does not serve as prominent or privileged in the language. On the other hand, positional faithfulness constraints play an important role in obtaining position-sensitive trigger control and certain other kinds of position-sensitive resistance to neutralization.

In future research on vowel patterns, a natural question to pursue is whether these functions of positional faithfulness could be obtained through some other means. In a related direction, a study of licensing in multiple contexts by Jesney (in press b) in the model of Harmonic Grammar (Legendre *et al.* 1990; Smolensky and Legendre 2006; Pater 2009b) finds that the typology derived using positional markedness constraints alone is more restrictive than one in classic OT that uses both positional markedness and positional faithfulness constraints, and it eliminates undesirable effects of positional faithfulness.[9] While this does not resolve the problem of position-sensitive trigger control, it is suggestive that new scrutiny be applied to areas where positional faithfulness constraints appear to be necessary. Perhaps new advances in the theory could cause them to be obviated, leading to a more uniform approach to position-sensitive featural phenomena in the constraint set.

Let us delve more closely into vowel patterns that involve licensing in multiple contexts. The study by Jesney centers on the distribution of voicing in consonants. An example involving vowels is found in the northern Mantuan dialect, described by Miglio (2005). A pattern of vowel reduction in unstressed syllables in this language was discussed in §7.2.1. The full range of vowel qualities can occur in stressed syllables. A further particular of the vowel distribution in this dialect is that [y] occurs in stressed syllables (e.g. [] 'fool') and the word-initial syllable even if unstressed (e.g. [] 'boy'), but it does not occur in non-initial unstressed syllables (2005: 28). This distribution could be considered a case of licensing in multiple contexts: [y] is licensed by stressed syllables and initial syllables, and its membership in either of these positions will cause it to escape being assigned a penalty by whatever constraint drives the licensing effect. As Jesney points out, a conceivable way of handling this type of distribution is to employ positional faithfulness constraints for each of the positions in which the marked segment is licensed. In this case, the positional faithfulness constraints would be IDENT constraints for the initial syllable and the stressed syllable, and they would dominate the constraint that penalizes [y], e.g. *[+round, +high, −back]. However, as mentioned above, Jesney argues that positional faithfulness constraints introduce some unwanted effects, and they present some redundancy with positional markedness licensing constraints. Reinforcing the redundancy problem, in §7.2.1 it was suggested that vowel reduction in unstressed syllables in northern Mantuan could be handled using prominence-based licensing constraints. A generalization would seem to be missed if the licensing capability of stressed syllables were obtained using a prominence-based licensing constraint, and a positional faithfulness constraint were used to obtain the same distributional effect for [y] in word-initial position. In addition, if positional faithfulness were used to obtain the licensing distribution in northern Mantuan with respect to word-initial syllables and/or stressed syllables, a commonality would be overlooked with patterns of vowel neutralization in non-initial syllables or unstressed syllables in other languages for which this was captured using prominence-based licensing (e.g. Ola Lamut, Belarusian; §7.2).

This provokes the question whether positional markedness constraints could capture licensing in multiple contexts without appeal to positional faithfulness. Jesney demonstrates that in their existing formulation they do not, at least within classic OT. The problem is illustrated in (5). The prominence-based licensing constraints used here penalize [+round] in a front vowel that is not licensed by a stressed syllable, and [+round] in a front vowel that is not licensed by a word-initial syllable. Both of these constraints dominate IDENT-IO(round) to drive a licensing distribution. A hypothetical form with an input that contains /y/ in each of three syllables is considered. All of the candidates considered have stress assigned to the final syllable. With respect to vowel quality, the expected output according to Miglio's description is candidate (a), where [y] is retained in the initial and stressed syllable. However, this candidate loses to (e) (called out by '×☞'), where /y/ maps to [i] in all contexts. The problem is that [y] in a stressed syllable incurs a violation of the licensing constraint for the initial syllable, and likewise [y] in an initial syllable incurs a violation of the licensing constraint for the stressed syllable. Thus, the licensing constraints together predict that /y/ should only survive when it occurs in a syllable that is both initial and stressed, a phenomenon that Jesney calls "licensing in doubly-privileged context." Other candidates that retain [y] in one or more syllables, in (5b–d), are ruled out by the licensing constraints. It is assumed that [+round] is not shared across syllables in these candidates, i.e. the language permits direct licensing only.

(5)   The problem of licensing in multiple contexts

/bygyty/	LICENSE ([+round]/[−back], σ́)	LICENSE ([+round]/[−back], σ$_{Initial}$)	IDENT (round)
a. bygitý	*(!)	*(!)	*
b. bigitý		*!	**
c. bygití	*!		**
d. bygytý	*(!)*	*(!)*	
✗☞ e. bigití			***

A possible way to obtain licensing in multiple contexts, as in (5a), would be to adjust the formalism of prominence-based licensing constraints. Specifically, the π argument, which represents the prominent position that serves to license the marked element, could be modified so that it represents a *set* of prominent positions. A further adjustment would be required so that a penalty would be assigned to a marked element whose chain did not coincide with some $p \in \pi$. With this modification, a single licensing constraint would be invoked: LICENSE([+round]/[−back], {σ, σ$_{Initial}$}). Candidate (5a) would satisfy this constraint, because each occurrence of [y] coincides with a member of the π set, and this candidate would then be selected over the alternatives, as shown in (6).

(6)   Resolving the problem of licensing in multiple contexts

/bygyty/	LICENSE ([+rd]/[−bk], {σ́, σ$_{Initial}$})	IDENT (round)
☞ a. bygitý		*
b. bigitý		**!
c. bygití		**!
d. bygytý	*!	
e. bigití		**!*

Under the modified licensing constraint being considered, the prominence-based licensing constraints considered in prior analyses in this paper would have a single element in π, that is, only one position would be available to serve as a licensor in those patterns.

Other cases of licensing in multiple contexts involving vowels include the distribution of color features in Esimbi (see §7.4, n. 20), which appear to be licensed by word-initial and root-initial syllables, and the distribution of round in Hungarian, where [+round] in a short mid front suffix vowel is prevented unless it is licensed by association with a root vowel or a suffix vowel that is not short and mid (Ringen and Vago 1998).

Another possible strategy for obtaining licensing in multiple contexts would be to leave the formulation of prominence-based licensing constraints unaltered and instead make use of the formalisms of Harmonic Grammar, as Jesney proposes. Potential advantages of that approach are that it would retain a simpler statement of licensing constraints, and achieve licensing in multiple contexts in a modular fashion through additive effects of separate licensing constraints. Whether the Harmonic Grammar approach or an approach using a modified statement of the licensing constraint would be preferable is a question to be illuminated by further investigation.

In closing, it is valuable to observe that many aspects of the issues and possible solutions discussed in this section are not specific to licensing constraints as formalized in this work, rather they have broader-based relevance for linguistic theory. This suggests that these matters do not undermine the results achieved by the licensing approach advanced here, and highlights the fact that the investigation of licensing-driven phenomena intersects with fundamental issues in theoretical phonology.

9.3   Final remarks

To conclude, the aim of this book was to illuminate vowel patterns, both their description and analysis, with emphasis on the role played by word position and grounding in factors of speech perception and production. The formalism proposed in this work makes novel claims about a common grammatical imperative for diverse vowel patterns and makes testable typological predictions. While making advances on a number of fundamental issues that span description, typology, and formal theory, the investigation also opens significant new research questions. Looking to the future, a basic question that is a natural follow-up to these results is how consonant patterns in language show parallels or differences from vowel patterns. Study of this issue would further our understanding of the nature of a basic opposition in the sounds of speech.

Notes

1 Introduction

1. The label 'metaphony' has been used in reference to various vowel raising phenomena in Romance dialects, including not just (morpho)phonological patterns but also emerging phonetic processes and historically frozen forms. In this book I focus on cases where metaphony is a productive phonological pattern, in some dialects restricted to certain morphological categories.

2 Preliminaries: functional grounding

1. Phenomena that involve licensing of distinctive phonological properties may be distinguished from augmentation phenomena for prominent positions, which show different characteristics, including certain kinds of neutralization. See Smith (2005) for a typological study.
2. For additional contributions relevant to this topic, see Jun (1995, 2004), Kaun (1995, 2004), Silverman (1997), Gafos (1999), Hume (1999), Côté (2000, 2004), Crosswhite (2001, 2004), Kirchner (2001, 2004), Ní Chiosáin and Padgett (2001), Flemming (2002, 2004), Zhang (2002, 2004), Frisch (2004), Gordon (2004, 2006), Padgett (2004), Wright (2004), Fleischhacker (2005), Walker (2005), and Zuraw (2007). As Hayes and Steriade point out, the notion that phonological markedness has roots in phonetics finds precursors in the theory developed in *The Sound Pattern of English* (Chomsky and Halle 1968) and in *Natural Phonology* (Stampe 1973).
3. Additional research that pursues a chiefly diachronic perspective on the role of phonetics in phonology (for particular cases) includes Hyman (2001), Hansson (2004, 2007b), Yu (2004, 2007), Barnes (2006), and Mielke (2008). For related discussion, see Anderson (1981), Ohala (1981, 1993, among other work), and Boersma (2008).
4. See Hume and Johnson (2001a) for discussion of another model that postulates an indirect connection between functional factors and formal theory. Yu (2007) posits a model along similar lines.
5. Citing de Jong (1995), Fougeron (1999: 19) reports that oral obstruents (e.g. [t]) can exhibit a "lower jaw position" under stress. I infer that this was intended to read "higher jaw position", since de Jong reports finding that speakers "tend to have higher jaw positions in stressed alveolar consonants" (p. 501).
6. For discussion of surrounding issues, see Crosswhite (2001, 2004), Flemming (2004, 2005), and Barnes (2006).

7. This perspective is in line with other work suggesting that (certain) patterns of vowel harmony have origins in vowel-to-vowel coarticulation (e.g. Boyce 1988; Ohala 1994; Manuel 1999; Beddor *et al.* 2001, 2002; Kaun 2004; Barnes 2006; Mielke 2008).
8. For related discussion, see Berg (1998) and MacEachern (1999).
9. Beckman (1997: 35, n.3) points out that for the most part psycholinguistic studies have not systematically studied the distinctions of word-initial prominence in prefixed versus unprefixed forms.
10. For some related observations, see Howe and Pulleyblank (2004). See also studies of vowel systems in Dresher (2009).
11. Rice lists increased perceptual salience as a diagnostic that has been used for a more marked feature, but where perceptual difficulty is under consideration, this criterion will not be applicable.
12. Lehiste notes that higher vowels tend to have a higher fundamental frequency. That might serve to increase their salience, but it may be dependent on the overall pitch pattern of the context in which the vowel is embedded.
13. For a different perspective, see Rice (2007), who lists retention in deletion as a diagnostic of a marked feature.
14. Nevertheless, more research on coarticulation in the languages in question would be valuable.

3 Generalized licensing

1. For additional work developing this kind of approach, see Harris (1997), Piggott (1997, 2000), Itô and Mester (1993), Itô, Mester, and Padgett (1995). Applications to vowel patterns include Flemming (1993), Majors (1998), Ringen and Vago (1998), Crosswhite (2001, 2004), and Walker (2004, 2005).
2. A similar concept of 'correspondence chains' is proposed by Hansson (2006, 2007a) to refer to any sequence of corresponding segments within an output.
3. For further work relevant to this topic, see Lamontagne and Rice (1995), Kitto and de Lacy (1999), Zuraw (2000, 2002), Clements (2001), Struijke (2002), Krämer (2003), Archangeli and Pulleyblank (2007), Jiménez and Lloret (2007), McCarthy (2007a), Rhodes (2008), and Coon and Gallagher (2009).
4. While the locus of violation is postulated to be occurrences of λ in a chain that does not coincide with the given prominent position, the same effects would largely result from instead assigning a violation to the chain itself. If future studies should find an empirical reason to support assigning violations to chains rather than their constituents, the constraint could be modified accordingly without significant alteration. For unlicensed autosegments (features, tones), it is also conceivable that violations of the licensing constraint could be assigned to each dominating segment. However, this would complicate the statement of the constraint schema across different types of phonological constituents.
5. In the markedness-based version of the Licensing-by-Cue approach (Steriade 1999a, b), it is contexts that license segments and segmental properties, not prosodic constituents (see Boersma 1998 for a proposal with some similarities). This approach is also assumed by Crosswhite (2001, 2004). For the vowel patterns that

Crosswhite examines, the context is a prosodic one, such as a stressed position, during which the vowel is produced. Like Crosswhite's work, the main focus here is on patterns in which vowels are licensed by certain prominent positions. In keeping with Zoll's formalism, affiliation with that position will be assessed through formal relations between units of structure. On substantive restrictions in licensing effects, see §3.4.2.

6. Prominent and weak positions are largely complementary. However, the final syllable has the capacity to show aspects of strength and weakness (see chapter 2). It would be surprising to see the same position called out as strong and weak within a single constraint. Nevertheless, if the final syllable served as the licensing position as well as a weak position in a restriction in the same licensing constraint, the constraint would be vacuous in effect.
7. As discussed in §2.6, which particular feature value serves as marked can be sensitive to the contrasts into which that vowel enters in the language. Such effects have been handled in Dispersion Theory (e.g. Padgett 1997, 2003; Flemming 2002, 2004), among other approaches. I will not attempt to obtain those effects using the constraints under focus here, but interactions among constraints governing the contrast system and prominence-based licensing would be fruitful to pursue. The sensitivity of licensing constraints to whether a feature serves as contrastive in a particular vowel is taken up in §3.4.2.
8. The assumption that seven-vowel inventories of Romance make use of the feature [ATR] follows Calabrese (1988). Approaches that instead use a scalar height feature are discussed by Nibert (1998) and Krämer (2009) (with foundation from Clements 1991). The debate surrounding the treatment of height features is an area that deserves continued investigation. A positive aspect of using [ATR] is that it serves to encode the markedness of the vowels [ɪ ʊ] (high and [–ATR]) and [ą] (low and [+ATR]), vowel qualities that are actively avoided in various vowel patterns, as discussed by Calabrese and by Archangeli and Pulleyblank (1994). For that reason, I assume [ATR] as part of the height feature system here.
9. Dyck's account of Lena shares with the generalized licensing analysis the theme that the pattern is driven by an asymmetry between a vowel in a strong position and one in a dependent (weak) position. However, her formal treatment of the assimilation and the role of contrast is developed along rather different lines, as is her implementation of the observation that only distinctively high vowels trigger raising.
10. A refinement of faithfulness using existential quantification (Struijke 2002) is discussed in §5.3.
11. As Wolf (2007) points out, non-identical segments can correspond because it is the segment roots that stand in correspondence, not their features. He proposes discarding the representation of roots as containing the features [consonantal] and [sonorant], instead handling the special behavior of these features by other means.
12. The lack of correspondence between + and – specifications for the same feature could be prevented by assuming privative feature specifications (Keer 1999). I leave open that possibility, but will continue to use binary features for exemplification and assume that values must be identical in corresponding features.

13. *DUPLICATE(X) could have more general utility in blocking the formation or retention of (vacuous) correspondence relations between other elements in an output, in the absence of evidence of interaction among those elements.
14. Krämer (p. 93) at first characterizes indirect correspondence as holding between an underlying feature specification and 'assimilated feature bearers' in the output. However, in elaborating, it becomes clear that he posits correspondence between feature specifications.
15. In the case study of Ascrea in §6.4, this constraint is argued to be morphologically indexed so that it holds specifically of height features in affixes.
16. The preference for indirect licensing in adjacent syllables assumes that the vowel feature in question can also be present on any intervening consonants, i.e. it assumes that the vowels are articulatorily adjacent with respect to that feature. If particular consonants were to block a shared feature specification for flanking vowels, then identity licensing could occur when those consonants intervene.
17. Pater (2007) suggests that lexical indexation of a markedness constraint for the general morphological category 'affix' is possible. He notes that indexation of markedness for the category 'root' could make problematic typological predictions. Indexation to 'root' or 'stem' is not necessary for licensing effects, as these categories can instead serve as an argument π in the licensing constraint.

4   Typological predictions

1. See de Lacy (2007a) for a similar claim that positional markedness and positional faithfulness constraints are both warranted. In §9.2.3 I return to the status of positional faithfulness constraints in the theory.
2. As mentioned in §3.5, n. 16, this result assumes that no blocking segment intervenes between the vowels in adjacent syllables. If a blocker did intervene, such as a blocking consonant, then identity licensing could arise.
3. The absence of harmony patterns that show majority-rule effects could have a basis in learner biases. Artificial learning paradigm experiments reported by Finley (2008) and Finley and Badecker (2008) suggest that learners show a bias towards harmony patterns that display directionality over unattested majority-rule patterns.
4. Whether there are limits as to which constraints can be locally conjoined is open to debate. For discussion, see Crowhurst and Hewitt (1997), Itô and Mester (1998), Baković (2000), Łubowicz (2002), and Smolensky (2006).
5. See Itô and Mester (2003) for further discussion surrounding majority-rule effects and the use of symmetric IDENT(F) constraints in a constraint-conjunctive approach.

5   Indirect licensing

1. The simple existence of blocking or multiple vowels undergoing assimilation is not necessarily diagnostic of an indirect licensing pattern that excludes identity licensing. For example, multiple targets of assimilation could emerge in a language with identity licensing if what caused an intervening segment to be skipped was a markedness constraint that prevented only certain segments from undergoing harmony. On the issue of blocking, Hansson (2007a) discusses how assimilation mediated by

correspondence chains could produce opaque segments. However, unlike the kind of correspondence considered here for identity licensing, he deals specifically with similarity-driven correspondence at the segmental level. Formal issues surrounding the potential for blocking effects in identity licensing remain to be explored.
2. The constraint that prevents feature insertion could be DEP(high). Alternatively, it may be possible to formulate a constraint that penalizes a feature that lacks any faithful association.
3. Carson (1982) also notes vowel assimilation in some unaccented suffixes, e.g. /–ri/ 'det.' and /–ki/ 'poss.' However, the suffixes appear to show some differences in height and rounding assimilation. These together with pitch effects at word endings need further study.
4. The data in (8) are also compatible with licensing by an accented syllable rather than the stem, but the existence of assimilation to an unaccented syllable for backness and rounding in some suffixes suggests that it is the stem rather than accent that is targeted, e.g. [po-ro] 'here' (/po-/ 'loc.,' /–ri/ 'one.').
5. Since inflected forms are generally vowel-final, there are no forms with which to test whether /a/ in a closed syllable undergoes copy harmony. If such forms were identified, and they were not to show harmony, then the notation for the word-final syllable in the constraint could be elaborated to indicate that the syllable must be open.
6. Spotts (1953: 254) reports some additional blocking effects by non-laryngeal consonants: after [a] in a root the affix vowel is [ə], after [ɛ] in a root, the affix vowel is [i].
7. In addition to oral vowels [i e ɛ a ə ʌ ɔ o u], Mazahua has several nasal vowels [ĩ ẽ ɔ̃ ã õ ũ]. Vowel nasalization assimilates in vowel harmony across consonants, even if the consonant is oral, e.g. [hẽ1tʃʔẽ] 'to spin' [thɔ̃ʔ51tʔɔ̃] 'to tie'. This is suggestive that identity licensing is available for [+nasal] in vowels, because it does not appear to continue during the consonant. This could arise from ranking LICENSE([+nasal]/V, Root) over *DUPLICATE(F).
8. It is conceivable that the vowel in the third syllable undergoes assimilation to the vowel in the second syllable, but, as mentioned above, assimilation for [–round] only is typologically unexpected.
9. For some forms, the effect of this conjunction overlaps with that of initial syllable faithfulness in this pattern.
10. [ᵊ] is described by Dettweiler as "a short transition between certain occurrences of consonants in clusters" (2000: 4). He describes it as often seeming to be "an echo of the full vowel preceding the consonant" (2000: 4, n. 4).
11. There were no forms in the source with an intervening suffix with a mid vowel. Such forms might not occur: according to Dettweiler, the only vowels that form class marker affixes are /i a u/ (2000: 14).
12. The only disyllabic direct object pronoun is [tʃinna] 'we (all)' (Rikoto 2001). The high vowel in this suffix does not seem to alternate, which is expected, because it is in non-final position.
13. An apparent exception to this generalization is the non-alternating third person plural pronoun, which is realized with a high central vowel: [fumtᵊkᵊ nɨ] 'pulled them,' [batkᵊ nɨ] 'released them,' but as Pulleyblank notes, [ɨ] in this pronoun

could be regarded as epenthetic. The neutrality of epenthetic high vowels is discussed later.
14. The question of the role of morphology has been raised in the literature. Klein (1995: 124) contrasts OHG forms *magati:n* 'maiden (dim.)' versus *zahar/zahiri* 'tear (sg/pl)' and *magad/magedi* 'maiden (sg/pl).' He interprets these data (as well as pairs like *apful/epfili* 'apple (sg/pl)') as indicating that the plural suffix *–i* triggered umlaut in OHG via a floating [–back] feature in its representation, whereas the diminutive suffix *–ti:n* did not. While a correlation between umlaut and the plural suffix did indeed eventually develop in the history of German, it is unlikely that this was systematically the case as early as OHG. First, variation is documented in plural forms, e.g. *magadi* versus *magedi*, *zahari* versus *zahiri* (Braune 1987: 29; Klein 1995: 124; Iverson and Salmons 1996: 71). Second, medial vowels in trisyllabic words were likely reduced in quality, as indicated by high variability in their spelling. This calls into question whether medial vowels whose spelling suggests they are fronted and sometimes raised are indeed the product of umlaut. The spelling could instead have signaled reduction or perhaps a variable assimilation that affected reduced vowels. Further careful study of variation in the relevant forms is necessary to address this issue.
15. Hypothesized phonetic motivations for primary umlaut are touched on in a body of related work that includes Iverson *et al.* (1994), Iverson and Salmons (1996, 2003, 2004, 2009), Howell and Salmons (1997), and Holsinger and Salmons (1999).
16. An alternative approach to trigger control in OHG that uses a local conjunction of markedness and faithfulness, *[+back] &$_l$ IDENT(back), does not capture the specific coarticulatory strength of /i/ versus other front vowels. A conjunction *[+back, +high] &$_l$ IDENT(back) could more closely call out high vowels, but this too does not directly reflect /i/'s coarticulatory strength.
17. For simplicity, I follow Crosswhite in referencing the category 'unstressed syllable' (ŏ) in *ŏ/a,e•o. De Lacy (2002) proposes a formalism where sonority markedness constraints instead reference categories defined in terms of 'designated terminal elements,' essentially whether they are heads or non-heads of prosodic categories. Under that approach, the analysis of reduction in unstressed syllables that may be footed or unfooted is somewhat more complicated, but it could be substituted here.
18. I do not have direct information that the high tone is contained within the lexical entry for this suffix.
19. Smolensky assumes that AGREE(ATR), which drives unbounded spreading, is the harmony imperative. He focuses on issues other than the bounded nature of harmony in this system.
20. If it were desirable to ensure that the constraint only had the potential to operate over material in affixes (no matter what morphemes it were indexed to), that restriction could be added to the licensing constraint, but the indexation is sufficient for present purposes.
21. Rodolfo Cerrón-Palomino (personal communication) observes that vowel copy harmony in the added vowels seems to be becoming less productive.
22. Specifically, the element at the right edge of the root is required to have a correspondent with an element at the right edge of a vowel. Because a vowel is itself a corresponding element, I assume that it is an element at its own right edge.

23. Quantification is not at issue for INTEGRITY-IO because this constraint itself penalizes multiple correspondence (Struijke 2002: 35).
24. In order to concentrate on issues pertinent to mechanisms of vowel copy and licensing, I do not analyze the assignment of exceptional antepenultimate stress in certain unsuffixed loans.
25. See Anttila (2007) for an overview of treatments of variation and optionality in phonological patterns in OT.
26. In borrowings that end in a nasal, the vowel added in root-final position is generally [a], e.g. [butuŋa] < botón (Spanish) 'button,' [pantaluŋa] < [pantalón] (Spanish) 'pants,' [isquɲa] < [isqun] (Quechua) 'nine,' but [siɲi] < [sien] (Spanish) 'temple' (Cerrón-Palomino 2000: 176; Adelaar and Muysken 2004: 314). (No examples were provided with Jaqaru [n] or [m], but Cerrón-Palomino's description portrays the pattern as true of base-final nasals.) Elsewhere the added vowel is a copy of the preceding vowel, e.g. [atuqu] < atuq (Quechua) 'fox,' [hintili] < gentil (Spanish) 'gentle, nobleman,' [kuntiri] < cóndor (Spanish) 'condor' (last example from Beas 2000) and examples in (52). There is no reason to expect nasals alone to block harmony. In fact, vowel harmonies that show transparency of coronal sonorants have led to proposals that sonorant consonants are *more* receptive to participating in vowel harmony (McCarthy 1994; Gafos and Lombardi 1999). In addition, the pattern does not seem to be dictated by consonant place, e.g. /x/ does not prevent harmony (52). These considerations suggest that the operative generalization is that sequences of a nasal followed by a high vowel are avoided: *V[+high]/[+nasal]_, perhaps due to perceptual effects of the nasal on the neighboring vowel height (Beddor 1982, 1993; Wright 1986; Kingston 2007; note also Beddor *et al.* 1986). Sequences of a nasal plus a high vowel are prevented specifically when the vowel is added, for example, the suffix [-ni] is well-formed, but a nasal+i sequence is avoided in repairing a nasal final root. This is obtained by the local conjunction *V[+high]/[+nasal]_ &$_l$ INTEGRITY-IO. The conjunction will be violated when a high vowel that follows a nasal stands in multiple correspondence, i.e. when it is duplicated.

   For loans ending in a nasal plus added [a] that show antepenultimate stress in isolation, what transpires when they combine with a harmony-triggering suffix remains to be explored. Consider a hypothetical loan /pisuɲ/ → [písuɲa] (< [písun]). The question is whether under suffixation, the contracted alternative form shows the quality of the last input vowel of the root in the penultimate syllable or [a], that is, [pisɲú-ʃi] or [pisɲá-ʃi]. As it stands, the analysis proposed for Jaqaru predicts [u] will be realized in the penult. If [a] occurs here instead, then a constraint preventing a faithful realization of the root vowel in this circumstance must dominate ∃-IDENT(V-FEATURE)$_{L2}$. A possible analysis could employ the local conjunction *V[+high]/[+nasal]_ &$_l$ ∃-LINEARITY-IO. This would prevent a singly realized high vowel from occurring after a nasal out of its input sequence, and instead the final root vowel would be realized as [a].
27. Struijke proposes that input–output faithfulness constraints only demand preservation of the input; therefore DEP-IO, which penalizes output segments that lack input correspondents, is absent from her constraint inventory. She substitutes a constraint M-SEG, which assigns a violation to segments that lack a morphological

affiliation. Existential quantification of faithfulness constraints does not necessitate an assumption of unidirectional faithfulness, and I will continue to assume that DEP-IO is part of Con. However, M-SEG could be used in place of DEP, where I call upon it.

6 Identity licensing

1. In some patterns of vowel harmony, instrumental research has revealed that certain vowels that had been reported to be transparent may actually present the harmonizing property. For studies on this issue, see Gordon (1999), Gafos and Benus (2003, 2006), Benus et al. (2004), Gick et al. (2006), and Benus and Gafos (2007). It would be useful to extend instrumental investigations to other vowel patterns with reported transparent vowels. Nevertheless, many of the transparency effects discussed in this chapter involve features that are expected to be clearly perceptible by speakers if they were present on the transparent vowel, because they are not neutralizing contexts for that feature.
2. Vaysman states that [æ] does not occur underlyingly (2009: 61), but she represents [æ] in the underlying form of some stems.
3. Vaysman distinguishes back and round harmonies that affect underlying full vowels from harmony affecting reduced vowels that are vocalized to full in metrically determined contexts. I deal here with the harmony patterns that affect underlying full vowels, which I propose to be licensing-driven. Vaysman characterizes vocalized schwa as copying "the relevant features of a preceding full vowel" (2009: 86). Different from the harmony that affects underlying full vowels, harmony that governs vocalized schwa lacks restrictions on the position of the trigger, and it produces assimilation for more vowel properties.
4. The consonant of the suffix /-ta/ is allophonically voiced in this example.
5. Vaysman states that the suffix vowel is fronted in this form because of the palatal [ʎ] (2009: 92, n. 34).
6. See Majors (1998) for a related treatment of transparent [ə] in back and round harmony from stressed syllables in the Eastern Mari dialect described by Sebeok and Ingemann (1961).
7. In this form, the [ə] in the suffix is epenthetic (Vaysman 2009: 95). The same is true in later examples of this suffix that begin with [ə].
8. See van Oostendorp (1995) for the claim that schwa lacks vocalic features in various languages. Crosswhite (2001, 2004) also makes this claim for reduced [ə], including in Mari dialects.
9. Vaysman (2009) transcribes the root as [ímne] 'horse' on p. 93 but [ímɲe] on p. 79.
10. Vaysman notes that this suffix shows progressive devoicing when following a voiceless obstruent (2009: 93).
11. When the stressed vowel is /ɛ/ and there is an intervening palatalized velar consonant, metaphony does not occur, e.g. [vékkʲi] 'old (pl).' Following Sluyters (1988: 169), I assume that this is not an occurrence of blocking by a consonant but rather an instance of avoidance of [i]-initial diphthongs in adjacent syllables.
12. Apart from lexical/morphological restrictions, Sluyters (1988: 165) suggests that metaphony occurs only in derived environments.

13. The neutralization of mid vowels to [−ATR] in stressed syllables (in the absence of metaphony) could be handled by ranking *[+ATR, −high] >> IDENT-IO(ATR).
14. A complication in the metaphony of Francavilla Fontana arises in particular forms with antepenultimate stress. In forms of this kind with a metaphony-triggering suffix, height assimilation in the stressed syllable usually occurs, e.g. /mɛtik-u/ → [miétuku], /mɛtik-i/ → [miétitʃi] 'physician (m sg/pl)'; /sɛkul-u/ → [siékulu], /sɛkul-i/ → [siékuli] 'century (m sg/pl).' However, if the vowel in the penultimate syllable is underlyingly /a/, height harmony only transmits to the stressed syllable from metaphonic suffixes with /−i/ and not ones with /−u/: /mɔnak-u/ → [mɔ́nuku], /mɔnak-i/ → [muénitʃi] 'monk (m sg/pl)'. These forms also show evidence of independent harmonies for [back] and [+round] in post-tonic syllables. Evidence that the underlying vowel in the penult is underlyingly /a/ comes from [munatʃiéddu] 'monk-like ghost'. The blocking effect of /a/ seems to indicate that metaphony cannot skip a syllable (see Sluyters 1988: 172 for a related interpretation). At the same time, under the identity licensing analysis, metaphonic raising can skip a vowel in contexts where diphthongs are formed in the stressed syllable. In this dialect, identity licensing configurations that skip a syllable could be prevented by a constraint that restricts the phonological exponents of a morpheme to contiguous syllables: MORPHOLOGICAL-O-CONTIGUITY-σ. See §7.3 for discussion of this constraint. (See also §6.4 for discussion of another dialect with identity licensing where /a/ might serve as a blocker for metaphony.) The cause for the blocking effect by /a/ in metaphony from /−u/ but not /−i/ could plausibly be treated as the effect of a kind of derivational opacity (Calabrese 1985; Sluyters 1988). However, I will not pursue an analysis here.
15. Hualde (1989) was unable to find examples with the environment for raising in a form with antepenultimate stress and a mid vowel in the penult.
16. Neira Martínez, a native speaker of the dialect, characterizes /e/ and the vowel to which /a/ raises as the same (1955: 5). However, Dyck (1995: 57, n. 30) cites Galmés de Fuentes (1960a: 21) as describing these vowels as distinct. The transcriptions that I use are consistent with those of Neira Martínez and Hualde. If the vowel to which /a/ raises is indeed distinct from /e/, the raised quality of /a/ would still be attested elsewhere in the language − in stressed syllables. Instrumental investigation is warranted. Depending on the findings for /a/, the analysis of metaphony for this vowel may require some modification.
17. As discussed in §3.4.2, effects of systemic contrast involve candidates that represent languages, i.e. sets of possible word forms, rather than individual forms. See §7.2.2 for an evaluation of these kind of candidates within a tableau. For ease of exposition, candidates are presented here as individual word forms, because the constraints under focus are not ones that require evaluation across word forms in a set.
18. Fanti represents the 'd' in this word with a stroke through it (1940: 106).
19. Trigger control in the Ascrea and Lena patterns would also be compatible with an analysis using the conjunction that was active in central Veneto: *ŏ/a,e•o &$_l$ IDENT-IO(high).
20. Other work on proximity-type restrictions includes Odden (1994), Suzuki (1998), Rose (2000), Pulleyblank (2002), Struijke (2002), and Uffmann (2004) (note also Wolf 2007 for a related proposal).

21. This approach would fall roughly in line with the observations of Nevins (2004, 2010), who finds that vowels with greater sonority are less prone to be transparent in vowel harmony. However, Nevins argues that sonority rather than duration is the relevant dimension to consider.
22. Word-final /h/ also triggers [–ATR] allophones of vowels, but examples are very limited.
23. See Jiménez and Lloret (2007) for arguments against an analysis with a floating [spread glottis] or [–ATR] feature that expresses a particular grammatical category.
24. When a final /s/ is not deleted, Jiménez and Lloret propose that [spread glottis] spreads to the preceding vowel because this feature is licensed by association with a syllable nucleus or onset.
25. Howell and Salmons (1997) discuss evidence for an intermediate stage during which umlaut of /u/ was blocked by geminates and certain clusters. The /u/-specific blocking effects could perhaps be analyzed in terms of the combined markedness of the derived front high round vowel [y] and a duplicated [–back] feature, which would be necessary to skip the intervening material.
26. In the case of two output segments that correspond with the same input segment, the constraints in question could be Struijke's 'surface faithfulness' constraints.
27. Some similar issues are faced by the analysis of Lena by Wolf (2007), who also posits a floating height feature ([+high] or [–low]) plus a suffix vowel /–u/.
28. See Piggott (1997, 2000) for a licensing-based analysis of floating-feature phenomena that is implemented rather differently from its development in this work.
29. Specifically, Dillon analyzes metaphony in Lena as a case of "double morphemic exponence," building on an approach that Kurisu (2001) proposes for umlaut in German plurals. A complication of that approach is that it treats metaphony and umlaut as involving a kind of morphological opacity.

7   Direct licensing

1. The dominated IDENT(F) constraint is not necessarily for the same feature as that subject to licensing.
2. Citing Czekman and Smułkowa (1988), Barnes (2006: 87) notes that in pretonic positions other than immediate pretonic, /e o a/ neutralize to [ɐ]. For discussion of this kind of reduction, see Crosswhite (2001), Padgett (2004), Padgett and Tabain (2005), and Barnes (2006).
3. It would also be possible to characterize the λ argument in this constraint as [–low]/[–high]. The reference to two features here in characterizing a mid vowel is a consequence of the particular system of vowel height features assumed; it may be possible to adopt a different system in which mid vowel height was represented by a single feature.
4. Miglio observes that [ɪ] is probably a contextually conditioned allophone of /i/ and likewise [ʌ] of /e/.
5. Dyck posits that the non-low vowel phonemes in desinences are /e o/ (1995: 47). She notes a marginal, archaic desinence /(i)/, which, she concludes, does not stand in full contrast with desinential /e/.

6. Another possible formulation of the licensing constraint is LICENSE$_L$([high]/V$_h$ [–low], σ́), which equally penalizes a high specification in a mid or high vowel. However, the formulation that I have adopted is consistent with the tendency for licensing-driven metaphony initiated by high vowels only, in related dialects.
7. Padgett (2003: 58) observes that there is a partial overlap in the labor of IDENT(F) and *MERGE. A violation of *MERGE implies a violation of IDENT, but the reverse entailment does not hold.
8. I have assigned a violation for *MERGE for each word with a suffix that merges a height contrast. If instead the constraint were assessed by morpheme, just two violations would be accrued in (14a).
9. Rohlfs refers to such dialects as 'antico'.
10. Other research that has proposed some version of a constraint that prevents discontinuous morphemes includes Wolf (2007), Finley (2009), and Łubowicz (2009).
11. I leave open the possibility that these morphemes are unordered in the input, and that the suffixing status of /–i/ is determined by a constraint, such as alignment (McCarthy and Prince 1993b). If the stem and suffix were ordered in the input, then infixation would also violate LINEARITY-IO (see §5.3).
12. Stress is marked in outputs based on comparison with the Standard Italian form, which matches where it would be expected to be assigned according to the usual orthographic conventions.
13. Alternatively, the realization of the coalesced high and low vowels as mid could perhaps be analyzed using a local conjunction of the constraints IDENT-IO(high) and IDENT-IO(low) within the domain of a single correspondent segment. The realization of the coalesced vowel as mid would avoid violating this conjunction because it earns a violation of IDENT(high) from its correspondent /a/ and a violation of IDENT(low) from its correspondent /i/. Alternative realizations would violate the local conjunction. The realization of the coalesced vowel as /a/ would violate IDENT(high) and IDENT(low) for the input correspondent /i/ and the realization of the coalesced vowel as /i/ would violate IDENT(high) and IDENT(low) for the input correspondent /a/. However, the theoretical ramifications of this type of domain for local conjunction require further consideration.
14. Féry considers non-umlauted *Frauchen* as a lexicalized hypocoristic (1994: 15). See Iverson and Salmons (1992) for a different proposal in which there are two *–chen* suffixes, an umlauting one and a non-umlauting one, which are also distinguished in their semantics and, they suggest, in the resulting word's prosodic structure. Either approach would be compatible with a licensing analysis.
15. Klein (1995, 2000) lists a few forms where umlaut with *–chen* affects an unstressed vowel, e.g. Póp[a]nz/Póp[ɛ]nz-chen 'scarecrow/– (dim),' Ámb[ɔ]ß/ Ámb[œ]ß-chen 'anvil/– (dim).' Given Féry's findings and my own preliminary investigation on this topic, such forms do not seem to reflect the effect of a categorical, regular, and productive process. It is possible that umlaut is lexicalized in these words, although further research is needed. Klein (1995) hypothesizes that umlaut targets a root-final syllable rather than a stressed syllable. If further research were to reveal firm evidence for this, a licensing constraint could be framed along such lines.

16. As Wolf (2007) points out, MAX(FLOAT) does not entail a commitment to MAX(F) governing featural faithfulness in general. See Walker (2001a) and de Lacy (2006) for discussion of some surrounding issues.
17. I assume that another constraint that penalizes floating features in the output is undominated in the grammar of MSG.
18. Alternatively, if the glide in *–lein* were actually specified [–back], possibly the floating feature could dock to this segment and an identity licensing configuration could be posited for this suffix (see discussion of umlaut in OHG in chapter 6). That option would not be available for *–chen*, as docking in this suffix would incur an extra violation of IDENT (see [32b]).
19. A third kind of prefix vowel alternates in height at a step below the prefix vowels illustrated in (35), showing alternants [o]/[ɔ/ɛ]/[a], an effect referred to as 'downstep' by Hyman. Stallcup (1980b) reconstructs this prefix vowel as */a/. Downstep will not be analyzed here; see Hyman (1988) and Clements (1991) for possible approaches.
20. It is also conceivable that color harmony in Esimbi could be analyzed as the effect of a licensing constraint for color features by the root-initial syllable. However, since the prefix vowel can display color features distinct from the root, the word-initial syllable would also have to be a possible licensor for color features. For discussion of formal issues surrounding patterns with licensing in multiple contexts, see §9.2.3.
21. Struijke (2002) analyzes the phenomenon without floating features using existential faithfulness and vowel fission. That would also be compatible with the main claims of the prominence-based licensing approach developed here. But see discussion in §6.6 of the drawbacks of treating licensing in general as potentially mediated by segment correspondence, of which fission is an instance.
22. Koenig *et al.* (2007) transcribe the central stem vowel as [ə] rather than [ɨ]. This would be compatible with the present account if stem [ə] in the output represented a central vowel unspecified for height.
23. Apart from reduplication, no data with multiple prefixes are provided in the sources. According to Hyman (personal communication), such forms do exist in Esimbi. Hyman reports that in these forms each prefix displays the vowel height conditioned by the root. If initial syllable licensing for height were the only factor in vowel height realization, this distribution would be unexpected. The consistency of vowel height in prefixes across their occurrence in initial or non-initial positions could possibly be considered a paradigm uniformity effect, like that suggested for unprefixed verbs. However, in the absence of concrete data, an analysis would be premature.
24. Brad Koenig (personal communication) informs me that he has not seen the secondary person marker prefix in any construction other than the reduplicated progressive in Esimbi.

8 Maximal licensing

1. Li (1996: 209, n. 2) reports that [ɔmɔlɩɛ-xal] was confirmed by most of his consultants, but some reported [ɔmɔlɔ-xɔl], [ɔmɔlɔ-xal], [ɔmɔlɩɛ-xɔl]. See Li (1996) for discussion.

2. Apart from borrowed stems, Li (1996: 139–40) lists two exceptions to this generalization. The derivational suffix [–mkɔːk] and a plural suffix [–nɔr] are always realized as round, even following a syllable with a preceding high vowel or an unround vowel. The vowels in these suffixes also do not show alternations in their tongue root quality. The suffix [–mkɔːk] is always word final, so it is not possible to test its effect on following vowels; however, [–nɔr] can trigger round harmony in a following suffix: [ətʃəxə-nɔr-wo̪-t] 'paternal uncles (def. acc.).' I assume that a morpheme-specific IDENT-IO(round) constraint for these suffixes preserves their rounding quality independent of the usual restrictions in the language.
3. In §9.2.3, an overgeneration issue in OT is discussed concerning this and various other constraints that drive unbounded harmony phenomena.
4. See McCarthy (2003: 129) for a critique of the local statement of AGREE(F) along other lines.
5. Because Baiyinna Orochen is a suffixing language, the root-initial syllable generally coincides with the word-initial syllable, so there is no need to distinguish those positions in the forms under consideration.
6. Notice that a prominence-based licensing constraint, LICENSE([+round]/[–high], $\sigma_{Initial}$) could also serve to restrict the free occurrence of non-high round vowels in non-initial syllables. However, the positional faithfulness constraint IDENT-IO-$\sigma_{Initial}$(round) is independently needed to obtain trigger control in the pattern, which obviates the necessity for a position-sensitive statement of markedness with respect to the distribution of [+round]. In the interests of simplicity, I will favor the use of context-free constraints where possible.
7. Alternatively, it could be driven by ranking *ŏ/a,ɛ•ɔ over IDENT-IO(ATR), with IDENT-IO(low) invoked to prevent raising of /a/.
8. Other work that has discussed vowel harmony in Servigliano includes Leonard (1978), Kaze (1991), Maiden (1991a, b, 1997), Flemming (1993), Penny (1994), Clements and Hume (1995), Dyck (1995), Parkinson (1996), Vogel (1997), Canalis (2009), and Krämer (2009).
9. The texts in Camilli's article (1929: 232–47), which appear to be drawn from local poetry, were not included in the database.
10. Transcriptions of initial geminates follow Camilli.
11. These mappings could alternatively be prevented by *[–ATR, +high], which is not violated in the language.
12. Camilli (1929) gives this form as *stómmucu* ([stómmuku]) on p. 225 but as *stòmmucu* ([stómmuku]) on p. 269. I infer that the latter entry had an error in the accent mark, since it is unexpected given the pattern of metaphony.
13. Nibert (1998: 74) glosses this form as 'he marks it (m pl) down for you (sg).' I have interpreted [lu] as 'it (m sg),' consistent with its gloss elsewhere.
14. This partial gloss is as given by Nibert (1998: 75).
15. Other work that postulates clitic attachment by adjunction to PWd for particular cases includes Selkirk (1995), Booij (1996), Peperkamp (1996, 1997), Anderson (2005), Krämer (2009), and Itô and Mester (2009a, b).
16. It might be appropriate to further differentiate between vowels assigned primary stress and those assigned a secondary stress, but that awaits further investigation.

17. Recasens also found that two of three speakers of Catalan whom he studied showed greater length in immediate post-tonic syllables.
18. The immediate pretonic syllable is not strong in all languages. For example, see Kaplan (2008a) on Chamorro, a system discused briefly in §5.3. See also Trubetzkoy (1969: 236) on neutralizations that differently affect pretonic and post-tonic syllables across languages.
19. I consider the IDENT-BA relation as distinct from positional faithfulness. Although the stem plus its closest proclitic forms the base for attachment of the next outermost clitic, basehood does not directly translate into a prominent position. Further, the proclitic that controls harmony is external to the stem of the word to which it cliticizes, so positional faithfulness to the stem is not applicable here.
20. Possibly [kummunikíno] means 'we communicate,' although the suffix in that case is expected to be –*imo*. I infer that this is the assumption of Nibert, who gives the form [kummunik-ímo] with the gloss 'we communicate' (1998: 87). The closest form that I found in Camilli was [kummunikíno] (1929: 225).
21. Nibert gives the form [predik-á] 'to preach' (1998: 73), but it did not appear in the database. I also did not find this word in Camilli's texts, but I may have missed it.
22. Camilli does not indicate whether there is a difference in the meanings of [tʃitʃeró] and [tʃitʃeróttu].
23. A northwest Tuscan Romance dialect spoken near Castelnuovo Garfagnana shows a similar raising harmony that affects pretonic vowels and is triggered by high vowels, whether stressed or unstressed (Venturelli 1974; Maiden 1988, 1991b), e.g. [vistíto]/[vestáλλa] 'suit'/'dressing gown,' [du̬rmí]/[do̬rmján] 'to sleep'/'we sleep,' [sintúto]/[se̬ntján] 'felt (past part.)'/'we feel,' [ti̬livi̬sión] (It. *televisióne*) 'television.' The Pasiego dialect may present another possible case, although there is debate regarding specifics of the unstressed height harmony pattern, on which see Penny (1969), McCarthy (1984), Vago (1988), Hualde (1989, 1992), and Flemming (1993).
24. Another difference between metaphony and unstressed vowel raising that could give reason to treat them as distinct processes is the behavior of vowels that are underlyingly [–ATR]. In unstressed vowel raising, /ɛ/ and /ɔ/ become high (see [55]), whereas metaphony causes /ɛ/ and /ɔ/ to raise only to their [+ATR] counterparts. Also, unstressed /a/ can be transparent to the unstressed vowel raising (63a), whereas raising harmony triggered by a post-tonic vowel cannot propagate across /a/, e.g. [so̬prán-u] 'airplane (m sg),' [pe̬kkát-u] 'sin (m sg).' However, these effects could possibly be attributed to differences in the stressed versus unstressed status of these vowels.
25. Cf. Kaze (1989) who analyzes metaphony and unstressed vowel raising as the same process, for which the triggers are high vowels that are stressed or post-tonic.
26. The database did not contain examples with the conditions to demonstrate vowel copy harmony feeding metaphony that in turn feeds unstressed vowel raising; however, that vowel copy harmony feeds metaphony was independently established (see [33–34]).

9   Conclusion and final issues

1. In some maximal licensing patterns, the vowel properties that are subject to a licensing restriction occur contrastively only in a strong position (e.g. initial syllable,

1988. *Towards a Theory of Phonological Alphabets*. Ph.D. dissertation, MIT.
1998. "Metaphony revisited," *Rivista di Linguistica* 10: 7–68.
Camilli, Amerindo. 1929. "Il dialetto di Servigliano," *Archivum Romanicum* 13: 220–71.
Campos-Astorkiza, Rebeka. 2009. *The Role and Representation of Minimal Contrast and the Phonetics–Phonology Interaction.* Munich: Lincom Europa.
Canalis, Stefano. 2007a. "When a feature is metrical: vowel harmony in two Romance dialects," paper presented at the 15th Manchester Phonology Meeting, May 24–26, 2007.
    2007b. "Total vowel harmony in two Romance dialects," paper presented at Phonetics and Phonology in Iberia, Universidade do Minho, Braga, June 25–26, 2007.
    2009. "Post-tonic vowel harmony in some dialects of central Italy: the role of prosodic structure, contrast and consonants," in Marina Vigário, Sónia Frota, and M. João Freitas (eds.), *Phonetics and Phonology: Interactions and Interrelations.* Amsterdam: John Benjamins.
Carson, Neusa M. 1982. *Phonology and Morphosyntax of Macuxi (Carib).* Ph.D. dissertation, University of Kansas.
Casali, Roderic. 1997. "Vowel elision in hiatus contexts: which vowel goes?" *Language* 73: 493–533.
    1998. *Resolving Hiatus.* New York: Garland.
Causley, Trisha. 1997. "Featural correspondence and identity: the Athapaskan case," *North East Linguistic Society* 27, 93–105.
Cerrón-Palomino, Rodolfo. 2000. *Lingüística Aimara.* Cuzco: Bartolomé de Las Casas.
Cerrón-Palomino López, Alvaro. 2003. "A case of weak triggers: vowel harmony in Jaqaru," ms., University of Southern California.
Chitoran, Ioana and José I. Hualde. 2007. "From hiatus to diphthong: the evolution of vowel sequences in Romance," *Phonology* 24: 37–75.
Cho, Taehong and Sun-Ah Jun. 2000. "Domain-initial strengthening as enhancement of laryngeal features: aerodynamic evidence from Korean," *UCLA Working Papers in Phonetics* 99: 57–79.
Chomsky, Noam and Morris Halle. 1968. *The Sound Pattern of English.* New York: Harper and Row.
Christdas, Prathima. 1988. *The Phonology and Morphology of Tamil.* Ph.D. dissertation, Cornell University.
Clements, G. N. 1980. *Vowel Harmony in Nonlinear Generative Phonology.* Bloomington: Indiana University Linguistics Club.
    1991. "Vowel height assimilation in Bantu languages," *Berkeley Linguistics Society* 17: 25–63.
    2001. "Representational economy in constraint-based phonology," in T. Alan Hall (ed.), *Distinctive Feature Theory*, 71–146. Berlin: Mouton de Gruyter.
Clements, G. N. and Elizabeth V. Hume. 1995. "The internal organization of speech sounds," in Goldsmith (ed.), 245–306.
Cole, Jennifer. 1995. "The cycle in phonology," in Goldsmith (ed.), 70–113.
    1998. "Deconstructing metaphony," *Rivista di Linguistica* 10: 69–98.

Cole, Jennifer and Charles Kisseberth. 1995. "Restricting multi-level constraint evaluation: opaque rule interaction in Yawelmani vowel harmony," in Suzuki and Elzinga (eds.), 18–38.
Cole, Ronald A. and Jola Jakimik. 1980. "How are syllables used to recognize words?" *Journal of the Acoustical Society of America* 67: 965–70.
Coon, Jessica and Gillian Gallagher. 2009. "Similarity and correspondence in Chol Mayan," *North East Linguistic Society* 38, 203–16.
Côté, Marie-Hélène. 2000. *Consonant Cluster Phonotactics: A Perceptual Approach.* Ph.D. dissertation, MIT.
  2004. "Syntagmatic distinctness in consonant deletion," *Phonology* 21: 1–41.
Crosswhite, Katherine. 2001. *Vowel Reduction in Optimality Theory.* New York: Routledge.
  2004. "Vowel reduction," in Hayes *et al.* (eds.), 191–231.
Crowhurst, Megan and Mark Hewitt. 1997. "Boolean operations and constraint interactions in Optimality Theory," ms., University of North Carolina, Chapel Hill and Brandeis University. [Available as ROA 229.]
Curtin, Suzanne. 2002. *Representational Richness in Phonological Development.* Ph.D. dissertation, University of Southern California.
Czekman, Walery and Elżbieta Smułkowa. 1988. *Fonetyka i Fonologia Języka Białoruskiego z Elementami Fonetyki i Fonologii Ogólnej.* Warsaw: Państwowe Wydawnictwo Naukowe.
de Jong, Kenneth. 1995. "Supraglottal articulation of prominence in English: linguistic stress as localized hyperarticulation," *Journal of the Acoustical Society of America* 97(1): 491–504.
de Lacy, Paul. 2002. *The Formal Expression of Markedness.* Ph.D. dissertation, University of Massachusetts, Amherst.
  2006. *Markedness: Reduction and Preservation in Phonology.* Cambridge University Press.
  2007a. "The interaction of tone, sonority, and prosodic structure," in de Lacy (ed.), 281–307.
de Lacy, Paul (ed.). 2007b. *The Cambridge Handbook of Phonology.* Cambridge University Press.
Delattre, Pierre. 1966. "A comparison of syllable length conditioning among languages," *International Review of Applied Linguistics* 4: 183–98.
Dettweiler, Stephen H. 2000. "Vowel harmony and neutral vowels in C'Lela," *The Journal of West African Languages* 18: 3–18.
Dillon, Caitlin. 2004. "Metaphony as morpheme realization, not vowel harmony," *IULC Working Papers Online*, Volume IV, www.indiana.edu/~iulcwp.
Downing, Laura. 2006. *Canonical Forms in Prosodic Morphology.* Oxford University Press.
Dresher, B. Elan. 2009. *The Contrastive Hierarchy in Phonology.* Cambridge University Press.
Dressler, Wolfgang. 1997. "'Scenario' as a concept for the functional explanation of language change," in Jadranka Gvozdanović (ed.), *Language Change and Functional Explanations*, 109–42. Berlin: Mouton de Gruyter.

Dyck, Carrie. 1995. *Constraining the Phonology–Phonetics Interface with Exemplification from Spanish and Italian Dialects*. Ph.D. dissertation, University of Toronto.
Ellis, Jeffrey. 1953. *An Elementary Old High German Grammar*. Oxford: Clarendon.
Fanti, Renata. 1938; 1939; 1940. "Note fonetiche e morfologiche sul dialetto di Ascrea (Rieti)," *L'Italia dialettale* 14: 201–18; 15: 101–35; 16: 77–140.
Farnetani, Edda, Kyriaki Vagges, and Emanuela Magno-Caldognetto. 1985. "Coarticulation in Italian /VtV/ sequences: a palatographic study," *Phonetica* 42: 78–99.
Fay, David and Anne Cutler. 1977. "Malapropisms and the structure of the mental lexicon," *Linguistic Inquiry* 8: 505–20.
Feldman, Laurie B. and Jasmina Moskovljević. 1987. "Repetition priming is not purely episodic in origin," *Journal of Experimental Psychology: Learning, Memory, and Cognition* 13: 573–81.
Féry, Caroline. 1994. "Umlaut and inflection in German," ms., University of Tübingen.
Finley, Sara. 2008. *Formal and Cognitive Restrictions on Vowel Harmony*. Ph.D. dissertation, Johns Hopkins University.
  2009. "Morphemic harmony as featural correspondence," *Lingua* 119: 478–501.
Finley, Sara and William Badecker. 2008. "Analytical biases for vowel harmony languages," *West Coast Conference on Formal Linguistics* 27: 168–76.
Flack, Kathryn. 2007a. *The Sources of Phonological Markedness*. Ph.D. dissertation, University of Massachusetts, Amherst.
  2007b. "Templatic morphology and indexed markedness constraints," *Linguistic Inquiry* 38: 749–58.
  2007c. "Inducing functionally grounded constraints," ms., University of Massachusetts, Amherst.
Fleischhacker, Heidi. 2005. *Similarity in Phonology: Evidence from Reduplication and Loan Adaptation*. Ph.D. dissertation, University of California, Los Angeles.
Flemming, Edward. 1993. "The role of metrical structure in segmental rules," Masters thesis, University of California, Los Angeles.
  1995. "Vowels undergo consonant harmony," paper presented at the Trilateral Phonology Weekend (TREND) 5, University of California, Berkeley.
  2002. *Auditory Representations in Phonology*. New York: Routledge.
  2004. "Contrast and perceptual distinctiveness," in Hayes *et al.* (eds.), 232–76.
  2005. "A phonetically-based model of phonological vowel reduction," ms., MIT.
Fónagy, Iván. 1966. "Electro-physiological and acoustic correlates of stress and stress perception," *Journal of Speech and Hearing Research* 9: 231–44.
Forner, Werner. 1975a. "Metatesi, metafonesi, o alterazione nei dialetti liguri?" *L'Italia dialettale* 38: 77–89.
  1975b. *Generative Phonologie des Dialekts von Genua*. Hamburg: Buske.
Fougeron, Cécile. 1999. "Prosodically conditioned articulatory variations: a review," *UCLA Working Papers in Phonetics* 97: 1–73.
Fougeron, Cécile and Patricia A. Keating. 1996. "Articulatory strengthening in prosodic domain-initial position," *UCLA Working Papers in Phonetics* 92: 61–87.
Fowler, Carol A. 1981. "Production and perception of coarticulation among stressed and unstressed vowels," *Journal of Speech and Hearing Research* 46: 127–39.

Fowler, Carol A., Shirley E. Napps, and Laurie Feldman. 1985. "Relations among regular and irregular morphologically related words in the lexicon as revealed by repetition priming," *Memory and Cognition* 13: 241–55.
Frisch, Stefan. 1996. *Similarity and Frequency in Phonology*. Ph.D. dissertation, Northwestern University.
  2000. "Temporally organized representations as phonological units," in Michael Broe and Janet Pierrehumbert (eds.), *Papers in Laboratory Phonology V: Acquisition and the Lexicon*, 283–98. Cambridge University Press.
  2004. "Language processing and segmental OCP effects," in Hayes *et al.* (eds.), 346–71.
Gafos, Adamantios. 1998. "Eliminating long-distance consonantal spreading," *Natural Language and Linguistic Theory* 16: 223–78.
  1999. *The Articulatory Basis of Locality in Phonology*. New York: Garland.
Gafos, Adamantios and Stefan Benus. 2003. "On neutral vowels in Hungarian," *Proceedings of the 15th International Congress of Phonetic Sciences*, 77–80. Universitat Autònoma de Barcelona.
  2006. "Dynamics of phonological cognition," *Cognitive Science* 30: 1–39.
Gafos, Adamantios and Linda Lombardi. 1999. "Consonant transparency and vowel echo," *North East Linguistic Society* 29: 81–96.
Galmés de Fuentes, Alvaro. 1960a. "Más datos sobre la inflexión metafonética en el centro-sur de Asturias," in Galmés de Fuentes (ed.), 11–26.
Galmés de Fuentes, Alvaro (ed.). 1960b. *Trabajos sobre el dominio románico leonés*, Vol. II. Madrid: Editorial Gredos.
Gick, Bryan, Douglas Pulleyblank, Fiona Campbell, and Ngessimo Mutaka. 2006. "Low vowels and transparency in Kinande vowel harmony," *Phonology* 23: 1–20.
Goad, Heather. 1993. *On the Configuration of Height Features*. Ph.D. dissertation, University of Southern California.
Goldsmith, John A. 1989. "Autosegmental licensing, inalterability, and harmonic rule application," *Papers from the 25th Annual Meeting of the Chicago Linguistic Society, Part I, The General Session*, 145–56.
  1990. *Autosegmental and Metrical Phonology*. Oxford: Blackwell.
Goldsmith, John A. (ed.). 1995. *The Handbook of Phonological Theory*. Oxford: Blackwell.
Goldstein, Louis. 1977. "Three studies in speech perception: features, relative salience, and bias," *UCLA Working Papers in Phonetics* 39.
  1992. "Comments on chapters 3 and 4," in Gerard J. Docherty and D. Robert Ladd (eds.), *Papers in Laboratory Phonology II: Gesture, Segment, Prosody*, 120–4. Cambridge University Press.
González, Carolina. 2003. *The Effect of Stress and Foot Structure on Consonantal Processes*. Ph.D. dissertation, University of Southern California.
Gordon, Matthew. 1999. "The 'neutral' vowels of Finnish: how neutral are they?" *Linguistica Uralica* 35: 17–21.
  2001. "Laryngeal timing and correspondence in Hupa," in Adam Albright and Taehong Cho (eds.), *UCLA Working Papers in Linguistics 7, Papers in Phonology* 5: 1–70.

2004. "Syllable weight," in Hayes *et al.* (eds.), 277–312.

2006. *Syllable Weight: Phonetics, Phonology, Typology.* New York: Routledge.

Gordon, Matthew and Peter Ladefoged. 2001. "Phonation types: a cross-linguistic overview," *Journal of Phonetics* 28: 383–406.

Granda Gutiérrez, Germán de. 1960. "Las vocales finales del dialecto leonés," in Galmés de Fuentes (ed.), 27–117.

Grandgent, C. H. 1927. *From Latin to Italian.* Harvard University Press.

2002. *An Introduction to Vulgar Latin.* Honolulu: University Press of the Pacific. [Reprint of the 1907 edition.]

Hagland, Jan Ragnar. 1978. "A note on Old Norwegian vowel harmony," *Nordic Journal of Linguistics* 1: 141–7.

Hall, Christopher J. 1988. "Integrating diachronic and processing principles in explaining the suffix preference," in Hawkins (ed.), 321–49.

Hansson, Gunnar Ólafur. 2001. *Theoretical and Typological Issues in Consonant Harmony.* Ph.D. dissertation, University of California, Berkeley.

2004. "Long-distance voicing agreement: an evolutionary perspective," *Berkeley Linguistics Society* 30: 130–41.

2006. "Understanding harmony as agreement," paper presented at the annual meeting of the Linguistic Society of America, Albuquerque, January 2006.

2007a. "Blocking effects in agreement by correspondence," *Linguistic Inquiry* 38: 395–409.

2007b. "On the evolution of consonant harmony: the case of secondary articulation agreement," *Phonology* 24: 77–120.

2008. "Diachronic explanations of sound patterns," *Language and Linguistics Compass* 2: 859–93.

Hardman, M. J. 1966. *Jaqaru: Outline of Phonological and Morphological Structure.* The Hague: Mouton.

Harris, John. 1997. "Licensing inheritance: an integrated theory of neutralisation," *Phonology* 14: 315–70.

Hawkins, John A. (ed.). 1988. *Explaining Language Universals.* Oxford: Blackwell.

Hawkins, John A. and Anne Cutler. 1988. "Psycholinguistic factors in morphological asymmetry," in Hawkins (ed.), 280–317.

Hayes, Bruce. 1989. "The prosodic hierarchy in meter," in Paul Kiparsky and Gilbert Youmans (eds.), *Phonetics and Phonology, Volume I: Rhythm and Meter*, 201–60. San Diego: Academic Press.

1999. "Phonetically driven phonology: the role of Optimality Theory and inductive grounding," in Michael Darnell, Edith A. Moravcsik, Michael Noonan, Frederick J. Newmeyer, and Kathleen M. Wheatley (eds.), *Formalism and Functionalism in Linguistics*, Vol. I, General Papers, 243–85. Amsterdam: John Benjamins.

Hayes, Bruce and Donca Steriade. 2004. "The phonetic bases of phonological markedness," in Hayes *et al.* (eds.), 1–33.

Hayes, Bruce, Bruce Tesar, and Kie Zuraw. 2003. OTSoft 2.1, software package. www.linguistics.ucla.edu/people/hayes/otsoft/.

Hayes, Bruce, Robert Kirchner, and Donca Steriade (eds.). 2004. *Phonetically-based Phonology.* Cambridge University Press.

Hermann, József. 1997. *Vulgar Latin*. Translated by Roger Wright. University Park: Pennsylvania State University Press.

Herrick, Dylan. 2003. *An Acoustic Analysis of Phonological Vowel Reduction in Six Varieties of Catalan*. Ph.D. dissertation, University of California, Santa Cruz.

Holsinger, David J. and Joseph C. Salmons. 1999. "Toward 'a complete analysis of the residues': on regular vs. morpholexical approaches to Old High German umlaut," in Sheila Embleton, John E. Joseph, and Hans-Josef Niederehe (eds.), *The Emergence of the Modern Language Sciences: Studies on the Transition from Historical-comparative to Structural Linguistics in Honour of E.F. Konrad Koerner*, Vol. II, 239–53. Amsterdam: John Benjamins.

Howe, Darin and Douglas Pulleyblank. 2004. "Harmonic scales as faithfulness," *Canadian Journal of Linguistics* 49: 1–49.

Howell, Robert B. and Joseph C. Salmons. 1997. "Umlautless residues in Germanic," *American Journal of Germanic Linguistics and Literatures* 9: 83–111.

Hualde, José I. 1989. "Autosegmental and metrical spreading in the vowel-harmony systems of northwestern Spain," *Linguistics* 27: 773–805.

1992. "Metaphony and count/mass morphology in Asturian and Cantabrian dialects," in Christiane Laeufer and Terrell Morgan (eds.), *Theoretical Analysis in Romance Linguistics*, 99–114. Amsterdam: John Benjamins.

1998. "Asturian and Cantabrian metaphony," *Rivista di Linguistica* 10: 99–108.

2004. "Quasi-phonemic contrasts in Spanish," *West Coast Conference on Formal Linguistics* 23: 374–98.

2005. *The Sounds of Spanish*. Cambridge University Press.

Hualde, José I. and Ioana Chitoran. 2003. "Explaining the distribution of hiatus in Spanish and Romanian," *Proceedings of the 15th International Congress of Phonetic Sciences* 1,683–6. Universitat Autònoma de Barcelona.

Hume, Elizabeth. 1998. "Metathesis in phonological theory: the case of Leti," *Lingua* 104: 147–86.

1999. "The role of perceptibility in consonant/consonant metathesis," *West Coast Conference on Formal Linguistics* 17: 293–307.

Hume, Elizabeth and Keith Johnson. 2001a. "A model of the interplay of speech perception and phonology," In Hume and Johnson (eds.), 3–26.

Hume, Elizabeth and Keith Johnson (eds.). 2001b. *The Role of Speech Perception in Phonology*. San Diego: Academic Press.

Hume, Elizabeth and Misun Seo. 2004. "Metathesis in Faroese and Lithuanian: from speech perception to Optimality Theory," *Nordic Journal of Linguistics* 27: 35–60.

Hyman, Larry. 1988. "Underspecification and vowel height transfer in Esimbi," *Phonology* 5: 255–73.

1998. "Positional prominence and the 'prosodic trough' in Yaka," *Phonology* 15: 41–75.

2001. "The limits of phonetic determinism in phonology: *NC revisited," in Hume and Johnson (eds.), 141–85.

2008. "Directional asymmetries in the morphology and phonology of words, with special reference to Bantu," *Linguistics* 46: 309–50.

Itô, Junko. 1988. *Syllable Theory in Prosodic Phonology*. New York: Garland.

1989. "A prosodic theory of epenthesis," *Natural Language and Linguistic Theory* 7: 217–59.
Itô, Junko and Armin Mester. 1993. "Licensed segments and safe paths," *Canadian Journal of Linguistics* 38: 197–213.
1998. "Markedness and word structure: OCP effects in Japanese," ms., University of California, Santa Cruz. [Available as ROA 255.]
1999. "Realignment," in René Kager, Harry van der Hulst, and Wim Zonneveld (eds.), *The Prosody–Morphology Interface*, 188–217. Cambridge University Press.
2003. *Japanese Morphophonemics: Markedness and Word Structure*. Cambridge, MA: MIT Press.
2009a. "The extended prosodic word," in Janet Grijzenhout and Baris Kabak (eds.), *Phonological Domains: Universals and Derivations*, 135–94. The Hague: Mouton de Gruyter.
2009b. "The onset of the prosodic word," in Parker (ed.), 227–60.
Itô, Junko, Armin Mester, and Jaye Padgett. 1995. "Licensing and underspecification in Optimality Theory," *Linguistic Inquiry* 26: 571–613.
Iverson, Gregory K. and Joseph C. Salmons. 1992. "The place of Structure Preservation in diminutive formation," *Phonology* 9: 137–43.
1996. "The primacy of primary umlaut," *Beiträge zur Geschichte der deutschen Sprache und Literatur* 118: 69–86.
2003. "The ingenerate motivation of sound change," in Raymond Hickey (ed.), *Motives for Language Change*, 199–212. Cambridge University Press.
2004. "The conundrum of Old Norse umlaut: regular sound change versus crisis analogy," *Journal of Germanic Linguistics* 16: 77–110.
2009. "Naturalness and the lifecycle of language change," in Patrick Steinkrüger and Manfred Krifka (eds.), *On Inflection: In Memory of Wolfgang U. Wurzel*, 89–105. Berlin: Mouton de Gruyter.
Iverson, Gregory K., Garry W. Davis, and Joseph C. Salmons. 1994. "Blocking environments in Old High German umlaut," *Folia Linguistica Historica* 15: 131–48.
Jaberg, Karl and Jakob Jud. 1928–1940. *Sprach- und Sachatlas Italiens und der Südschweiz* (AIS). Zofingen: Ringier.
Jakobson, Roman, Gunnar Fant, and Morris Halle. 1952. *Preliminaries to Speech Analysis*. Cambridge, MA: MIT Press.
Jarvella, Robert J. and Guust Meijers. 1983. "Recognizing morphemes in spoken words: some evidence for a stem-organized mental lexicon," in Giovanni B. Flores d'Arcais and Robert J. Jarvella (eds.), *The Process of Language Understanding*, 81–113. New York: John Wiley and Sons.
Jesney, Karen. In press a. "Positional faithfulness, non-locality, and the Harmonic Serialism solution," *North East Linguistic Society* 39.
In press b. "Licensing in multiple contexts: an argument for Harmonic Grammar," *Proceedings of the 45th Meeting of the Chicago Linguistic Society*. Chicago, IL: University of Chicago.
Jiménez, Jesús. 1998. "Valencian vowel harmony," *Rivista di Linguistica* 10: 137–61.
Jiménez, Jesús and Maria-Rosa Lloret. 2007. "Andalusian vowel harmony: weak triggers and perceptibility," paper presented at the 4th Old World Conference in

Phonology, Workshop on Harmony in the Languages of the Mediterranean, Rhodes, January 18–21, 2007.
Johnson, Keith and Jack Martin. 2001. "Acoustic vowel reduction in Creek: effects of distinctive length and position in the word," *Phonetica* 58: 81–102.
Joseph, Brian. 1990. "A non-bleeding rule in Modern Greek," *Glotta: Zeitschrift für griechische und lateinische Sprache* 68: 124–9.
Jun, Jongho. 1995. *Perceptual and Articulatory Factors in Place Assimilation: An Optimality Theoretic Approach.* Ph.D. dissertation, University of California, Los Angeles.
   2004. "Place assimilation," in Hayes *et al.* (eds.), 58–86.
Kager, René. 1997. "Rhythmic vowel deletion in Optimality Theory," in Iggy Roca (ed.), *Derivations and Constraints in Phonology*, 463–99. Oxford University Press.
   1999. *Optimality Theory*. Cambridge University Press.
   2001. "Rhythmic directionality by positional licensing," handout of a paper presented at the fifth HIL Phonology Conference, University of Postdam, January 11, 2001. [Available as ROA 514.]
   2007. "Feet and metrical stress," in de Lacy (ed.), 195–227.
Kaplan, Aaron F. 2008a. *Noniterativity is an Emergent Property of Grammar*. Ph.D. dissertation, University of California, Santa Cruz.
   2008b. "Licensing and noniterative harmony in Lango," *North East Linguistic Society* 37, 311–22.
Karabay, Fetiye. 2004. "Exploiting motivations of reduplication: the Turkish case," *Proceedings of the 1st Workshop on Altaic Formal Linguistics – 2003, MIT Working Papers in Linguistics* 46.
Kaun, Abigail. 1995. *The Typology of Rounding Harmony: An Optimality Theoretic Approach*. Ph.D. dissertation, University of California, Los Angeles.
   2004. "The phonetic foundations of the rounding harmony typology," in Hayes *et al.* (eds.), 87–116.
Kawahara, Shigeto. 2003. "Root-controlled fusion in Zoque: root-faith and neutralization avoidance," ms., University of Massachusetts, Amherst. [Available as ROA 599.]
   2008. "On the proper treatment of non-crisp edges," *Japanese/Korean Linguistics* 13: 55–67. Stanford: CSLI Publications.
Kaze, Jeffery. 1989. *Metaphony in Spanish and Italian Dialects Revisited*. Ph.D. dissertation, University of Illinois, Urbana-Champaign.
   1991. "Metaphony and two models for the description of vowel systems," *Phonology* 8: 163–70.
Keating, Patricia A., Taehong Cho, Cécile Fougeron, and Chai-Shune Hsu. 1999. "Domain-initial strengthening in four languages," *UCLA Working Papers in Phonetics* 97: 139–51.
Keer, Edward. 1999. *Geminates, the OCP, and the Nature of Con*. Ph.D. dissertation, Rutgers University.
Kehoe, Margaret and Carol Stoel-Gammon. 1997. "The acquisition of prosodic structure: an investigation of current accounts of children's prosodic development," *Language* 73: 113–44.
Kempley, S. T. and John Morton. 1982. "The effects of priming with regularly and irregularly related words in auditory word recognition," *British Journal of Psychology* 73: 441–54.

Kingston, John. 2007. "The phonetics–phonology interface," in de Lacy (ed.), 401–34.
Kingston, John and Randy Diehl. 1994. "Phonetic knowledge," *Language* 70: 419–53.
Kirchner, Robert. 1993. "Turkish vowel harmony and disharmony: an Optimality Theoretic account," paper presented at the Rutgers Optimality Workshop I (ROW I), October 22. [Available as ROA 4.]
    1996. "Synchronic chain shifts in Optimality Theory," *Linguistic Inquiry* 27: 341–9.
    2001. *An Effort-Based Approach to Consonant Lenition*. New York: Routledge.
    2004. "Consonant lenition," in Hayes *et al.* (eds.), 313–45.
Kitto, Catherine and Paul de Lacy. 1999. "Correspondence and epenthetic quality," *Austronesian Formal Linguistics Association* 6: 181–200. Toronto Working Papers in Linguistics.
Klein, Thomas B. 1995. *Umlaut in Optimality Theory*. Ph.D. dissertation, University of Delaware.
    2000. *"Umlaut" in Optimality Theory*. Tübingen: Niemeyer.
Koenig, Brad, Arnie Coleman, and Karen Coleman. 2007. "Notes on Esimbi phonology and orthography," private ms., Denver, CO.
Koriat, Asher and Israel Lieblich. 1974. "What does a person in a 'TOT' state know that a person in a 'don't know' state doesn't know," *Memory and Cognition* 2: 647–55.
Krämer, Martin. 2003. *Vowel Harmony and Correspondence Theory*. Studies in Generative Grammar 66. Berlin: Mouton de Gruyter.
    2009. *The Phonology of Italian*. Oxford University Press.
Krivitskii, A. A. and A. I. Podluzhnyi. 1994. *Uchebnik belorusskogo iazyka dlia samoobrazovaniia* (Textbook of the Belarusian Language for Self-study). Minsk: Vyshèishaia Shkola.
Kurisu, Kazutaka. 2001. *The Phonology of Morpheme Realization*. Ph.D. dissertation, University of California, Santa Cruz.
Ladefoged, Peter. 1993. *A Course in Phonetics*. Third Edition. Fort Worth, TX: Harcourt Brace.
Lamontagne, Greg and Keren Rice. 1995. "A correspondence account of coalescence," in Beckman *et al.* (eds.), 211–23.
Landman, Meredith. 2003. "Morphological contiguity," in Angela Carpenter, Andries Coetzee, and Paul de Lacy (eds.), *Papers in Optimality Theory II: University of Massachusetts-Amherst Occasional Papers in Linguistics*. Amherst: Graduate Linguistic Student Association Publications.
Lausberg, Heinrich. 1939. *Die Mundarten Südlukaniens*. Beihefte zur Zeitschrift für Romanische Philologie 90. Halle: Niemeyer.
Lavoie, Lisa M. 2001. *Consonant Strength: Phonological Patterns and Phonetic Manifestations*. New York: Routledge.
Legendre, Géraldine, Yoshiro Miyata, and Paul Smolensky. 1990. "Can connectionism contribute to syntax? Harmonic Grammar, with an application," *Proceedings of the 26th Meeting of the Chicago Linguistic Society*, 237–52. Chicago, IL: University of Chicago.
Lehiste, Ilse. 1970. *Suprasegmentals*. Cambridge, MA: MIT Press.
Lehiste, Ilse and G. E. Peterson. 1959. "Vowel amplitude and phonemic stress in American English," *Journal of the Acoustical Society of America* 31: 428–35.

Leonard, C. S. 1978. *Umlaut in Romance: An Essay in Linguistic Archeology*. Grossen-Linden: Hoffman.
Li, Bing. 1996. *Tungusic Vowel Harmony*. HIL dissertations 18. The Hague: Holland Academic Graphics.
Lieber, Rochelle. 1987. *An Integrated Theory of Autosegmental Processes*. Albany: State University of New York Press.
Lindblom, Björn. 1963. "Spectrographic study of vowel reduction," *Journal of the Acoustical Society of America* 35: 1,773–81.
  1986. "Phonetic universals in vowel systems," in John J. Ohala and Jeri J. Jaeger (eds.), *Experimental Phonology*, 13–44. Orlando: Academic Press.
  1990. "Explaining phonetic variation: a sketch of the H&H theory," in William J. Hardcastle and Alain Marchal (eds.), *Speech Production and Speech Modelling*, 403–39. Dordrecht: Kluwer.
Lodge, Ken. 1989. "A non-segmental account of German umlaut," *Linguistische Berichte* 124: 470–91.
Lombardi, Linda. 1994. *Laryngeal Features and Laryngeal Neutralization*. New York: Garland.
  1995. "Laryngeal neutralization and syllable wellformedness," *Natural Language and Linguistic Theory* 13: 39–74.
  1999. "Positional faithfulness and voicing assimilation in Optimality Theory," *Natural Language and Linguistic Theory* 17: 267–302.
  2001. "Why Place and Voice are different: constraint-specific alternations in Optimality Theory," in Linda Lombardi (ed.), *Segmental Phonology in Optimality Theory*, 13–45. Cambridge University Press.
Loporcaro, Michele. 2000. "Stress stability under cliticization and the prosodic status of Romance clitics," in Lori Repetti (ed.), *Phonological Theory and the Dialects of Italy*, 137–68. Amsterdam: John Benjamins.
Łubowicz, Anna. 2002. "Derived environment effects in Optimality Theory," *Lingua* 112: 243–80.
  2003. *Contrast Preservation in Phonological Mappings*. Ph.D. dissertation, University of Massachusetts, Amherst.
  2009. "Infixation as morpheme absorption," in Parker (ed.), 261–84.
  2010. *The Phonology of Contrast*. London: Equinox.
MacEachern, Margaret. 1999. *Laryngeal Cooccurrence Restrictions*. New York: Routledge.
Magen, Harriet S. 1997. "The extent of vowel-to-vowel coarticulation in English," *Journal of Phonetics* 25: 187–205.
Mahanta, Shakuntala. 2007. *Directionality and Locality in Vowel Harmony*. Ph.D. dissertation, Utrecht University.
Maiden, Martin. 1987. "New perspectives on the genesis of Italian metaphony," *Transactions of the Philological Society* 85: 38–73.
  1988. "Armonia regressiva di vocali atone nell'Italia meridionale," *L'Italia dialettale* 51, 111–39.
  1991a. *Interactive Morphonology: Metaphony in Italy*. New York: Routledge.
  1991b. "Armonia regressiva di vocali atone nell'Italia centromeridionale: la sua importanza per la teoria della fonologia prosodica," in Luciano Giannelli, Nicoletta

Maraschio, Teresa Poggi Salani, and Massimo Vedovelli (eds.), *Tra Rinascimento e strutture attuali. Saggi di linguistica italiana*, 233–9. Turin: Rosenberg and Sellier.

1995. "Evidence from Italian dialects for the internal structure of prosodic domains," in John Charles Smith and Martin Maiden (eds.), *Linguistic Theory and the Romance Languages*, 115–31. Amsterdam: John Benjamins.

1997. "Vowel systems," in Maiden and Parry (eds.), 7–14.

Maiden, Martin and Mair Parry (eds.). 1997. *The Dialects of Italy*. New York: Routledge.

Major, Roy C. 1992. "Stress and rhythm in Brazilian Portuguese," in Dale A. Loike and Donald P. Macedo (eds.), *Romance Linguistics: The Portuguese Context*, 3–30. Westport: Bergin and Garvey.

Majors, Tivoli. 1998. *Stress-dependent Harmony*. Ph.D. dissertation, University of Texas, Austin.

Mancarella, G. B. 1974. *Note de storia linguistica salentina*. Lecce: Milella.

Manuel, Sharon. 1999. "Cross-language studies: relating language-particular coarticulation patterns to other language-particular facts," in William J. Hardcastle and Nigel Hewlett (eds.), *Coarticulation: Theory, Data and Techniques*, 179–98. Cambridge University Press.

Marcato, Gianna and Flavia Ursini. 1998. *Dialetti veneti: Grammatica e storia*. Padua: Unipress.

Marslen-Wilson, William D. 1975. "Sentence perception as an interactive parallel process," *Science* 189: 226–8.

Marslen-Wilson, William D. and Alan Welsh. 1978. "Processing interactions and lexical access during word recognition in continuous speech," *Cognitive Psychology* 10: 29–63.

McCarthy, John J. 1984. "Theoretical consequences of Montañes vowel harmony," *Linguistic Inquiry* 15, 291–318.

1988. "Feature geometry and dependency: a review," *Phonetica* 43: 84–108.

1994. "On coronal 'transparency'," paper presented at the Trilateral Phonology Weekend, January 22, 1994, University of California, Santa Cruz.

1999. "Sympathy and phonological opacity," *Phonology* 16: 331–99.

2000. "The prosody of phase in Rotuman," *Natural Language and Linguistic Theory* 18: 147–97.

2002. *A Thematic Guide to Optimality Theory*. Cambridge University Press.

2003. "OT constraints are categorical," *Phonology* 20: 75–138.

2004. "Headed spans and autosegmental spreading," ms., University of Massachusetts, Amherst. [Available as ROA 685.]

2007a. "Consonant harmony via correspondence: evidence from Chumash," in Bateman *et al.* (eds.), 223–37.

2007b. *Hidden Generalizations: Phonological Opacity in Optimality Theory*. London: Equinox.

2008a. "The serial interaction of stress and syncope," *Natural Language and Linguistic Theory* 26: 499–546.

2008b. "The gradual path to cluster simplification," *Phonology* 25, 271–319.

2009. "Harmony in Harmonic Serialism," ms., University of Massachusetts, Amherst. [Available as ROA 1009.]

In press. "Autosegmental spreading in Optimality Theory," in John Goldsmith, Elizabeth Hume, and Leo Wetzels (eds.), *Tones and Features*. Berlin: Mouton de Gruyter.

McCarthy, John J. and Alan Prince. 1993a. *Prosodic Morphology I: Constraint Interaction and Satisfaction*. Rutgers Technical Report TR-3. New Brunswick, Rutgers Center for Cognitive Science. [Available as ROA 482.]

   1993b. "Generalized alignment," in Geert Booij and Jaap van Marle (eds.), *Yearbook of Morphology*, 79–153.

   1994a. "An overview of prosodic morphology," papers presented at the OTS/HIL Workshop on Prosodic Morphology, University of Utrecht.

   1994b. "The emergence of the unmarked: Optimality in Prosodic Morphology," *North East Linguistic Society* 24: 333–79.

   1995. "Faithfulness and reduplicative identity," in Beckman *et al.* (eds.), 249–384.

Meijer, Paul J. A. 1996. "What speech errors can tell us about word form generation: the roles of constraint and opportunity," *Journal of Psycholinguistic Research* 26: 141–58.

Mielke, Jeff. 2008. *The Emergence of Distinctive Features*. Oxford University Press.

Mielke, Jeff and Elizabeth Hume. 2001. "Considerations of word recognition for metathesis," in Elizabeth Hume, Norval Smith, and Jeroen van de Weijer (eds.), *Surface Syllable Structure and Segment Sequencing*, 135–58. Leiden: Holland Institute of Generative Linguistics (HIL).

Miglio, Viola. 2005. *Markedness and Faithfulness in Vowel Systems*. New York: Routledge.

Milberg, W., S. Blumstein, and B. Dworetzky. 1988. "Phonological factors in lexical access: evidence from an auditory lexical decision task," *Bulletin of the Psychonomic Society* 26: 305–8.

Morén, Bruce. 1999. *Distinctiveness, Coercion and Sonority: A Unified Theory of Weight*. Ph.D. dissertation, University of Maryland at College Park.

Moreton, Elliott and Paul Smolensky. 2002. "Typological consequences of local constraint conjunction," *West Coast Conference on Formal Linguistics* 21: 306–19.

Mpiranya, Fidèle and Rachel Walker. 2005. "Sibilant harmony in Kinyarwanda and coronal opacity," paper presented at 28th annual conference of Generative Linguistics in the Old World, University of Geneva, March 31, 2005.

Neira Martínez, Jesus. 1955. *El habla de Lena*. Oviedo: Instituto de Estudios Asturianos.

   1983. "De dialectología asturiana. La metafonia por /-i/ en los Bables centrales," *Philologica Hispaniensia in Honorem M. Alvar*, Vol. I, 485–97. Madrid: Gredos.

Nelson, Nicole A. 2003. *Asymmetric Anchoring*. Ph.D. dissertation, Rutgers University.

Nespor, Marina and Irene Vogel. 1986. *Prosodic Phonology*. Dordrecht: Foris.

Nevins, Andrew. 2004. *Conditions on (Dis)Harmony*. Ph.D. dissertation, MIT.

   2010. *Locality in Vowel Harmony*. Cambridge, MA: MIT Press.

Nibert, Holly. 1998. "Processes of vowel harmony in the Servigliano dialect of Italian: a comparison of two non-linear proposals for the representation of vowel height," *Probus* 10: 67–101.

Ní Chiosáin, Máire and Jaye Padgett. 2001. "Markedness, segment realization and locality in spreading," in Linda Lombardi (ed.), *Segmental Phonology in Optimality Theory*, 118–56. Cambridge University Press.

2009. "Contrast, comparison sets, and the perceptual space," in Parker (ed.), 103–21.
Noonan, Michael. 1992. *A Grammar of Lango*. Berlin: Mouton de Gruyter.
Nooteboom, S. G. 1981. "Lexical retrieval from fragments of spoken words: beginnings vs. endings," *Journal of Phonetics* 9: 407–24.
Nooteboom, S. G. and N. J. van der Vlugt. 1988. "A search for a word-beginning superiority effect," *Journal of the Acoustical Society of America* 84: 2,018–32.
Odden, David. 1991. "Vowel geometry," *Phonology* 8: 261–89.
  1994. "Adjacency parameters in phonology," *Language* 70: 289–330.
Ohala, John. 1981. "The listener as a source of sound change," *Papers from the Parasession on Language and Behavior*, 178–203. Chicago, IL: Chicago Linguistic Society.
  1993. "The phonetics of sound change," in Charles Jones (ed.), *Historical Linguistics: Problems and Perspectives*, 237–78. London: Longman.
  1994. "Towards a universal, phonetically-based theory of vowel harmony," *Proceedings of ICSLP 94* [International Conference on Spoken Language Processing, Yokahama, Japan, Sept. 18–22, 1994], 491–4.
O'Keefe, Michael. 2007. "Transparency in Span Theory," in Bateman *et al.* (eds.), 239–58.
Oostendorp, Marc van. 1995. *Vowel Quality and Phonological Projection*. Ph.D. dissertation, Tilburg University.
Padgett, Jaye. 1995. "Partial class behavior and nasal place assimilation," in Suzuki and Elzinga (eds.), 145–83.
  1997. "Perceptual distance of contrast: vowel height and nasality," in Rachel Walker, Dan Karvonen, and Motoko Katayama (eds.), *Phonology at Santa Cruz* 5: 63–78.
  2002. "Feature classes in phonology," *Language* 78: 81–110.
  2003. "Contrast and post-velar fronting in Russian," *Natural Language and Linguistic Theory* 21: 39–87.
  2004. "Russian vowel reduction and Dispersion Theory," *Phonological Studies* 7: 81–96. Tokyo: Kaitakusha Publishing Co.
Padgett, Jaye and Marija Tabain. 2005. "Adaptive Dispersion Theory and phonological vowel reduction in Russian," *Phonetica* 61: 14–54.
Parker, Steve (ed.). 2009. *Phonological Argumentation: Essays on Evidence and Motivation*. London: Equinox.
Parkinson, Frederick. 1996. *The Representation of Vowel Height in Phonology*. Ph.D. dissertation, Ohio State University.
Paster, Mary. 2004. "Vowel height harmony and blocking in Buchan Scots," *Phonology* 21: 359–407.
Pater, Joe. 2000. "Nonuniformity in English stress: the role of ranked and lexically specific constraints," *Phonology* 17: 237–74.
  2007. "The locus of exceptionality: morpheme-specific phonology as constraint indexation," in Bateman *et al.* (eds.), 259–96.
  2009a. "Morpheme-specific phonology: constraint indexation and inconsistency resolution," in Parker (ed.), 123–54.
  2009b. "Weighted constraints in generative linguistics," *Cognitive Science* 33: 999–1,035.

Payne, David. 1990. "Accent in Aguaruna," in Doris L. Payne (ed.), *Amazonian Linguistics: Studies in Lowland South American Languages*, 161–84. Austin, TX: University of Texas Press.

Penny, Ralph J. 1969. "Vowel-harmony in the speech of the Montes de Pas (Santander)," *Orbis* 18: 148–66.

1994. "Continuity and innovation in Romance: metaphony and mass-noun reference in Spain and Italy," *The Modern Language Review* 89: 273–81.

Peperkamp, Sharon. 1996. "On the prosodic representation of clitics," in Ursula Kleinhenz (ed.), *Interfaces in Phonology*, 102–27. Berlin: Akademie Verlag.

1997. *Prosodic Words*. Ph.D. dissertation, Amsterdam University. The Hague: Holland Institute of Generative Linguistics.

Petrova, Olga, Rosemary Plapp, Catherine Ringen, and Szilárd Szentgyörgyi. 2006. "Voice and aspiration: evidence from Hungarian, German, Swedish, and Turkish," *The Linguistic Review* 23: 1–35.

Pierrehumbert, Janet and David Talkin. 1992. "Lenition of /h/ and glottal stop," in G. Doherty and D. R. Ladd (eds.), *Papers in Laboratory Phonology II*, 90–117. Cambridge University Press.

Piggott, Glyne L. 1997. "Licensing and alignment: a conspiracy in harmony," *Phonology* 14: 437–77.

2000. "Against featural alignment," *Journal of Linguistics* 36: 84–129.

Poser, William J. 1982. "Phonological representation and action-at-a-distance," in Harry van der Hulst and Norval Smith (eds.), *The Structure of Phonological Representations, Part II*, 121–58. Dordrecht: Foris.

Prince, Alan and Paul Smolensky. 2004. *Optimality Theory: Constraint Interaction in Generative Grammar*. Oxford: Blackwell.

Pulleyblank, Douglas. 1996. "Neutral vowels in Optimality Theory: a comparison of Yoruba and Wolof," *Canadian Journal of Linguistics* 41: 295–347.

2002. "Harmony drivers: no disagreement allowed," *Berkeley Linguistics Society* 28: 249–67.

Recasens, Daniel. 1991. "Timing in Catalan," *Proceedings of the 4th International Congress of Phonetic Science*, 230–33.

Revithiadou, Anthi. 1999. *Headmost Accent Wins: Head Dominance and Ideal Prosodic Form in Lexical Accent Systems*. Ph.D. dissertation, University of Leiden.

Rhodes, Russell. 2008. "Vowel harmony as Agreement by Correspondence: the case of Khalkha Mongolian rounding harmony," paper presented at Trilateral Linguistics Weekend (TREND), University of California, Santa Cruz, May 10, 2008.

Ribezzo, Francesco. 1912. *Il dialetto apulo-salentino de Francavilla Fontana*. Martina Franca.

Rice, Keren. 1999. "Featural markedness in phonology: variation – Parts 1 and 2," *GLOT* 4.7: 3–6; 4.8: 3–7.

2007. "Markedness in phonology," in de Lacy (ed.), 79–97.

Rikoto, Bulus Doro. 2001. *C'Lela–English – Hausa Dictionary*. Nigeria: Lelna Language Development/Trans. Association Details.

Ringen, Catherine O. and Orvokki Heinämäki. 1999. "Variation in Finnish vowel harmony: an OT account," *Natural Language and Linguistic Theory* 17: 303–37.

Ringer, Catherine O. and Robert M. Vago. 1998. "Hungarian vowel harmony in Optimality Theory," *Phonology* 15: 393–416.

Rizzi, Fabio. 1989. "Le ricerche sul dialetto padovano contemporaneo," in M. Cortelazzo (ed.), *Guida ai dialetti veneto XI*, 131–49. Padua: Cooperativa Libraria Editrice Università de Padova.

Rohlfs, Gerhard. 1956–1961. *Vocabolario dei dialetti salentini (Terra d'Otranto)*. (3 vols.) München: Beck'schen Verlagsbuchhandlung.

 1966. *Grammatica storica della lingua italiana e dei suoi dialetti: Fonetica*. Torino: Einaudi.

Rose, Sharon. 2000. "Rethinking geminates, long-distance geminates and the OCP," *Linguistic Inquiry* 31: 85–122.

 2004. "Long-distance vowel–consonant agreement in Harari," *Journal of African Languages and Linguistics* 25: 41–87.

Rose, Sharon and Rachel Walker. 2004. "A typology of consonant agreement as correspondence," *Language* 80: 475–531.

 In press. "Harmony systems," in John A. Goldsmith, Jason Riggle, and Alan Yu (eds.), *The Handbook of Phonological Theory*, second edition. Basil Blackwell.

Rosenberg, Sheldon, Paul J. Coyle, and Walter L. Porter. 1966. "Recall of adverbs as a function of the frequency of their adjective roots," *Journal of Verbal Learning and Verbal Behavior* 5: 65–76.

Rosenthall, Sam. 1997a. *Vowel/Glide Alternation in a Theory of Constraint Interaction*. New York: Routledge.

 1997b. "The distribution of prevocalic vowels," *Natural Language and Linguistic Theory* 15: 139–80.

Sakellariades, George. 1985. "A bleeding rule in Modern Greek," *Glotta. Zeitschrift für griechische und lateinische Sprache* 63: 111–13.

Salvioni, Carlo. 1894. "L'influenza della tonica nella determinazione dell'atona finale in qualche parlata della valle del Ticino," *Archivio Glottologico Italiano* 13: 355–60.

Sanders, Nathan. 2003. *Opacity and Sound Change in the Polish Lexicon*. Ph.D. dissertation, University of California, Santa Cruz.

Sands, Kathy L. 2004. *Patternings of Vocalic Sequences in the World's Languages*. Ph.D. dissertation, University of California, Santa Barbara.

Sasa, Tomomasa. 2009. *Treatments of Vowel Harmony in Optimality Theory*. Ph.D. dissertation, University of Iowa.

Savoia, Leonardo and Martin Maiden. 1997. "Metaphony," in Maiden and Parry (eds.), 15–25.

Schwartz, Jean-Luc, Louis-Jean Boë, Nathalie Vallée, and Christian Abry. 1997. "The dispersion-focalization theory of vowel systems," *Journal of Phonetics* 25: 255–86.

Sebeok, Thomas A. and Frances J. Ingemann. 1961. *An Eastern Cheremis Manual*. Bloomington, IN: Indiana University.

Selkirk, Elisabeth O. 1978. "On prosodic structure and its relation to syntactic structure," in T. Fretheim (ed.), *Nordic Prosody*, Vol. II, 111–40. Trondheim: TAPIR.

 1995. "The prosodic structure of function words," in Beckman *et al.* (eds.), 439–69.

Sevald, Christine A. and Gary S. Dell. 1994. "The sequential cuing effect in speech production," *Cognition* 53: 91–127.
Shattuck-Hufnagel, Stefanie. 1986. "The representation of phonological information during speech production planning: evidence from vowel errors in spontaneous speech," *Phonology Yearbook* 3: 117–49.
  1992. "The role of word structure in segmental serial ordering," *Cognition* 42: 213–59.
Silverman, Daniel. 1997. *Phasing and Recoverability*. New York: Garland.
Sluyters, Willebrord. 1988. "Vowel harmony, rule formats and underspecification: the dialect of Francavilla-Fontana," in Harry van der Hulst and Norval Smith (eds.), *Features, Segmental Structure and Harmony Processes, Part II*, 161–84. Dordrecht: Foris.
Smith, Jennifer. 2005. *Phonological Augmentation in Prominent Positions*. New York: Routledge.
Smolensky, Paul. 1993. "Harmony, markedness, and phonological activity," paper presented at the First Rutgers Optimality Workshop (ROW 1), Rutgers University, New Brunswick, New Jersey.
  1997. "Constraint interaction in generative grammar II: local conjunction," paper presented at the Hopkins Optimality Theory Workshop/Maryland Mayfest 1997, Baltimore, Maryland.
  2006. "Optimality in phonology II: harmonic completeness, local constraint conjunction, and feature domain markedness," in Paul Smolensky and Géraldine Legendre, *The Harmonic Mind: From Neural Computation to Optimality-theoretic Grammar*, Vol. II, 27–160. Cambridge, MA: MIT Press.
Smolensky, Paul and Géraldine Legendre. 2006. *The Harmonic Mind: From Neural Computation to Optimality-theoretic Grammar*. Cambridge, MA: MIT Press.
Spaelti, Philip. 1997. *Dimensions of Variation in Multi-pattern Reduplication*. Ph.D. dissertation, University of California, Santa Cruz.
Spotts, Hazel. 1953. "Vowel harmony and consonant sequences in Mazahua (Otomí)," *International Journal of American Linguistics* 19: 253–8.
Stallcup, Kenneth L. 1980a. "Noun classes in Esimbi," *Noun Classes in the Grassfields Bantu Borderland. (SCOPIL 8)*, 139–53. Los Angeles: University of Southern California.
  1980b. "A brief account of nominal prefixes and vowel harmony in Esimbi," in Luc Bouquiaux (ed.), *L'expansion bantoue*, Vol. II, 435–41. Paris: Société d'Etudes Linguistiques et Anthropologiques de France.
Stampe, David. 1973. *A Dissertation on Natural Phonology*. Ph.D. dissertation, University of Chicago. [Distributed 1979 by Indiana University Linguistics Club, Bloomington.]
Stanners, Robert F., James J. Neisner, William P. Hernon, and Roger Hall. 1979. "Memory representation for morphologically related words," *Journal of Verbal Learning and Verbal Behavior* 18: 399–412.
Steriade, Donca. 1995a. "Positional neutralization," ms., University of California, Los Angeles.
  1995b. "Underspecification and markedness," in Goldsmith (ed.), 114–74.
  1999a. "Phonetics in phonology: the case of laryngeal neutralization," *UCLA Working Papers in Linguistics* 2: 25–146.

1999b. "Alternatives to the syllabic analysis of consonantal phonotactics," in O. Fujimura, B. Joseph, and B. Palek (eds.), *Proceedings of the 1998 Linguistics and Phonetics Conference*, 205–42. Prague: Charles University Press.

2001. "Directional asymmetries in place assimilation," In Hume and Johnson (eds.), 219–50.

2009. "The phonology of perceptibility effects: the P-map and its consequences for constraint organization," in Kristin Hanson and Sharon Inkelas (eds.), *The Nature of the Word: Studies in Honor of Paul Kiparsky*, 151–79. Cambridge, MA: MIT Press.

Stevens, Kenneth. 1989. "On the quantal nature of speech," *Journal of Phonetics* 17: 3–45.

Stevens, Kenneth and Samuel Jay Keyser 1989. "Primary features and their enhancement in consonants," *Language* 65: 81–106.

Struijke, Caro. 2002. *Existential Faithfulness: A Study of Reduplicative TETU, Feature Movement, and Dissimilation*. New York: Routledge.

Suomi, Kari. 1983. "Palatal vowel harmony: a perceptually motivated phenomenon?" *Nordic Journal of Linguistics* 6: 1–35.

Suzuki, Keiichiro. 1998. *A Typological Investigation of Dissimilation*. Ph.D. dissertation, University of Arizona.

Suzuki, Keiichiro and Dirk Elzinga (eds.). 1995. *Proceedings of the South Western Optimality Theory Workshop*. Tucson: University of Arizona Coyote Papers.

Svantesson, Jan-Olof. 1985. "Vowel harmony shift in Mongolian," *Lingua* 67: 283–327.

Temkin Martinez, Michal. 2010. *Sources of Non-conformity in Phonology: Variation and Exceptionality in Modern Hebrew Spirantization*. Ph.D. dissertation, University of Southern California.

Trubetzkoy, N. S. 1969. *Principles of Phonology*. Translated by Christiane A. M. Baltaxe. Berkeley: University of California Press.

Uffmann, Christian. 2004. *Vowel Epenthesis in Loanword Phonology*. Ph.D. dissertation, University of Marburg.

Urbanczyk, Suzanne. 2001. *Patterns of Reduplication in Lushootseed*. New York: Garland.

2006. "Reduplicative form and the root–affix asymmetry," *Natural Language and Linguistic Theory* 24: 179–240.

2007. "Reduplication," in de Lacy (ed.), 473–93.

Ussishkin, Adam and Andrew Wedel. 2002. "Neighborhood density and the root–affix distinction," *North East Linguistic Society* 32: 539–49.

Vago, Robert M. 1988. "Underspecification in the height harmony system of Pasiego," *Phonology* 5: 343–62.

Vaysman, Olga. 2009. *Segmental Alternations and Metrical Theory*. Ph.D. dissertation, MIT.

Venturelli, G. 1974. "Varietà di armonizzazioni vocaliche nella Garfagnana centro-meridionale," *Atti del XIX Congresso internazionale de linguistica romanza* 3: 101–4. Naples: Macchiaroli and Amsterdam: John Benjamins.

Vignoli, Carlo. 1925. *Il vernacolo di Veroli in provincia di Roma*. Rome: Società Filologica Romana.

Vogel, Irene. 1997. "Prosodic phonology," in Maiden and Parry (eds.), 58–67.
Walker, Rachel. 2000a. *Nasalization, Neutral Segments, and Opacity Effects*. New York: Garland.
  2000b. "Long-distance consonantal identity effects," *West Coast Conference on Formal Linguistics* 19: 532–45.
  2000c. "Yaka nasal harmony: spreading or segmental correspondence?" *Berkeley Linguistics Society* 26: 321–32.
  2001a. "Positional markedness in vowel harmony," in Caroline Féry, Antony Dubach Green, and Ruben van de Vijver (eds.), *Proceedings of HILP 5. Linguistics in Potsdam* 12: 212–32. University of Potsdam.
  2001b. "Round licensing, harmony, and bisyllabic triggers in Altaic," *Natural Language and Linguistic Theory* 19: 827–78.
  2004. "Vowel feature licensing at a distance: evidence from Northern Spanish language varieties," *West Coast Conference on Formal Linguistics* 23: 787–800.
  2005. "Weak triggers in vowel harmony," *Natural Language and Linguistic Theory* 23: 917–89.
  2009. "Similarity-sensitive blocking and transparency in Menominee," paper presented at the annual meeting of the Linguistic Society of America, San Francisco, CA, January 9, 2009.
  2010. "Nonmyopic harmony and the nature of derivations," *Linguistic Inquiry* 41: 169–79.
Walker, Rachel and Bella Feng. 2004. "A ternary model of morphology–phonology correspondence," *West Coast Conference on Formal Linguistics* 23: 773–86.
Wiese, Richard. 1996. *The Phonology of German*. Oxford University Press.
Wilson, Colin. 2000. *Targeted Constraints: An Approach to Contextual Neutralization in Optimality Theory*. Ph.D. dissertation, Johns Hopkins University.
  2003. "Analyzing unbounded spreading with constraints: marks, targets and derivations," ms., University of California, Los Angeles.
  2006. "Unbounded spreading is myopic," paper presented at the workshop on Current Perspectives on Phonology, Indiana University, Bloomington, June 23, 2006.
Wolf, Matthew. 2007. "For an autosegmental theory of mutation," in Bateman *et al.* (eds.), 315–404.
Woock, Edith B. and Michael Noonan. 1979. "Vowel harmony in Lango," *Papers from the 15th Annual Meeting of the Chicago Linguistic Society*, 20–9.
Wright, James T. 1986. "The behavior of nasalized vowels in the perceptual vowel space," in John. J. Ohala and Jeri J. Jaeger (eds.), *Experimental Phonology*, 45–67. Orlando: Academic Press.
Wright, Richard. 2004. "A review of perceptual cues and cue robustness," in Hayes *et al.* (eds.), 34–57.
Yu, Alan C. 2004. "Explaining final obstruent voicing in Lezgian," *Language* 80: 73–97.
  2007. *A Natural History of Infixation*. Oxford University Press.
Zhang, Jie. 2002. *The Effects of Duration and Sonority on Contour Tone Distribution: Typological Survey and Formal Analysis*. New York: Routledge.
  2004. "The role of contrast-specific and language-specific phonetics in contour tone distribution," in Hayes *et al.* (eds.), 157–90.

Zoll, Cheryl. 1997. "Conflicting directionality," *Phonology* 14: 263–86.
  1998a. *Parsing Below the Segment in a Constraint-based Framework*. Stanford: CSLI Publications.
  1998b. "Positional asymmetries and licensing," ms., MIT. [Available as ROA 282.]
Zuraw, Kie. 2000. *Patterned Exceptions in Phonology*. Ph.D. dissertation, University of California, Los Angeles.
  2002. "Aggressive reduplication," *Phonology* 19: 395–439.
  2007. "The role of phonetic knowledge in phonological patterning: corpus and survey evidence from Tagalog infixation," *Language* 83: 277–316.

Language Index

Aguaruna. *See* Awajún
Andalusian dialects, Eastern, 142, 147, 166, 167, 177–80, 183, 192, 255, 294, 301
Ascrea dialect, 43, 53, 55, 57, 77, 146, 147, 166, 167, 171–7, 183, 185, 192
Asturian dialects
    Aller (central), 203
    eastern, 204
    Lena (central). *See* Lena Asturian dialect
    Western, 194, 200–7, 231, 302
Awajún, 211

Baiyinna Orochen. *See* Orochen, Baiyinna
Belarusian, 5, 78, 79, 194, 195–7, 199, 231, 234, 235, 236, 303, 311
Bolognese dialect, 29
Buchan Scots, 70, 91, 92, 117, 136, 142, 143, 301, 302

C'Lela, 6, 91, 99, 104–9, 110, 117, 136, 142, 186, 237, 302
Castelnuovo Garfagnana dialect, 327
Catalan, 16, 255, 270
    Valencian dialects. *See* Valencian Catalan dialects
Chamorro, 135, 301, 327
Chumash, 207–8, 236, 303
Cortona dialect, 270
Czech, 21

Dutch, 16, 23, 25

English, 1, 15, 16, 17, 18, 20, 21, 23, 25, 28, 30
Esimbi, 30, 194, 216, 221–30, 232, 237, 303, 304, 313

Finnish, 21
Francavilla Fontana dialect, 79, 139, 146, 147, 158, 159–66, 183, 191, 192, 233, 237, 269, 299
French, 15, 21, 23

German, 10, 17, 21, 23, 28, 30, 60, 113, 141, 228, 304
    Middle High, 181, 304
    Modern, 10, 78, 79, 182, 185, 189, 194, 207, 216, 230, 232, 236, 304
    Old High, 10, 30, 91, 110, 111–15, 118, 135, 137, 138, 139, 140, 142, 147, 166, 167, 180–2, 183, 185, 191, 192, 216, 299, 301, 304
Germanic, 20, 142, 304
Goajiro, 31
Greek
    Modern Standard, 208
    northern dialects, 4, 78, 79, 194, 208, 231, 236, 302

Hungarian, 28, 313

Italian, 1, 5, 10, 25, 30, 184, 212, 213, 262, 266, 268, 269, 276

Japanese, 37, 38
Jaqaru, 62–3, 69, 91, 111, 127–35, 135, 137, 138, 139, 140, 141, 301, 302

Korean, 21
Kullo, 31
Kwara'ae, 215

Lango, 5, 75, 91, 98, 111, 115, 121–7, 135, 138, 139, 140, 143, 190, 301
Latin, 10, 29, 197
Lazio dialects, 270
    Sant'Oreste. *See* Sant'Oreste dialect
    Veroli. *See* Veroli dialect

Lena Asturian dialect, 30, 49–52, 147, 166, 167–71, 183, 185, 188–90, 192, 204, 322
Ligurian dialects, 79, 213–15, 232

Macuxi, 5, 70, 91, 92, 95–6, 136, 186, 301
Malay, 31
Mantuan dialect, northern, 199–200, 303, 310
Mari, 321
  Eastern Meadow, 77, 147, 148–58, 182, 184, 186, 192, 301, 302
Mazahua, 98–9, 301
Mongolian, Classical, 6, 42–3, 47, 91, 99–104, 136, 140, 144, 186, 302
Montefalcone dialect, 269
Muinane, 31

Navajo, 28
Neopolitan dialect, 268
Norwegian, Old, 296
Nova Siri dialect, 195, 197, 231, 236, 269

Ola Lamut, 6, 42, 47, 58, 70, 194, 200, 231, 235, 236, 302, 310, 311
Orochen, Baiyinna, 240–51, 255, 294, 295, 296, 302

Pasiego dialect, 283, 327
Piedmontese dialects, Old, 5, 212, 232
Polish, 23
Portuguese, Brazilian, 269, 270
Portuguese, European, 270

Quechua, 128

Ragusa dialect, 60

Romance, 10, 18, 29, 30, 50, 52, 59, 72, 117, 140, 141, 142, 184, 188, 197, 212, 236, 262, 267, 268, 269, 275, 285, 287, 304, 305, 316
Rotuman, 215
Russian, 1, 16, 31

Sant'Oreste dialect, 269
Serbo-Croatian, 25
Servigliano dialect, 11, 240, 255, 256–93, 294, 295, 296, 302
Slavic, 18, 270
Spanish, 10, 18, 20, 23, 28, 128, 270
Stabiese dialect, 268
Swedish, 16, 28

Taiwanese, 21
Tamil, 207
Thai, 28
Ticinese, 91, 92, 96–8, 136, 302, 303
Turkish, 21
Turkmen, 22

Umbertide dialect, 270

Valencian Catalan dialects, 207, 251, 255
  Sueca, 207
  València, 207, 252
  Vinalopó Mitjà. *See* Vinalopó Mitjà dialects
  Xaló, 207
Veneto dialect, central, 5, 10, 48, 56, 69, 75, 91, 111, 115–21, 135, 136, 138, 139, 140, 143, 162, 189, 190, 237, 299, 301, 302, 322
Veroli dialect, 72, 195, 197–9, 231, 236, 302
Vinalopó Mitjà dialects, 240, 251–5, 294, 295, 296

Subject Index

accent, 24, 70, 95–6, 136
affix
  different trigger strengths, 175
  evidence for weakness of, 25–6
  subject to licensing, 43, 75, 87, 98, 106, 107, 109, 128, 136, 138, 159, 168, 173, 183, 203, 212, 218, 231, 232, 233
AGREE(F), 247
ALIGN, 245, 247, 307
aspiration
  and ATR harmony, 177–9
  of /s/ in Eastern Andalusian, 177, 178
assimilation
  active assimilation versus passive licensing, 6, 70, 91, 99, 100, 103, 106, 110, 136, 148, 152
  consonant assimilation, local, 19, 22, 24
  consonant harmony, 24, 191
  metrical approach, 185–7
  vowel harmony. *See* vowel harmony
augmentation, 5, 14, 15, 19, 21, 22, 301

blocking
  and licensing, 34, 98, 106, 112, 114, 119, 135, 155, 158, 177, 209, 249, 289, 317
  and vowel harmony. *See* vowel harmony, blocking
  morpheme-specific, 131, 133, 174, 290
  of deletion, 208

categorical assessment. *See* constraint, categorical assessment
chain, 7, 44, 45, 47, 48, 53, 54, 55, 57, 59, 66, 78, 90, 143, 145, 146, 190, 193, 194, 238, 245, 246, 271, 312
child language, 13, 14, 15, 22, 23
clitic, 96, 104, 138, 264, 265–6, 269, 270, 271, 276–8, 281, 285, 293, 294

and prosodic structure, 246, 267–9, 271, 288
coalescence, 78, 79, 178, 213–15, 232, 233
coarticulation, 16–17, 18, 30, 113–14, 118, 137, 139, 142, 181, 182, 191, 215, 296, 299, 300, 304
Coincide relation, 45, 247
constraint
  categorical assessment, 247
  local conjunction. *See* local conjunction
contrast
  and licensing, 30, 46, 50, 52, 169, 204, 206, 298
  and triggers for harmony, 29, 50, 153, 169, 203, 204, 206, 239, 255, 295
  ATR and mid vowels, 52, 116, 159, 162, 316
  Contrast Coindexing. *See* Contrast Coindexing
  Dispersion Theory. *See* Dispersion Theory
  final syllable privilege, 22
  initial syllable privilege, 6, 19, 200, 243, 294
  reduction in unstressed syllables. *See* reduction
  root privilege, 24, 200, 222, 243
  static lack of, 6, 200, 211, 233, 302, 303
  stressed syllable privilege, 15
Contrast Coindexing, 50–2, 203, 205
cooccurrence restriction, consonant, 19
correspondence
  among segments in an output, 165, 187
  and chains, 44, 54, 190
  feature. *See* feature correspondence
  morpheme-specific, 189
  multiple output segments. *See* fission
CRISPEDGE constraint, 57–8

353

354 Subject index

deletion, 4, 15, 18, 22, 24, 26, 29, 78, 79, 122, 129, 132, 134, 188–309
desinence, 201, 203
diphthong, 5, 78, 79, 158, 159, 160, 162, 163, 164, 165, 183, 212, 213, 214, 216, 232, 233, 265, 321
 derived versus underived, 164
diphthongization, 60, 79, 158–60, 162–6, 183, 192
Dispersion Theory, 204, 316
duplication constraint, 54–5

emergence of the unmarked, 164
epenthesis, 26, 28, 79, 99, 106–8, 109, 134, 165, 233, 307
evolution of licensing. *See* licensing, evolution of
Evolutionary Phonology, 12

factorial typology, 9, 64
faithfulness constraint
 base-affixed form, 276
 existential, 129–35, 162–5
 final syllable, 65
 for floating features, 218
 for primary vowels, 141–2
 positional. *See* positional faithfulness
 sensitive to segment type, 114, 142, 299
 stressed syllable, 65
feature
 chain. *See* chain
 correspondence, 44, 53, 55, 169, 190
 duplication, 7, 53
 floating. *See* floating feature
 substitution, 70, 106, 110
Feature-Driven Markedness, 140–1
feeding, 264, 274, 287, 293
final position and syllable
 contrast. *See* contrast, final syllable privilege
 evidence for prominence of, 22–3
 evidence for weakness of, 24, 31
 faithfulness constraint. *See* faithfulness constraint, final syllable
 subject to licensing, 97, 106, 136, 149, 152, 182, 207, 302
fission, 79, 129–30, 131, 158, 162–3, 165, 166, 183, 187, 191, 325
floating feature, 78, 79, 188, 189, 190, 216, 218–21, 223–9, 230, 232, 233, 303, 304, 319

faithfulness. *See* faithfulness constraint for floating features
fortition, 15, 19
fusion, 24

GESTURALUNIFORMITY constraint, 103, 254
gesture, 40, 43, 44, 45, 56, 103, 186

Harmonic Grammar, 310, 313
Harmonic Serialism, 309, 328
hiatus, 18, 22, 24, 172

infixation, 5, 13, 15, 19, 22, 78, 79, 212–15, 232, 233
initial position and syllable
 as a licensing position, 6, 42, 99, 136, 149, 182, 200, 207, 224, 231, 233, 301
 contrast. *See* contrast, initial syllable privilege
 evidence for prominence of, 18–22

lenition, 15, 19
Lexical Indexation approach, 60, 190
LICENSE constraint
 maximal, 246
 precedence-sensitive, 271
 prominence-based, 45
 prominence-based morpheme-specific, 61
 restriction on, 46–7
licensing
 and contrast. *See* contrast and licensing
 and non-directional harmony, 68, 90, 123, 127
 concept of, 36–40, 238–40
 constraint. *See* LICENSE constraint
 direct, 7, 41, 42, 57, 58, 193–4
 evolution of, 182, 185, 216, 230, 304
 identity, 7, 41, 43, 55, 145–6
 in multiple contexts, 310–13
 indirect, 7, 41, 42, 56, 89–90
 maximal, 8, 238–40
 passive, 6, 70, 99
 perception-driven hypothesis, 2–3
 prominence-based, 2, 4, 6, 41, 238
Licensing by Cue, 315
local conjunction, 74–5, 102, 114, 118, 123, 127, 140, 155, 170, 214, 232, 254, 260, 272, 286, 290, 299, 324
local constraint conjunction. *See* local conjunction
locality
 articulatory adjacency, 43, 186

Subject index

gapped representation, 186
non-local vowel interaction in Baiyinna Orochen, 247
proximity constraint. *See* proximity constraint
transparent segment. *See* transparent segment
locus of violation, 45, 57, 61, 232, 247

majority rule effect, 71, 72–4, 102
markedness
   and ATR, 27, 123, 126, 161, 179, 241, 252, 316
   and rounding, 26, 75, 99, 114, 164, 200, 302
   and vowel backness, 27, 155
   and vowel color, 224, 303
   and vowel height, 27, 28–32, 207, 209, 212, 224, 285, 293, 302
   context-free, 27, 120, 140, 147, 179, 235
   diagnostics for, 26–32
   positional, 6, 10, 38–40, 64, 141, 309, 310, 311
   variable, 27, 32, 34, 42, 75, 179, 196, 302, 303
metaphony, 10, 30, 43, 50, 52, 56, 59, 115–21, 139, 141, 142, 143, 158–66, 167–77, 184, 185, 188–90, 203–4, 206, 212, 213, 257–61, 264, 273–4, 279, 280, 285, 287, 292, 293, 304–5, 314
metathesis, 4, 5, 13, 15, 19, 78, 129, 134, 212, 213, 215, 307, 328
metrical approach to assimilation. *See* assimilation, metrical approach
metrical strength hierarchy, 98
morpheme realization, 189
morphemic harmony approach, 188–9

Natural Phonology, 314
neutralization, 2, 6, 8, 21, 26, 29, 31, 37, 40, 49, 65, 67, 68, 70, 71, 72, 77, 78, 79, 91, 94, 98, 99, 100, 106, 107, 110, 117, 142, 152, 159, 195–200, 202, 204, 206, 207, 211, 223, 237, 294, 295, 299, 301, 302, 303, 304, 310, 311
   reduction. *See* reduction

Optimality Theory, 7, 9, 44, 64, 80, 134, 234, 237, 297, 307, 309, 310, 311

perception-driven hypothesis. *See* licensing, perception-driven hypothesis

phonetic knowledge, 12, 13, 49
phonetically-based phonology
   diachronic origins, 12, 14, 49, 215, 314
   synchronic functional grounding, 12, 13–14, 49
positional faithfulness, 8, 10, 39–40, 57, 64–5, 68, 69, 72, 90, 120, 136, 138, 140–1, 182, 191, 235, 255, 270, 287, 299, 302, 310–11
procedural markedness constraint, 307
process-based approaches, 127, 234
prominence
   as a basis for licensing. *See* licensing, prominence-based
   metrical strength hierarchy. *See* metrical strength hierarchy
   reduction. *See* sonority minimization
   scale, 269
prosodic hierarchy, 267
   and clitics. *See* clitic and prosodic structure
   maximal and minimal category projections, 268
proximity constraint, 176, 185, 220

reduction, 1, 4, 5, 15, 16, 21, 31, 115, 195, 197–9, 233, 252, 256, 261–4, 269, 270, 295, 299, 311, 323
   sonority minimization. *See* sonority minimization
   unstressed vowel raising. *See* unstressed vowel raising
reduplication, 14, 15, 19, 24
root
   as a licensing position, 5, 61, 98, 106, 122, 135, 136, 207, 301
   contrast. *See* contrast, root privilege
   evidence for prominence of, 24–5

sonority
   maximization, 234
   minimization, 107, 111, 118, 160, 262, 263, 299
Sound Pattern of English, The, 314
Span Theory, 309
stem
   as a licensing position, 5, 61, 70, 95, 136, 203, 301
   evidence for prominence of, 24–5, 26
stressed syllable
   as a licensing position, 4, 5, 43, 50, 62, 92, 97, 112, 117, 128, 136, 152, 160, 169, 173, 179, 181, 182, 183, 195, 198, 199,

stressed syllable (*cont.*)
    203, 207, 209, 212, 214, 218, 231, 232, 258, 301
    contrast. *See* contrast, stressed syllable privilege
    evidence for prominence of, 14–15, 16–18
    faithfulness constraint. *See* faithfulness constraint, stressed syllable

tone, 15, 22, 44, 45, 46, 54, 80
too-many-solutions problem, 306
transparent segment, 7, 41, 145, 146, 148, 151, 166, 167, 171, 172, 177, 178, 180, 182, 190, 192, 239, 284, 285, 289, 292, 294, 295, 321, 327
trigger
    and contrast. *See* contrast and triggers for harmony
    control, 8, 40, 65, 68, 90, 93, 110, 114, 118, 123, 126, 133, 135–40, 141, 142, 166, 167, 169, 173, 183, 191, 286, 288, 290, 296, 299, 302, 310
    morpheme-specific, 60, 128, 173, 176, 188, 290
    weak, 10, 40, 91, 110, 116, 140, 142, 191, 240, 245, 247, 255, 290, 294, 296, 299
truncation, 14, 15, 19, 22, 23

umlaut, 30, 111–15, 135, 142, 216–21, 299
    and syllable adjacency, 115, 217
    evolution of, 10, 60, 113, 141, 182, 185, 216, 230, 304
    lexicalization, 217, 230
    morpheme-specific triggering, 60, 189, 217, 218
    non-primary, 180–2
    primary, 181
    productivity of, 217
    secondary. *See* umlaut, non-primary
unstressed syllable
    evidence for weakness of, 15–17
    immediate post-tonic, 18, 327
    immediate pretonic, 18, 135, 270, 287, 323
    non-final post-tonic, 72, 167, 172, 178, 180, 183, 197, 231, 236, 270
    post-tonic, 10, 18, 29, 48, 69, 70, 72, 97, 116, 117, 118, 138, 159, 172, 173, 184, 197, 231, 236, 257, 258, 261, 264, 269–70, 275, 293, 294, 304, 305, 322
    pretonic, 18, 31, 48, 98, 197, 265, 269, 270, 280, 282, 284, 323, 327
    subject to licensing, 117, 197, 231
unstressed vowel raising, 29, 49, 160, 199, 207, 210, 254, 261, 299
    in height harmony. *See* vowel harmony, height
    interaction with vowel harmony, 160, 255

vowel harmony
    and contrastive status of triggers.
        See contrast and triggers for harmony
    and different affix trigger strengths.
        See affix, different trigger strengths
    ATR, 5, 98, 121, 138, 177, 183, 255, 301
    backness, 5, 30, 95, 111, 135, 138, 148, 181, 182, 183, 216, 233, 301
    blocking, 93, 99, 106, 110, 112, 117, 143, 176, 239, 243, 266, 274, 285, 294, 295
    color, 5, 95, 136, 222, 301
    copy, 62, 96, 98, 127, 136, 138, 251, 264, 294, 301, 303
    directional. *See* License constraint, precedence-sensitive
    domain, 92, 115, 142, 246, 267, 268, 272, 279, 285, 288, 295
    dominant vowels, 75, 121, 123, 190
    height, 5, 29, 30, 43, 48, 50, 92, 115, 136, 138, 158, 167, 171, 183, 204, 221, 233, 257, 279, 294, 296, 301, 302, 327
    interaction with unstressed vowel raising.
        See unstressed vowel raising, interaction with vowel harmony
    majority rule effect. *See* majority rule effect
    metaphony. *See* metaphony
    non-directional. *See* licensing and non-directional harmony
    round, 5, 95, 151, 182, 241, 294, 301
    transparent segment. *See* transparent segment
    trigger. *See* trigger
    umlaut. *See* umlaut
vowel hiatus. *See* hiatus
vowel raising
    in height harmony. *See* vowel harmony, height
    in unstressed syllables. *See* unstressed vowel raising
    stepwise, 50, 167, 170, 171, 260, 285